Richard Cobden, Independent Radical

Portrait of Richard Cobden, by Lowes Dickinson, 1861, courtesy of the Governors of Dunford House.

Richard Cobden
Independent Radical

NICHOLAS C. EDSALL

Harvard University Press
Cambridge, Massachusetts
London, England   1986

Library of Congress Cataloging in Publication Data

Edsall, Nicholas C.
    Richard Cobden, independent radical.

    Bibliography: p.
    Includes index.
    1. Cobden, Richard, 1804–1865. 2. Legislators—Great Britain
—Biography. 3. Great Britain.
Parliament. House of Commons—Biography. 4. Social
reformers—Great Britain—
Biography. 5. Great Britain—
Politics and government—1837–1901. I. Title.
DA536.C6E37 1986   942.081'092'4 [B]   86-366
ISBN 0-674-76879-5 (alk. paper)

To my brother David
and in memory of my brother Lawrence

Preface

The most important nineteenth-century British politician never to have held national government office, Richard Cobden is also perhaps the most important such figure not to have been accorded a major biographical study since World War II. And this despite the fact that it has been just over a hundred years since the publication of the official *Life of Richard Cobden* by John Morley. The present would appear to be a good time to look at Cobden anew. Many of the issues that most deeply concerned him—the relative economic development of different countries within and without the industrialized world, the role of the state in the economy, the nature of the arms race, and the dangers of an interventionist foreign policy, for example—are again at the center of public debate. Cobden himself and the particular mix of ideas and policies that went under the label Cobdenism, however, have long since ceased to be an influence and therefore, in themselves, an issue. Hence it is now possible to view him dispassionately.

This would have been difficult until quite recently. When Morley's study was published in 1881, sixteen years after its subject's death, Cobden's influence was at its height: the Gladstonian Liberal party had just won an electoral victory on a platform of economy in government and opposition to imperialism. Over the next generation all the positions with which Cobden was most closely associated were abandoned or put under siege; but such reverses only increased the devotion of his disciples, and when the political pendulum at long last swung back, many radicals viewed the change as a vindication of Cobdenism. A quarter century after the publication of Morley's *Cobden*, the Liberals won their greatest electoral victory on a wave of disillusionment with imperialism and renewed support for free trade.

The senseless slaughter of World War I also served to enhance Cobden's reputation as critic and prophet—and not only among radical politicians. At one point in Siegfried Sassoon's war novel, the *Complete Memoirs of George Sherston,* Cobden's writings were recommended to the wounded Sherston by a radical journalist who, happening to notice a bust of Cobden at his club, regretted "that the man himself wasn't above ground to give the present Government a bit of his mind." And to those who looked beyond the war to the hope of a new kind of peace, Cobden served even more directly as guide and mentor. J. A. Hobson, the first systematic critic of imperialism, wrote his study of Cobden's role in the peace movement only secondarily as a contribution to historical scholarship; *Richard Cobden, the International Man* was very much a book of its year, 1919. In domestic policy as well Cobdenism survived the war, apparently in good health. As late as 1923 free trade was still a sufficiently potent battle cry around which to reunite the Liberal party and restore it to a semblance of its old importance.

If the twenty-fifth anniversary of the publication of Morley's *Cobden* marked a resurgence of his reputation and influence that continued into the postwar world, the fiftieth anniversary witnessed the near total eclipse of Cobdenism. In 1931 the Liberal party was all but destroyed electorally and acquiesced in the abandonment of free trade as a central principle of British economic policy. Cobdenism, it seemed, could thrive only in a world expanding economically and in the arts of civilization. After 1929 that world was collapsing in upon itself. During the Great Depression the doctrines of laissez-faire liberalism seemed merely cruel where they were not simply beside the point. The growth of the role of the state was no longer a matter of choice; it had to take place if democratic capitalist society was not to disintegrate. Similarly, in the context of the aggressive totalitarianism of the 1930s and 1940s, policies of nonintervention and economy in arms spending, as central to Cobden's thinking as free trade, were once again irrelevant—that is, if they were not felt to be clearly irresponsible. Cobden, who had been looked to as an inspiration for more than half a century after his death, suddenly came to seem as distantly, even naively, Victorian as any of his contemporaries.

During the past two decades, however, as the rhetoric and policies of the welfare state and the cold war era have gradually lost much of their vitality, the limitations of Cobden's thinking have come to seem less important than the fact that he was among the first practical politicians to attempt to come to grips with the wider implications of the economic revolution of his time for government and society, for international relations and war. It is this breadth of vision, rather than its validity or invalidity, that makes him still—and again—a fascinating and important man.

Acknowledgments

First and foremost I should acknowledge my debt to the staffs of the archives where the greater part of the research for this book was done: the West Sussex Record Office in Chichester, the Department of Manuscripts of the British Library, and the Archives Department of the Manchester Central Library. In addition I should like to thank the following for permission to quote from the manuscript collections in their care: the Governors of Dunford House, the West Sussex County Record Office, and the County Archivist for the papers of Richard Cobden; the Department of Manuscripts of the British Library for the papers of John Bright, Richard Cobden, William Ewart Gladstone, Francis Place, and Joseph Sturge; the Leisure Services Committee of the City of Manchester for the papers of Richard Cobden, John Benjamin Smith, and George Wilson; the Trustees of the Broadlands Archives Trust for the papers of Lord Palmerston; and Sir William Gladstone for the papers of William Ewart Gladstone.

Unfair as it may be to single out individuals from among the many with whom I have discussed this work over the years, I should like particularly to acknowledge the help of W. H. Chaloner in its formative stages and my colleague Norman Graebner in everything to do with Anglo-American relations. But my greatest debt is to four people outside the profession: Carlton Dickerson for his support through a period when I was uncertain this work would ever be finished; James Miskovsky, who, with the help of two dogs, ensured that I would keep the work in perspective once I was sure it would be finished; Gerald Trett of the University Press of Virginia for his invaluable advice on the craft of writing; and my cousin Mary Deutsch Edsall for her insights into the character of the subject of this book—and its author.

Contents

PART I

Manchester Manufacturer
1832–1838

CHAPTER 1

Family and Finances

When Richard Cobden settled in Manchester in the autumn of 1832, he was, at the age of twenty-eight, still far in outlook and experience from being the man who entered Parliament nine years later at the head of what was to be the most successful of Victorian mass agitations. The calico printing firm he had founded the year before was still struggling; his father and his elder brother had both recently failed financially, and the future of his younger brothers and sisters was a source of constant worry; he had not yet married. Although he was to become one of the best-traveled public figures of the nineteenth century, he had only once and briefly left the British Isles; having had little formal education, he was still doggedly pursuing self-education; he had never spoken publicly or written for publication; and the beginning of his political career was still five years away. Cobden was not, however, a newcomer either to his adopted city or to the textile trade. He had first visited Lancashire as the traveling representative of his uncle's London-based firm of textile wholesalers seven years before. In 1828 he and two friends had gone into business for themselves as London agents working on commission for Lancashire textile manufacturers. And finally, three years later, they had expanded operations to Lancashire itself, taking over a calico printing works at Sabden, near Clitheroe, and opening a Manchester office.

Thus, by the time he came to live in the North, Cobden was, and felt himself to be, already in part a Mancunian. It is worth recalling how quickly a young man of ability and a bit of nerve could make contacts and develop a reputation in early nineteenth-century Lancashire. In later years Cobden enjoyed recounting how he had gone about setting himself up in business in 1828:

I began business in partnership with two other young men, and we only mustered a thousand pounds amongst us, and more than half of it was borrowed . . . We were literally so ignorant of Manchester houses that we called for a directory at the hotel, and turned to the list of calico printers, theirs being the business with which we were acquainted, and they being the people from whom we felt confident we could obtain credit. And why? Because we knew we should be able to satisfy them that we had advantages from our large connexions, our knowledge of the best branch of the business in London, and our superior taste in design, which would ensure success. We introduced ourselves to Fort Brothers and Co., a rich house, and we told our tale, honestly concealing nothing. In less than two years from 1830 we owed them forty thousand pounds for goods which they had sent to us in Watling St., upon no other security than our characters and knowledge of our business.[1]

It was little different four years later, except that now sheer luck seemed to conspire with his own talents to ease Cobden's final entry into the city. The Fort brothers, who owned the calico printing works at Sabden, proved willing to let it go on favorable terms, largely because they were in the process of reorganizing their business. Cobden was at first less sure of his good judgment in the purchase of a residence in Manchester itself, in Mosley Street, on the edge of the commercial district; but within less than a year of buying it, there was no doubt he had made a coup. "I have given such a start to Mosley St., that all the world will be at my heels soon," he gleefully informed his brother Fred:

My next door neighbor . . . has sold his house to be converted into a warehouse . . . The house immediately opposite to me has been announced for sale, and my architect is commissioned . . . to bid 6000 guineas for it . . . The architect assures me that if I were to put up my house tomorrow, I might have 6000 guineas for it. So as I gave but 3000, and all the world is talking of the bargain here, and there being but one opinion or criterion of a man's ability—*the making of money*—I am already thought a clever fellow.[2]

Small wonder that Cobden was exhilarated by the city. "Manchester is the place for money making business," he wrote, pressing Fred to join him. "It is there that every one of us must sooner or later go."[3] To live in Manchester was like living in the future; it was, in one historian's famous phrase, "the shock city of the age."[4] Every commentator of Cobden's generation would have agreed to that, even those who were the city's most savage detractors. And Cobden was not one of these, certainly not in the sense that Engels and Carlyle were, or in any sense for some time. For one thing, his early years in Manchester coincided with a period of prosperity and relative social peace, very different in temper from the hungry forties, which spawned visions of "sooty Manchester . . . built on the infinite abysses."[5] Not that the social critics of the thirties, although less apocalyptic, were any less trenchant. Cobden was well aware of the darker side of life in Manchester; the first surveys of the city's slums were published about the time he settled there, and, like all newcomers, he was struck by the stark contrasts of the place. Yet despite its deficiencies—even because of them—Manchester seemed to many "the most wonderful city of modern times,"[6] "every whit as wonderful, as fearful, unimaginable as the oldest Salem or Prophetic City."[7] Tocqueville explained this paradox better perhaps than anyone. The Manchester he described in 1835—a year of prosperity—was ugly, dirty, unplanned and ill-governed, squalid—a sewer; yet "from this foul drain the greatest stream of human industry flows out to fertilise the whole world. From this filthy sewer pure gold flows. Here humanity attains its most complete development and its most brutish; here civilisation works its miracles, and civilised man is turned back almost into a savage."[8]

In that contradiction there was as much room for hope as for horror, and everything in Cobden's experience of the city inclined him to be hopeful. For him Manchester was a challenge to be overcome and a source of personal liberation, not of degradation. There, if anywhere, careers were open to talent. "I am sure from what I have seen," he informed his father, "that if you were to strip me naked and turn me into Lancashire with only my experience for capital, I should make a large fortune."[9] To his less confident brother Fred, he wrote: "I wish I could impart to you a little of that Bonapartian feeling with which I am imbued,—a feeling that spurs me on with a conviction that all the obstacles to fortune with which I am impeded will (nay, *shall*) yield if assailed with energy."[10]

If Cobden had any doubts at this stage, they concerned not Manchester, let alone his ability to make his way there, but something less tangible. He was at times disturbed by the intensity of his drive for success: "Sometimes I confess I allow this sort of feeling to gain a painful and harassing ascendency over me. It disquiets me in the night as well as the day. It gnaws my very entrails (a positive truth), and yet if I ask, What is all this yearning after? I can scarcely give myself a satisfactory answer. Surely not for money; I feel a disregard for it, and even a slovenly inattention to its possession, that is quite dangerous."[11]

This may seem odd, indeed hardly credible, in view of Cobden's childhood and youth. To be sure, his early years had been happy and comfortable enough; but from the age of ten until his business was firmly established nearly two decades later, Cobden and his family knew little stability or financial security. For his first five years Richard lived at Dunford, near Heyshott, in West Sussex, the farm where he was born, and although that was sold when his grandfather died in 1809, his father, William, took a smaller farm nearby. From then on, however, the Cobdens fell victim to every downturn in the economic cycle. William Cobden was forced to abandon farming when agricultural prices collapsed near the end of the Napoleonic wars. He ultimately turned to shopkeeping but failed in that as well, first in the panic of 1826 and again soon thereafter. He spent his last years dependent on his children, living first with his eldest son, Frederick, until he too failed in business, and then under the care of two of his daughters.

Each of these crises forced William Cobden to move: from Dunford to a farm nearer Midhurst in 1809; from Sussex to Westmeon in Hampshire after the second farm was lost; and then, in rapid succession, to Farnham in Surrey in 1827, on to Barnet, north of London, two years later, and finally, briefly, to central London in 1832. Although the family remained close through all these changes, it proved impossible for Richard's parents to keep their eleven children together once they abandoned farming. In 1814 Richard was sent to London to live with his mother's brother-in-law, who in turn sent him away to boarding school and later trained him as a clerk in his London warehouse. Throughout this period Richard saw his parents and brothers and sisters only during holidays or when he could arrange a day's outing to meet them somewhere between London and Westmeon.

Life with his uncle was hardly compensation. Although they got along reasonably well before Richard left school in 1819, the years of apprenticeship in his uncle's warehouse were unhappy. All too often his uncle saw Richard's presence as an unwanted responsibility, and Richard felt burdened by obligations he could neither avoid nor, apparently, satisfactorily fulfill. "If I chance to err in any one point of business, I am . . . accused of ingratitude," he told his father in 1822. "Now how is it possible to escape that character if every fault I may happen to fall into makes me liable to be accused of it?"[12] Desperate to find "some place where the prejudices of Relatives and the obligations of Benefactors no longer pressed upon me,"[13] Richard accepted a position with a clothing merchant in Belgium. When he broke the news to his parents, however, they would not hear of his leaving the country (his elder brother, Fred, having earlier emigrated to the United States). Reluctantly, Richard—still a month shy of his eighteenth birthday—acceded to his parents' wishes and stayed on in his uncle's warehouse.

This unhappy episode may not have been entirely fruitless. Richard's differences with his uncle had been aired and became the subject of a lengthy correspondence between uncle and father. Moreover, Richard had found a firm ally in his uncle's partner, Partridge. In any event, Richard's threatened departure marked the beginning of a significant improvement in relations with his uncle. Early in the following year he was placed in charge of the firm's accounts and, although he could still write a year later of those who "inflict rather than bestow their bounty on us,"[14] he had become a valued member of the business even before he was first sent on the road in the autumn of 1825. Also at this time, in 1824, Richard's isolation from his immediate family was ended: the first of his younger brothers moved to London and his elder brother, Fred, returned to England and also settled in London.

Even at this point, however, the catalogue of family misfortunes was by no means complete. The year before his father lost the shop at Westmeon, Richard's mother died of typhoid—all her children were present at the end—and the same crisis that ruined the shop also bankrupted his uncle in London. Richard was out of a job and, like virtually everyone in his family in 1826, had neither money nor prospects. Thereafter, his circumstances, which gradually became divorced from those of the rest of his family, began to improve. He had done well as a commercial traveler, and when his uncle's former partner, Partridge, resumed operations in a new firm, Richard was taken on in his old capacity. Indeed, his qualifications were so highly regarded that when he and his two friends decided to start out on their own, he was able to raise most of his share of the capital by approaching one of the firm's best customers for a loan. This generous customer and benefactor was John Lewis, the founder of the London department store of that name, who was said to have agreed to lend the money, despite Cobden's lack of collateral, simply because "Lewis conceived a liking for the young man on account of the smart and business-like manner in which he used to come to his house and transact whatever he had to do."[15]

Financially at least the worst years were over; Cobden had managed to break the cycle of failure that had defeated all his close relatives. But, understandably, he looked back on the twelve years from the loss of the family farm in 1814 to his first employment outside the family in 1826 as the unhappiest of his life. It was a period to which he rarely referred in later years and from which he was determined to distance himself and, so far as he could, his family completely. "If I am spared," he promised his father in 1829, "our family shall yet live to see the tables turned."[16] That, unfortunately, proved to be an impossibly ambitious goal, because just as Cobden was laying the foundations of his own prosperity, both his father and his elder brother suffered irretrievable financial reverses: his father in 1829, his brother two years later. (Moreover, as if that were not enough, the pattern of family tragedy coinciding with financial disaster was repeated: in 1830, within a few months of each other, an especially beloved younger brother and then a younger sister died.)

Cobden was not involved in his father's failure, but he did have money invested in Fred's business. The financial loss was only the most obvious of his concerns, however; the emotional toll was far greater. The transformation to dependency of the father on the son and of the elder on the younger brother would have been a source of strain within the family, even had Cobden handled the situation perfectly. Unhappily, torn between the demands of his business in Manchester and the responsibility to his relatives in London, he was often impatient and insensitive. Toward his father he was at least always gentle if sometimes patronizing, but with Fred he frequently lost his temper. After the collapse of Fred's business, Cobden lectured him on the importance of positive and aggressive attitudes in business, as in life, and pressed him to make up his mind between staying in London to retrieve what he could of his business, making a fresh start in America, or joining Cobden's firm in Manchester.

Eventually, at the end of 1832, Fred chose the last alternative, but that raised yet another problem: what to do with their father, who had gone to live with Fred after the failure of his shop. In the end his sons managed to place him with one of his married daughters in London, but it was not a happy solution. The old man had nothing to occupy his time and he disliked the city. Coincidentally or not, this last of William Cobden's many retreats marked the beginning of an inexplicable physical decline, which, despite a last-minute move back to the quiet of rural Hampshire, ended in his death in the summer of 1833. Although Cobden had hurried south when his father's condition grew serious, he found that he could not take the strain of the death watch and wrote to Fred in Manchester asking him to come to London in his stead. "I feel a presentiment," he explained, "that to attend the funeral of my father at the grave of my mother would be more than my fortitude is equal to. These trials unfit my nerves and spirits for the world's conflict, which I am compelled to fight for the very existence of those dependent on me."[17]

Luckily for Cobden this was the last time for many years that he would be faced with so harsh a conflict between his personal obligations and the demands of his career. Indeed, he was already well on the way to achieving a degree of financial security that seemed likely to ensure him against such conflicts, for he could hardly have picked a better place and time than Manchester in the early 1830s in which to seek his fortune. The unsettled years between 1829 and the passage of the great reform bill were succeeded by a period of prosperity, and early in 1831, just before he and his partners took over the calico printing works at Sabden, the duty on calicos was repealed. Their firm grew rapidly over the next five years, and risks that in other times might have proved disastrous paid off handsomely. Always impatient with conservative business practices, Cobden, as one of his contemporaries later recalled,

> introduced a new mode of business. The custom of the calico trade at that period was to print a few designs, and watch cautiously and carefully those which were most acceptable to the public, when large quantities of those which seemed to be preferred would be printed off and offered to the retail dealer . . . [Cobden] and his partners did not follow the cautious and slow policy of their predecessors, but fixing themselves upon the best designs, they had these printed off at once, and pushed the sale energetically throughout the country. Those pieces

which failed to take in the home market were at once shipped to other countries, and the consequence was that the associated firms became very prosperous.[18]

The results were indeed impressive: by the end of 1836 the firm had a capital of some £80,000, an annual turnover of about £150,000, and net profits for the year of £23,000.

Yet at that very moment Cobden's interest in the business flagged, and he began to seek out ways of divesting himself of some of his financial responsibilities in order to turn to other pursuits. It is possible that his decision to shift to a public career at a point when the business still required close attention reflected something in his makeup that held him back from achieving a degree of success that had eluded both his father and his elder brother. In view of the fact that twice in later life he failed financially and was rescued only through the intervention of friends, such speculation is at least legitimate. Perhaps a more likely explanation of his growing lack of interest in business and, for that matter, of some of his later financial problems—which were due primarily to overoptimistic speculations in Manchester property and American railroads—was the rapidity with which he had achieved financial success in the first place. Only eight years earlier he had been a commercial traveler and had had to borrow money in order to start a business; now he was at the head of a prosperous firm and had already ventured into the Manchester property market. In the long run this turn in his fortunes may have hurt as much as helped Cobden by giving him an exaggerated view of his business acumen and of his ability to manage his affairs on a part-time basis. More immediately, however, it relieved him of the worry of having to care for his family, gave him the freedom to pursue other goals, and proved to him his capacity to succeed where others in his family had failed.

By comparison, wealth in itself was relatively unimportant to him, and Cobden never appears to have regretted his decision not to seek the great fortune he surely could have made. What had chiefly excited him about the business world was the challenge it offered, but when that challenge had been met and security and independence were apparently assured, his drive in that direction slackened, to be replaced by a sense of frustration. His misgivings about the long-term value of a business career were far from new; they dated back to a time well before he had even the prospect of success. He frequently complained that he found the business world as confining as it was challenging, and the detached humor with which he often commented on the foibles of his fellow businessmen was usually touched with a dose of disdain. On one of the earliest of his business trips Cobden took time out to visit the birthplace of Robert Burns. In an account of it written to his brother Fred, he contrasted his own enthusiasm with the reaction of a manufacturer from Paisley:

> Our worthy Paisley friend remarked to us, as we leaned over the Bridge of Doon, and as its impetuous stream rushed beneath us, "How shamefully," said he, "is the water-power of this country suffered to run to waste—here is the force of twenty horses running completely idle." He did not relish groping amongst ruins and tombstones at midnight, and was particularly solicitous that we should leave matters of discussion until we reached Burns's birthplace, where he had understood they kept the best whiskey in that vicinity.[19]

The side trip was as characteristic of Cobden as the comments on his traveling companion. One of the reasons he enjoyed his work as a commercial traveler was the opportunity it offered to make such excursions and escape, however briefly, from the pressures of buying and selling. "Oh! that I had money," he wrote after a brief visit, between coaches, to Shrewsbury Abbey, "to be deep skilled in the mysteries of mullions and architraves, in lieu of black and purples and pin grounds! How happy I should be."[20] Even after he settled in Manchester and was occupied with the demands of establishing his own firm, his letters were sprinkled with references to his other interests. All too often he felt personally isolated in the business world, and the passage of time, far from softening his youthful strictures on that world, if anything hardened them. In 1838 he wrote to Frederick from Germany: "Our countrymen, if they were possessed of a little of the *mind* of the merchants and manufacturers of Frankfort, Chemnitz, Elberfeld, etc., would become the De Medicis, and Fuggers, and De witts of England, instead of glorying in being the toadies of a cloddish aristocracy, only less enlightened than themselves!"[21]

Precisely when Cobden's dissatisfaction stiffened into a resolve to quit business for a career in public life is uncertain, but it cannot have been much later than the autumn of 1834, only two years after he settled in Manchester. That summer he took his first nonbusiness trip abroad, and in 1835 he wrote his first political pamphlet and his earliest letters to the press. Considerations of a private nature added to his sense of urgency at this time. His health had never been particularly good, and at times he was almost morbidly preoccupied with it. He had suffered severely from the cold during his school years in Yorkshire, and when he first set out on the road in 1825, illness, not the possibility of failure, was his chief worry. Even when he went to live in Manchester and could imagine no other insurmountable barrier to success, the question of his health was always on his mind; his most optimistic letters were likely to be prefaced by the phrase, "If I live . . ." It was a legitimate concern. He fell ill more than once during his time as a traveling salesman. He caught cold easily, suffered from earaches, and was prone to bronchitis. The winters of Lancashire affected him badly, and he was so seriously ill late in 1835 that his doctor recommended he spend the whole of the following winter abroad. As Cobden put it to Fred a couple of years later: "With reference to health . . . we are not made for rivalling Methusaleh, and if we can by care stave off the grim enemy for twenty years longer, we shall do more than nature intended for us. At all events let us remember that to live usefully is far better than living long. And do not let us deprive ourselves of the gratification at last . . . that we have not embittered our whole lives with heaping up money, but that we have given a part of our time to more rational and worthy exertions."[22]

In any case, by the autumn of 1836 Cobden had begun to plan the transition. His hope was to dissolve the old partnership and get out of the London end of the business, retaining only the office in Manchester and one of the firm's calico printing works. Since the business would then be a personal one, Cobden would be free to bring his brothers into it, thus simultaneously ensuring the security of his family and freedom for himself. The realization of Cobden's scheme did not come easily, however. Frederick, rightly uncertain of his ability to carry his share of the burden, constantly urged delay, and relations between the brothers became strained. "One word as to your own private feelings," Cobden wrote warningly to Fred early in 1837,

> which may from many causes be rather inclined to lead you to wish that my entrance into public life were delayed a little. I shall only say that on this head it is now too late to parley; it is now useless to waver . . . Your temperament and mine are unequal, but in this matter I shall

only remind you that my feelings are more deeply implicated than your own, and that whilst I can meet with an adequate share of fortitude any failure which comes from insuperable causes . . . yet if in this case my defeat should spring from your timidity or sensitiveness (shall I say disinclination?), it would afflict me severely, and I fear lastingly.[23]

Despite his impatience, Cobden was not inclined to act precipitously. Even if all went well, it seemed likely that it would be as much as two or three years before he and Fred could accumulate sufficient capital and train their younger brothers. Until then he realized that he would have to devote much of his time to the business, but he also hoped to be able gradually to shift most of the day-to-day burden onto his brothers' shoulders. Indeed, spread over this long a period, the transition would, Cobden believed, take place almost imperceptibly, so that the actual reorganization of the firm would involve little more than making official what had evolved in practice. That, at any rate, is how he outlined the future to Fred, to whom he promised "to give a few years of entire exertion towards making the separation successful to ourselves. But," he also made it clear, "at the same time all my exertions will be with an eye to make myself independent of all business claims on my time and anxieties."[24] And with that understanding, the new arrangements were consumated in the summer of 1839.

Whether or not Cobden seriously intended to give those "few years of entire exertion" to the business in its new form, he did not do so. A few months after making that promise in the fall of 1838, circumstances and his own inclinations drew him into the agitation against the Corn Laws. The business suffered accordingly. Frederick proved as uncertain a businessman in partnership with Richard as he had been on his own. The new firm was small, deficient both in capital and trained personnel, and in any case its early years were difficult ones in the British economy as a whole. Nonetheless, for the time being at least, Cobden had gained what he most wanted: freedom from the responsibilities of partnership, apparent financial security for himself in association with his brothers, and the opportunity "to give part of . . . [his] time to more rational and worthy exertions."

CHAPTER 2

Education, Travel, and Authorship

If financial independence was the first prerequisite of a public career, it was not, at least in the long run, the most important to Cobden. There was a purpose behind the reading and the brief excursions with which he diverted himself during his early years in business. He felt keenly his lack of background and education and was as determined to make good those deficiencies as to achieve financial security. His formal schooling had been spotty at best and had ended at the age of fifteen. Until he was ten he attended school in Midhurst; after the family farm was lost, his uncle sent him to a boarding school in the north Yorkshire dales, some five miles in distance and even closer in character to the model for Dickens's Dotheboys Hall. Cobden spent five miserable years there and escaped only when his father was informed of his circumstances by a sympathetic usher at the school.

Remarkably, his love of learning survived this experience, although certainly not through any encouragement from his uncle, who showed no understanding of his nephew's intellectual interests. Even so, life in his uncle's warehouse was preferable to his school years; he now had some spending money, access to London, close contact with his brother Frederick, who settled in London when Richard was twenty, and, despite his uncle, sufficient time to pursue self-education. It was a serious business, undertaken with industry and method apparently from the outset; but it was emphatically neither joyless nor narrow. Young Cobden gambled a bit, went now and then to Vauxhall Gardens, learned to dance, and became an inveterate theatergoer. He developed a lifelong habit of haunting bookshops and began to build a personal library.

Perhaps because he had had little formal schooling, Cobden's knowledge of the classics was limited; he was, however, fluent in

French and widely read in modern literature. Cervantes and Le Sage; Shakespeare, Spenser, Byron, and Burns; Irving and Cooper were among the authors quoted or referred to in his early political pamphlets or travel diaries. There was nothing perfunctory about his relationship with the works of literature he loved. It was not by chance that his second journey as a commercial traveler took him to Burns's birthplace; when he sailed to the Mediterranean and first saw Cadiz, it was Byron's description he recalled in his letter home; and on his first trip to the United States, he did not regard an excursion up the Hudson as complete without a visit to the scene of Rip Van Winkle's dream. For a time, around the age of twenty, Cobden even considered a literary career and went so far as to write a play which he submitted—unsuccessfully—to the manager of Covent Garden.

His interest in literature and, as he traveled more widely, in the visual arts never waned, but increasingly the failed playwright turned to other subjects: modern history, serious travel literature, the works of the French and British Enlightenment philosophers and, above all, political economy. Adam Smith, as Cobden readily acknowledged, was the greatest single influence on his thought. Cobden regarded him as the most important practical philosopher of the age and hoped for a future in which the great cities of England would "possess their Smithian Societies, devoted to the purpose of promulgating the beneficent truths of the 'Wealth of Nations.' "[1]

Cobden's choice of mentor among living thinkers is more surprising—and has caused some discomfort to his biographers ever since. George Combe, the chief British exponent of phrenology, was enormously influential in the early Victorian era, and Cobden was by no means unusual when he declared, after reading Combe's *Constitution of Man*, that it seemed "like a transcript of his own familiar thoughts."[2] Despite this, Donald Read, in his study of Cobden and Bright, belittled the influence of phrenology on Cobden, citing for example Cobden's humorous treatment of the new science in his one venture at playwrighting.[3] In fact Combe's influence on Cobden was as long lasting as it was important. The two men corresponded for years. Cobden tried with limited success to found a phrenological society in Manchester in the 1830s, and throughout his life he rarely recorded his impressions on first meeting an important public figure without commenting on the man's character as revealed by the shape of his head.

John Morley, although he too underplayed the influence of this aspect of phrenology on Cobden, was closer to the mark in stressing the broader philosophical implications of Cobden's attraction to Combe.[4] To many phrenology appeared to be the latest chapter in the scientific revolution stretching back to the seventeenth century. It was an attempt to construct a science of the mind, to study human personality and therefore human relationships and institutions as one would study any other natural phenomenon. Moreover—and this was clearly of primary importance to Cobden—phrenology, at least in the hands of George Combe, was a reformist doctrine. For although it taught that personality was the result of brain physiology and thus hereditary, it did not argue that personality was immutable. On the contrary, Combe believed that through physical exercise, self-discipline, education, and social reform the physical and psychological makeup of the individual could be improved. Phrenology in this sense seemed to provide a link and a basis in the natural sciences for the newly emerging social sciences of economics and utilitarianism. Small wonder that Cobden, like many reform-minded men of his generation on both sides of the Atlantic, was attracted to it.

What we know of the development of Cobden's thought prior to 1835 must be gleaned from passing remarks in his correspondence or from literary and historical references in his early political writings. Quite the opposite is the case with the other major facet of his self-education, his travels, which assumed increasing importance in the last years before he entered public life. During all of his early trips abroad he wrote frequent letters to his brothers and sisters and kept detailed journals. These are certainly the best evidence of the importance Cobden attached to his travels, but it is the sheer extent of those travels that most dramatically illustrates what they meant to him. Cobden had in fact been something of a compulsive traveler ever since going on the road for his uncle in 1825, and although these early business trips had taken him no farther afield than Ireland, that in itself made him a rarity among nineteenth-century British politicians.

The requirements of establishing a business kept him close to Manchester or London after 1828, but he did manage one brief business trip to Paris, his first as an adult outside the British Isles, in 1833. In the spring of the following year, however, the business was sufficiently secure that Cobden felt free to embark on the first of many private trips abroad, in this case to France and Switzerland. This was followed in quick succession by journeys to the northeastern United

States in the summer of 1835, to the eastern Mediterranean in the winter of 1836–7, and to Germany in the summer of 1838. In all Cobden spent nearly a year in a period of just over four years away from England. Although his longest absence, six months on the Mediterranean voyage, was undertaken largely for his health, it is unlikely he would have traveled much less even had his health been excellent; he might, indeed, have traveled more, or at least more frequently. In any case his journeys, including that to the Mediterranean, could hardly be called restful, since quite apart from the problems inherent in traveling on the eve of the age of steam, Cobden traveled with a purpose.

Even in his most anecdotal letters, dramatic evocations of the sublimities of nature often led to observations on the uses to which the local inhabitants had—or had failed to—put their natural environment; and Cobden almost always used his vivid descriptions of local color as pegs on which to hang political or social commentary. The great monuments of the ancient world led to similar reflections. Although awed by the pyramids, he could not resist comparing the labor expended in building them unfavorably with the construction of that wonder of modern and useful engineering, the Plymouth breakwater. Not that the moderns, least of all his own countrymen, always got the better of comparisons with the ancients. Parting shots apparently directed at one time and place often found their way to a different target. "What famous puffers those old Greeks were!" he wrote from Smyrna. "Half the educated world in Europe is now devoting more thought to the ancient affairs of these Lilliputian states, the squabbles of their tribes, the wars of their villages, the geography of their rivulets and hillocks, than they bestow upon the modern history of the South and North Americans, and the charts of the mighty rivers and mountains of the new world."[5]

Compared with the chatty letters home, the travel diaries, written for his own eyes, were more impressionistic, summing up a place or person or local custom in a few phrases. Now and then his enthusiasm, usually for a place of natural beauty, spilled over into an entry of essay length. He spent as much time at—and wrote as copiously about—Niagara Falls as any other place in the United States, for example. But for the most part his longer entries dealt with practical matters: wage, price, and trade figures, reports of conversations with local businessmen or resident Englishmen, descriptions of visits to factories, schools, prisons, and the like. Factual though they often were, the diaries were never dull or dry. He had an excellent sense of place and an eye for the telling detail that could bring to life the record of a chance encounter or conversation. Always the diaries were more descriptive than analytical, and for good reason. In his travels Cobden was seeking out not the raw material of his political and economic thought but rather a means of fleshing out his ideas, of making the abstract concrete. He was, as it were, accumulating additional ammunition for weapons already forged against targets he had already chosen. Significantly, he made his first visit to the United States not before but after, and immediately after, writing a pamphlet devoted largely to America. Similarly, the publication of his pamphlet on the Eastern question preceded, again immediately, rather than followed his Mediterranean journey.

Like most travelers at most times, Cobden found just about what he had anticipated before setting out, and travel changed his views only to the extent of strengthening them. His visit to Turkey made him more anti-Turkish, while first-hand experience of the United States transformed admiration into affection. Cobden found nothing good to say of the "ruined, worn out" Turkish empire, no reason to suppose it would not continue to fall to pieces.[6] In America, however, he felt quite at home, comparing the cities he visited in terms of which he would most like to live in. "You know," he wrote Fred near the end of his journey,

> I predicted when leaving England for this continent, that I should not find it sufficiently to my taste to relish a sojourn here for life. My feelings in this respect are quite altered . . . My estimate of the American character has improved, contrary to my expectations, by this visit. Great as was my previous esteem for the qualities of this people, I find myself in love with their intelligence, their sincerity, and the decorous self-respect which actuates all classes. The very genius of activity seems to have found its fit abode in the souls of this restless and energetic race.[7]

Cobden did not like some aspects of the United States, however. He thought American women too pale and thin, and American children spoiled; he disliked the national habits of spitting in public and boasting about everything American; he was appalled by the summer climate. More important, every encounter with slavery made him profoundly uncomfortable, and he was relieved to quit Maryland for Pennsylvania. But America's scale and resources and the energy and democratic spirit of its people impressed Cobden greatly, and he returned to England convinced that the United States, which many Europeans patronized when they did not ignore it, would soon surpass Europe in wealth and power.

Among the smaller European nations he singled out Switzerland and Greece for praise: Greece for its promise now that it was free from Turkish misrule and Switzerland for its achievements under peace and free trade. Of the greater states of Europe he admired Prussia especially: for its leadership in the Zollverein, for its commitment to popular education, and above all for the quality of its government, which he thought the best, the most "simple and economical," in Europe. That it was an autocratic government did not bother Cobden: "I would gladly give up my taste for talking politics," he declared, "to secure such a state of things in England."[8] Cobden was careful to keep that sentiment private, of course, but he made no secret of his admiration for Prussia and America, or of his antipathy toward the Turks. These were far from being majority sentiments in England in the 1830s, and surely one purpose of Cobden's travels was to establish his credentials as a knowledgeable critic of established opinions and policies.

By the time he began to pursue a public career, Cobden was already one of the best-read and best-traveled political figures of the Victorian era. The importance he attached to these accomplishments was considerable. His fame as an agitator is in a way misleading; Cobden's politics were above all the politics of ideas, and it is no accident that his first venture into public life involved not running for office or taking part in some agitation but the writing of two long pamphlets on general questions of public policy: the first, *England, Ireland and America*, published in 1835, the second, *Russia*, following a year later. No less characteristic of their author than that he chose to write the pamphlets in the first place was Cobden's approach to the issues of the day in these early writings. Although the most recent Russian threat to the decaying Turkish empire was what prompted him to rush into print, the pamphlets ranged beyond that topic from their very first pages. Indeed, together they contained almost all the ingredients of his political and economic thought and, moreover, in a form that was to remain remarkably constant throughout his public career.

They did not, of course, have the polish of his later writings and speeches. *England, Ireland and America* in particular, perhaps because it was Cobden's first work, attempted to deal with too much. Nonetheless, underlying the sometimes confused surface of this pamphlet—and more immediately apparent in the better organized second one—are a few central themes to which he often was to return.

Cobden made perhaps the best and certainly the most succinct statement of his basic thesis almost in passing halfway through the second pamphlet. Whatever may have been the case in former times, he argued, it is "labor, improvements and discoveries that confer the greatest strength upon a people . . . by these alone and not by the sword of the conquerer can nations in modern and all future times hope to rise to power and grandeur."[9] This was the lesson Cobden hoped to teach through the pamphlets, a lesson that in his view England's governors failed to understand. They did little to enhance and much to inhibit discovery, improvement, and the productive use of labor, and they wasted millions of pounds in the defense of England's past conquests or in anticipation of the possible conquests of others. Unless and until this order of priorities was reversed, Cobden feared, England stood in danger of forfeiting her present position in the world.

This issue was the overriding concern of the pamphlets, the source of the sense of urgency that pervades them, and understandably they consist largely of a catalogue of misdeeds and misconceptions on the part of England's governors. No area of public policy escaped Cobden's critical attention, from domestic taxation and education through the administration of Ireland and the empire to naval policy and tariffs. But his favorite target and the opening subject of both pamphlets was the doctrine of the balance of power. That shibboleth of British foreign policy and in particular its application to the unanswerable Eastern question seemed to Cobden to epitomize all that was misguided and dangerous in the conduct of national policy. Far from being a principle of statecraft or foundation of policy, it was a chimera without real meaning or definition, a source not of stability but of conflict, a goal that could never be achieved—a will o' the wisp. For a century and a half Britain had fought under that banner, yet "empires have arisen unbidden by us; others have departed despite our utmost efforts to preserve them."[10]

It therefore followed that if now, in the nineteenth century, Turkey was to collapse through her own incompetence and backwardness, Britain should not attempt to stop the process because, in the end, there was little she could do. That was realism; it was also, in Cobden's view, sound policy. He had no fears of the consequences of Turkish collapse. Even if the worst happened and Russia occupied Constantinople, he did not believe that this would threaten the security of the rest of Europe or the safety of British commerce and the British empire. Conquest, the mere addition of territory, did not necessarily add to a nation's power. On the contrary, Russia in possession of Turkey would be tied down for years by the task of subduing and developing these backward lands. As for the conquered territories themselves, Russian occupation could only bring about their advancement, and that in turn, Cobden asserted, could not help but work to Britain's advantage. For, in the end, "whatever tends to advance the civilisation and augment the wealth of any part of the world must be beneficial . . . to us who are the greatest commercial and manufacturing people."[11]

As for the argument that Russia would close any conquests to foreign commerce, that, Cobden believed, was nonsense. Experience was against it: Russian expansion to the Black Sea, so feared in the late eighteenth century, had actually led to increased British trade in the area. More important, economic self-interest was against it. In an increasingly competitive world no nation could cut itself off from international commerce and hope to prosper. Not even Napoleon at the height of his power had been able to break the British economy or exclude British trade from the continent. The key to any nation's prosperity and power lay not in conquest but in commercial and industrial supremacy, and the way to that was simply and only through the ability to undersell other nations: "Cheapness . . . will command commerce; and whatever else is needful will follow in its train."[12]

Those who failed to recognize this truth, Cobden believed, were the prisoners of outmoded mercantilist views of commercial rivalry as a kind of economic warfare. Such views had perhaps been tenable in the past when the bulk of world commerce was in the hands of a few imperial powers all pursuing mercantilist policies backed by large navies. It was tenable no longer. The emergence of an independent western hemisphere had revolutionized the world economy and world politics, rendering the closed economies of Europe and its empires vulnerable. More than a dozen new states were now free to buy in the cheapest market and sell in the dearest; "the new world is destined to become the arbiter of the commercial policy of the old."[13] Compared with the growth of New York on the eastern shore of a vast and developing continent, it mattered little whether Constantinople was or was not in Russian hands. The Atlantic, not the Mediterranean, was the fulcrum of a new balance of power, a fact that parochial Europeans failed to recognize at their peril. Already British policies such as tariffs on American food exports and wartime restrictions on neutral shipping had unwittingly provided incentives for American industrial development at the expense of British exports. If present trends and policies continued, Cobden believed, the United States would surpass Britain as the world's leading economic power well before the end of the century.

America, to Cobden, was not, however, merely an economic rival of enormous potential; she also by her example provided an opportunity and a goad to the British in setting their own economic policy. Already American competition or the need to trade in the American market had compelled Britain to abandon many of the regulations governing colonial commerce. It was Cobden's hope that ultimately Britain would be led to realize the futility of all imperial bounties and monopolies, the effects of which were merely to subsidize uneconomic enterprise and inhibit the natural development of the colonial economies. For much the same reason, he believed, England would be pushed into abandoning protective tariffs, especially on food and raw materials, because, in the end, these measures reduced the incomes of the primary producing nations which were Britain's natural customers and also made Britain less competitive abroad by raising the cost of living and the costs of production at home. In the long run, Cobden was certain, Britain had little choice. Incapable of economic self-sufficiency, it could increase its national wealth only through expanded trade based on greater industrial efficiency and specialization. This was or would soon become so obvious that Cobden had little doubt of the ultimate course of national economic policy. It was only a matter of time; but time, as he pointed out, was one luxury Britain had less of than its leaders imagined.

Although changes in national economic policy seemed inevitable to Cobden, the same could not be said of reforms in the other area of greatest concern to him, foreign and military policy. England's rulers and most of her people regarded an interventionist foreign policy backed by a strong navy as essential to national security and the protection of commerce. To Cobden just the opposite was true. Free and expanding trade and a noninterventionist foreign policy were not separate goals but two aspects of the same policy. Each tended to foster—indeed was ultimately indispensable to—the other, and together they promised in the long run to provide the surest foundation for national security. But this, Cobden realized, was far from being self-evident. The contradictory results of traditional economic policy were even then becoming apparent, but it was no easy matter to demonstrate that the risks involved in abandoning traditional foreign and military policy were not greater than the alleged benefits.

Hence, once more, the importance to Cobden of the American example. By rendering mercantilist policy outmoded, the growth of an independent western hemisphere had also in effect made traditional foreign and military policy unnecessary and even detrimental to Britain's national interests. With the old colonial system a nullity and the empire itself therefore increasingly an economic burden, of what use were the far-flung military establishments designed to protect that empire? Since in time of peace Britain could no longer enforce its commerce or exclude that of others in independent states, why should it any longer maintain the fleets and bases built in another time to serve a trade it now commanded freely by its industry or not at all? Under these new circumstances the costs of servicing its war-related national debt and of the ships built to protect its commerce were unnecessary taxes on the nation's industry. In the past and in competition with its European rivals, all of whom maintained large military establishments, Britain could afford such burdens. America, by contrast, presented a different kind of challenge. Self-sufficient, free of national debt, and unencumbered with imperial responsibilities, it alone among the major powers combined nearly free trade with an economical noninterventionist foreign policy. With a navy smaller than Britain's and designed, as Cobden believed Britain's should be, solely for national defense and the protection of shipping, America nonetheless enjoyed a secure and steadily growing commerce. That was an example that Britain simply could not afford not to follow.

Furthermore, and this was the heart of Cobden's argument, it was an example that Britain could afford to follow both easily and safely. Wealthy and productive beyond any other nation, secured by geography against invasion, and uniquely placed to dominate the richest sea lanes, Britain alone among the states of Europe could risk turning its back on the quarrels of Europe. And that in essence was what Cobden was asking of his countrymen—that they take such a risk, that they gamble on a future different from the past. All his criticisms of traditional policy were designed ultimately to demonstrate that the risks involved in abandoning past policies were not that great; his use of the American example was designed to prove that the risks involved in not abandoning such policies were far greater. Such a gamble was really no gamble at all, and beyond that, Cobden passionately believed, for England to take that risk was to open up for it and for the world a unique historical opportunity. For just as the example of America's peaceful prosperity was bound to draw or drive England to similar policies, so the adoption of a noninterventionist, economical, and free trade policy by Great Britain would lead to such an increase in its prosperity that no nation in the world would dare ignore the lesson. Britain's power and authority—not military but economic— were so great, so unexampled in human history, that it could by its leadership and example do more than any other nation to bring about that future different from the past, a future in which "states will turn moralist, in the end, in self defense."[14]

CHAPTER 3

The Political Setting

Important though the pamphlets were in the development of Cobden's political philosophy, they had another more immediate purpose: they were propaganda pieces designed to ease his path—by way of Manchester—into national politics, and sprinkled through them were none too subtle appeals to the interests and prejudices of a provincial middle-class audience. In a sense, of course, the whole of both pamphlets was a paean of praise for manufacturing as against other interests, but Cobden took care to point up the message lest anyone miss it. Again and again he emphasized that England's greatness derived entirely from the inventiveness and productivity of its manufacturing population, so much so in fact that he enjoyed playing with the notion of the North and Midlands as almost a nation unto themselves. He talked of "Liverpool and Hull with their navies, and Manchester, Leeds and Birmingham with their capitals."[1] He speculated that "even the four counties Lancashire, Yorkshire, Cheshire, and Staffordshire could, at any moment, by means of the wealth drawn, by the skill and industry of its population, from the natural resources of this comparative speck of territory, combat with success the whole Russian empire." Yet this England, this industrial nation, was hostage to other interests in society: "This great and independent order of society . . . is deprived of the just reward of its ingenious labour by the tyranny of the corn-laws . . . it possesses no representation . . . in one of the Houses of Parliament . . . and . . . it still lies under the stigma of feudal laws, that confer rights, privileges, and exemptions upon landed possessions, which are denied to personal property."[2]

Here in embryo was the political argument Cobden was to develop over his next ten years as an agitator. However, although clearly written with the response of the manufacturing interest in mind and signed, simply, "by a Manchester manufacturer," the pamphlets were not in subtle and important ways of Manchester. Cobden's commitment to classical economic thought and his identification with the interests of his adopted city do not suffice to account for the intensity with which the pamphlets were written, let alone for the personal quirks that surfaced here and there throughout them. His loathing for the Turks was almost matched by his disdain for England's tendency to romanticize the Poles, who he believed were better off under Russian rule (a view that set him apart from almost all other radicals). Cobden's most startling outburst was a six-page attack on Catholicism as an enemy to progress. But the most persistent and important subtheme of the pamphlets was his loathing for the great landed proprietors of England.

Scattered through both pamphlets are nasty asides directed against the aristocracy: at their "prodigality and insolence abroad . . . which . . . disgraced . . . their native country,"[3] at their selfish interest in the high price of food, and at their love of "the honors, the fame, the emoluments of war; the battle plain," he concluded in his most savage comment, "is the harvest field of the aristocracy, watered with the blood of the people."[4] Attacks on the aristocracy as a parasitic class living off the industry of others were, of course, part of the rhetoric of the age and remained a useful weapon in the radical arsenal until the time of Lloyd George. But Cobden's private correspondence proves what the pamphlets indicate, that he truly hated the aristocracy—that he did indeed believe that as a privileged military and political caste they were the chief practitioners of and only beneficiaries from patronage, corruption, foreign adventurism, and war; that as a privileged economic class they were the scourge of Ireland and the chief obstacle to an open society in England; and that, if England was ever to become a democratic, educated, prosperous, well-governed, and, above all, peaceful society, their enormous power would first have to be broken.

What lay at the root of this often bitter obsession can only be guessed at, but it is not too much to say that, in part, the Manchester manufacturer of thirty-one was speaking for the boy of ten whose father had lost his farm. Certainly there is no denying the importance of that event in Cobden's life; it marked the dividing line between a childhood he idealized in later years and a humiliating and often lonely youth. Despite his years in Manchester and London, Cobden liked to think of himself as a countryman; he never lost his Sussex accent and was proud of his rural heritage. He came of yeoman stock—his grandfather had been a maltster and local bailiff as well as a farmer—and the Cobden connection with Midhurst dated back two hundred years (and there had been Cobdens in West Sussex three centuries before that). One of Cobden's yearnings, an occasional subject of his correspondence even in his early years in Manchester, was to replant his roots in his native soil. Among the first things he did after the successful completion of the campaign to repeal the Corn Laws gave him the personal freedom and financial resources to settle down was to arrange for the purchase of his birthplace at Dunford. Although he had not lived there since the age of five, he clearly felt that he was coming home and always spoke of it with a sense of belonging that he felt nowhere else. "I have been for some weeks in one of the most secluded corners of England," he wrote a close friend soon after moving in:

> The roof which now shelters me is that under which I was born, and the room where I now sleep is the one in which I first drew breath. It is an old farm-house, which had for many years been turned into labourers' cottages. With the aid of the whitewasher and carpenter, we have made a comfortable weather-proof retreat for summer; and we are surrounded with pleasant woods, and within a couple of miles of the summit of the South Down hills, where we have the finest air and some of the prettiest views in England.[5]

For the rest of his life Cobden spent as much time at Dunford as possible. The tendency, then and since, to identify him with Manchester is misleading. He was closely associated with that city for less than half his sixty years and lived there only fifteen years. He spent more even of his adult life in Sussex than in Lancashire. As with William Cobbett, much of Cobden's urban radicalism can only be understood in terms of his rural background and his nostalgia for the English countryside. "We were born and bred up," he wrote in his first pamphlet, amidst "the pastoral charms of the south of England, and we confess to so much attachment to the pursuits of our forefathers ... that, had we the casting of the role of all the actors on the world's stage, we do not think we would suffer a cotton mill or a manufactory to have a place in it."[6]

The rural England Cobden loved was a very particular rural England, however. It was the world of the smallholder. There was in his view no single landed interest but two competing and incompatible interests: that of the working farmer and that of the great landowner. The prosperity of the farmer depended on low rents, tenant rights, and, in the long run, the general prosperity of the country; if he but knew it, he was the natural ally of the urban middle class. The prosperity of the great landowner rested on high rents and high food prices; he was the enemy equally of the farmer and of the city dweller. Not the farmer but only the landlord benefited from agricultural protection; not the farmer but only the landlord would suffer from its removal—and about time too.

Probably because the pamphlets were addressed primarily to an urban audience, Cobden did not use them to develop this line of argument, but its relevance to his personal history is clear. Ordinary farmers such as Cobden's father had borne the brunt of the price fall in agriculture beginning in 1813. Tenants experienced a disastrous drop in incomes without a commensurate decrease in rents, and freeholders by the thousands sold out to the great landlords, who in turn used their political power to protect themselves through the passage of the Corn Laws. How fitting it was to seem to Cobden therefore that Dunford came into his possession as a direct result of his agitation against the Corn Laws, the money he used to purchase it having been raised by public subscription as a testimonial to his efforts. Dunford was not merely his home; its purchase represented a personal vindication, even a kind of revenge, and he clearly regarded it as his by more than merely the right of ownership. Once, in answer to some heckling about where the money for Dunford had come from, he declared:

> Yes; I am indebted for that estate, and I am proud here to acknowledge it, to the bounty of my countrymen. That estate was the scene of my birth and of my infancy; it was the property of my ancestors; it is by the munificence of my countrymen that this small estate, which had been alienated by my father by necessity, has again come into my hands, and that I am enabled to light up again the hearth of my fathers; and I say that there is no warrior duke who owns a vast domain by the vote of the imperial Parliament who holds his property by a more honourable title than that by which I possess mine.[7]

Cobden's hatred of oligarchy colored his views of urban society as well and posed some problems for him in Manchester. He always felt most comfortable politically with the middling to lower middle class—shopkeepers, small-scale manufacturers, independent artisans, and the like—what might well be called the urban yeomanry and he himself termed the shopocracy. Early on he recognized that a comparatively egalitarian city such as Birmingham, with its specialized trades and a skilled working population, offered perhaps the most fertile field for his ideas. Manchester was an altogether trickier proposition. He often complained that "the huge factories of the Cotton district, with three thousand hands under one capitalist, give to our state of society the worst possible tone, by placing an impassable gulf between master and operative."[8] Manchester, to be sure, was healthier in this regard than the almost exclusively manufacturing cities surrounding it; as the metropolis and commercial center of southern Lancashire, it had a large shopocracy. Nonetheless, even in Manchester the atmosphere of local society and politics was all too often pervaded by the conflict between its poles, and the shopocracy, fearful of one extreme, looked uneasily to the other for leadership. And that, in Cobden's view, was precisely the source of many of Manchester's political problems, for the upper middle class of the city, the small elite of great manufacturing, mercantile, and banking families, was too exclusive, too timid, too little aware of its real interests. Instead of providing a model and leadership for the productive classes as a whole in the struggle against oligarchy, they tended to regard themselves as a kind of urban aristocracy and, more dangerously, to ape the customs of the landed aristocracy. As he commented in one of the pamphlets, "Of what conceivable use . . . would it be to strike down the lofty patricians that have descended to us from the days of the Normans and Plantagenets, if we of the middle class . . . are prepared to lift up, from amongst ourselves, an aristocracy of mere wealth—not less austere, not less selfish—only less noble than that we had deposed."[9]

Whatever the justice of Cobden's strictures on the upper middle class of Manchester, there was no denying the disunity and lack of adequate leadership of the reform interest in the city. Where Birmingham, for example, had a single dominant reform tradition, Manchester had no less than three separate Liberal or radical strains, and, just to confuse the matter further, a fourth, Tory reform tradition as well. On the whole, since the end of the Napoleonic wars, it had proved impossible to bring more than two of them together at any time or for long. At the top of the political as of the social scale was the upper-middle-class elite Cobden so distrusted. Variously termed Whig Liberals, *Manchester Guardian* Liberals, or simply moderate reformers, they were, although slow to act, reasonably sound, in Cobden's view, on economic issues. They had supported all the economic reforms of the past generation: repeal of the Orders in Council, resumption of specie payments, abolition of the income tax, the lowering of import duties, and so forth. But toward any movement for political reform, indeed toward any measure that did not touch their economic interests, they were either indifferent or, if it smacked of radicalism, hostile. Indeed, whenever an independent radical reform movement threatened to develop, they tended to opt out of active politics or be frightened into a tacit alliance with the Tories. That, to a great degree, is what had happened following the end of the Napoleonic wars, culminating in the Peterloo massacre.

Much the same thing had come close to happening just before Cobden settled in Manchester during the crisis leading to the passage of the reform bill of 1832. That it did not happen again was due in part to the reform bill's having been a moderate government measure, in part, presumably, to the moderates' determination not to be outflanked again, but also, surely, to the fact that the working-class radicals were preoccupied with other, nonpolitical issues in the early stages of the reform bill controversy. This opened up a political vacuum into which even the most cautious reformers could safely step. Not that they stepped very far, even then, or that this was a sign that the social gap in Manchester was narrowing. The moderates backed off at every indication of ultraradical activity, and two separate reform movements emerged. Moreover, the issues that had temporarily diverted working-class attention from political agitation—trade unionism and factory reform—were as much anathema to the moderates as democratic political reform.

In theory the gap between the upper-middle-class Whig Liberals and the working-class ultraradicals should have been bridged by the shopocracy. But they too were alarmed by the ultraradicals and in any case lacked the wherewithall to dominate Manchester politics. They had, it is true, played a key role in the agitation for the reform bill, but that was largely by default. With the cautious Whig Liberals and preoccupied ultraradicals both entering the field late, a group of moderate radicals, led by Archibald Prentice, the proprietor of the *Manchester Times*, was able to take the initiative in founding a political union in support of the reform bill. Nonetheless, this group proved incapable of building a base of support broad enough to allow them to ignore or overawe potential rivals from right and left, and, largely because of this, they had to be content with seconding the activities of the unified and confident Birmingham Political Union.

The costs of such disunity were high. At best the reformers of Manchester could summon up a variety of special interest agitations pressing for limited goals or, alternatively, broader but cautious movements following in the wake of better organized reformers elsewhere. At worst their efforts tended to cancel each other out or disintegrate in mutual suspicion, thus handing the city's Tories an influence out of proportion to their numbers. Indeed the Tories had learned to play skillfully on these divisions, either aligning themselves with the moderates when things threatened to get out of hand or, in some cases, lending their support to the ultraradicals on such nonpolitical, humanitarian social questions as factory reform. Whatever the particular outcome, the reformers of Manchester had forfeited much of the political influence to which the wealth and population of their city entitled it.

It was Cobden's ambition to change all this and give to Manchester what it had hitherto lacked, a central reform tradition. Specifically he hoped to mobilize the city's middling classes as the core of a broad reform alliance untainted by Whiggism or ultraradicalism and strong enough to overwhelm the Tories not only in Manchester but, under Manchester's leadership and example, throughout the manufacturing districts and beyond. As late as 1836 he appears to have been optimistic about achieving this goal in the near future. As a result of the reform bill, he declared (although he undoubtedly overstated his faith for propaganda purposes), "the governing power is now wholly transferred to the hands of the middling class."[10] He recognized that "time may be necessary to develop the effects of the complete submission of the former dominant influence," but he had little doubt that it could happen within the existing political framework. What was needed above all was to educate the new electorate as to their real interests, and the pamphlets—his contribution to that process—made it clear that he did not underestimate the difficulty of the task or the danger of delay. Nonetheless, once that was achieved, he believed, the rest—a majority in Parliament and control of government personnel and policy—would follow.

Such optimism was not peculiar to Cobden at this time; most

middle-class radicals shared in it. The reform bill had begun a process that appeared to have no ending. The balance of constitutional power had continued to shift against the monarchy and the House of Lords, Parliament was still passing measures of reform, and the radical gains in the general election of 1835 held out the promise of more to come. The future seemed to be in their hands; they needed only the knowledge and the will to shape its course correctly.

CHAPTER 4

Political Beginnings

Cobden's optimism concerning the likely future course of British politics was not to survive for long. Reformers in general—-and Cobden personally—suffered a series of reverses in 1837 that substantially altered his outlook. By then, luckily for him, Cobden had already taken his first tentative steps in public life and was beginning to establish a reputation among reformers. Since he did not venture into local politics until late in 1835, after the publication of his first pamphlet and his visit to the United States, that was no small achievement. Even before the prospects for reform began to dim in 1837, however, Cobden had difficulty finding his feet politically. He tended, once he had made the decision to divert some of his energy from business to public affairs, to become too deeply involved too quickly. The air of expectancy among reformers combined with his own impatient enthusiasm to lead him into a number of dead ends and to spread himself too thin. Not content with concentrating on one or two primary goals, he pursued a variety of interests simultaneously and, almost inevitably, with mixed results.

For the most part this was due to inexperience and lack of public recognition, but there were personal reasons as well. It was characteristic of Cobden throughout his career that he was drawn to two or three causes at once and had great difficulty deciding which should have priority. As in his first pamphlet, so also in practical politics there were often digressions that, however interesting in themselves, tended to vitiate his effectiveness. At this time, public education, fiscal and economic questions, and political reform all attracted his attention. Each appeared important and full of potential in 1835 and 1836, but none to the exclusion of the others. As was to happen again and again in later years, circumstances ultimately decided the issue for Cobden, but for the moment circumstances only compounded the problem. Although the prospects for reform seemed promising, their direction was by no means clear. No dominant issue emerged, and reformers of various stripes attacked on all fronts. Cobden's varied activities in Manchester during these years were as much an indication of political uncertainty—and opportunism—as of the wide-ranging nature of his concerns.

Politically the most important issue in Manchester—and, as it turned out, to Cobden—was local government reform. It was with this issue that ultimately, in 1838, he had his first success as a political leader; it was on this issue also that he made his inauspicious political debut three years earlier. The circumstances were curious. *England, Ireland and America* was not Cobden's only anonymous publication in 1835. He also wrote a series of letters to the *Manchester Times* over the pseudonym Libra, in which he urged his fellow citizens to take advantage of the provisions of the recently passed Municipal Corporations Act allowing unincorporated boroughs such as Manchester to petition for local self-government. The proprietors of the *Times*, Archibald Prentice and William Cathrall, were impressed with the letters, and all the more so when they found out by accident that *England, Ireland and America* had also been written by their mysterious correspondent. Eventually they were able to discover his identity and arrange a meeting or (there are conflicting accounts) arrange a meeting and discover his identity. In any case, they were so taken with Cobden that they asked him to address a meeting in support of the incorporation of Manchester arranged and chaired by Prentice. Cobden was extremely reluctant, and for good reason. Cathrall recalled that "his speech on this occasion was a signal failure. He was nervous, confused, and, in fact, practically broke down, and the chairman had to apologize for him."[1]

Nothing more was heard of municipal reform in Manchester for some time. Prentice's attempt to launch an agitation appears to have died with this meeting, and Cobden, it was obvious, was far from ready to take on the leadership himself. All the same, his political debut was not without its benefits. He had found an ally in Prentice and a platform in Prentice's *Manchester Times*. Prentice, in fact, needed Cobden as much as, if less obviously than, Cobden needed him. The *Times* occupied an uncomfortable position among reformist newspapers between the Whig-Liberal *Manchester Guardian* and the ultraradical *Manchester and Salford Advertiser*. One of Prentice's ambitions was to launch a moderate radical reform movement in the city. He had come closest to succeeding during the reform bill agitation in 1831, but even then his achievement was limited, and most of his other efforts were failures. Essentially Prentice was a political busybody, intervening in print and in person in every aspect of local affairs; but he was no great agitator nor, for that matter, an especially skilled newspaperman, as Cobden quickly realized. Nonetheless he was able to spot talent when he saw it, and in Cobden he immediately recognized a man whose goals were close to his own and who could perhaps, for all his early deficiencies as a speaker, galvanize the middling middle class.

Cobden, for his part, as assiduously cultivated Prentice, in some measure surely out of gratitude for Prentice's attention to him but primarily because the *Manchester Times* spoke for, or at least to, his natural constituency. The nature of their relationship as it evolved over the next couple of years was well—if acidly—observed by Absolom Watkin, one of the city's leading reformers and later an ally of Cobden's in the anti–Corn Law agitation. Watkin was dining at Cobden's one evening late in 1837 and the conversation turned to local electoral politics:

> Speaking of Mr. S. J. Lloyd and his unsuccessful attempt to get into Parliament from Manchester ... Mr. Cobden, adverting to the prejudice against Mr. Lloyd which had been produced by the questioning of Mr. Prentice, observed, "Prentice should have been bought over. Not," he added, "that I mean to say that our friend is on sale, but he should have been won over ... *he should have been consulted; that would have been enough.*" ... Not long after Mr. Cobden's man entered the room and told his master that a person from Mr. Prentice wished to speak to Mr. Cobden about a paper. Mr. Cobden apologised to us, and went to him. Now Prentice eulogizes Mr. Cobden in the *Times* and, I have no doubt, *has been consulted.* In such manner reputation is maintained, and the way to distinction is smoothed.[2]

Not that Cobden was beholden to Prentice even at the start of his public career; luckily for his reputation and his self-esteem, the embarrassing debut as a public speaker received virtually no publicity and was, in any case, of secondary importance to him. His main energies in 1835 were directed elsewhere—and with better results—in support of education. Because he was so closely identified with economic causes and because all his efforts on behalf of national education ended in failure, it is easy to forget how important the education question was to Cobden. There was no issue that he regarded as more central to the solution of England's problems. Self-improvement and improvement in the condition of the mass of the population were, he believed, next to impossible in the absence of a system of universal education. Like most radicals, he regarded England's failure to provide such a system as a national scandal and, potentially, as a national danger. Without a well-educated electorate England might well not get the reforms she needed; and even if she did, their full benefits were likely to remain unrealized. There was, moreover, an external threat, from England's better-educated foreign rivals. As in so many things, Cobden looked to the American example and found his own country seriously deficient by comparison. On his visit to the United States in 1835, and in Germany three years later, one of the things that most impressed him was the attention devoted to public education. "If knowledge be power and education give knowledge," he warned in *England, Ireland and America*, "then must the Americans become the most powerful people in the world."[3]

Cobden's first opportunity to give practical expression to his educational ideas came in the small village of Sabden surrounding his calico works, where he supported local efforts to found an infant school. In Manchester itself his first step was to join a number of the learned societies that were the mainstay of the city's cultural life. He became active in the venerable Manchester Literary Society, was a frequent participant in its discussions, and early in 1836 was elected its vice-president. Of greater importance to his later public career was his membership in the local statistical society, the earliest in England, to which he was admitted near the end of 1835. This small and selective group—there were only fifty members—was only two years old when Cobden joined, yet already it was engaged in two major surveys in south Lancashire: one of the condition of the working classes, the other of the state of education. For all their faults as scientific surveys and despite the tendentiousness of their final reports, these studies were the most ambitious of their kind undertaken by a private agency in the post–reform bill era. And, besides, their tendencies were Cobden's tendencies.

In the other members of the Manchester Statistical Society Cobden found a group of like-minded men, concerned with the same problems and inclined to similar solutions. The founders of the society were all middle-class reformers little different in outlook from the Cobden of *England, Ireland and America*. Indeed it is likely that the publication of that pamphlet earlier in the year provided Cobden with his entree to the society. They were, moreover, activists, as they took care to point out, "not associated merely for the purpose of collecting facts concerning the inhabitants of this district" but intent on gathering the raw material of informed social action.[4] Again and again over the next five years members of the society formed the nucleus of committees in support of any number of reforms, from the incorporation of Manchester to the repeal of the Corn Laws. But education, as their meeting ground in a statistical society and the nature of its studies suggest, was the issue on which they were most passionately agreed, and Cobden's association with them at the outset of his public career must have reinforced his own inclination to see educational reform as the root reform, the surest basis for progress in other areas.

It was not therefore by chance that Cobden's earliest attempt at generating a popular agitation came, more than a year before the foundation of the Anti–Corn Law League, in support of a scheme for national education; nor is it surprising that he emerged as an important figure in the city's life as a result of his part in the foundation of the Manchester Atheneum in the autumn of 1835. John Morley mentioned Cobden's participation in the early history of the atheneum only in passing, as yet another example of the widening scope of his activities at the time and as the occasion of his first major public speech. But Cobden did far more than merely move or second resolutions at organizational meetings or serve as one of a couple of dozen members of the planning committee and, thereafter, of the atheneum board; he was one of the two or three most important founders of the atheneum. At the laying of the cornerstone of its permanent home, Cobden opened the occasion by presenting a ceremonial silver trowel to its president, James Heywood, and Heywood in his reply praised Cobden as "more than anyone else . . . the father of the Manchester Atheneum . . . with whom the idea of the institution originated."[5]

Cobden's idea of an atheneum was ambitious. The prodigious growth in the wealth and population of Manchester had outstripped its cultural resources. "It would be a shame," as he put it at the first public meeting in support of the atheneum in October, "that, while they were erecting mills in every direction for the manufacture of cotton, they could not have one manufactory for working up the raw intelligence of the town."[6] Membership fees in this "factory of the raw intelligence" were to be kept low in order to attract the participation of unmarried men starting out on their careers. The social as much as the intellectual needs of the members were to be met by providing a coffee room and restaurant as well as lecture halls, classrooms, a library, and a periodicals reading room. Limited participation by the wives of members was also envisioned. Furthermore, in addition to evening classes and visiting lecturers, the founders of the atheneum hoped ultimately to engage permanent teachers and lecturers.

The public response was all that Cobden could have desired, not only for the atheneum but for his own career. The meeting to launch the atheneum was the first at which he addressed a large audience in Manchester, and, although he was nervous at first, the speech was well received. Excellent press coverage, the steady influx of subscriptions and memberships, and the impressive roster of names on the atheneum's planning and governing boards all attested not only to the timeliness of his original proposal but also, presumably, to his skills in politics and persuasion at a time when his name meant little. Henceforward Cobden as well as the atheneum was considered newsworthy—and not only in the *Manchester Times*. The atheneum opened in January 1836 only three months after it was first projected, and little more than a year later the cornerstone of its new headquarters was laid. The list of its supporters included many of the most important names in the city: Birley, Callendar, Heywood, Nield, Potter, Rawson, Watkin, Wood. Many of these men were to be Cobden's political allies over the next decade; others, to be sure, became his political enemies, but to Cobden that was further evidence of the soundness of the atheneum project. On political and economic questions he was always suspicious of compromise; indeed he tended to state issues in a way that made prevarication and compromise next to impossible. In anything pertaining to education, however, he sought to cooperate with potential opponents, emphasizing points of agreement and seeking out the means of blurring differences. At the first public meeting of the atheneum committee, in October 1835, as in every speech he gave on education in later years, he stressed the need to keep to their goal and avoid any hint of exclusiveness—political, religious, or social.

Early in 1836 he took much the same message to the annual general meeting of the Mechanics Institute, to which, as a sort of unofficial emissary from the atheneum, he pledged his best efforts toward co-operation. But, characteristically, his main concern was with the institute itself and what he saw as its failure to live up to its purpose. Too many of its members were drawn from the middle not the working classes; indeed it had done too little to reach its intended audience. The only remedy, he believed, was for the institute to move out actively into the city, sponsoring lectures and classes on a regular basis in working-class neighborhoods.[7]

A few months later an even better opportunity to promote the cause of popular education arose when James Simpson, a Scottish educational reformer, was invited to give a series of lectures in Liverpool. Immediately, "a number of gentlemen, friends of enlightened education, residing in Manchester" formed a committee to bring Simpson to lecture in Manchester.[8] It is likely that Cobden was the main inspiration behind the Friends of Education; seven of Simpson's ten lectures in Manchester were given at the atheneum, and Cobden was the sponsor of a dinner held in Simpson's honor following the lecture series. The actual arrangements, however, were almost certainly the work of George Wilson, the secretary of the Friends of Education and soon to become the master wire puller of radical politics in Lancashire. Although he had dabbled in local politics for some time, Wilson, not yet thirty, was even less well known than Cobden at this time. The two men already knew each other well, however, if only through their shared interest in phrenology, but the education campaign marked the beginning of their long political association.

Nothing followed directly from Simpson's visit to Manchester, but the next step was inevitable, although it did not come until a year later, after Cobden's winter in the Mediterranean and the general election of 1837. In the autumn a larger committee with the original Friends of Education as its core was formed to rouse the cotton districts in support of a reformed system of national education. They moved with care, since the education question in Lancashire had become primarily a religious issue. Cobden believed that a compromise of religious differences could be worked out that would satisfy all but the most extreme Anglican claims for the role of the established church in national education and at the same time allay Dissenters' fears of Anglican control sufficiently to prevent them from abandoning a national system in favor of voluntary efforts. The solution appeared to lie in the creation of a nonsectarian system of state-financed schools in which Bible reading and religious instruction would be provided in such a way that no sect would be favored or excluded. This could be done, indeed was already being done in some places, Cobden noted in a letter to the *Guardian*, by inviting ministers into the schools "at a time to be agreed upon for that purpose."[9]

In supporting a solution along these lines, Cobden was far closer to Dissenting than to Anglican opinion, but as a member of the Church of England he was perhaps in a better position than most of his Manchester friends to win some Anglican support for it. Not that he thought this would be an easy task; the year before, in conjunction with Simpson's visit to Manchester, he invited to his "counting-house in Mosley Street the ministers of religion of every denomination . . . to try . . . to bring them to some sort of agreement on the system of education," only to find that there was no basis for common action.[10] Clearly, therefore, if any proposed compromise was to have a chance of acceptance, education itself rather than religion would first have to be made the focus of debate, and to that end the Friends of Education proposed holding a public meeting in support of national education in October. The organizing committee was deliberately made very large so as to include a wide range of potential supporters. All of the surrounding manufacturing towns were represented, as was every major religious group in Manchester. An equally impressive array of local dignitaries, civic, religious, and business leaders, together with educators and members of Parliament was recruited for the meeting itself. Some two thousand people attended and special sections of the hall were set aside for women and representatives of the Mechanics Institute. The guest of honor was Thomas Wyse, M.P. for Waterford and chairman of the recently founded Central Society for Education, who had also spoken at the dinner for Simpson the year before. Although a leading advocate of nonsectarian education, Wyse, in keeping with the spirit of the meeting, limited himself to demonstrating the need for a national system and avoided any specific proposals.

If the Friends of Education hoped by these means to forestall opposition, they were disappointed. Shortly before the meeting a local Anglican minister, the Reverend Hugh Stowall, published an attack on the Friends of Education, accusing them of seeking to exclude religion in general and the established church in particular from its proper place in the schools and warning that the meeting was only a stalking horse for Dissenters and secularists. Cobden responded with an open letter, published in the *Manchester Guardian*, in which he accused Stowall of "falsehood" and "meanness" and of arguing at "the basest level."[11] Cobden denied that the meeting was a cloak for the interests of any group and reaffirmed his support for a nonsectarian system. However, although the education meeting was still carefully limited to general support for an undefined national system, the Friends of Education no longer felt constrained to limit themselves, perhaps because Stowall's attack had demonstrated the impossibility of compromise, perhaps because they did indeed see the meeting as a stalking horse. In any case, three weeks later they announced the formation of a new group, the Manchester Society for Promoting National Education, and for the first time came down unequivocally on one side in the religious controversy. They declared that the practice by the largely Dissenting British and Foreign Schools Society "of prescribing Bible classes for every school and placing the Holy Scripture without note or comment in the hands of every child . . . is the best system hitherto devised for meeting the difficulties arising out of the varieties of religious sects in the country."[12]

The new society was very active over the next year or so, getting up petitions to Parliament and, more concretely, supporting a number of nonsectarian schools in the city. But, although the society unquestionably did much to further the cause of education in Manchester, its formation also served to reduce what little chance there had been for compromise. Shortly after the society was founded, a group of Anglican clergy, led by Stowall, met to reaffirm their support for control of national education by the established church. Clearly the struggle for a comprehensive national system was going to be long, bitter, and perhaps inconclusive. Unhappily for Cobden, and certainly through no fault of his own, his earliest efforts to find a common ground on education happened to coincide with a growing tendency by Anglicans and Dissenters alike to decamp in opposite directions from what little common ground there was.

CHAPTER 5

Advances and Setbacks

National education was not the only issue that Cobden began to pursue more actively late in 1837; nor was it the only issue the solution to which seemed to recede the more actively he pursued it. Much the same thing happened when he first became involved with the cause that was to become, above all others, his cause—the repeal of the Corn Laws. His connection with the free trade movement began early in 1836 with his election to the board of the Manchester Chamber of Commerce. This recognition of his growing importance in the Manchester business world was welcome, if only because it enhanced his status as a critic of economic policy (he worked a reference to his new position into his second pamphlet).[1] But the chamber itself was a disappointment to Cobden. It met infrequently and was cautious in taking positions on controversial topics. It seemed, indeed, to be suffering from that tendency toward undue deference, that unwillingness proudly to assert its interests that Cobden in his pamphlets decried in the manufacturing classes generally. A few in the chamber shared his sentiments, and one in particular, John Benjamin Smith, had earned a reputation as resident gadfly. For years he had tried unsuccessfully to get the chamber to declare itself for the total repeal of the Corn Laws, and Cobden's election to the board followed by his own a year later at long last opened up the possibility that he might succeed.

The two men first met through Prentice, who, apparently at Cobden's request, called on Smith with the suggestion that he call on Cobden. Precisely when this happened is not certain, although a date much after Cobden's election to the board of the Chamber of Commerce seems unlikely. In any event, they did not immediately become allies. Cobden was not yet the single-minded advocate of repeal Smith had long been. He was still feeling his way on some economic issues and on the relative merits of these issues; he regarded government expenditure and the burden of the national debt as no less important or exploitable questions than Corn Law repeal. Indeed, as recently as 1835, in his first pamphlet, he had accepted the argument for a small fixed duty on imported grain: "We object no more to a tax on corn than on tea and sugar, for the purpose of revenue, but we oppose a protective duty."[2] Smith was horrified at this heresy when he read the pamphlet, of which Cobden gave him a copy at their first meeting, and he immediately and, he claimed, successfully set about persuading his new friend of the error of his ways. At lunch at Cobden's the following day Smith pressed the argument that any duty, however small, on the importation of an article that could be produced at home amounted to a subsidy to domestic producers. On hearing this, Cobden, as Smith remembered it, "in his accustomed manner held his head on one side and his chin on his chest and after a short pause exclaimed you are right, you are right and from that time became a total repealer."[3]

Cobden never denied that he was a convert to total repeal, although he recalled the circumstances differently and gave the credit not to Smith but to an unnamed "gentleman, a stranger to him, but a friend to truth," who, after reading Cobden's pamphlet, "wrote to him and called his attention to the great difference there was in levying a duty on corn grown at home and on foreign produce such as sugar and tea." After that, he confessed in a speech to his fellow aldermen and councillors of Manchester at the height of the struggle against the Corn Laws, "a little inquiry satisfied his mind that he was entirely wrong."[4] The two stories are not entirely incompatible; perhaps Cobden sought out Smith as part of his little inquiry. In any event, he had become an absolute free trader probably well before the end of 1836. But, although converted to total repeal, he was not yet committed to actively pursuing it. He was embroiled in the education question and at the time of the next annual general meeting of the chamber early in 1837—a meeting at which, over Smith's objections, nothing was said of the Corn Laws—he was out of the country on his Mediterranean voyage. The general election of 1837 imposed a further delay, but in the autumn, simultaneously with the beginning of the national education campaign, he and Smith decided to press the issue in the Chamber of Commerce.

Cobden adopted this new cause with his usual enthusiasm, a characteristic disdain for half measures, and an apparent suddenness that was equally typical. Actually there was nothing sudden about it. By the autumn of 1837 England was well into a serious recession, and Cobden was increasingly concerned with problems of economic policy that had seemed far less urgent in the high prosperity of 1836. Smith, as always, was pressing the Corn Law question, and the board of the Chamber of Commerce would soon be preparing its report for the next annual general meeting. As was to be true at other times on other issues, it was not Cobden's determination to support repeal that came suddenly, only the decision as to when and how to press the issue.

A fascinating glimpse of Cobden at this particular moment of decision was left to us by a close friend, Henry Ashworth, the head of Bolton's leading political and manufacturing family. In September 1837 Cobden accompanied Ashworth to Liverpool, where, on behalf of the Manchester Statistical Society, Ashworth was to read a paper on conditions in Lancashire to the annual meeting of the British Association. They had not known each other long at this point. Cobden first became aware of Henry Ashworth as a potential kindred spirit while he was in Egypt, where he met the manager of the state-owned cotton works near Cairo, a young Englishman formerly employed by the Ashworth brothers. Shortly after his return to England, Cobden took advantage of an early opportunity to meet Ashworth when they both happened to be in the same Manchester club one day and Cobden asked a mutual friend to introduce them. They hit it off immediately and rapidly developed a friendship that was to be one of the most intimate of Cobden's adult life. Certainly on the excursion to Liverpool they were inseparable, and in the private discussions with other delegates that followed the gloomy reports of the Manchester Statistical Society, Ashworth observed that Cobden was becoming increasingly agitated. Again and again their conversation turned to the Corn Laws, protection, and monopoly—"the great hindrances to commercial progress in the country"—and this "so aroused his feelings that it became almost a constant topic of conversation with him; and one evening, after a soiree at the Liverpool Town Hall, he stopped suddenly as we were walking quietly at midnight up Pembroke Place, and with some abruptness, said: 'I'll tell you what we will do; we'll use the Chamber of Commerce for an agitation to repeal the Corn Laws.' "[5]

J. B. Smith was delighted that Cobden had come round to his views, and together they were able to persuade the board of the Chamber of Commerce to adopt a petition to Parliament in favor of total repeal. (The wording of the petition—strong, clear and concise—has all the earmarks of Cobden's prose.)[6] But if Smith's many years of isolated effort were now vindicated, Cobden was more frustrated than satisfied. It quickly became clear that the chamber was not about to go beyond a petition. Ashworth had predicted this when Cobden raised the issue in Liverpool, pointing out that the chamber had neither the will nor the funds nor, under its rules, the power to launch an agitation. At the annual general meeting in February 1838 Cobden did attempt to get the chamber to agree at least to more frequent general meetings and a more activist role in commenting on government economic policy. But in the face of only limited support, reservations even from his friends, and much outright opposition, he withdrew his proposal.

Frustrating half-victories, which were all that Cobden could show for his efforts on behalf of national education and Corn Law repeal in 1837, were not his only disappointments that year. Indeed he had taken up these campaigns in the backwash from an even more clear-cut defeat in the general parliamentary election in July. It is not certain who initiated the process that led to Cobden's adoption as a reform candidate in nearby Stockport. Prentice probably had a hand in it and certainly supported Cobden in the *Manchester Times* from the moment his candidacy was first mooted. But by the summer of 1836 Cobden was a likely parliamentary candidate in any case. As a successful businessman, a member of the board of the Manchester Chamber of Commerce, and a founder of the Manchester Atheneum, he had a solid, if recent, local reputation. His second pamphlet, *Russia*, published in the spring of 1836, was even better noticed than the first and laid the foundation for national recognition. For example, Lord Durham, whose up-and-down career included a stint as British minister in St. Petersburg, was greatly impressed by the pamphlet's approach to the Eastern question and wrote his friend Joseph Parkes to find out who the author was. Parkes, one of the leaders of the Birmingham Political Union during the reform bill agitation and, after 1832, perhaps the most effective lobbyist for radical causes in London, always made it his business to keep track of rising talent and was equally impressed with Cobden's credentials. Hence, when James Coppock, the Liberal election agent and town clerk of Stockport, wrote Parkes about Cobden's prospective candidacy, Parkes assured him that Cobden "would be an honour to them, not they to him."[7]

Whatever role this particular set of connections may have played in the adoption of Cobden as a candidate, the nucleus of an election committee was formed in the autumn of 1836. Because Cobden was about to sail for the Mediterranean, his supporters asked him to leave behind an address to the electors of Stockport, which the committee could release when it saw fit—a step they took in December. It was a long address, outlining Cobden's position on almost every issue of the day and prefaced with a call to the reformers of England to make full use of the power that had been theirs since 1832. He advocated, in haphazard order, a liberalization of English policy toward Ireland, political reform (including household suffrage, the secret ballot, and shorter Parliaments), the abolition of church rates and the separation of church and state, action in support of those issues—free trade and national education—that were to occupy so much of his attention the following year, a more humane legal system, an overhaul of Britain's relationship with her colonies, cheaper government and a reduction of the national debt to meet the economic challenge of the United States, and careful scrutiny of those bastions of aristocratic privilege, the standing army and the conduct of foreign policy. Interestingly, he closed with an attack on the powers of the House of Lords, for which he, like many radicals at this time, blamed the faltering momentum of reform. Indeed, he predicted that it was "a subject which will very soon, and above all others, engross the attention of the public mind."[8]

Had Cobden been planning to launch an agitation at this point, the Lords might well have been his issue. As it was, he spent the next six months abroad, and almost from the moment of his return the prospect of a general election rather than any particular issue was the chief topic of political speculation. The serious illness of the king, added to the usual uncertainties about the future of Lord Melbourne's government, produced a flurry of electoral preparations. Cobden's primary concern at this point was to ensure that he would emerge as the unchallengeable second reform candidate in a constituency in which the representation was divided between the major parties. His strategy was a mix of personal predilection and political necessity. Many moderate Liberals and factory owners distrusted his radical views, and few such men would serve on his election committee when it was formed. Therefore, he and his agents deliberately courted the shopocracy and the nonelectors as an indirect route to more powerful support. "The low party cannot bring a man in," he explained to his brother Charles, "still it is everything to secure that party, because the others will concede rather than divide the liberal interest."[9] Whether or not it was this approach that brought the hoped-for dividends, by late spring his election committee, now much enlarged, felt strong enough to move formally. In mid-May Cobden visited Stockport for the first time as a prospective candidate to address and answer questions from his election committee, which then, as expected, officially -endorsed him. All this took place before the king's illness was generally known, so that at the time a general election occasioned by the accession of a new monarch became a possibility, Cobden was the only declared candidate in Stockport, apart from the sitting members.

With the death of the king at the end of June and the election of Queen Victoria's first Parliament set for late July, rival claimants emerged, but good preparations by Cobden's committee and the lucky timing of those preparations had placed him in such a commanding position that all his challengers quickly withdrew. That left his supporters with an equally serious obstacle, however: relations with the sitting Liberal member, Henry Marsland. He had headed the poll in 1835 but the Conservative member, Major Thomas Marsland, had represented Stockport since the reform bill, and many local Liberals feared that they were not sufficiently strong to elect two reformers and that a good showing by Cobden might knock off the wrong Marsland. After lengthy negotiations and a public meeting in mid-July, however, the two election committees decided to make the attempt and merged. Even so, their doubts were proved well founded on polling day: the Marslands won in a dead heat, and Cobden, although he did respectably, was the clear loser.

Local loyalty to the Marslands as well as an understandable inclination on the part of the electors to keep a foot in both political camps certainly played a part in Cobden's loss. So perhaps did his status as an outsider. Furthermore, some Liberals thought Cobden too radical; even the *Manchester Guardian*, which backed him, had misgivings about some of his views. Other reformers voted only for Henry Marsland to ensure that he at least would be victorious. There may also have been corruption; that certainly was Cobden's view. In an angry letter to the electors of Stockport he accused Major Marsland of buying votes, although he reserved his most scathing comments for those among the Tories' supporters whom he regarded as traitors to their class interests: "The Wesleyan Tories, also, (those brawlers in favor of a state church, with bishops and a monarch for its temporal head—all of which they have themselves consistently renounced!) threw their perverse influence into the scale of misgovernment and ignorance. And the Tory millowners, who raised their infatuated and frantic voices through their worthy representative at the hustings, in favor of the Corn Laws, combined to a man against the cause of reform and improvement in the machinery of government."[10]

Cobden had not sought the nomination at first and maintained all along that "I shall be quite happy whichever way the die falls."[11] But as the tone of his letter to the electors of Stockport and his conduct of the campaign indicated, he very much wanted to win and was disappointed at the loss. Nonetheless, as he was certainly aware, he had used the campaign to excellent effect and emerged from his defeat with a much enhanced reputation. He had come close to winning and was now accepted as a certain future member of Parliament, and not only in Lancashire. In June the hopeful candidate had gone up to London to meet his prospective colleagues from the North and make contact with the leaders of the radical interest nationally. He was not much impressed with the northern M.P.s—"a sad lot of soulless louts"[12]—and little more so with the leading radicals, apart from Joseph Parkes, whom he thought "one of the cleverest men I have ever met."[13] Of the others, he considered William Molesworth "not a man of superior talents," John Arthur Roebuck undeniably "a clever fellow" but with a "mind...more active than powerful," and George Grote a "man possessing the highest order of moral and intellectual endowments, but wanting something which for need of a better phrase I shall call devil." Of his own M.P., C. P. Thompson, Cobden simply noted the London view that "he is not the man of business we take him for in Manchester." Some of Cobden's acerbity, especially in Thompson's case, may have been due to the fact that his calls were not promptly returned—he was, after all, only a potential M.P.; on the other hand, the wily Parkes "has been most kind to me," and John Easthope, the proprietor of the *Morning Chronicle*, was very solicitous in ensuring that Cobden met the right people.

That Cobden had impressed others besides Parkes and Easthope was made clear only a few months later. In November his supporters in Stockport decided to give a banquet in honor of Cobden and Henry

Marsland, and Daniel O'Connell was invited and agreed to attend. It was quite an occasion. O'Connell and Cobden were met at the edge of the city and escorted in triumph to the main square, where both spoke to the crowd. A special pavilion had been set up for the dinner, the presentation of testimonial silver salvers, and a full evening of speeches. In both his speeches Cobden sounded a new theme for him, the central importance of the secret ballot. Reiterating his charges of corruption at the recent election, he argued that only the ballot could end such practices. Indeed, he asserted, without the ballot all the other reforms for which they hoped would either remain beyond their grasp or prove of little value.

Cobden had been moving toward this view of the ballot as the first item on the radical agenda for some time. He had first raised it publicly as a separate issue in September at a meeting of the Bolton Reform Association, founded only the month before by the Ashworth brothers. Other meetings on the ballot, in Bolton and elsewhere, followed Cobden's speech in Stockport. Clearly he and the Ashworths hoped that it might become the focus of a new radical agitation. In his biography of Cobden, John Morley dismissed this sudden concern with the ballot as an "inversion of his usual order of thinking," in that Cobden normally "paid much less heed to the machinery, than to the material objects of government."[14] But to Cobden at this time, as on many later occasions, the secret ballot was more than merely a piece of the machinery of government. Like all the issues for which he had a particular penchant, it was both clear-cut and of great symbolic as well as practical importance. More than any other reform it would loosen the bonds of social deference in politics, freeing the individual voter from the pressures of patronage and the temptations of corruption. Moreover, unlike the other major political reforms—an enlarged suffrage, shorter Parliaments, and more equal electoral districts—the ballot was not subject to compromises that would render it meaningless. One was either for it or against it. It was the perfect test of the genuineness of any man's radicalism. Small wonder that, whenever the political climate seemed especially murky or directionless, Cobden sooner or later raised the issue, if only to clear the air.

That the air urgently needed clearing was apparent to every reformer by the end of 1837. The radicals' assumption that their numbers would inexorably increase as a result of the reform bill, an assumption confirmed in the elections of 1832 and 1835 and shared in by Cobden in 1837, was dashed in that year's election, when half a dozen radicals lost their seats. This, combined with the enhanced strength of the Conservative opposition, reinforced Lord Melbourne's inclination toward moderation. The Whigs, once so receptive to radical influences, were ceasing even to fear their radical allies. For the radicals this turnabout had been devastatingly quick. Only two years before they had been pressing forward with confidence, undecided only as to which of the reforms on their agenda should have pride of place. Cobden, in seeking entry to their ranks at that time, assumed that he was joining a movement gaining in strength. Now he, in common with the dwindling corps of national radical leaders, was searching desperately through that same agenda in the hope of finding some issue through which they could regain their lost momentum. Yet, as Cobden was just then discovering, this was no more easily done on the local than on the national level. Each of the issues he raised in the closing months of 1837—national education, Corn Law repeal, the ballot—encountered stiffening resistance from an increasingly confident Conservative opposition or, even more disturbing, a Whig-like caution from potential allies. There had been measurable achievements to be sure—the Manchester Society for the Promotion of National Education and the Chamber of Commerce petition in favor of Corn Law repeal—but both fell short of what he had hoped for when he first took up these issues. As for his advocacy of the secret ballot, that was even less successful; the Bolton and Stockport meetings produced nothing.

For all his personal achievements, and they were considerable, Cobden was still floundering politically. In only two years he had gained access, although not full admission, to the inner circle of Manchester reformers; he had good contacts and prospects in London; he was seen as a coming figure in the world of radical politics. Unfortunately for him that world was no longer expanding. If anything it was contracting, and Cobden, as much as anyone, was at a loss to know how to proceed.

CHAPTER 6

The Incorporation of Manchester

Cobden's dilemma, the dilemma of every middle class radical in the latter half of 1837, was about to be resolved. Developments in another city, Birmingham, and an unexpected turn of events in local politics combined to hand him an issue ideally suited to his needs. The issue, the reform of local government, was not a new one for Cobden, who had been drawn into Prentice's attempt to develop an agitation in support of municipal incorporation two years before. In 1837, however, the issue was raised in a more urgent form by the threatened breakdown of local government. A crisis in the management of Manchester's affairs had long been inevitable. Like many of England's new industrial cities, Manchester had no borough charter, and its government had therefore not been reformed under the Municipal Corporations Act of 1835. The act did afford unincorporated cities the opportunity to petition the Privy Council for a charter, but because no such action had been taken in Manchester, its government remained a manorial government—complete with boroughreeve, court leet, and other ceremonial trappings—totally unsuited to the needs of a city of 200,000 inhabitants. Understandably, many of Manchester's leading citizens were reluctant to serve in this archaic government, and the problem of recruiting able candidates was growing more acute every year, as the wealthy suburbs spread beyond the boundaries of the increasingly commercial township of Manchester from which the manorial officers had to be drawn. In 1836 and again in the autumn of 1837 the problem was suddenly transformed into a crisis when the man selected by the jurors of court leet to serve as boroughreeve refused to accept the office.

Cobden was perfectly placed to take advantage of the situation, for he had been selected by the lord of the manor to serve on the court leet jury in 1837—yet another sign of his growing importance in Manchester. Had Cobden not been a juror, the problem would likely have been solved by pressing the reluctant boroughreeve elect into accepting office or, failing that, by fining him and selecting someone else (as had happened the year before). But Cobden was not willing to let it go at that. The reluctant candidate, William Nield, was a friend and a colleague in the education campaign. When the jury voted to censure Nield for refusing to serve, Cobden dissented and proposed instead that the jurors should pass a resolution pointing out the difficulty of recruiting officers under the manorial government and supporting the incorporation of Manchester. The jurors unanimously endorsed the first half of the resolution, and although they divided on the issue of incorporation, the majority supported that as well. With that support Cobden decided to take the issue directly to the ratepayers of Manchester, and during the next few weeks he wrote a pamphlet and began to lay the groundwork for a popular agitation.

Nine months later Manchester had its charter and Cobden his first triumph as an agitator, but at the time he undertook the agitation it was no less a gamble than any of his ventures that autumn. That it paid off where the ballot, Corn Law repeal, and national education campaigns did not was due primarily to the obvious difference that this was a local issue. Success or failure depended on Manchester alone, rather than anyone else's response to a lead taken in Manchester. Nonetheless the movement would probably have failed in hands other than Cobden's. Municipal incorporation was a cause that he was especially well equipped to exploit, for, characteristically, he saw in it a significance, a symbolic importance, which raised it to the level of a great issue and won for the campaign a breadth and intensity of support—and opposition—it might otherwise not have had.

His pamphlet, *Incorporate Your Borough*, set the tone. The incorporation of Manchester was not, he argued, an end in itself; it was an issue of democracy versus privilege, of the rights and powers of the productive classes against a rapacious aristocracy:

The Lords of Clumber, Belvoir and Woburn, although they can no longer storm your towns and ransack your stores and shops at the head of their mailed vassals, are as effectually plundering your manufacturers and their artisans; for, by the aid of their parchment votes and tenant at will serfs, they are still enabled to levy their infamous bread tax upon your industry. And you must tamely submit to the pillage, or, like your ancestors of old, will you not resist the aristocratic plunderers? If the latter, then imitate your forefathers by union and cooperation; amalgate all ranks in your town, by securing to all classes a share in its government and protection; give unity, force and efficiency to the intelligent and wealthy community of Manchester, and qualify it by organisation, as it already is entitled by numbers, to be the leader in the battle against monopoly and privilege. In a word, INCORPORATE YOUR BOROUGH.[1]

The implication was clear; victory in this endeavor could be a step toward victory in other, greater causes. Here the example of Birmingham was crucial to Cobden's thinking. Thomas Attwood, still the most influential spokesman for provincial radicalism, was at this time attempting to revive the Birmingham Political Union, which had disbanded after the passage of the reform bill of 1832. The incorporation of Birmingham was an integral part of his plan, for he envisaged the new borough councils as, in effect, permanent and government-sanctioned radical caucuses—"real and legal political unions" as he put it—which would be unrestrained by such things as the Corresponding Societies Act. Cobden took Attwood's words as his own, and expanded on them, calling the new corporations "trades' unions in opposition to the Corn Law tyrants—the landed interest . . . normal schools of agitation for the education of orators and patriots . . . real and legal political unions."[2]

In the particular context of Manchester the municipal incorporation campaign had additional attractions for Cobden. It provided a perfect opportunity to drag the moderate Liberals out of their lethargy, unite all shades of reform opinion, and push the Tories into isolated opposition. To these ends he skillfully played on the interests and prejudices of the groups he sought to win over—or alienate. The pamphlet opened with a scornful attack on the manorial government, its titles and trappings, its leaders and their minions. Tory baiting was as easy as it was fun; uniting the disparate reform groups of the city was neither. To the Liberal elite he talked of pride—in their class and in their city—and urged them to take on their natural role of leadership. He reminded Dissenters and the shopocracy that they had been excluded from any role in the manorial government and that incorporation was therefore peculiarly in their interest. The Irish, he argued, should back it as a step toward similar reforms in their homeland. And as for the ultraradicals, Cobden hoped to enlist their support by stressing the democratic nature of the new corporation and by recalling the bitterest chapter in the city's recent history. The massacre at Peterloo, he claimed, "could not have occurred if Manchester had been incorporated . . . and why? Because the united Magistrates of Lancashire and Cheshire . . . would in such a case have no more jurisdiction in Manchester than in Constantinople."[3]

All in all, the pamphlet was a first-rate piece of political propaganda. Shorter than his earlier pamphlets and directed to a specific goal, it was the most effective thing he had yet written. As to the campaign itself, that too was remarkably sophisticated, in view of the lack of experience of its most active leaders in the arts of agitation. Cobden and Henry Ashworth decided to mount a parallel incorporation campaign in Bolton and agreed that smaller and more manageable Bolton should be the object of the initial effort as a sort of pilot project. It was a wise move. From start to finish the Bolton campaign went smoothly, despite some fierce local opposition. Manchester required much greater effort. Up to a point the campaign followed the usual pattern of agitations at this time. Small private meetings of sure supporters were followed by a well-publicized and larger but still closed meeting late in January 1838. From that point on, however, the requirements for gaining a borough charter and the exigencies of local politics required greater risks and careful planning. To meet the requirements of the Municipal Corporations Act, the incorporationists would have to demonstrate to the Privy Council that they had the support of the bulk of the ratepayers for a change in their form of government. Clearly the incorporationists would have to hold and dominate open public meetings and raise a petition of formidable size. Equally clearly they were bound to encounter bitter opposition not only from the entrenched Tories but also from the outlying townships that would be incorporated with Manchester into the new borough.

Cobden believed that the incorporationists' best hope of overcoming this opposition was to mobilize the middling middle class, the shopocracy. That he was able to do so was due primarily to the organizing ability of George Wilson, who, although he and Cobden had worked together only in the education campaign, was nonetheless entrusted with control over the organization of the incorporation agitation. Wilson's most important contribution was his thoroughness in canvassing. By mid-March the incorporation petition had almost 12,000 signatures, a good many more than in any of the other cities seeking a charter at this time.

Beyond that, he was able to thwart the opposition in what proved to be the two key turning points of the campaign. The agitation opened with a mass public meeting in February. Exactly a year before, an attempt to launch a municipal reform movement had collapsed when the Tory-led opposition packed a similar meeting. This time, however, drawing on poll books and electoral registers, the incorporationists "sent a circular to every one of the £10 parliamentary electors who support liberal men calling on them to aid us at the public meeting and they came forward to our rescue. The shopocracy," Cobden gleefully reported, "carried the day."[4] Wilson's other critical contribution involved the near-destruction of the opposition's counterpetition. It was a huge document, almost three times the size of the incorporationists' petition. But Cobden and Wilson suspected fraud, and Wilson embarked on a name-by-name check of the opposition petition against the tax assessment roles of the city. By the time the commissioners sent by the Privy Council to assess the authenticity of the two petitions arrived in Manchester in May, Wilson was in a position to prove that more than 70 percent of the signatures on the opposition petition were invalid. Although nearly one third of the signatures on the incorporationists' petition were also disallowed, the credibility of the opposition petition and to a degree of the opposition itself was all but destroyed.

With this kind of organizational backing Cobden was left free to concentrate on the strategy and public conduct of the campaign. In his speeches he reiterated the themes of his pamphlet: civic pride, democracy, the need for unity among reformers, and the significance of incorporation as a harbinger of other reforms. He sought to ensure that it would be seen as an issue and a campaign of national not merely local importance by linking the agitation directly to Bolton and, at least in spirit, to Birmingham. To ensure success and maximize pressure on the Whigs, he secured the services of Joseph Parkes as the incorporationists' London agent. Parkes, who had headed the Royal Commission that recommended the Municipal Corporations Act to the government, was already performing the same function for Birmingham. Cobden was not only the chief strategist; he was also the most visible leader of the agitation. He headed the delegation that carried the petition to the Privy Council in March and the committee that received the Privy Council commissioners in Manchester two months later. Thus, when the charter was finally granted that summer, it was rightly regarded as a personal triumph for Cobden. The rewards were therefore considerable, the most tangible of these being his election late in the year as a borough councillor and then as one of the first aldermen under the new charter. But the intangible rewards were, of course, far greater. He was now widely recognized as a major provincial reform leader; he had gone a long way toward building a new social base for reform politics in Manchester; and he had restored his adopted city to a position of equality in provincial politics with Birmingham.

Cobden had every reason to be pleased, yet if anything he became less hopeful as the year progressed. He had expected a bitter campaign but nothing like what the incorporationists had in fact encountered. Even more distasteful to Cobden was the air of corruption surrounding the whole campaign, and not only on the opposition side. He went along with it, even to the point of bribing disaffected opposition canvassers to reveal the details of their fraudulent petition, but he took no pleasure in it, as Wilson clearly did. "It is the kind of work which makes public matters about as pleasant as scavenging and not so cleanly either," he told Wilson in May. Not that Cobden advocated turning back, even at this point. "Since we have begun, there is no help but to go on," he concluded; but, he warned Wilson, "we must not be rash in future enterprises of this kind."[5] On a number of occasions that summer he seriously considered quitting public life altogether once the campaign was over.

Cobden might not have minded all this so much had the future looked brighter, but on the whole he was more impressed by the near failure of the incorporation campaign than by its ultimate success. For one thing, he, like Attwood in Birmingham, was all but certain that the Privy Council would have turned down the incorporationists had not Wilson's organization demolished the opposition petition and the radicals hinted (through Parkes) that they might desert the Whigs in Parliament if incorporation was denied. There is in fact no hard evidence to support this charge, and some evidence (from Parkes) that tends to refute it. Cobden, like many radicals, almost always imputed to the aristocracy malevolently reactionary motives, when in reality he was often faced with nothing more sinister than indifference and inertia. But these, as the difficulty of the incorporation campaign had demonstrated, were obstacles enough, and by the summer of 1838 Cobden was becoming convinced that further reforms would require almost intolerable effort and delay.

Even more dispiriting was the near failure of the campaign in Manchester itself. He had expected Tory opposition, although not as well-organized an opposition. But he had also hoped for substantial support from all reformers, and this he did not get. Early in the campaign, after the distribution of 5,000 copies of his pamphlet brought little response, he nearly despaired. "Shall we give it up?" he asked Wilson. "So little public spirit in a place that ought to be at the head makes me almost inclined to turn hermit and let my beard grow."[6] Only the shopocracy turned out in force and with the hoped-for enthusiasm. Many moderate Liberals, led by the *Manchester Guardian*, were cautious and skeptical, although they did at least support the movement. Not so the ultraradicals, most of whom steadfastly opposed incorporation. For all Cobden's emphasis on the democratic nature of the proposed charter, the borough franchise would be limited to ratepayers. The bulk of the working class would remain excluded from municipal government, and many ultraradicals understandably dismissed the whole thing as a middle-class sham.

Furthermore, unfortunately for Cobden, the incorporation campaign coincided with the most militant phase of opposition to the Poor Law of 1834, which was just then being introduced into the manufacturing districts of the North. Cobden made no secret of his support for the underlying principles of the act or of his contempt for its ultraradical opponents—"Poor Law lunatics,"[7] he called them—who found their only allies in the textile districts among the humanitarian Tories (much as had happened earlier with the movement to limit the hours of adult factory labor, which Cobden had publicly opposed as a parliamentary candidate). This in itself made cooperation between Cobden and the ultraradicals on any other issue next to impossible in 1838, and in addition many ultraradicals saw sinister links between incorporation and the social causes with which they were concerned at this time. They feared that the police powers that incorporation would grant the largely middle-class government of Manchester would be used to ensure rigorous enforcement of the New Poor Law, wink at evasions of the existing factory acts, and,

more generally, suppress ultraradical political activity. Far from supporting incorporation, in short, the most militant working-class leaders were willing to cooperate with whoever opposed it.

Thus, the alliance between northern Tories and working-class
ultraradicals, begun in the factory reform campaign and continued
into the anti–Poor Law agitation, spilled over into the incorporation
controversy. Cobden's calculation that this alliance, founded on humanitarian social questions, would break down on a political issue
proved fallacious, and the Tory opponents of incorporation were
provided with the mass backing they otherwise would have lacked.
But for Wilson's organizational skills and the support of the shopocracy, the incorporationists might have been overwhelmed at their
public meeting in February and out-petitioned in March. As it was,
although the signers of the incorporation petition had higher average
property assessments than their opponents and were therefore accepted as representing a more substantial segment of the community,
the number of legitimate signatures on the opposition petition remained, for all the deletions, larger than the number of valid signatures the incorporationists had been able to muster. It was an ironic
ending to a campaign based on a call to greater democracy, and
Cobden was at once angry and perplexed by this turn of events.

For all his efforts, it seemed that he was back where he had been the
year before. Manchester had won its borough council, its "real and
legal political union." But a political union was useless without some
broad agreement as to its purpose, and that did not exist in
Manchester. If the Whig Liberals and ultraradicals could not be drawn
together in enthusiastic support for a measure of local semidemocratic
self-government, there seemed to be no issue on which unity was
possible. To be sure, as the incorporation campaign wound down in
the summer of 1838, Cobden returned to the issues of 1837—Corn
Law repeal, national education, the secret ballot—and discussed their
relative merits in his correspondence. But where, only three years
before, at the outset of his public career, each of these issues had
seemed full of promise and only a year before had seemed at least
possible, now all three appeared increasingly remote and fatally dependent one on another.

In Cobden's view the best and perhaps the only means of securing
Corn Law repeal was through the secret ballot. Yet an agitation for
the ballot would not be enough to satisfy the ultraradicals of the

North, who were just then being drawn into the movement for the People's Charter. As for himself, he did not fear the Chartists or their program, including universal suffrage, but since most of the present electorate did, he recognized that peaceful progress toward the enfranchisement of the masses required that the masses first be educated. Anything approaching an adequate system of national education was, however, unlikely for the foreseeable future. There seemed, in short, to be no way out, and although he was inclined to see Corn Law repeal as the most important issue of the day, there is nothing to suggest that he was close to resolving his doubts about the possibility of achieving it. "You cannot pander to the new poor law delusion," he complained in August, "or mix up the Corn Laws with the currency quackeries of Attwood"; yet, he concluded gloomily, "Nothing but these cries will go down with the herd at present."[8] Exhausted and pessimistic, Cobden left Manchester for a tour of Germany immediately after the city charter was granted. So far as we can tell, he did so with no clear idea of what he would do on his return.

PART II

Agitator
1838–1846

CHAPTER 7

Founding the Anti–Corn Law League

Fortunately for the future of radicalism and for Cobden, there were others in Manchester who did not share his gloomy assessment of the political outlook in the autumn of 1838. Failing to see or willing to overlook the obstacles Cobden saw all too clearly, a number of his friends were determined to use the recent agitation and the corporation it had won for Manchester as the legal political union and school for agitation Cobden had envisaged. Bypassing the apparently hopeless questions of the ballot and national education and inspired by a series of free trade lectures in Lancashire that summer, they determined at a meeting in September to found a Manchester Anti–Corn Law Association.

Cobden took no part in these opening moves. He was abroad at the time and his name was not among the thirty-eight on the provisional committee of the association. He and twenty-nine others were added to the list the following week, however, and from the moment of his return to Manchester in late October, he was one of the most active members of the association. This sudden and total commitment to a cause that only a few months before he had viewed with considerable pessimism was completely in character and symptomatic as much of his weaknesses as of his strengths as an agitator. In the years before he finally committed himself to the repeal campaign—and again after that campaign was over—Cobden often seemed indecisive, largely because he lacked the single-mindedness of a J. B. Smith or the instinct for action of a John Bright. He found it next to impossible to see an issue apart from related issues, from the obstacles ahead, or from his longer-run goals. He therefore found it difficult to commit himself wholly to a particular cause or course of action. In the late summer of 1838, as had been the case the year before and was to be again in later years, he hesitated, torn between alternatives and acutely conscious of the pitfalls ahead. Usually it took some external event to overcome this, to make open commitment unavoidable or preferable to further indecision. The crisis in local government in Manchester had done the trick in 1837; the initiative of his friends in founding the Anti–Corn Law Association served the same purpose in 1838.

Once committed, however, Cobden's whole attitude changed, for the qualities of mind that had held him back now became his greatest assets as an agitator. His tendency to see his immediate goals in the context of his long-run ambitions gave him, if not always patience, at least perspective. His tendency to see the obstacles that lay ahead meant that he was rarely taken by surprise and usually moved to anticipate difficulties. His tendency to see issues symbolically, as encompassing and serving other issues, allowed him to stick to one thing at a time. And, perhaps most important, because he saw all the issues of the day as interconnected, he sought out ways of enlisting the broadest support, of making what could have been merely local and class questions into national and international matters.

It was this above all that appealed to him about an anti–Corn Law agitation, once it had been launched by others. He quickly recognized that Corn Law repeal was potentially the most important issue of post–reform bill politics. Like the ballot but unlike national education, it was clear, it was precise. Better than any other issue, it could be made to embody all the arguments in his early pamphlets against existing foreign and economic policy. Moreover, unlike the divisive issues of educational and political reform, it could be made to serve the political ends he had hoped but failed to achieve through the incorporation campaign. As a free trade question repeal could enlist the support of commercial and industrial interests. As a cheap bread question it could win the support of the working classes. As an assault on special economic privilege it could unite urban England and portions even of rural England against the aristocracy and oligarchic government. If the Corn Laws could be made the central issue of politics, then the divisions among reformers and the flirtations between Tories and ultraradicals would break down. Reformers of all classes could unite, regain their influence over the Whigs, place the Tories on the defensive, and set about the realization of the promise of the great reform bill.

From the moment he joined the ranks of the Manchester Anti–Corn Law Association Cobden aimed at nothing less than this, and over the next seven years he directed the movement not only toward its ostensible goal of repeal but in the service of these broader ends. This vision of what the anti–Corn Law agitation should be was Cobden's special contribution to the movement, and largely because of it he was able to assume a central role in the campaign from its inception. Not that the other leaders of the Anti–Corn Law League—Smith, Wilson, Bright—took a less broad view of what they were about, but, as most contemporaries recognized, it was largely Cobden's view they shared. Their special contributions lay elsewhere. J. B. Smith brought to the question a dedication, a fanaticism even, without which there might never have been an Anti–Corn Law League. John Bright had a missionary zeal and combativeness that were indispensable in keeping the league alive through so many years of agitation. Wilson was gifted with an uncanny ability to translate ideas into concrete courses of action and for structuring a volatile mass movement.

Cobden, who certainly lacked neither passion nor organizing ability, appears nonetheless to have regarded their greatest strengths and his as complementary. Although he clearly dominated the later history of the league, it was Smith who was accorded the leadership of the movement at the outset. Ten years older than Cobden, he was the son of a Manchester manufacturer and himself well established in the local business community and in the free trade cause before Cobden settled in the city. As much as anyone Cobden acknowledged Smith's special status as the father of the league and normally, if sometimes impatiently, deferred to him, at least until illness forced Smith into retirement during 1841. Cobden's relationship with Bright during the league years was almost the opposite. Seven years younger than Cobden, Bright did not emerge as a major figure in the agitation until about the time Smith began to withdraw from active leadership. "I have always had a sort of selfish share in his career," Cobden recalled many years later, "for I have felt as though, when passing the zenith of life, I was handing over every principle and cause I had most at heart to the advocacy of one not only younger and more energetic but with gifts of natural eloquence to which I never pretended."[1]

If Cobden saw Bright as his natural successor, he regarded Wilson as almost the practical extension of his own thinking. They were not intimate personally. Wilson was a wheeler dealer, not a thinker, and socially he lacked the standing and manner of Cobden and his closest associates. Indeed, one long-term colleague of both guessed that Cobden did not like Wilson "over much. He [Cobden] . . . had an inherent aversion to any sort of ambidexterity."[2] But ambidexterity, as Cobden recognized, was necessary to the unique contribution Wilson could make to the repeal movement, and, as in the incorporation campaign, he was entrusted from the first with control over its organization. Although he gradually emerged from behind the scenes to take a leading public part in the agitation, it was his manipulative skills that made him indispensable to Cobden, who, whatever his personal feelings, always acknowledged that he had never made a move without first consulting Wilson. Luckily that side of the repeal movement's history, the story of the league as an organized mass movement, has been excellently told.[3] It is therefore legitimate, in a study of Cobden, to look at the league primarily as he saw it and sought to direct it, in terms of the complex relationship between ideology and political power. "The ultimate triumph of our cause," he declared, "may depend upon accident or upon further political changes. But our only claim is in the enlightenment of the public mind, so as to prepare to take advantage of such an accident when it arises."[4]

All agreed that their first goal must be to secure their home base in Manchester. This was surprisingly easily done, the momentum from the incorporation campaign being the biggest factor in their success. In the election for the first borough council in December the Tories did not even challenge the reformers; they preferred instead to fight a rear-guard action by challenging the validity of the new city charter in the courts. The ultraradicals did put up a slate of candidates in the central ward of the city but they were hopelessly outclassed. The incorporationists beat them almost two to one. Elsewhere the reform ticket was elected unopposed, as were all of the aldermen. The election of the first mayor of Manchester, who, like the aldermen, was appointed by the borough council, was closely contested. But the minority, led by Cobden, closed ranks and unanimously endorsed the successful candidate, Thomas Potter. And whoever won, it was a victory for the repealers. Both candidates for mayor, William Nield as well as Potter, were members of the provisional committee of the Anti–Corn Law Association, as were more than a third of the borough councillors and half the alderman.

This impressive show of strength prepared the way for the repealers' next victory, won only a few days later at an extraordinary general meeting of the Manchester Chamber of Commerce. The meeting was called in response to a requisition from nineteen members of the chamber to consider petitioning Parliament for a repeal of the Corn Laws. Most of the requisitionists were not members of the Anti–Corn Law Association, and a few were inclined toward a low fixed duty on imported grain. Even so, the repealers, led by Cobden and Smith, were determined to use the meeting for their own purposes. The day before the general meeting, the directors of the chamber agreed to petition for repeal, but the wording of the crucial paragraph of their resolution, written by the president of the chamber, G. W. Wood, was ambiguous. Thus, when Wood moved its adoption at the general meeting, Smith immediately objected that it did not reflect the wishes of the directors as a body. In the often acrimonious debate that followed, a number of members urged compromise, but the repealers would have none of it.

Cobden was particularly aggressive. He accused the chamber of backsliding and demanded that they adopt a petition at least as strong as that which he and Smith had steered through the board of directors the year before. To this end he moved that they postpone action for a week in order to reconsider their position, and after a few face-saving gestures by Wood and his allies, Cobden's motion was passed. It was a shrewd maneuver by the repealers, who now had ample time to marshal their forces and, not incidentally, ensure maximum publicity for their efforts. By the time the chamber met again it was clear the repealers had the votes, and Cobden, who dominated the meeting, was in no mood for conciliation. Although he opened with an apology to any members he might have offended the week before, he later subjected one of the directors to a searching inquisition concerning his views on free trade. As to the main purpose of the meeting, the chamber overwhelmingly rejected an amended version of Wood's petition in favor of one written by Cobden. The repealers had, it appeared, secured their home ground.

Along the way Cobden had antagonized a considerable minority in the Chamber of Commerce, but it is unlikely that many of these enemies were newly made. Although no one doubted his abilities, Cobden had long since acquired a reputation for abrasiveness. He had risen too rapidly in the affairs of Manchester not to be thought pushy by some of the established families of the city. His early pamphlets ridiculed the pseudoaristocratic pretension of the urban upper middle class, and he did not bother to hide his disdain for the ritualistic trappings of manorial government, some of which to his dismay were adopted by the new borough council. It was the tone as much as the substance of his radicalism that disturbed the *Manchester Guardian* and presumably many of its readers. Not that Cobden was always inclined toward the politics of confrontation in his early years. When it suited his purposes, as was the case in anything to do with education, he was the first to seek to blur differences. Nor was he prone to push a point when it served no greater goal to do so. In the summer of 1837, for example, he had been appointed to serve on a committee charged with drafting an address of loyalty from the city of Manchester to Queen Victoria at her accession. A number of radicals, including Prentice, hoped to include some reference to reform in the address, but Cobden fended them off on the grounds that anything of that sort would be pointlessly divisive.

When—as with anything touching the Corn Laws—a matter of principle or power was at stake, however, Cobden could be as ruthless as he was impatient. It was perhaps as much because of this as because of J. B. Smith's seniority that he, not Cobden, assumed the role of spokesman for the repeal movement in its early stages. Indeed, as its president, Smith was the Anti–Corn Law Association to most people. He introduced the first anti–Corn Law lectures under association auspices in Manchester in October and was largely responsible for recruiting the lecturer, Abraham Paulton. Smith also was the only association leader to carry the word personally outside Manchester, by accompanying Paulton on a lecture tour of five Midlands cities in November (although Cobden was apparently the first to suggest the journey).[5] Smith conducted most of the early correspondence with sympathetic M.P.s and repealers in other cities, and he presided at a banquet and conference of free trade parliamentarians and delegates from other associations held in Manchester in January. Inevitably, he headed the Manchester contingent to the first London meeting of anti–Corn Law delegates, timed to coincide with the opening of Parliament in February 1839.

Cobden, meanwhile, was concerned primarily with shaping the strategy of the movement, both internally and in relation to other movements and to Parliament. From the outset both problems were sources of fundamental divisions among repealers, divisions that were to recur throughout the history of the movement. And on both issues, also from the outset, Cobden took an uncompromising line. As far as the movement itself was concerned, once its base of support in Manchester began to expand and still more as Manchester's efforts inspired the formation of anti–Corn Law associations elsewhere, the founders of the movement were subjected to increasing pressure to dilute or diversify their program. Even some of its supporters in Manchester feared that total and immediate repeal was an impossibly ambitious goal or one that, pursued by itself, could never attract a broad enough base of support. In addition, reformers in other cities and in Parliament, many of whom were primarily concerned with other causes, especially political reform, looked on the Corn Laws as either a secondary or a rival issue and feared that Manchester's single-minded pursuit of repeal might weaken the cause of reform generally.

Neither Cobden nor his closest colleagues were impervious to such arguments. Indeed they shared all of these concerns, differing from their more timid supporters only in the practical conclusions they drew. Thus, although they recognized that they might have to settle for less than total and immediate repeal, they were certain that the best way of ensuring that they would get less would be to demand less. As for mixing repeal with other issues, they believed that such a strategy would weaken not strengthen the movement. Individual repealers might join other movements or engage in partisan politics, just as individual supporters of other causes might join the repealers, but for the repeal movement as a body to associate itself with any other cause or faction would ensure the alienation of some of its most dedicated supporters, the creation of factions within the movement, and potentially crippling debates on the relative merits of repeal and other issues. Instead, as Cobden liked to put it, there should be free trade in agitations, from which the best organized and most popular would emerge as the most likely to succeed. That in the end would serve the interests of all reformers.

On this fundamental point of strategy there was no disagreement among the leading founders of the anti–Corn Law movement; like the leaders of most successful agitations, they refused to depart from their single issue, simply stated. The Manchester association's plan of campaign, presented by Cobden to the January delegates conference, contained a strong admonition to all other associations to follow

Manchester's example in "prohibiting the discussion of any party or political topic."[6] The rules of the Manchester association adopted a few days later were even more sweeping. After declaring that the sole purpose of the association was to win "the total and immediate repeal of the Corn and provision laws," they stated: "No party political discussion shall, on any account be allowed at any of the general or committee meetings of the association; nor shall any resolution be proposed, or subject entertained which shall be at variance with the declared object of the association."[7] Furthermore, as a means of ensuring that the leadership and its program would be free from the vagaries of popular pressure, the structure of the association was made as hierarchical as was possible in an ostensibly democratic movement. Whatever the future problems of the repeal movement might be, an internal coup or successful pressure for sudden changes in policy were not among them. From first to last the repeal movement was a disciplined movement.

This unanimity on matters of doctrine and internal structure did not extend to tactics, however. In seeking a model for the agitation, J. B. Smith understandably looked back to the successful agitation for the repeal of the Orders in Council. He therefore proposed as a first step that the repealers seek a hearing at the bar of the House of Commons. Their chief ally in Parliament, Charles Villiers, was to move for such a hearing, and the anti–Corn Law associations flooded Parliament with petitions, gathered evidence to present to the Commons, and elected delegates to meet as a body in London when the new session of Parliament opened. Smith was not naive enough to suppose that victory would be won without a struggle, but he went to London at the head of the Manchester delegation expecting that the House of Commons would afford the repealers a hearing.

Cobden had no such illusions. He perhaps knew more of national politics than Smith; he also knew Joseph Parkes. And Parkes confirmed what Cobden already suspected: that the Corn Laws touched the vital interests of the governing class as the Orders in Council had not; that, despite the reform bill, the House of Commons was still a house of landlords; and that Parliament as presently constituted would never grant the repealers a hearing, let alone repeal. For Cobden, then, this phase of the campaign was a charade. It had its uses: in particular it afforded the repealers the opportunity to identify and recruit potential allies at the national level. Parkes had already set about that business on Cobden's behalf and had managed to catch, among others, the leader of the agitation against the Orders in Council more than twenty years before, Lord Brougham. But in Cobden's view the real value of Villiers' motion—or, rather, of its inevitable defeat—was that it would clearly define the lines of battle, rouse the ire of the repealers, and send them back to their proper task, the organization of the provinces.

"My hopes of agitation are anchored in Manchester," he wrote to J. B. Smith in London a few days before the vote on Villiers' motion:

> We have money and also business habits; but if joined with a numerous body in London, who don't understand the matter as well, or feel so ardently, we might . . . fall into the claws of some jackall of the ministry. They will not agree to your being heard at the bar. Don't let us lose our time and money over the members of a committee . . . You will perhaps smile at my venturing thus summarily to set aside all your present formidable demonstrations as useless, but I formed my conviction upon the present constitution of the House of Commons, which forbids us hoping for success. *That House must be changed before we can get justice.* All our efforts must therefore be directed upon the constituencies, and, to strike a blow that will be responded to by every large town, let us begin in Manchester. I propose that on the return of our delegates (unsuccessful of course)—, our association call a meeting of the electoral body of Manchester, by which a pledge shall be entered into . . . not to return any man to represent them in the future who will not vote for . . . total and immediate repeal.[8]

This, Cobden believed, was the only effective means of serving notice on other reformers and on the Whigs that the repealers were determined to remain independent, even to the point of threatening the life of the government, in pursuit of their goal.

Almost no one else in the movement was prepared to follow Cobden in advocating such a policy in 1839. Soon after the defeat of Villiers' motion, Cobden proposed that the Manchester association express its "regret that . . . the Queen's ministry declared their neutrality . . . upon this great national question."[9] Mildly worded though it was, this resolution nonetheless provoked opposition from a minority in the association that feared alienating the government. Anything stronger would probably not have been adopted, for many of Cobden's colleagues continued to hope for as much from the Whigs as he feared from them. As long as this was the case, the majority of repealers preferred the politics of persuasion to the politics of confrontation. In the long run, of course, Cobden was right; M.P.s would have to be "made uncomfortable in their seats" before the opposition to the Corn Laws was taken seriously at the national level.[10] But if the advocates of caution were perhaps naive in their thinking, they, not Cobden, were probably correct in practice in 1839. Nowhere outside of Manchester, and perhaps not even there, could the repealers have mustered the organization and popular backing to make Cobden's proposed electoral policy stick. Moreover, most rank-and-file repealers were Liberals, disappointed with the government perhaps but supporters of most of its policies nonetheless. For the repealers to have suggested that they risk splitting the anti-Tory vote in pursuit of any one issue might have destroyed the movement. It was a long way from a single-issue mass movement to single-issue politics, and neither the Anti–Corn Law Association nor provincial public opinion was yet ready to make the jump.

Just how divisive open intervention in the electoral process would have been at this stage was demonstrated a few days after Cobden suggested this strategy to Smith, when, led by Cobden, the association decided to carry out a purge of the Manchester Chamber of Commerce. As in December, the occasion of the confrontation was the behavior of G. W. Wood, who was not only president of the chamber but M.P. for Kendal. Unfortunately for the repealers and, as it turned out, for Wood, his loyalty to the Whig government outweighed his opposition to the Corn Laws. Deputed to second the address from the throne in the opening debate of the new session of Parliament, he performed his duty to his constituents by denouncing agricultural protection; but then, in performing his duty to the ministry, he proceeded to undermine his earlier arguments by minimizing the severity of the two-year-old economic depression. If the Whigs were relieved at this, the Tories were jubilant, and the radicals aghast. J. B. Smith nearly despaired. Parkes, who had witnessed the fiasco from below the visitors' gallery, immediately fired off a letter to Cobden urging him to depose Wood as president of the Chamber of Commerce.

Cobden hardly needed prompting. This, unlike any parliamentary battle, would be a fight on home ground and one they could win. On the same day Parkes wrote him, Cobden wrote Smith urging him not to waste time in London gathering evidence on the effects of the Corn Laws while there was a chance of "getting up a row"[11] in Manchester.

Providentially the chamber was about to hold its annual general meeting, and Cobden planned to offer an amendment to the annual report or, if he could get sufficient backing, a direct vote of censure on Wood, in addition to proposing a free trade slate of directors. To ensure victory he canvassed the membership of the chamber and recruited at least sixty new members.

As expected the meeting was bitter. John Edward Taylor, the editor of the *Manchester Guardian*, proposed a mixed list of directors for the following year. J. C. Dyer, seconded by Edmund Ashworth, countered with a free trade list containing only eight of the twenty-four names on Taylor's list. In the debate that followed, the repealers were accused of imposing a partisan political test, a charge that Dyer and Cobden legitimately denied. What they could not deny was that they were attempting to impose a loyalty test on the chamber, based solely on one issue. And although the repealers won handily—by a majority of at least four to one—the losers and the *Guardian* never entirely forgave Cobden. Although they had to wait for many years, they ultimately exacted appropriate political retribution.

For the moment, however, the repealers dominated middle-class politics in Manchester, and in view of what was happening in London that was of critical importance. Even before the Wood fiasco, it had become clear to Smith that Manchester's enthusiasm did not translate to the capital where anti–Corn Law meetings were poorly attended and it often seemed as if local radical leaders were concerned with almost everything other than free trade. By the time the repealers' request to be heard at the bar of the House of Commons was rejected, one week after the purge of the Manchester Chamber of Commerce, the argument that they must anchor their agitation in the provinces seemed unanswerable. Some of the delegates, close to despair, were prepared to moderate their demands as the only means of keeping the movement alive.

Cobden, on the other hand, was probably relieved that this phase of the campaign, and with it any illusions about Parliament, was done with. Although officially a member of the Manchester delegation, he had kept his distance from the proceedings in London. When the delegates first assembled at Westminster, he was in Leamington, presumably for his health. Soon thereafter he had returned to Manchester to manage the Chamber of Commerce coup and did not come up to London until a day or two before the vote on Villiers' motion. At the critical meeting of the delegates following Villiers' defeat, however, he took a central role. In a fiery speech he urged them to return to the provincial sources of their strength and band together in a modern "Hanseatic League against the feudal Corn Law plunderers. The castles which crowned the rocks along the Rhine, the Danube, and the Elbe, had once been the strongholds of feudal oppressors, but they had been dismantled by a League, and they now only adorned the landscape as picturesque memorials of the past, while the people below had lost all fear of plunder, and tilled their vineyards in peace!"[12]

It was especially important that the repealers' retreat from London should appear as a new beginning, not a rout. Considering that almost no plans had been made beyond the London delegates meeting, this redirection of the movement was carried off remarkably smoothly. The delegates dispersed immediately, thus avoiding the divisive debates that so debilitated the Chartist movement that summer. The return of the delegates to their home cities was made the occasion for a series of meetings at which the authority of the delegates was reconfirmed. This was followed by a new delegates conference in Manchester, which hinted darkly at things to come and then adjourned to London to wait upon the result of a new motion by Villiers. Modestly (and in the hope of catching as many votes as possible), it did not seek repeal but only "that the House resolve itself into a Committee of the whole House to take into consideration the act . . . regulating the importation of foreign grain."[13] This time there were no illusions. Defeat was expected and planned for. On Wednesday, March 20, 1839, the day after the defeat of Villiers' motion, the assembled delegates voted to form a national Anti–Corn Law League.

CHAPTER 8

Building an Agitation

The league was new in name only; in every important respect it was simply the Manchester Anti–Corn Law Association writ large. It was, if anything, even more oligarchical. In addition to adopting the same hierarchical structure of councils and committees, the league rules accorded individual members and local associations an influence directly proportionate to the size of their financial contribution. Furthermore, although the league purported to be a national organization, its headquarters were to be in Manchester, and day-to- day management was in effect reserved to the Manchester association. This had obvious advantages: as a league of but not by its many associations, it proved resistant to the centrifugal forces that threatened Chartism as a national movement. As an agitation run by a small local elite, it was almost free from the rivalries that all but destroyed Chartism.

These advantages were not without their price, however. The triumvirs of the league in its early years—Smith, Cobden, and Wilson— often complained that they had to do almost all the work, and that fund raising, difficult in Manchester, was almost impossible anywhere else. A more open, national, and popularly based organization might have rendered this problem, which nearly killed the league in its first two years, less potentially lethal. Worse still perhaps, the tightness of its organization tended to reinforce the popular suspicion from which the league never entirely freed itself, that it was little more than a special interest group of Manchester manufacturers masquerading as a national movement.

To many of its supporters as well as its opponents, this, no doubt, is precisely what the league was at its inception. "I am afraid, if we must confess the truth," Cobden admitted four years later, "that most of us entered upon this struggle with the belief that we had some distinct class interest in the question, and that we should carry it by a manifestation of our will in this district against the will and consent of other portions of the community."[1] John Morley was certain that "it was not of himself . . . that Cobden was speaking," but Morley wrote with the knowledge of Cobden's later, mellower, and more wide-ranging arguments for repeal.[2] In 1839 he was both more dogmatic and less politically sensitive than he later became. Not that he ever thought the task would be easy or quick. As his skepticism about the early parliamentary phase of the campaign demonstrated, he understood the power of their opponents better than most leaguers. Even had his proposed electoral policy been adopted, and still more in its absence, he assumed that the struggle would be long. About the time the league was founded he asked Wilson to devote six months to the agitation; a year later he admitted to Wilson that he had always known it would take far longer. Yet, as he often remarked even before repeal was passed and many times thereafter, he had never dreamed that success would demand so much time and effort.

In common with all his colleagues, Cobden misread not so much the political power of their opponents as the extent of support for the Corn Laws and of popular distrust of the league. He overestimated the ability of the league to mobilize public opinion and the weight that opinion would carry once organized; conversely he underestimated the unity and perseverance of the enemy. He too readily assumed that the supporters of protection acted from motives of narrow self-interest and that their followers followed out of ignorance; he therefore too optimistically believed that, once it could be demonstrated that the Corn Laws served the interests of the landlord class alone and that the interests of the league coincided with those of all other classes, public support for the Corn Laws would erode.

Hence, since an electoral strategy had been ruled out, the almost exclusive reliance of the league on propaganda early on. Hence also, in large measure, the peculiar nature—and ultimate failure—of that propaganda campaign. In its first address the league called specifically only for "engaging and recommending competent lecturers, obtaining the co-operation of the public press, and the establishing and conducting of a stamped circular."[3] These aims and methods were sound and reasonable, as far as they went. Until substantial additional public support could be assured, a new parliamentary initiative (let alone an electoral strategy) was out of the question. The middle classes of the industrial North and Midlands, from whom alone a spontaneous response could be expected, were already organized or in the process of being organized. For the most part they were to be left to their own devices. Clearly, if the league was to overcome its reputation as a regional special interest group, it would have to concentrate on extending the movement to new classes and new areas of the country.

In this effort the leadership in Manchester saw itself as having two functions. First, it was to act as a center of communications: with the public press, between existing associations, and with potential supporters elsewhere. To this end, as well as churning out the usual flood of tracts, the league took a major gamble. Less than a month after the league was founded it launched its own newspaper, the *Anti–Corn Law Circular*, which quickly settled on a mix of league news, extracts from other papers, vituperative attacks on its enemies, and general political and economic articles with a free trade slant. In a daring and expensive move, the first issue of the *Circular* promised free copies to all newspapers, local anti–Corn Law associations, and individual members. In its early days most of the articles appear to have been written by Smith or Cobden, who had been particularly anxious for the league to have a paper. Both men also shared with Wilson and the league secretary the growing burden of correspondence.

Beyond that, the leadership envisioned Manchester as a center of missionary activity. Cobden and Smith did not intend to undertake this work themselves; Smith's foray into the Midlands at the end of 1838 was not repeated elsewhere. Instead they hired itinerant lecturers. One, Paulton, was already in the field. Two others were added early in 1839, one of them, James Acland, suggested by Parkes, the other, Sidney Smith, recruited by Cobden through his Edinburgh publisher, William Tait. In itself this reliance on lecturers was not mistaken; they were an accepted means of public education and propaganda. This, indeed, was the golden age of the lecture circuit in England. Nor, on the whole, were the lecturers poorly chosen; a couple of them remained with the league until the end. But their early use was poorly thought out. Since the leadership did not travel, the lecturers were the league to most of the areas they visited. They should, therefore, have served a period of apprenticeship, perhaps at first lecturing only to friendly audiences and accompanied by one of the leaders of the league, as Paulton had the year before. Instead they were sent out on their own into uncharted territory. They learned their job on the road, often with unfortunate results. A speech that might have gone down well with the true believers in Manchester could seem irrelevant, even inflammatory, in parts of England where repeal was an alien issue or not yet an issue.

Furthermore, to be effective, their appearances had to be well planned and followed up. Yet only Sidney Smith was provided with an advance man at first; for the rest, local sympathizers or the lecturers themselves had to arrange publicity, hire halls, and lay the basis for local associations. This was a sufficiently chancy proposition even in friendly territory, but in large areas of England only hostility could be expected, and the greatest mistake of the league in 1839 was to concentrate its missionary efforts in precisely those areas. All three lecturers spent the bulk of their time in the rural south, and for all of them the results were nearly disastrous. Often they could not even hire a hall, almost all their meetings were disrupted, and on occasion they were manhandled and driven out of town.

Cobden was largely responsible for this fiasco. Deeply committed to the rural campaign, he believed in the necessity and possibility of shattering the apparent unity of the agricultural interest and recruiting the farmer as an ally against the landlord. The underlying class conflicts of rural England as well as the farmer's interest in free trade were major themes of the *Anti–Corn Law Circular* from its first issue: "These laws have occasioned deep distress to the farmer and profound suffering to the peasantry, whilst, if they have secured increased revenues to the landowner, they have been derived from the capital of the tenant and not from the high price of his produce."[4]

For Cobden, given his family background, this was an intensely personal matter. Repeal, he argued, could not hurt the farmer. It would not lead to a collapse of agricultural prices, throw land out of cultivation, or inundate the Poor Law authorities with a vast new pool of unemployable farm labor. On the contrary, by opening up the English market to foreign grain, it would tend to raise foreign grain prices as much as lower English ones. Furthermore, free trade not protection was the best assurance of general rural, indeed national, prosperity. By providing an expanding English market for foreign agricultural countries, repeal would open up in these same countries a market for English manufactures. The resulting commercial and industrial prosperity would directly contribute to rural prosperity both by increasing the demand for domestic as well as foreign grown food and by offering alternative employment to the surplus rural population. This, in turn, would enhance the bargaining position of tenants in the setting of rents and of laborers in the setting of wages. Only those who lived by rent needed to fear the effects of free trade.

It was a beguiling argument but, as Cobden only belatedly recognized, it failed to meet the immediate fears of farmers. Even if his arguments were correct, the benefits he promised were long-term ones. Rents might fall and foreign grain prices rise in a few years; industrial prosperity might solve the problems of rural poverty and overpopulation eventually. In the short run, however, repeal seemed likely to mean a fall, perhaps a catastrophic fall, in domestic agricultural prices. In that context Cobden's arguments appeared at best conjectural, at worst duplicitous. After all, in addressing its original middle-class constituency, the league's most persuasive and often repeated argument against the Corn Laws was their inflationary effect on the price of food and, hence, on the money wages of labor and the price of manufactures. Understandably, farmers (and urban workers) as well as landlords concluded that the real intention of the league was to force down the price of manufactured goods, if necessary at the expense of workers and agricultural producers.

The league's early emphasis on the high price of English manufactures and on the problems this posed in foreign markets was inevitable. Founded during a depression and aimed first and foremost at enlisting the support of industrial interests, it could do nothing else. But the results were disastrous when the league tried to reach out beyond its home base, for it appeared to be pitting interest against interest and class against class. Thus, far from enlisting support against protectionist landlords, the league succeeded primarily in forging an alliance against itself. In later years, in different political and economic conditions, the league was able gradually to alter its message and repair most of the early damage; but in 1839 its much-hoped-for rural campaign was misconceived and doomed before it started.

So too, and for the same reasons, was a missionary effort in the league's own back yard, aimed at enlisting the support of the industrial working class. Working-class opposition to the league was always an embarrassment; at times it was a good deal more. When the repealers held their regional rallies following the defeat of Villiers' first motion in February, the Chartists disrupted many of them. Worst of all, the Manchester association was forced to abandon a public meeting in its native city and reconvene in a closed meeting a few days later. This was intolerable, and Cobden was determined to put an end to it. As in his approach to the farmers, however, he misjudged the temper of working-class politics in Manchester. Sensibly he avoided any public criticism of the Chartists and ascribed the disturbances to an unspecified rabble, which, he warned, threatened the aspirations of the laboring classes as well. In private, however, he pinned most of the blame on a handful of self-serving Chartists, perhaps backed by Tory money, who played on the fears of ignorant working men in order to maintain their own political influence against the rivalry of the league.

That the league might be seen by honest men as a smokescreen to divert the working classes from their real interest, the People's Charter, hardly entered Cobden's calculations. Nor did he credit the genuineness of popular suspicion of the league's intentions, a suspicion born not so much of ignorance as of fear. At a time when the North was again moving into economic recession, with the peak of opposition to the New Poor Law only recently passed, and in view of the emphasis of the league on the dangers of foreign competition, it would have been remarkable if working-class radicals had not believed that the repealers hoped to push down costs by pushing down wages. The league did what it could to counter such suspicions. The second and subsequent issues of the *Anti–Corn Law Circular* contained a column entitled "The Operative," which set out to dispel workers' misconceptions. The first of these columns was devoted to the most sensitive question, the effect of repeal on wages, and set forth what was always to be the official league position: "Taking into account the increased demand which must arise in the labor market, owing to the stimulus which . . . [repeal] would impart to our foreign trade, it is quite impossible that the wages of the operative can fall so much as the necessaries of life, and therefore he will be in a better position, not only by the increased reward of, but also by the more constant demand for, his labor."[5]

Yet, however often the league reiterated the argument that real if not money wages would rise with repeal and that the long-run effects of free-trade-induced prosperity would be more jobs and a better standard of life for all, it is clear that this was not widely believed. Thus, when Cobden appointed young Edward Watkin, the son of

Absolom Watkin, to organize an Operative Anti–Corn Law Association, the results were mixed. The association held a number of large meetings and aided in the creation of similar groups elsewhere, but the Chartists condemned it as a pawn of the league, and the Chartists, not the league, continued to command the streets and meeting halls of Manchester for another two years.

By the early summer of 1839 the league was in trouble. It had failed to broaden its base significantly and had overextended itself in attempting to do so; the *Circular* and the lecture tours had proved expensive, and there were growing signs of friction between the lecturers, the advance men, and headquarters back in Manchester; money was not coming in. There were even rumors that the league was about to collapse. At the very least some economies would have to be made. The lecture campaign and the number of paid staff in Manchester were cut back, fund raising became a central feature of the lecture tours, and the *Circular* started accepting advertising. Yet no fundamental rethinking of league strategy followed. The plans for 1840 were essentially a replica of those for 1839, only, or so the league council hoped, a bit bigger and much better. The campaign was certainly bigger, but it was little better. As in 1839, it began with a banquet and delegates conference in Manchester. In addition there was a second banquet for working men and their families, sponsored by the Operative Anti–Corn Law Association. This was followed by the trek to London in support of Villiers' second annual motion for the House of Commons to resolve itself into a committee to debate the Corn Laws. But when it finally came to a vote, the result, in a thinner house than the year before, was nearly identical. Once again the assembled delegates responded by pledging their support for a nationwide campaign, and once again the campaign centered on propaganda.

There were changes. More lecturers were hired, including two specifically for working-class audiences, and there was less emphasis on rural areas. An attempt was also made to integrate the lecture campaign more fully with the other aims of the league. The lecturers played an important role in getting up petitions to Parliament preparatory to the debate on Villiers' motion, and the league council proposed the creation of regional lecture circuits, which would have the advantages of being closely tied to local needs, local organization, and, not incidentally, local sources of funding. However, not much appears to have come of this or any of the league's plans in early 1840. The petition drive produced impressive results, but the rural lecture campaign fell flat again, and a major effort to rouse London collapsed through a combination of internal rivalries and lack of popular enthusiasm. To be sure, the league was not in danger of dissolution as it had been the year before. Contributions from beyond Manchester were now coming in, and a few wealthy supporters had emerged who could be relied on in an emergency. This, plus more careful management, assured the survival of the league. But a mass movement that does not grow is bound to wither sooner or later, and the league was not growing.

All the same, Cobden was happy that summer. In May he married a young Welsh woman, Catherine Anne Williams, whom he had met through one of his sisters, and somehow they managed to get away from Manchester for a two-month-long honeymoon through France, Switzerland, and Germany. This respite could not have come at a better time for Cobden. With his business affairs settled and the full pressure of the repeal campaign still ahead of him, this was, however brief, the most carefree period he had known or was to know for many years. For the historian as well his marriage and honeymoon came at an opportune time. Because the leaders of the league worked together in Manchester during the league's first year, they left few private reflections on the condition and prospects of the agitation in its first phase. During his two months abroad in the summer of 1840, however, Cobden wrote long letters of just this kind to Wilson and J. B. Smith.

Compared with the combativeness of everything he wrote or said in the early months of 1839, these letters were subdued. Undoubtedly he was tired, and in any case the minutiae of league business must have appeared particularly unappetizing as seen from Paris. Even so, the tone is striking. Not that he was pessimistic. He expressed no fears for the survival of the league; as he noted, there were now "a certain number of real friends upon whom we can rely permanently for an income sufficient to enable us to keep alive the League."[6] But he appears to have had no master plan in mind and no sense that a significant advance was close at hand. "Years will probably pass before anything can be done," he commented to Wilson; the important thing was to keep going and, whatever the realities, "to indicate that we have a plan"[7] and the resources to carry it out. As to the means, "there is nothing for it then but lectures, tracts and the Circular."[8]

He no longer looked on the rural south as a major field of operations; securing their base in the industrial towns of England was his new highest priority, because without them the movement had no weight and the "landlords may laugh at us." Once again he raised the subject of an electoral policy, expressing the "hope that when another election comes we shall make some important advances in the large towns," but beyond that he offered nothing specific. Indeed, for the moment he was inclined to see the role of the league in modest terms: "Perhaps, after all, some accident of an extraordinary nature will carry the question. But in the mean time we are preparing the public mind for taking advantage of such an accident when it comes."[9]

CHAPTER 9

The League and Electoral Politics

The sense of drift, so evident in league policy and from Cobden's letters in the summer of 1840, ended abruptly that autumn. Shortly after Cobden returned from the continent, the league executive decided on two major policy innovations in preparation for the next year's campaign and for a general election everyone assumed was imminent. The first involved the participation of the leadership of the league in missionary activity beyond Manchester; the second took the league into electoral politics. Both changes had been a long time in coming. In his *History of the Anti–Corn Law League* Archibald Prentice claimed that it was he who originated missionary sorties by members of the league council.[1] And so it very likely was. Prentice, whatever his limitations as a newspaper editor, had a better idea than most of his colleagues of the value of publicity for its own sake. He also enjoyed the hustle and bustle of the political tour. When he discovered at the delegates meeting in London that spring that officers of some local associations were already moving about their districts, he urged the leadership in Manchester to follow suit, and early in 1840 he made a number of forays into nearby towns, apparently on his own initiative.

Other members of the league executive were reluctant to commit themselves to a new area of activity that could easily consume almost any amount of time. Yet the pressures to do so were increasing. The itinerant lecturers served an important but limited purpose; as personal links binding the movement together in the intervals between delegates conferences, they were poor substitutes for the leadership. In May the Glasgow association asked the council to send a representative to a conference of Scottish repealers, and once again it was

Prentice who volunteered to go. Sooner or later others were bound to follow, but when they did, it was not on the ad hoc basis pioneered by Prentice. The missionary work of the leaders of the league was made an integral part of a larger shift in policy, the decision to engage in electoral politics.

Late in September the *Anti–Corn Law Circular* announced that the Council of the league was waiting "only for the completion of the year's registries . . . to carry into operation the plan which has long occupied their attention—of appealing directly and personally to the constituencies of the kingdom . . . Beginning with those boroughs in the immediate vicinity of Manchester whose representatives have voted in favor of the Corn Laws, the Council will respectfully solicit an interview, by deputation from their own body with the electors."[2] The Council hastened to reassure its more timid supporters that it "entered upon the field of electoral agitation with the determination to recognise no political partisanship" but equally it made clear its intention "of creating in every borough an anti–corn law party . . . whose united strength shall be sufficient to prevent the return of any candidate at the next election, whatever his political party may be, who supports the landowners bread tax."

The plan was not quite as ambitious as this public announcement implied. The leadership of the league had no intention of moving either rapidly or far beyond its base in Manchester. The attempt to create an anti–Corn Law party in selected boroughs was a calculated risk, as Cobden noted a week earlier when giving a preview of what was afoot to the veteran leader of London radicalism (and chief liaison for the league in the capital), Francis Place: "If we can only succeed in a few boroughs to get a hearing from the electors, we shall frighten the representatives in other places."[3] Nonetheless, for all their private caution in launching the new move, the leaders of the league were right to announce it in dramatic terms. It was the most important innovation in the policy of the movement since the formation of the league itself eighteen months before.

This move, too, had been brewing for some time. In March a delegation from the league conference was accorded an interview with the prime minister, whose position on the Corn Laws proved so unsatisfactory that a number of delegates came away determined to adopt some sort of electoral policy. When Villiers' motion was delayed a few days later and finally defeated two months later, the majority at the conference felt that they had to respond with something more forceful than a renewal of the propaganda campaign. On both occasions they resolved "that, disassociating ourselves from all political parties, we hereby declare that we will use every exertion to obtain the return of those members to Parliament alone who will support a repeal of the Corn Laws."[4] Cautiously worded though they were, both resolutions were opposed by a minority of delegates, who still wanted to avoid mixing in electoral politics, particularly if that might further weaken the Whig government. Perhaps because of this—perhaps also because of Cobden's marriage and wedding trip—nothing more was heard of an electoral policy for some months. But the dangers of avoiding the issue were beginning to outweigh the dangers of taking it up. During the spring and summer reports filtered back to headquarters of growing frustration in the provinces, and in what may have been a decisive development, proposals for political action of another kind appeared to threaten the unity of the repealers.

Ominously, the new move sprang up in Leeds, hitherto one of the most active centers of opposition to the Corn Laws. Now, in the wake of the defeat of Villiers' motion, a number of radicals there concluded that repeal could never be carried in existing political circumstances. With the Chartists and the league each attacking the other as bitterly as both attacked the government, Parliament could comfortably continue to ignore both movements. The reformers' only hope appeared to lie in unity in support of a compromise proposal for household suffrage, which, once passed, would open the way for free trade. It was a naive hope, as the subsequent history of the Leeds Household Suffrage Association, founded in the spring of 1840 and all but dead a year later, demonstrated. For the most part, Chartists and repealers were united only in their disdain for this attempt to divert them from their primary goals; even in Leeds it was attacked from both sides.

At first, however, fearful that this new rival might gain momentum, the leadership of the league was cautious in its public comments. The *Circular* criticized the Leeds association only for its criticism of the league; and Cobden declined to attend an association conference in December solely on the grounds that the league was barred by its charter from supporting any issue other than repeal. In private, however, Cobden was scathing in his criticism of a movement he regarded as unrealistic and divisive. All the same, he was well aware of the dangers it posed. A number of prominent radicals, including Daniel

O'Connell, Joseph Hume, and John Roebuck, supported the Leeds association, and whatever the fortunes of that group might be, its approach to the frustrations of radicalism was always the greatest threat to the primacy of the league. The formation of the association was a clear warning that unless the league charted its own course politically, it risked being swallowed up or shunted aside.

In charting that course, however, the league moved cautiously. In November a deputation from the league council visited Bolton, which, as the stronghold of the Ashworth brothers, was a safe place in which to try out the new policy. To avoid any suggestion of political dictation, much was made of the fact that the deputies came at the invitation of local reformers. To avoid any suggestion of exclusiveness, all local electors regardless of party were invited to meet with them. To avoid any suggestion of secretiveness, anti–Corn Law tracts were sent to each elector before the deputies arrived. At the meeting J. B. Smith was frank about the purpose of the visit: "Till they could point to the representatives of the manufacturing towns as united in their opinions on the question, all the efforts of the League would be insufficient."[5] The electors were requested and agreed to lobby their present M.P.s and to support only anti–Corn Law candidates at the next general election. During the next seven months similar visits were arranged to eight other boroughs in Lancashire and Cheshire. With only minor variations the procedures tried out in Bolton were repeated elsewhere with similar results. Here and there the preparations were not as smoothly handled; occasionally the deputies ran into Tory or Chartist heckling; and in a few places the deputies had to settle for vaguely worded promises of greater cooperation. But in most of the boroughs the all important electoral pledge was overwhelmingly agreed to.

All in all, it was a major success for the league—its first in many months—and particularly for Cobden. More than anyone else he was identified with this new policy. Alone among the leaders of the league, he was a member of every deputation. A policy that, prematurely, he had advocated eighteen months before was now, of necessity, emerging as the centerpiece of the repeal movement. The result was almost a new league: more aggressive, more willing to take risks, less fearful of making enemies. As good an illustration as any of the nature and rapidity of this change was the way that the league dealt with the immediate threat of the Leeds Household Suffrage Association. As late as December 1840 the leaguers had suppressed their private anger and adopted a live-and-let-live policy. In late January 1841, however, in the wake of a stormy conference of the association and with the league's electoral policy under way, the leaguers went on the attack.

Repeal, not political reform, the *Anti–Corn Law Circular* declared, was the practical issue of the day, and the league, not the Leeds association, was the practitioner of realistic politics. As the recent conference in Leeds had shown, there was no basis for united action between Chartists and household suffragists. Distrust and disagreement ran too deep. Repeal, however, was a source of potential unity among those divided on political reform. It was, moreover, a matter of urgent necessity, which could not wait for a further reform of Parliament. Change of any kind depended on working within the system as it existed, and that only the league was now doing. All else must give way to that effort. "To those who think there are other questions of equal or more urgent pressure," the *Circular* issued a challenge: "Get such a body of voters to stand out, in any constituency, for a candidate anxious to promote your reform as . . . can carry the election and we will join with you to carry an advocate of both our wishes; but until you by such means make it worth our while to court your alliance in elections, we will throw our own weight at the scale of the Whig, aye, or of the Tory, who . . . will work sincerely and earnestly in Parliament for the abolition of the corn laws."[6]

Clearly the league was now confident that it had closed off the possibility of attrition from that quarter, but in moving to shore up its left flank, it opened itself to attack from the right. Even in Manchester many nominal supporters of the league had criticized its policies and tactics from the beginning and with increasing vehemence all through 1840. After the defeat of Villiers' motion in May, the *Manchester Guardian* chastised the league for its unwillingness to water down its program. As for the league's electoral policy, that was anathema. To make opposition to the Corn Laws a shibboleth, the sole grounds on which to decide support of or opposition to a candidate, was, the *Guardian* argued, irresponsible and potentially self- defeating. Many members of the league agreed, and as the leadership moved toward adopting an electoral policy, the moderates became restive. Once the league council began sending out its deputations and extracting pledges in November, a showdown within the league was inevitable. It came two months later, when, with the electoral policy just getting under way, the league was given its first opportunity to apply that policy in practice.

The occasion was a by-election in Walsall, a borough just north of Birmingham and even closer to Charles Villiers' constituency at Wolverhampton. It was a marginal seat; the Tories had won it in 1832 and again, unopposed, three years later, and were beaten by a mere twenty votes in 1837. The retiring Liberal member was a free trader, but the official Whig nominee to replace him was an uncertain quantity, and the league council therefore decided to send a deputation to Walsall to question the candidates. When their answers proved unsatisfactory, the deputation began to promote free trade sentiment and talk of alternative candidates among the Liberal electors. This sufficed to drive the official Liberal from the contest and opened the way to a momentous decision by the league council to intervene in the selection of a free trade candidate. Finding a sufficiently prestigious and willing candidate proved almost impossible, however, and in the end J. B. Smith, dispatched to Walsall to give advice, agreed to stand himself.

To the moderates of the league this was intolerable. In a matter of months the repeal agitation had been transformed from a pressure group primarily concerned with propaganda into a quasi political party, willing to put at risk a marginal Liberal seat in Parliament. The Whig-Liberal press was furious, and some moderate members of the league hoped to reverse the course of league policy before it proved disastrous. It was too late. The meeting of the council at which the issue was finally fought out was held just after Smith had agreed to stand in Walsall. Even many who feared and opposed what was happening had to agree that it was more dangerous now to back off than go on. Moreover, the dissidents were mostly peripheral figures in the league. The inner circle had either, like Cobden, long believed in an electoral strategy or, like Smith, come to see its necessity. Thus, when it came to canvassing votes on the league council, the leadership and old hands at the business like Cobden were bound to win. Despite the fact that Smith was away in Walsall and Cobden was ill and could attend the crucial meeting only briefly, the issue was never in doubt.

Even so, their victory was sure to take its toll. Some members dropped out and, of greater concern to Cobden, some financial support dried up. Intent on minimizing the damage, the council went out of its way to reassure the moderates. During and after the Walsall campaign, the league insisted that it was not using general funds (as opposed to a special subscription) to fight the election. The council also claimed that it was not acting as an election machine but only cooperating with the free traders of Walsall in attempting to persuade the voters. Neither assertion was true. The league masterminded the campaign and used whatever funds it could lay its hands on. Indeed, as Sidney Smith put it, the "League virtually adjourned" to Walsall for the duration.[7] And with good reason: since the future policy of the league—indeed, perhaps, the future of the league itself—hung on the outcome, no rules were observed on either side. For all the league's claims to represent a higher standard of public morality than their monopolist adversaries, its leaders plunged effectively, if not always happily, into a campaign as corrupt as any in an age when corrupt elections were still commonplace. According to Sidney Smith,

> the working men and their wives blockaded the shopkeepers—and those who declared for the Tory, had their customers turned from their shop doors . . . Staid and sober Quakers presided at convivial meetings . . . Others bottled voters or carried them off drunk to places many miles off and by darkening windows persuaded them to sleep until the poll was over . . . I saw two men come up after a third. One was asked his name and on giving it a man exclaimed, "Why, that man is in America!" When the second gave his name another cried, "I buried that man on the third of last month!" They however voted and the third man said with a wink, "Come away to your graves again!"

Wilson and Parkes were in their element. Cobden, on the other hand, felt distinctly uncomfortable, although he too played his part, hiring election agents of dubious reputation, and so on. "If we lose," he noted uneasily, "it will be because we won't take the usual way to win."[8] He did draw the line, however, at corruption of the most blatant sort. "I am more or less convinced," he wrote Smith, "that we ought not to buy illegally a single vote to save the election. It would be a lasting stigma on our cause and be the ruin of the League."[9] More to his taste and more important in determining the future character of league election efforts was his work in soliciting endorsements from prominent figures in nearby Birmingham and Wolverhampton, in overseeing a methodical review of the local electoral register, and, above all, in canvassing. He and Smith personally undertook a thorough canvass of Walsall, working the constituency like any professional party organization. Cobden, it appears, was a forceful canvasser:

> One of the electors called upon was a corn merchant who was looked upon as a very religious man . . . After a few introductory words

J. B. S. asked the corn merchant for his support. The man replied that he would consult his broker on the subject. "Consult your broker," cried Mr. Cobden, "on the justice of the Corn Laws! Consult your Bible, sir, and see what it says on the subject." With these words he opened the Bible at Proverbs XI verse 26: "He that withholdeth corn, the people shall curse him; but blessing shall be upon the head of him that selleth it.", and pointing to it with his finger excitedly and striking the table he exclaimed, "That is what the Bible says."[10]

It would be nice to report that the corn merchant then and there saw the light and supported Smith, but although duly shaken by the encounter, he was observed to be among the first to cast a Tory vote on polling day.

The Tory, indeed, won but by a margin of less than thirty votes in seven hundred. Considering how late they had come into the field, how much they had had to improvise, and that, in running a single-issue campaign, they were challenging both major parties, the leaguers rightly claimed Walsall as a moral victory. More even than that, in the heady aftermath of Walsall, it seemed that the league had finally found the means of circumventing partisan politics and placing the issue of repeal inescapably on the agenda of public debate. At the annual meeting of the Manchester Anti–Corn Law Association, held less than three weeks after polling day in Walsall, Cobden explained what he regarded as the most extraordinary aspect of the campaign there: "In his address he [Smith] never mentioned one word of his political opinions, and all the time he was there I believe not an individual put a question to him as to party politics. This is a remarkable fact, and there cannot be a doubt that at the general election, come when it may, the great rallying cry will be, 'no bread tax.' "[11]

And so it might have been had the general election been delayed until the end of the year, for the movement was advancing on a broad front. In addition to adopting an electoral strategy, the league at this time set out to broaden the base of its appeal by placing greater emphasis on the humanitarian and moral aspects of the cause. The opening move involved the mothers, wives, and daughters of the league leadership. Hitherto relegated to the gallery at league functions, in late 1840 they gave a tea party, the first of a series of teas, galas, and bazaars sponsored by the ladies of the league. The idea—primarily George Wilson's—was an inspired piece of public relations. The speakers (all male) were afforded the opportunity of appealing for free trade as a question of the preservation of home and hearth, and by adding a social, even a familial, dimension to the agitation, the league was gradually able to soften its image.

Another example of the league's growing sensitivity to its audience was a change in the tone of its appeal to the working classes. Despite the operative anti–Corn Law associations and the hiring of lecturers specifically for working-class audiences, the league still encountered more distrust and hostility than support. This was a particular disappointment to Cobden, and in January 1841, tacitly admitting that the league's appeal to the working classes had been misjudged, he proposed changing the name of the league newspaper to the *Anti–Bread Tax Circular*. This new emphasis on repeal as "not so much a question of political economy as of justice and humanity"[12] was a sign of something more than greater awareness of the need for good public relations. The change, effected in April, coincided with a deterioration in the economy, as England plunged into the worst depression of the nineteenth century. The condition of England rapidly became the major theme of league propaganda, an aspect of the campaign that was to bear fruit in 1842.

The state of the economy was also a factor in another innovation in 1841, the attempt to recruit ministers of religion to the cause. Although sincerely believing that the repeal of the bread tax was a moral issue, Cobden was also conscious of the possible political benefits of emphasizing the moral dimension of the repeal movement. Even before joining the Manchester Anti–Corn Law Association he judged "that a moral and even a religious spirit may be infused into that topic [the Corn Laws] and if agitated in the same manner that the question of slavery has been it will be irresistible."[13] From time to time in its first two years the league urged individual ministers to preach and local groups of ministers to declare their abhorrence of the evil effects of the monopoly on food, but it was only in 1841 that the decision was made to launch a moral crusade. In June, George Thompson, the antislavery agitator, was recruited by the league with the intention, as Cobden put it, of launching "him versus white slavery."[14] Thompson joined the repeal campaign as part of an agreement—signed for the league by Cobden and Bright—with his employer at the time, the British India society, which in turn was promised the support of leading free traders once their agitation was over. That the league would enter into such an arrangement (which came close to violating its injunction against mixing other issues in with repeal) was itself perhaps the best testimony to Thompson's influence among human-itarian reformers, an influence the council of the league, made up overwhelmingly of businessmen, very much felt the need of early in 1841, when it first concocted the notion of holding a conference of ministers in August.

In the event, and largely as a result of Thompson's reputation and organizing skills, the conference exceeded the most optimistic expec-tations of its promoters. Nearly 700 ministers, mostly Dissenters, attended; for four days they heard evidence on the state of the nation and passed a series of resolutions condemning the Corn Laws. Os-tensibly the work of a group of Manchester ministers, in fact it was directed from league headquarters. The league had good reason to operate behind the scenes, quite apart from the fact that an indepen-dent meeting would carry more weight. The variety of sects repre-sented and the near absence of Anglicans and Methodists troubled some delegates, as did holding a religious conference on a political question. A more overtly league-dominated conference might in fact have been disastrous, but as the league leadership rightly judged, the advantages of support from the Dissenting sects outweighed the risks involved in trying to organize them.

The leaguers were looking well beyond the propaganda value of such meetings, however. The conference of ministers was a deliberate attempt to play on the prejudices of organized Dissent. The estab-lished church and its link to the Corn Laws through the tithes had often been a target of league invective. If repeal could be made not only a moral issue but another in the list of Dissenters' grievances, so much the better. The league's redoubled effort to reach a working-class audience was even more directly linked to an attack on its en-emies, in this case the Chartist movement. Heretofore the league had avoided criticism of the movement or its leaders by name. The newly christened *Anti–Bread Tax Circular* was not so cautious. In its first issue it accused the Chartists of having accepted Tory money to work against the league in Walsall. This marked the beginning of a sus-tained assault on the reputations of selected Chartist leaders in league propaganda.

In addition the league set about wresting control of the streets and meeting halls of Manchester from the Chartists. As in the founding of the Operative Anti–Corn Law Association two years earlier, the job was deputed by Cobden to Edward Watkin. His means was a disciplined corps of working-class repealers, aided by Daniel O'Connell's most reliable gift to the league, a phalanx of the Manchester working-class Irish. With unemployment increasing and a general election expected at any time, the political temperature in Manchester was bound to rise in any case. The league-Irish alliance, coupled with an attempt by Watkin to expand and tighten up the Operative Anti–Corn Law Association and inevitable Chartist efforts at counterorganization, ensured that there would be violence. In May, for the first time, supporters of the league took revenge for past Chartist disruptions of repeal meetings by successfully disrupting Chartist rallies. The climactic confrontation came a month later at an open-air meeting of the Manchester Operative Anti–Corn Law Association.

Both sides made elaborate preparations for this affair, but the league was at last in a position to out-organize its enemy. Working-class repealers and their Irish allies were scattered through the crowd, and at the first sign of trouble took on the disruptors, while Cobden calmly presided on the platform. In desperation, one of the opponents of repeal tried to win over the Irish, exclaiming, "at the height of the tumult . . . 'Irishmen, hear me, I am an Irishman!' " But one of O'Connell's "boys" immediately "retorted, 'So was Castle-r-a-a-y!' with," as Watkin noted, "prodigious effect."[15] The Chartists were driven from the square. This meeting marked an important turning point in the radical agitation of the 1840s. Never again did the league lose control of the public meeting places of Manchester or submit to interruptions at its meetings. As the *Circular* put it, actually in connection with Walsall, although the words could have been applied to the conference of ministers or the conflict with the Chartists, "the missionary period during which liberty of speech alone is asked, when 'he who is not against us is with us' has passed . . . and the time when a converted public opinion must act upon its convictions, when 'he who is not with us is against us' has arrived."[16]

That was also the approach the leaguers would like to have been able to take in fighting the general election of 1841 but, unfortunately for them, their plans were short-circuited by the political skills of Lord John Russell and Sir Robert Peel. When Parliament convened in January, the Whig government, which had managed to stand on its last legs for two years, seemed finally on the verge of collapse. To its normal problems of factionalized support, a disciplined opposition, and paper-thin majorities had been added the worsening economy, one of the effects of which was a chronic budget deficit. In 1840 the government had attempted—and failed—to balance the budget by raising taxes. A year later, not daring to raise them again, it took a leaf out of the book of free trade and proposed tariff reductions, in the hope that increased consumption would lead to increased revenue. Not incidentally, the government also hoped thereby to save itself by placing the Tories on the defensive and reenlisting the support of disaffected reformers.

It was a daring move, but it came too late to save the Whigs. Although the government's conversion to freer trade was likely to win over some radicals, it was certain to alienate important special interests. As for Peel, having been narrowly defeated in an attempt to unseat the Whigs the year before, he was determined to try again, at the right moment. That came on May 18, in response to the government proposal to reduce the duty on foreign sugar, the weakest link in the budget proposals. Not only the powerful sugar interests, but many antislavery advocates, who wished to retain the duty on slave-grown sugar, opposed it. With the Tories united, the number of Liberal defectors or abstainers was sufficient to hand the government a clear-cut defeat.

Although about to be deprived of office, the Whigs were not to be prevented from losing it in a manner as advantageous to themselves as possible. The budget had not staved off defeat, but it had helped to reinvigorate the Whig-Liberal-Radical coalition. Reduction of the sugar and timber duties would not, however, suffice to reverse the trend to Toryism. If the Whigs were successfully to renew their claim to being the party of reform, as Russell believed they must, then, he managed to convince his colleagues, they had to go further. On April 30, the day the budget was introduced, he announced his intention of moving for a committee of the whole House to consider the Corn Laws; a week later he informed the House that he would propose a low fixed revenue duty on imported grain in place of the existing protective duties.

Most of these developments were unexpected, and, not surprisingly, the league reacted with a sometimes confused mixture of elation, suspicion, and hasty improvisation. The decision to raise the issue of Corn Law revision as a matter of government policy was in itself a victory for the league, regardless of the government's motives. Whatever the outcome, the effect of Russell's announcement in legitimizing the question and enhancing the reputation of the league could not be undone. Cobden and his colleagues were determined to seize the initiative insofar as that was possible. If, as they believed and Parkes confirmed, the Whigs would not have moved so far without league pressure, then further pressure, not conciliation, was called for. Four days after Russell's first statement, the league council voted to send deputies to major cities all over the country, in the hope of generating funds, new members, and a new round of petitioning.

Although the league leadership saw the Whig initiative as a signal for greater militancy, the same was not true of all their followers. Simply by adopting Villiers' motion as their own, the Whigs threatened to draw moderate repealers into supporting an as-yet-unspecified revision of the Corn Laws. The hastily organized league deputations were designed as much to forestall that possibility as to put additional pressure on the government. Even after Russell announced the government's support for a low fixed duty, the league council was not at first inclined to moderate its commitment to total and immediate repeal. This, however, proved an impossible position to maintain. Pressures from within the league, although not its inner circle, to meet the Whigs halfway were irresistible. By the time of the general election, the league had compromised to the extent of urging its supporters to back advocates of a low fixed duty where no repeal candidate was available.

This in turn opened the league to the accusation from its hard-line supporters of trimming. Cobden neatly sidestepped this criticism, arguing that "it was not our business to attack them [the Whigs] whilst another party, more powerful than the Government and the people, was resolutely opposed to any concession."[17] In any case, Cobden was not unduly concerned with the long-run effects of the league's retreat from pure doctrine and an independent electoral strategy; he was rightly convinced that the league's awkward position was only temporary. Two days after Russell's first statement, he accurately predicted the political outcome: "The ministers can't carry a fixed duty . . . [The opposition] will probably destroy them by a vote of want of confidence. In that case we shall perhaps have a dissolution soon and Peel and the bread taxers would get a working majority."[18] In that event, of course, the league would be able to abandon its enforced alliance with the Whigs and return to the advocacy of total repeal. Even so, the league position just before and during the election was far less clear-cut than its leaders had planned since embarking on an electoral policy nine months before.

In other respects as well the election was a disappointment to the league. It came too soon. Deputations from the league council had visited fewer than a dozen boroughs, and the working of these constituencies for electoral purposes had hardly begun. In particular, there had not been time to screen the electoral registers to exclude unqualified Tories and enroll qualified repealers. The league had to make the best of an unpromising situation and concentrated its limited resources in a few constituencies, mostly in the Manchester area, but also including Walsall. In view of the size of the Tory victory nationally, however, the league did not do badly where it had to do well. In the cotton districts the Tories gained seats in two constituencies but lost ground in three. The league's sweetest victory came elsewhere, in Walsall. Their bitterest defeat was J. B. Smith's at Dundee. Cobden was returned from Stockport.

He had come close to being chosen as a candidate in Manchester. When one of the sitting members decided, in 1840, not to stand for reelection, a number of the younger repealers hoped that Cobden would be adopted as the reform candidate. He was sounded out but refused even to consider running; he could not, he explained, be a party man and, besides, "the country is not ready for my opinions."[19] Nor, for that matter, were many Manchester reformers. Cobden's reluctance to be a candidate opened the way for the establishment Liberals, led by Thomas Potter, to do what they had intended to do all along—choose a moderate candidate. Not that their man, Milner Gibson, was anything but sound on the major issues. But he was no agitator and came from an aristocratic family. That was his chief drawback for Cobden, who felt that Manchester should be represented by one of its own; but since he had no one else to suggest (and was abroad on his honeymoon), he was willing to go along. Gibson was selected and served Manchester loyally in Parliament for sixteen years.

Had the vacancy occurred a year later, Cobden's supporters would not have been so easily put off, either by Cobden or by Thomas Potter. The league was more visible and successful in 1841 than it had been in 1840, and Cobden was more clearly its leader. Indeed, whether he liked it or not, Cobden in the interim had become an inevitable parliamentary candidate. As the time for an election approached, three boroughs in the cotton districts vied for the honor of having him represent them; and all three refused to be put off by his reluctance to run or by his stringent conditions: that he be a totally independent M.P., free from normal constituency duties or other claims that might conflict with his work for the league. He could hardly hold out any longer, and once he accepted the inevitable, there was no doubt which constituency he would choose. Next door to Manchester and with a base of support left over from his unsuccessful candidacy four years earlier, Stockport had the best claim on his loyalty.

The Liberals of Stockport were also able to all but guarantee a victory. Two weeks before polling day Cobden reported to his brother Fred: "The Bolton and Stockport folks both got requisitions to me insuring my return. I declined. It was then that the Stockport people put the screw upon me, by a large deputation confessing their inability to agree amongst themselves upon any other man who could turn out the Major [Thomas Marsland]. They offered me carte blanche as to my attendance in London, and as to the time of my retaining the seat. I was over persuaded by my Manchester partisans and have yielded, and the election is secure."[20]

It was indeed. Cobden had to do little during the campaign; he had in any case prepared the ground some months before. Stockport was one of the boroughs visited by a deputation (including Cobden) from the league council early in 1841 and shortly thereafter he issued a letter to the working men and nonelectors of Stockport, urging them to back the decision of the electors' meeting to support only repeal candidates. Once his decision to accept their nomination ensured Liberal unity, his committee was able to do the rest on its own. "The Stockport affair was carried with unexpected éclat," he reported. "We drubbed the Major so soundly that at one o'clock he resigned. Two hundred electors were up all night previous to the polling, including the millowners," who, Cobden noted, "were against me at the former election."[21]

Cobden's reluctance to enter Parliament was not feigned. As he often said, he could not be a party man. That was less of a problem with the Whigs in opposition than it would have been before 1841 (and was to be after 1846). Even so, the position of an M.P. who represented a movement more than a constituency was anomalous. Most members of Peel's huge new majority and not a few Whigs as well saw Cobden, as he liked to put it, "as a gothic invader," come to destroy their empire[22]—which, indeed, he was. To others he seemed more like a "Saxon saint . . . meagre—a little melancholy, simple and earnest," as Disraeli remembered him during these years.[23] But whether gothic invader or Saxon saint or a bit of both, Cobden was an alien presence within the walls of Westminster, a constant reminder of the different sort of politics being practiced outside. Apart from this, however, the purpose of a league M.P. was not clear. Cobden's candidacy and election had come too suddenly for him to have developed a parliamentary strategy to go with the league's electoral policy. As he commented to his brother, "I shall be an observer for some time."[24]

Being an observer did not mean keeping silent, however. During the short six-week session of the new Parliament Cobden spoke five times, always on the Corn Laws or a related topic such as the condition of the poor, and usually briefly. Even his maiden speech was short. Unlike many of his contemporaries, Cobden was not given to lengthy speeches. He was, moreover, a restrained orator by the standards of the time. He rarely raised his voice or indulged in rhetorical flourishes. He did not harangue his enemies; his preferred weapons were sarcasm and cold contempt. Nor was he the sort of speaker who sought to bring audiences to their feet or to the verge of tears. He was most comfortable and most effective as an expository speaker appealing to reason. Above all he sought to persuade. It proved an effective parliamentary style, particularly so because so unexpected from a "gothic invader." Disraeli called him "the most persuasive speaker I have ever listened to."[25]

His maiden speech, although not a polished performance, was typical. Most of it was devoted to demonstrating the evils of the bread tax, as he now habitually called the Corn Laws, and to dealing yet again with the question that would not go away: the relationship between wages and the price of food. He warned the House of the dangers of inaction; he appealed to its conscience. Although his manner of illustrating an argument was often vivid, there was nothing especially noteworthy in the content of this or any of his early parliamentary speeches. What set them apart was that he so deliberately set himself apart from his audience. He was indeed an observer and made clear his disdain for much of what he observed. Again and again, he reiterated his indifference to party and to the ebb and flow of parliamentary debate. He was genuinely unconcerned with his standing in Parliament, at least as measured by the standards of Parliament, for his stature in the House had been established beyond its walls before he entered them.

His enemies were compelled to admit that. Even the mighty *Times* felt obliged to devote a leading article to a refutation of his maiden speech—an extraordinary compliment to a freshman member. And like most members elected under similar circumstances, Cobden tended to talk over the heads of both benches to his wider constituency. Implicit in all his speeches was an accusation against Parliament that it was not serious enough, that much of what went on there was irrelevant or self-serving, and that it was not in Parliament but in the councils of the league that the needs of the country were being addressed. As he said at the end his last major speech that session, "when I see a disposition among you to trade in humanity, I will not question your motives . . . but this I will tell you, that if you would give force and grace to your professions of humanity, it must not be confined to the Negro at the antipodes, nor to the building of churches, nor to the extension of Church establishments, nor to occasional visits to factories to talk sentiment over factory children—you must untax the people's bread."[26]

Hence Cobden's sense of frustration at being stuck in London, while the real business of the league as he saw it lay elsewhere. Feeling increasingly cut off, he wrote to Wilson near the end of the session, asking advice from the league council on how to proceed in Parliament. "We are not good judges of public feeling who are acting in a sphere of our own," he complained, "You are in a better position for forming a correct judgement as to the state of the public mind."[27] On the whole Cobden was inclined to press the issue, perhaps through a motion by Villiers, backed by petitions from the provinces. But he was no longer certain. During and immediately after the election, he had been optimistic. The Whigs in opposition would be more open to radical ideas and less sensitive (as well as less subject) to radical criticism, now that the future of a Whig government was not at stake. As for the new Tory government, it could not avoid dealing with the Corn Law question. The Whig initiative in opening it up could not be undone.

As the end of the session approached, however, it became clear that Peel, backed but also fettered by his huge majority, was not to be hurried, and that Parliament would be prorogued without any action on the Corn Laws. Cobden's appeal to the league council for aid was an act of desperation. Stymied in Parliament, he hoped that something might be done out of doors. "The question for you to decide really," he wrote, "is whether the feeling out of doors would back a small party in the House struggling for a hearing of our cause now." As the tone of his letter indicated he more than half expected, nothing was done. Manchester might move, but other cities could not be counted on to follow. Had the Tory majority been smaller or the Whig opposition vigorously led, the response might have been different, but as things stood in October 1841, the case for making a push in Parliament was poor.

Cobden could not deny that. His letter to Wilson was no clarion call, and irritated though he was at the failure of cities other than Manchester to come forward, he too felt ineffectual. In part the problem was simply a matter of the contrast between the expanding influence of the league early in 1841 and its present helplessness. In part the problem was a function of the perennial problem of any long-lived agitation: the need constantly to renew the movement and exceed its earlier achievements. The league had been faced with a similar crisis the year before and adopted an electoral policy as a way out. But that had been done in anticipation of a general election, now over. In addition, as was always the case at the end of the political year, the league was short of cash. There was no danger, as there had been two years earlier, that the league might go under, but a crisis of confidence ensued as the leadership searched for some means of restarting the engines of agitation.

CHAPTER 10

The Crisis of 1842

The crisis of confidence within the league could hardly have come at a more difficult time. Britain was just then entering the worst phase of a devastating economic depression. The price of wheat had averaged more than sixty shillings a bushel for four consecutive years. In almost every sector of mining and manufacturing, prices, employment, and real wages were declining dramatically. New investment was sharply down; bankruptcies were sharply up. The sustaining effects of the railway boom were petering out as lines projected in the prosperous mid-thirties neared completion. Despite the implementation of the New Poor Law of 1834, expenditure on poor relief in the manufacturing districts had grown inexorably, often more than doubling since 1837.

The human cost was appalling; the political cost was expected to be equally dramatic. With the Poor Law scheduled for debate and renewal in Parliament, a repetition of the popular opposition to it of 1837–38 seemed likely. The Chartists were reviving under the pressure of economic distress. As for the league, its leaders assumed that this should be their moment, that they more than any other popular movement or either political party held the key to solving the nation's economic crisis. Yet, at the outset of what should have been their time of triumph, the means of translating their support into effective political action seemed to be slipping from their grasp. Their maturing as a movement had come just too late; the political changes of 1841 had come just too soon. Somehow this gap had to be closed and the forward momentum of early 1841 restored or their greatest opportunity would be lost, perhaps irretrievably. That was the league's obsession—Cobden's obsession—for nearly a year, from the autumn of 1841 to the summer of 1842.

The nature of the league's practical dilemma was neatly stated by Cobden in a letter to Wilson written just after the prorogation of Parliament in October:

> It strikes me after a day or two of respite from the turmoil of London politics that the League wants a revival of some kind to give us a fresh impulse. I hardly know what to suggest but shall merely offer my opinion of the necessity of doing something . . . If we could find some work for our friends in all parts that would be the best plan for uniting us. But I question if the work of getting up petitions is a sufficient excuse for calling them together . . . Of one thing I am certain, that a new move is necessary.[1]

Nearly two months later neither Cobden nor anyone else had a clearer idea of what that new move should be. Reporting to J. B. Smith on an emergency conference of league leaders from all over the country, he concluded forlornly: "There was a general outcry for bold measures. But nobody was prepared to say what we were to do. And so we resolved to petition again."[2] No one was satisfied with that; indeed the leadership had trouble convincing the rank and file of the value of yet another round of petitioning in support of yet another motion by Villiers. But there was little else they could do. The ladies of the league were pressed into service again, this time to run a bazaar. (Although this was Wilson's pet project, Catherine Cobden was prevailed upon to preside over it.) The league council also came up with a way of injecting variety into the series of meetings and conferences preceding the opening of the new session of Parliament in 1842. At Cobden's suggestion it planned a number of regional gatherings representing the trades of the different manufacturing districts. "My object in suggesting this mode," he explained, "was to make the agitation more general and so to take away the stigma of its being a millowners' question." Cobden attended the first of these meetings, of the hosiery trades in Derby in December, and was pleased with the result. "It has already had the effect of giving a more *national* appearance to the agitation," he believed.

Hoping to appeal more directly for working-class support, the league came out in opposition to the New Poor Law. This was an especially blatant example of league opportunism, as Cobden acknowledged in his private correspondence. Like most of his Manchester colleagues, he favored the New Poor Law but was prepared to oppose its renewal on the grounds that, since the Corn Laws were largely responsible for the state of the poor; it would be unjust to restrict public welfare until repeal was passed. Properly handled, opposition to the New Poor Law on these grounds might neutralize working-class hostility toward the league, as well as play on the divisions on Poor Law policy within the Conservative government.

Like the bazaar and the regional meetings of trades, this was a clever piece of public relations, but everyone on the league council agreed that something more was needed. Throughout the winter of 1841–42, from the time Parliament was prorogued until it met again in February, the inner circle of the league acted as a clearinghouse for ideas, many of them very radical, some revolutionary in their implications. Wilson suggested petitioning the Queen to dismiss her ministers, but Cobden vetoed that as too partisan. Not so with a suggestion that the league lead a tax revolt. Cobden was very taken with the notion, which had an honorable place in the history of middle-class radicalism, from the threatened withholding of taxes in the final stages of the reform bill crisis in 1832 to the refusal of militant Dissenters to pay tithes. Cobden was wary on practical grounds, however: "As regards the declaration against paying taxes we must be very cautious about taking any step for which the middle class is not prepared . . . If the other large places were up to the mark with Manchester we could stop the wheels of government and convulse Threadneedle St. and Bond St. at any moment. But let us not shut our eyes to the fact that we stand in an advanced position."[3] The idea was therefore dropped, for the time being.

With the leadership of the league in Manchester unable to agree on any dramatic new initiative, the way was opened once again to the advocates of accommodation with the Chartists. This time the initiative came from Birmingham, where Joseph Sturge, a leader of the antislavery movement as well as a repealer, hoped to launch a new political reform movement combining elements from the league with the moderate wing of Chartism. A year before, Cobden had angrily held aloof from a similar movement in Leeds. It is a measure of the difference that Peel's election victory and the deepening economic depression had made in Cobden's thinking that now, for the first and last time in the history of the league, he was willing to go along, at least part way. He did not accept the view, to which Sturge and many others had resigned themselves, that repeal could not be passed without a further installment of parliamentary reform. Nor did he—or

Sturge for that matter—wish to see the league as the league involved. But he did accept Sturge's suggestion for holding a suffrage meeting immediately after the November conference of the league and agreed not only to lend his name to the new movement but to recruit others as well. "It would be desirable," he explained to J. B. Smith, "to get as many individuals prominently engaged in the Corn Law agitation as possible to sign in order to conciliate the people."[4]

Cobden had no illusions about the prospects of Sturge's Complete Suffrage Movement. A month before the conference in Manchester he visited Sturge in Birmingham, met with a number of local Chartist leaders, and came away as convinced as ever that "they are not a whit more reasonable upon our question than the O'Connorites. We must never expect any cooperation from these old leaders. Our only plan is to leave the two Chartist factions to fight with each other and raise up a working class party of repealers independent of both."[5] On the other hand, Cobden said little at this point about the other great weakness of attempts to create a united reform movement, the unwillingness of most middle-class reformers to associate with the Chartists. For the time being he was concerned with finding a way to revive the flagging morale of the league. "I am not sorry to see Sturge taking up the question," he told Smith, "It will be something in our rear to frighten the aristocracy."[6]

The willingness of Cobden and most of his colleagues to consider almost any expedient at this time was not entirely due to the growing sense of helplessness within the league. The movement was also changing as the nature of its leadership changed. Ill and largely out of sympathy with the direction the league was taking, J. B. Smith retired from an active role and went abroad after his defeat at Dundee. Cobden, increasingly the dominant figure in the league since the late months of 1840, was now its undisputed leader, and that in itself was bound to affect the temper of the agitation. He had always been more inclined than Smith to take risks and less concerned with the propriety of doing so. In addition, in almost direct proportion to the decline of Smith's role, the importance of John Bright increased, and Bright in 1841 was as much the impatient activist as Cobden had been two years before.

Their relationship at this stage was not the equal partnership it was later to become. That was not achieved until sometime after the repeal of the Corn Laws. Even at the moment of triumph in 1846 Bright remained a junior partner, and late in 1841 he could perhaps best be described as Cobden's chief lieutenant. All this is clear from the coverage of their activities in the league newspaper and from their extensive correspondence. The contrary impression, that their equal and intimate partnership dated back almost to the time of their first meeting, an impression dear to Victorian sentimentality and enshrined in radical mythology, was largely the product of Bright's reminiscences in the years after Cobden's death. They had first met four years earlier in connection with the education question. In October 1837 Jacob Bright, John's father, accepted a request from Cobden to be a sponsor of the national education conference in Manchester. Shortly thereafter Cobden returned the compliment; in response to a letter (followed perhaps by a personal visit) from John Bright, he agreed to attend an education meeting on Bright's home ground in Rochdale. In itself this meeting was of little importance and nothing followed from it. A year later Bright's name appeared (a week before Cobden's) on the list of members of the provisional committee of the Manchester Anti–Corn Law Association, and Cobden recruited Bright as a member of the Manchester Chamber of Commerce preparatory to the purge of G. W. Wood in February 1839. But Bright's early role in the agitation was limited to Rochdale and its surroundings.

That did not change until the spring of 1841, when, probably because of Bright's ability as a speaker, Cobden enlisted him as a member of the deputations to Birmingham, Bristol, Newcastle, and Liverpool, which the league organized in response to the Whig change of heart on the Corn Laws. This was the turning point in their relationship and the beginning of a central role for Bright in the agitation. It came, as a number of recent historians have noted, some months before the event that traditionally was viewed as the beginning of their political partnership: Cobden's visit to Bright at Leamington immediately following the death of Bright's first wife in September 1841. According to Bright's account, given many years later,

Mr. Cobden called upon me as his friend, and addressed me as you might suppose, with words of condolence. After a time he looked up and said, "There are thousands of houses in England at this moment where wives, mothers and children are dying of hunger. Now," he said, "when the first paroxysm of your grief is past, I would advise you to come with me, and we will never rest till the Corn Law is repealed" . . .

I accepted his invitation, and from that time we never ceased to labor hard on behalf of the resolution which we had made.[7]

Strictly speaking, Bright's account of what happened at Leamington is a myth; his great work for the league had begun before his wife's death. Emotionally, however, Leamington was a turning point. Cobden offered Bright release from private anguish through public service, and however great or small Bright's contribution to the league might otherwise have been, its meaning was altered and along with it the nature of his relationship with Cobden.

Bright now joined a small group of men—Henry Ashworth, J. B. Smith, and in a somewhat different way George Wilson and Joseph Parkes, all of them friends of longer standing—with whom Cobden corresponded unguardedly. To them, as to few others, he revealed his mind at work, mulling over their suggestions and airing ideas of his own, which he might partially retract later in the same letter. Bright's half of the correspondence provided a perfect foil for Cobden's and a nice balance as well to Cobden's correspondence with Wilson. Cobden and Wilson, no less than Bright, bristled with new ideas that winter. But Cobden, mindful of the responsibilities of overall leadership, and Wilson, enmeshed in the problems of administration, were ambivalent about the possibility, although not the need, for radical action. Bright, a comparatively new hand at the business and relatively free from responsibility, was the resident firebrand, willing to make a case for almost any course of action and willing to do almost anything himself. In February 1842, for example, he staged an anti–Corn Law demonstration in the Manchester exchange, to the disgust of its more staid members. That was just the sort of thing Cobden would have enjoyed back in 1839 but could no longer indulge in, given his new responsibilities.

Nothing had been decided by the time Parliament convened in February, largely because so much depended on what happened in Parliament. Cobden certainly felt this; he was more active in the House of Commons in 1842 than in any other year during the anti–Corn Law agitation. The league, of course, had made the usual preparations for the session. Villiers was to offer a motion for repeal; petitions were dispatched to Parliament; a delegates conference assembled in London and deputations waited upon government ministers and the leaders of the opposition. No one any longer set much store by these activities, but the league, having done as much in the past, could do no less in 1842. Cobden's hopes rested on the likelihood that Peel might make a mistake. The prime minister had managed to skirt the issues of economic distress and the tariff in the short session of 1841; he could do so no longer. And whatever course he took, Cobden believed, he was likely to play into league hands. "If he proposes a delusion or unsatisfactory scheme, which I suspect he will, then we shall be greatly strengthened in the manufacturing and trading community. If on the other hand he should dare to propose a useful measure he will split up his own party." Cobden's only worry was that Peel might offer "a bona fide concession," since "the middle classes are a compromising lot at best."[8]

Unfortunately for Cobden's calculations, that is precisely what Peel did. In a bold move, he coupled proposals for a reduction of the sliding scale duties on corn with the resumption of the income tax and a wholesale revision of import duties on hundreds of other articles. There was some Tory disaffection, but nothing like what Cobden had predicted or continued to hope for; the boldness of Peel's measures tended at first to unite his party behind him. It was the opposition that showed signs of disarray. The small band of repealers—and, for that matter, the Whigs—were therefore reduced to delaying tactics in Parliament backed by protest meetings in the provinces, in the expectation that public and parliamentary opinion would eventually turn against the government. After all, Cobden reasoned, the strengths of Peel's proposals were also, potentially, their weaknesses. In dealing evenhandedly with a variety of interests, they satisfied none. If Peel's cautious approach toward freer trade reassured protectionists and encouraged free traders, it could, upon reflection, be condemned by the latter as too little and too late and by the former as a dangerous precedent. And then there was the income tax, which was hardly likely to be a popular measure, particularly with the Corn Laws and sugar duties still in place. Here, certainly, were the elements of a potential negative majority, if only time could be won to develop and bring them together. Cobden hoped to buy that time by cooperating with the opposition leaders in obstructing the passage of legislation through the House.

Inevitably the result was an often unruly session: Cobden's attacks on the ignorance and selfishness of the monopolists were bound to provoke rejoinders. The protectionists' self-appointed spokesman was

William Busfield Ferrand, a maverick Tory representing a small northern constituency. Ferrand began a long career as an abuser of the league in the debate on Villiers' motion in February 1842. Directly following a speech by Cobden—and to the delight of the Tory back-benchers—he launched a savage attack on millowners in general, and a few of those prominently connected with the league in particular, for exploitation of their workers. He accused Cobden of "running his mill both day and night."[9] Cobden immediately rose to denounce Ferrand's language and to announce his own intention of not engaging in personalities or dignifying such attacks with a reply.

That was not a position he was able to maintain for long. Ferrand returned to the attack, and Cobden had no choice but to spend a good deal of time answering the charges. Gradually the issue narrowed to the prevalence of the truck system in the manufacturing districts, and in May the House agreed to appoint a select committee to inquire into the matter. Ferrand tried to stack the committee, but after yet another nasty exchange, Cobden was made a member. The committee hearings exonerated Cobden of any questionable practices as an employer. The worst that could be alleged against him was that he let out cows to some of his employees (cow dung was necessary in the dyeing process), but this practice, it was admitted, was of benefit to the employees, who could sell the milk for a profit. Indeed, "the only thing" one witness called by Ferrand had "heard against Mr. Cobden was that he employs too many Scotchmen." For the rest, he was "certain of one thing, that Mr. Cobden is greatly praised, for he does not keep a truck shop, nor does he tie any of his men to anything."[10]

Despite his eventual vindication, Cobden's running battle with Ferrand probably hurt his standing in the House and may have damaged the cause by diverting attention from the issues he wished to keep to the fore. No wonder Peel was quietly pleased at the fuss, for although it was not a major ingredient in his success that session, it helped to throw the opposition off balance and keep his own ranks together. In fact, no amount of tactical maneuvering by the Liberals could shake the Tory majorities for the new Corn Law and the income tax. The back-bench revolt, when it came, was directed against the reductions of other duties, and for them Peel could count on opposition support. In short, having seized the middle ground the moment Parliament opened, Peel was able to hold it throughout the session.

As their parliamentary prospects dimmed, the leaguers returned to their earlier schemes for bringing pressure from out of doors. In Cobden's view, they had no choice. "One thing is certain," he wrote to Wilson in February, "Unless we can strike a bold blow now, we shall be superseded very materially by the suffrage people."[11] The question, as it had been since September, was what that bold blow should be. For a time the league considered calling a mass meeting on Kersal Moor, the traditional site of radical demonstrations near Manchester; but no such meeting could be held without Chartist intrusions, and Cobden therefore opposed it as certain to alienate the middle class. However, he was not opposed to political meetings as long as they could be properly managed. In April Sturge staged the first public conference of the Complete Suffrage movement. Bright attended as the unofficial representative of the league, worked to paper over differences, and came away enthusiastic about the results. Cobden, who did not attend and remained as skeptical as ever, nonetheless welcomed the conference. "Nothing," he commented to Bright, "will frighten the aristocracy into free trade measures as soon as a threatened union of the classes upon the suffrage."[12]

The possibility of fomenting a tax revolt, first mooted in October, looked even more inviting during the spring, as Peel's budget progressed through the House of Commons. There was even talk of maneuvering in the House to stop supplies in conjunction with or as a means of triggering a movement to withhold taxes. Cobden was drawn to the idea as a means of bringing the government to heel. The "Poor Law—Suffrage—Corn Law parties are all alike disgusted," he suggested to Bright. "Now what should prevent all parties who are hostile to the present state of things attacking the system with the same weapon and that weapon the Quaker one of passive resistance."[13] But always there were second thoughts: "I see no prospect of raising a corps of desperados in the House to resist taxes," he told Ashworth. "We are a parcel of dunghill cocks good at nothing but crowing."[14] And beyond Parliament lay the real problem, the lack of adequate support in the country. As Cobden summed it up, again restating the central dilemma of the league, a move to stop supplies was feasible within the rules of the House of Commons, but few M.P.s would risk it unless supported outside; yet if popular support to that extent existed, such a move in Parliament would be superfluous.

It was to cut through this dilemma and give the initiative back to the leaders of the league, unencumbered by their more timid followers, that Bright suggested to Cobden a new and even more radical course of action. It would be possible, he believed, to get a meeting of manufacturers to declare that "they feel themselves merely the tools in the hands of the landowners to extract the greatest amount of labor for the smallest possible amount of food—that course they will no longer pursue, seeing that it will bring ruin to themselves and suffering to their workpeople and that unless the Government consent to open this trade by repealing the Corn Laws they will at a given time close their works ... This," Bright concluded, "would shake Peel either from office or into a new Bill or Total Repeal."[15] Indeed it might, Cobden agreed, but he never seriously considered Bright's proposal; the working classes would be alienated, and besides, the league did not possess the organization or sufficient backing from the millowners to carry it off.

This in the end was the insurmountable problem, the reason why Cobden finally abandoned every suggested means of precipitating a crisis out of doors. As he put it in opposing a meeting on Kersal Moor but could as easily have said of any number of suggested moves, "The middle classes must be still further pinched and disappointed before they will go to that."[16] This, indeed, was almost the sole ground for Cobden's ultimately cautious behavior in 1842. Not once did he oppose any suggestion, however extreme, because it would be wrong or would endanger the stability of the nation. On the contrary, he wished to discredit the government and Parliament, as a means of rousing the people to force a terrified governing class toward reform. The league lacked only the means, not, he believed, the right to do that. Cobden, Wilson, and Bright were all potential revolutionaries that summer, at least theoretically. Cobden and Wilson were only more moderate than Bright in the sense that they were more realistic. All three assumed that a crisis was coming and were prepared to do what they could to bring it about. In abandoning the notion of unilateral action by the league, they did not abandon the view that a crisis was imminent, or that the league should take full advantage of it when it came.

It came in August. On Friday, the fifth, workers in a mill in Staleybridge, ten miles east of Manchester, went on strike rather than accept a cut in wages. In its beginnings this was little different from other sporadic strikes that summer, but over the weekend plans were made to spread the stoppage. On Monday bands of strikers marched from Staleybridge to Ashton and Oldham, adding constantly to their numbers, turning out the workers in mill after mill, and pulling the plugs from the boilers in each factory as they went. On Tuesday they invaded Manchester. For the next two weeks the "Plug Plot" strikes spread throughout southern Lancashire, across the Pennines to Yorkshire, and down through the Potteries to the Black Country. Despite some destruction of property and occasional acts of violence by the strikers or by the authorities, the great wave of strikes advanced and then receded remarkably peacefully. In most cases, millowners and magistrates simply allowed the movement to take its course. As for the league and the Chartists, they hardly knew how to react to this largely spontaneous popular rising at first. The temptation to take advantage of it in some way had to be balanced against the dangers of being swept along and perhaps destroyed by a movement they could not control, or by its repression. In the end, the Chartists had little choice. They could not turn their backs on strikers who demanded the Charter almost as often as they demanded a fair day's wages, and on August 16 the Chartist executive voted to back the strike.

The league had greater freedom of action. Bright was all but certain that this was the moment the league had been waiting for. "I did not suppose our prophecies were so near their fulfillment," he wrote to Cobden on August 11.[17] After talking with his own workers in Rochdale, he was most impressed with their discipline and resolve; his only reservation, apparently, was that the movement lacked proper focus. The league's function, as he saw it, was to provide that focus, either by placarding Manchester with an address or by holding a great middle-class meeting, which would express sympathy with the worker's plight and blame the government and the Corn Laws for their desperation.

Had the strikers shown any inclination to adopt the cause of repeal, Bright might have carried the league with him. As it was, the Charter remained the political symbol of the striker's grievances, and that was perhaps decisive for Cobden and for the moderate leaders of the league. "I have written to Wilson who tells me the League meets tomorrow morning," Cobden informed his brother, "and have advised very strongly that they should be cautious and quiet just now . . . All that is necessary to rise higher than ever is for us to keep aloof in Manchester from all connection with the present commotions. The result of the present disturbances will be to weaken the government by the unpopularity which it will acquire in putting down the rioters.—The trades and Chartists will be weakened by their reverses."[18]

Cobden could not attend the league meeting—there were in fact four long meetings in two days (August 15-16)—but his intervention with Wilson was likely decisive. But for Wilson, Bright would probably haved prevailed, at least according to Bright's recounting of the second day's meetings to Cobden, evidently written on the assumption that Cobden would have backed him: "A majority were for the resolutions I proposed . . . but as a lot were against them—Greg, Wilson, Evans—Wilson sent for Brooks and Callender who spoke strongly against them. I kept my opinion but rather than sacrifice our union I consented to withdraw them . . . There is little pluck or firmness in this room."[19]

That was that, as far as the league was concerned; thereafter it limited itself to condemnations of government policy and expressions of sympathy with the plight of the strikers. That, however, did not prevent the enemies of the league, Tory and Chartist, from accusing it of being behind the turnouts. There was a good deal of circumstantial evidence to support the charge: in the increasingly radical rhetoric of the league during the preceding year, in ambiguous references to the possibility of factory closures from league members and lecturers, and in the accommodating response of many league member magistrates toward the strikers. The home secretary, Sir James Graham, was sufficiently suspicious to order the interception of Cobden's mail for a week in late August, and he also supplied the raw material for an article in the *Quarterly Review* outlining the case against the league. There were even rumors that the government was about to suppress the league, but there was too little hard evidence for that; unlike the Chartists, it escaped prosecution.

The league, of course, denied the allegations. "I will venture to say," Cobden assured a meeting of the Manchester association in late August,

> in the name of the Council of the Anti–Corn Law League, that not only did not the members of that body know or dream of anything of the kind . . . but I believe the very last thing which the body of our subscribers would have wished for or desired, is the suspension of their

business, and the confusion which has taken place in this district. And I pledge my honor as a man, and my reputation as a public man and a private citizen, that there is not the shadow of the shade of a ground for the accusation which has been made against us.[20]

Although substantially true, this was not the whole truth, as Cobden well knew. That 1842 was not the 1832 of Corn Law repeal was not due to want of hoping and trying on his part. The league under his direction had done much to create the atmosphere of crisis, and it was considerations of tactics not of principle that led him to step back from the brink in August.

Nonetheless, he did step back, and it is tempting to say that Cobden learned a lesson in moderation in 1842. To a degree, that was true. Where Bright was inclined to act quickly and worry about consequences later, Cobden always hesitated when he could not see and, to a degree, control the next step. Yet, had he commanded the means the league so clearly lacked in 1842, he might have acted differently. He was not so much moderate as deliberate. Nor did the crisis of 1842 mark a watershed in his conception of the league. The transformation of the movement from a traditional mass agitation into something akin to a lobby or a political party had begun in 1840 and was designed to prepare the league for any eventuality. The crisis of 1842 was not just an interruption in the process; like the election of 1841, it came too soon, before the league was ready to take advantage of it. That the late months of 1842 appeared in retrospect as a new beginning for the league was due largely to the fact that they marked the beginning of the end of the long economic crisis in which the league had been born. With the collapse of the Plug Plot strikes, the political fever broke, and a good harvest and the first signs of economic recovery ensured that it would not return. Cobden's actions in 1842 appear anomalous in his career and in the history of the league largely because the conditions of 1842 were not repeated.

In another sense as well it is misleading to treat the crisis of 1842 as a discontinuity in Cobden's life or, more generally, in the political life of England in the 1840s. Speaking of its effects on the prime minister, his greatest modern biographer noted:

What colored Peel's mind by the summer of 1842, and with it the whole statement of the case for his policy, was the social condition of Britain. It was not that the elements of that policy had changed, but that the balance had altered . . . Between the summer of 1841 and the summer of 1842 . . . the emphasis in his thinking steadily shifted from the financial and fiscal problems of government to the wider impact of government policy on the nation at large—to economic policy as a piece of social engineering . . . The Condition of England Question was a more savagely educative process than any economic textbook.[21]

For this change, the league and Cobden personally could take some credit, since they had evolved in parallel ways over the same period. The negative side of the league's tactically correct decision to limit itself to one issue was that it often seemed narrow, attributing most of England's ills to the Corn Laws and nearly magical consequences to their repeal. Particularly in circumstances as grave as those of 1842, this opened the league to the charge that it was taking a simplistic view of the nation's plight. In comparison with the government's wide-ranging fiscal proposals, the league's insistence on its single theme was indeed narrow. Cobden certainly sensed this. His speeches that session limited to the Corn Laws were not up to the quality of his maiden speech, and at one point he tacitly acknowledged the effectiveness of Tory and Chartist criticism of the league's monomania. "The people may not be crying out exclusively for the repeal of the Corn Laws," he admitted, "because they have looked upon that question, and have seen greater evils even than this . . . [but], now that the cries for 'Universal Suffrage' and 'The Charter' are heard, let not hon. Gentlemen deceive themselves by supposing that, because members of the Anti–Corn Law League have sometimes found themselves getting into collision with the Chartists, that therefore the Chartists or the working men generally, were favorable to the Corn Laws."[22]

Cobden, of course, had never been exclusively concerned with the Corn Laws; in attacking them, he always sought to expose those "greater evils" beyond that question. The combined effect of the economic crisis of 1842, the government's economic reform proposals, and renewed competition from Chartism was to bring Cobden and the league back to that task, which, in the day-to-day management of an agitation, had often been lost sight of. The best measure of this change was the contrast between the two assemblies of league delegates in London during the parliamentary session. The first was another of the familiar gatherings of deputies sent to London at the opening of Parliament in support of Villiers' annual motion. The second was an emergency meeting in July, convened at the request of the league council after consultation with parliamentary free traders. Both meetings were unruly; the first ended with a noisy demonstration outside the House of Commons, and the second threatened dangerous consequences—a juncture of the league with the Chartists, perhaps, or social unrest leading to strikes and factory closures—if the government did not act immediately.

But, whereas the first delegates meeting had been almost exclusively concerned with the Corn Laws, the main theme of the second was the social condition of England. For months, at least since the meeting of ministers of religion in August 1841, leaguers in the factory districts had been gathering statistics and case histories of economic distress. Day after day at the conference this evidence was laid before the delegates and printed in the national newspapers. Even allowing for the self-interested nature of this effort, it undoubtedly served to broaden the outlook of many leaguers and to soften public perceptions of the movement. Perhaps as much because of this as for reasons of political expediency, Peel agreed to receive deputations from the July conference, whereas he had declined requests for an audience in February.

While the July conference was meeting across the street at Palace Yard, Cobden was given an opportunity in Parliament to take an equally broad and lofty approach to the Condition of England question. During a two-day debate on the state of the country, the government, as governments will, tended to minimize the extent of distress. Cobden replied, in language of which Roebuck said that "he had never heard in his life . . . [a speech] more deeply interesting to the people of this country,"[23] with a sweeping overview of the causes and potential consequences of the depression. "What can be thought of a country which produces so much, and where the great mass of the inhabitants possess so little?" he asked. "Does it not show that there is some mal-distribution of production? . . . Those who are so fond of laughing at political economy, forget that they have a political economy of their own; and what is it? . . . That they will allow the productions of the spindle and loom to go abroad to furnish them with luxuries from the farthest corners of the world, but refuse to permit to be brought back in exchange what would minister to the wants and comforts of the lower orders."[24]

Of the inevitable results of maintaining this perverse political economy, he was equally certain: "I do not mean to threaten outbreaks—

that the starving masses will come and pull down your mansions; but I say that you are drifting on to confusion without rudder or compass. It is my firm belief that within six months we shall have populous districts in the north in a state of social dissolution . . . I do not believe that the people will break out unless they are absolutely deprived of food; if you are not prepared with a remedy, they will be justified in taking food for themselves and their families."

In addition to reminding the House what might happen in the country, while denying, of course, that either he or the league would have anything to do with precipitating it, he bluntly threatened Parliament itself (with a course of action the leaders of the league had already rejected as impractical): "I cannot give a stronger proof of the perils which I think surround us, than to say that I shall feel it my duty to stop the wheels of Government if I can, in a way [by stopping supplies] which can only be justified by an extraordinary crisis."

In all of this Cobden was speaking, as he had ever since entering Parliament, as the leader of a powerful movement out of doors. Yet he also seized the opportunity offered by this debate to become something besides the member of Parliament from the league. His theme throughout was distress, not repeal (although he still saw repeal as the only remedy), and he introduced overwhelming evidence of the depth and extent of distress. "I do not wish to mix up the Corn Laws with this question," he said at one point. "I care nothing for the Corn Laws, if you can provide me with a better remedy." More honestly, he denied any partisan motives: "I will take measures of relief from the right hon. Baronet [Peel] as well as from the noble Lord [Russell]," he declared in closing, "but upon some measures of relief I will insist . . . this question must be met and met fully; it must not be quibbled away; it must not be looked upon as a Manchester question; the whole condition of the country must be looked at and faced, and it must be done before we separate this session."

This was Cobden's finest speech that session or, for that matter, of his parliamentary career thus far. In his equally somber reply, Peel, although defending his policies and asking for time to let them take effect, admitted implicitly the force of Cobden's arguments by pledging that, should his revision of the Corn Laws prove inadequate, "I shall be the first to admit that no adherence to former opinions ought to prevent their full and careful revision."[25]

The depression of 1842 had pushed Cobden and Peel to remarkably similar views on economic policy. As early as April Cobden had become convinced that Peel was a free trader at heart and predicted, privately, that "Peel must head a milieu party soon."[26] By the end of the session he was saying as much in public and deliberately playing on the potential divisions between the Tory front and back benches. In response to Peel's promise of flexibility on the Corn Laws, Cobden angrily accused the old line Tories of having "killed Canning by thwarting him, and they would visit the same fate on their present leader, if he persevered in the same attempt to govern for the aristocracy, while professing to govern for the people. Yes, they had killed Canning by forcing him to try and reconcile their interests with those of the people, and no human power could enable the right hon. Baronet to survive the same ordeal."[27] Cobden's most optimistic hopes for Peel were premature. The prime minister was not yet a "whole hog" free trader, and it was to be nearly four years before he would finally throw over his followers—and they him. Indeed, for some time the different needs and outlook of a head of government and the leader of a popular agitation were to be a source of bitter personal and political division between the two men. All the same, Cobden's increasingly sympathetic assessment of Peel was not far wrong, and much of the new course adopted by the league after the crisis of 1842 had passed was predicated on that assessment.

CHAPTER 11

The Long Haul

Even at the worst of times in 1842, Cobden never lost sight of the longer run goals of the league or was tempted to abandon the policies assayed more than a year before. In a letter to Wilson in February, after rejecting the notion of holding a meeting on Kersal Moor and questioning the feasibility of a tax revolt, he returned to familiar topics, suggesting an extension of their electoral policy: "A well prepared account should be taken of the state of all the boroughs in the kingdom in reference to our question. They should be classified and put into lists of safe, tolerably safe, doubtful, desperate, hopeless. Our whole strength should then be thrown upon the doubtfuls. Electoral Committees should be formed in each borough to look after the registration."[1]

Three months later, while the leadership was discussing the possibility of a tax revolt in private, Wilson convened a general meeting of the league to announce a sweeping reorganization of its provincial machinery, coupled with new efforts to broaden the movement's popular base. The country was to be divided into twelve districts, each with its own lecturers and canvassers, whose first task would be the recruitment of thousands of new members. This in turn would provide the foundation for a campaign to enroll free traders on the electoral registers.

It was almost as if there two anti–Corn Law leagues during those months, one responding to the volatile moods of a nation in the midst of an economic crisis, the other going about the business of perfecting a strategy of agitation decided on before that crisis had hit. To this aspect of the league's activities in 1842 the strikes in August were at most an interruption—the lecturers and canvassers were temporarily called in—and the winter campaign, outlined by Cobden and Wilson in October, was not so much a new beginning as the extension of what was already under way. All the same, it initiated a process that radically altered the nature of the league during 1843. None of the traditional means of agitation was abandoned, but with the new Parliament only a year old, there was no need for a short-term electoral policy, and the size of Peel's majority dampened what little enthusiasm was left for further petitioning. In addition, after years of agitation, individual events such as banquets, mass meetings, delegates conferences, and Villiers' annual motion were likely to bring diminishing returns in publicity and popular support. So too were the efforts of itinerant lecturers and organizers. A crisis might arise to force the issue, but that could hardly be counted on. The league had to act on the assumption that it must outlast the present Parliament; it had, in effect, to become an agent of permanent agitation.

Hence Wilson's and Cobden's emphasis on the need for a saturation propaganda campaign and fund-raising efforts unprecedented in the history of mass agitations to back up a drive for new members. Hence also their decision to set ambitious goals, guaranteed to attract publicity. To give a central focus to the membership drive, they proposed hiring local agents to canvass every voter in the country and give each one a small library of anti–Corn Law tracts. In addition, these canvassers were to oversee the creation of machinery for working the electoral registers. To pay for all this the league council agreed that a war chest of at least £20,000 would be needed. When it came time to announce this publicly, however, Cobden upped the figure to an unheard of £50,000, "under the impulse of the moment,"[2] and without consulting the council. This bit of recklessness turned out to be an inspired move. The raising of such a sum inevitably became the focus of the league's winter campaign and, as it turned out, a means of breathing life into the round of conferences and meetings, which in the past had been devoted to getting up petitions.

If they were to achieve their goals within the alloted three months, however, the leaders of the league dared not rely on the local anti–Corn Law associations, whose generally lackluster support was one of Cobden's constant complaints. League headquarters would have to commit its resources to an unprecedented degree. In Manchester itself this meant transforming the weekly meetings of the league council into public gatherings, each one more impressive than the last, and each complete with constantly updated reports on the progress of the fund, visits from celebrities specially called to Manchester, and at least one speech by a popular leader of the league. Between October and late January the council meetings moved from their original cramped quarters in Newalls Buildings to a larger hall in the same building, to the Manchester Corn Exchange, and finally to Free Trade Hall, newly built for this purpose on a plot of land owned by Cobden in St. Peter's Fields.

Outside Manchester the demands on members of the league council were even greater. No official deputations from headquarters had attended provincial meetings away from Manchester since before the election of 1841, and most of those had gone to Lancashire or Cheshire. Between November 1842 and January 1843 deputations attended scores of meetings all over the country. Cobden, for example, traveled throughout Lancashire and to the West Riding of Yorkshire, the East Midlands, central Scotland, and Bristol. He and Bright were the most sought-after visitors; local repealers felt cheated if at least one of them did not appear. Now and then their paths crossed and they spoke from the same platform. But that was rare. Their later custom of traveling and speaking together, an expected part of the ritual at great meetings in the final years of the league, developed later in 1843. For both men, however, this short campaign marked the beginning of an all-consuming involvement in the public business of the league. Once committed to this kind of personal leadership, they quickly discovered that it was the most effective means of agitation and, soon thereafter, that it was expected of them. For a time they enjoyed it, but even after Cobden had ceased to do so, they were unable to give it up. For more than three years, until repeal was passed, Cobden and Bright were almost constantly on the road (or, more accurately, railroad) when they were not in Parliament.

This, coupled with its increasing reliance on the new penny postage as a means of overseeing fund raising and electoral policy on a regular basis, was perhaps the greatest of the league's contributions to the arsenal of popular politics. Well before any other mass movement, let alone the two major parties, Cobden, Wilson, and Bright understood the political significance of modern means of communication. Cobden had enthusiastically supported the agitation for a penny postage, which, significantly, was the only other cause he had been willing to devote any time to during the campaign for the incorporation of

Manchester. In May 1838 he traveled to London to give evidence on behalf of the Manchester Chamber of Commerce in favor of the penny postage before a select committee of the House of Commons, and two years later when the penny postage was introduced, he predicted to Villiers that "we shall radicalise the country in the process of carrying the repeal of the Corn Law, and we are effecting such an organisation by means of the penny postage (that destined scourge of the aristocracy) that we shall, by and by, be able to carry any measure by a coup de billet."[3]

Beginning in 1843, and with the railways for the first time accorded equal status as a means of communication for the league, Cobden's faith in the new technology of agitation was put to the test and vindicated. To the private, frequent, and above all inexpensive network of communication provided by the penny postage the railways added a necessary complement of personal contact between the leaders of the movement, its rank and file, and the general public. In the long run, this more than any other single factor was what established the league as a truly national movement; in the short run, it was the key ingredient in the ability of the league to emerge unscathed from the crisis of 1842. Indeed, but for the ability of its popular leaders to inspire and reassure their followers, the repeal movement might have withered away. "You are a most extraordinary agitator," Parkes commented to Cobden after this first great campaign was over, "and you have the great quality in a leader of public opinion, of sticking exclusively to your object. I must admit, as indeed I told you in August, that I had no idea you cd. keep up the balloon. I thought Peel's mock temporary law of affected concession, & Chartism, would paralyse any action this year on the Middle Classes."[4]

Cobden was not able to attend the climactic meeting of the campaign at the end of January, the first in Free Trade Hall. A few days earlier, while he was in Bristol, his youngest child died. In addition, as was the case in most of the winters of his adult life, he fell ill, in this instance with a recurrence of a childhood complaint, an inflammation of the eye. For three weeks he stayed with his family and did not appear in Parliament until mid-February, two weeks after the session opened. He might have done well to have stayed away longer. Near the end of his first speech, a defense of the recent tactics of the league, coupled with scathing attacks on the adequacy of government policy, Cobden turned on Peel directly and at length:

The right hon. Baronet acted on his own judgement, and he retained the duty on two articles on which a reduction of the duty was desired, and he reduced the duties on those on which there was not a possibility of the change being of much service to the country . . . It was folly or ignorance to amend our system of duties, and leave out of consideration sugar and corn . . . That is the scheme of the right hon. Baronet—the only plan he has to propose for the benefit of the country. Can he not try some other plan? . . . It is his duty, he says, to judge independently, and act without reference to any pressure; and I must tell the right hon. Baronet that it is the duty of every honest and independent Member to hold him individually responsible for the present condition of the country.[5]

It was a calculated assault. "He [Peel] is looking twenty percent worse since I came into the House," Cobden wrote his brother a few days later, "and if I had only Bright with me, we could worry him out of office before the close of the session . . . The whole thing turns upon their [the protectionists] finding a man to fill the office of executioner for them, and when Peel bolts or betrays them, the game is up. It is this conviction in my mind which induced me after some deliberation to throw the responsibility upon Peel, and he is not only alarmed at it, but indiscreet enough to let everybody know that he is so."[6]

Even Cobden could hardly have anticipated Peel's reaction, however. The prime minister, like Cobden, was under severe stress. Less than a month before, at the same time Cobden's child died, Peel's personal secretary had been shot and killed in Whitehall. There was no question that the bullet had been meant for Peel, and inevitably the incident spawned rumors of assassination plots. There had, after all, been two attempts on the queen's life the year before. Given the often violent rhetoric of the league and the allegations of league complicity in the Plug Plot strikes, it is hardly surprising that Peel overreacted to Cobden's attack.

The moment Cobden finished speaking, Peel rose. "Sir," he said, "The hon. gentleman has stated here very emphatically, what he has more than once stated at the conferences of the Anti–Corn Law League, that he holds me individually—[great excitement]—individually responsible for the distress and suffering of the country; that he holds me personally responsible; but be the consequences of these insinuations what they may, never will I be influenced by menaces either in this House or out of this House to adopt a course which I consider—[the rest of the sentence was lost in shouts from various parts of the House]."[7]

Cobden attempted to reply: "I did not say that I held the right hon. Gentleman personally responsible—[shouts of "Yes, yes," "You did, you did"—cries of "Order," and "Chair"] [Sir Robert Peel: "You did"] I have said that I hold the right hon. Gentleman responsible, by virtue of his office—["No, no," much confusion]—as the whole context of what I said was sufficient to explain—["No, no" from ministerial benches]."

A few minutes later, after being handed a note by Sir James Graham, Peel withdrew his charge that Cobden had used the phrase "personally responsible," but Cobden was far from satisfied. At the close of the debate he again attempted to explain his words: "I intended . . . to throw the responsibility of his measures upon him as the head of government . . . I treat him as the government," Cobden acidly concluded, "as he is in the habit of treating himself." Peel declared himself "bound to accept the construction which the hon. Member puts on the language he employed," but clearly he did not believe Cobden, who, he noted, had "used the word 'individually' in so marked a way that I and others put upon it a different interpretation."[8]

That exchange ended the matter, at least officially, but the legacy of hostility left over from 1842 was now out in the open, and within minutes Cobden was being attacked from a different quarter of the House by the radical member for Bath, J. A. Roebuck. Earlier in his speech that day, before launching his attack on Peel, Cobden had condemned Lord Brougham in even stronger terms. Brougham, formerly a supporter of the league, had become one of the strongest critics of its increasingly radical rhetoric, which, he had claimed in a recent speech, was largely responsible for the present ugly political climate. Brougham's words had been vague but their meaning was not, as Roebuck made clear. He reminded the House that the *Quarterly Review* article linking the league to the Plug Plot strikes, in commenting on the league conference in London a month before the strikes began, reported a speech by a Dissenting minister, who, hoping to convey some sense of the desperation to which people were being driven, told of a conversation he had overheard in which the assassination of the prime minister had been mentioned.

Bad enough in the context of 1842, this anecdote was especially damaging to the league in the light of recent events, and Roebuck criticized Cobden for not choosing his words to Peel with greater care.

Cobden regarded the whole matter as a piece of nonsense founded on innuendo. He did not even address himself to that aspect of Roebuck's speech, and in his earlier attack on Brougham, he had scornfully dismissed his accusations as "the ebullitions of an ill regulated intellect."[9] But Roebuck was no longer primarily concerned with defending Brougham. Earlier in the day, before Cobden spoke, Roebuck had asked him privately if he intended to attack Brougham and had warned Cobden that, in that event, he, Roebuck, would come to Brougham's defense. To this, according to Roebuck, Cobden had replied, "I would advise you not to have anything to do with him, for if you do the Corn Law Leaguers will go down to Bath and turn you out."[10] This, of course, Cobden denied. He had not, he stated, threatened Roebuck but simply advised him: "'If you justify Lord Brougham in this attack on the ministers who attend the conference of the Anti–Corn Law League, you will get into trouble at Bath, and you will be considered the opponent of that body, and you will have your Anti–Corn Law tea parties, and some members of the League visiting Bath' . . . So far from wishing to see him [Roebuck] out of Parliament, he is the last man I should wish to see removed from the seat which he now holds."[11]

Whatever the truth of the matter, this bit of radical infighting, coming on top of his confrontation with Peel, damaged Cobden's standing in the House of Commons. His enemies were jubilant. Brougham talked gloatingly of "the downfall of poor Mr. Cobden— the sole work of his own folly, which he might have avoided had his head not been turned by provincial applause."[12] Cobden, however, felt that Peel, in overreacting, had suffered greater damage. Indeed, he did not admit to any doubts about the rightness and effectiveness of his conduct. In one sense at least he was correct. He may have misread Parliament but he did not misjudge the reaction out of doors. What all his critics in the political world of London failed to understand was that incidents of this kind could only enhance his support in the provinces and reinforce provincial feelings of alienation from the capital. Far from marking "the downfall of poor Mr. Cobden," Peel's unprovoked attack, for that is how it was seen in Manchester, pro-

duced a flurry of indignant anti–Corn Law meetings and provided the
perfect setting for the next phase of the campaign.

For the next two months Cobden rarely attended Parliament; indeed he was less than half as active in the House during the 1843
session as he had been the year before. His confrontations with Peel
and Roebuck had something to do with this, but in the main they
served to reinforce a growing inclination to turn his back on Parliament. Cobden was coming to see the House of Commons as an adversary to be overcome rather than as a field of league operations.
Whatever gains were made would have to be made out of doors in the
fight for public opinion and in the constituencies before Parliament
could successfully be approached again. The great industrial towns
could now, he believed, take care of themselves and to some degree
aid their smaller neighbors.

London, as always, was a special problem. What little organization
there was in the capital had never worked comfortably with
Manchester. Partly to remedy this and partly to enhance the league's
status as a national movement, much of the league's machinery was
transferred to London. Thereafter, the management of the league
shifted between the two cities, depending on the season and the
whereabouts of George Wilson. London became the center of operations while Parliament was in session, although publicity not Parliament was the primary objective. Wilson staged a series of open
weekly meetings of the league on the model pioneered in Manchester
during the winter of 1842–43. Along with a succession of guest
speakers, most of them M.P.s, either Cobden or Bright usually attended. Behind the scenes Wilson carried out the more difficult task of
organizing the capital while at the same time working out a modus
vivendi with the London repealers whose inadequate organization he
was replacing.

Cobden meanwhile cultivated the press. The league had never had
adequate coverage in national newspapers, despite a policy of subsi-
dizing those that were favorable. Late in 1842, in conjunction with
the fund-raising campaign, the league council agreed to distribute
copies of eight London papers in return for favorable publicity and an
endorsement of the £50,000 fund. A few months later Cobden was
approached by James Wilson, one of the few effective London allies
of the league, who offered to start a free trade journal, *The Economist*, on condition that the league back him. After some hesitation,

Cobden endorsed the proposal, largely because it might allow the repealers to reach an audience hostile to the league itself. In August the league council agreed to purchase 20,000 copies of *The Economist*, which Cobden recommended should be distributed primarily to Tory voters in Lancashire. Before the appearance of *The Economist*, plans had been made to expand the *Anti–Bread Tax Circular* into a full-fledged newspaper. These plans were now abandoned but the *Circular* was substantially altered even so. Once again its name was changed—to *The League*; it was moved to London in September, and its coverage was broadened to include a digest of general news, financial reports, and even book reviews.

Although Cobden aided Wilson in working London and was himself largely responsible for working the London press, his most deeply felt commitment in 1843 was to a revival of the league's campaign in the countryside. The league's earlier efforts had ended in embarrassing failure, but in 1843 conditions at last seemed favorable, at least to Cobden. For one thing, he was now prepared to undertake the job himself. Moreover, he would not be working in isolation; the league district organization and the national distribution of anti–Corn Law literature had prepared the ground. Finally and most important, the economic climate had changed. An excellent harvest in 1842 had pushed agricultural prices down to their lowest levels in years. This in turn had contributed to the beginnings of a revival of industry, trade, and investment by giving the ordinary consumer more money to spend on goods other than food. Indeed, despite the fall in food prices, industrial wages were rising, as Cobden had predicted they would once the demand of industry for labor recovered.

With the vexing question of the relationship between wages and the price of food at last out of the way, the league suddenly found itself in a better position to appeal not only to the working classes but to the farmer. During the early years of the repeal movement, scarcity and high food prices had pitted the landed interest as a whole against the interests of consumers. For all the arguments of the league, the ordinary farmer understandably saw the Corn Laws as his security against an influx of cheap foreign grain at a time when only high prices compensated for low yields. After 1842, however, the price of grain fell to levels well below those that Peel had hoped to maintain through his sliding scale. The Corn Laws, in short, had failed once again to shore up agricultural incomes. This gave Cobden an opportunity he had never had before to appeal to the immediate economic interests of the farmer and to attempt to demonstrate that the rent-gouging landlord rather than the urban consumer was his real enemy, that his only security lay in long leases at reasonable rents, and that his economic salvation depended not on demonstrably failed attempts to regulate prices but on investment and improvement to increase production.

The change in the emphasis of league propaganda was startlingly abrupt and complete. In Parliament, in February, Cobden had framed his attack on the government largely in terms of continued urban distress: "I call attention to the condition of the country, and I ask you if it is not worse now than it was six months ago? ... Capital is melting away, pauperism is increasing, trade and manufactures are not reviving. What worse description can be given of our condition? And what can be expected, if such a state of things continues, but the disruption and dissolution of the State?"[13]

His speech in support of Villiers' annual motion, delivered only three months later, was totally different in tone. Gone were the predictions of the dissolution of urban society; instead Cobden concentrated on the plight of the farmer and of the rural laborer, both of them, in his view, even more the victims than the urban worker of exploitation by the rentier class. "The present condition of the farmers and laborers of this country is the severest condemnation of the Corn Laws that can possibly be uttered," he declared. "Let the farmer perfectly understand that his prosperity depends upon that of his customers—that the insane policy of this House has been to ruin his customers, and that acts to keep up prices are mere frauds to put rents into the landlord's pockets, and enable him to juggle his tenants."[14]

In the interim between these two speeches, during the Easter recess (and on Saturdays thereafter until the harvest season), Cobden carried this message to country towns throughout southern and eastern England. Bright echoed his efforts, usually in places farther from London. Apparently to good effect, Cobden made much of his background as the son of a farmer who had fallen victim to declining prices, a theme he also stressed in an autobiographical sketch he published in the *Circular* at the beginning of the campaign.[15] Temperamentally, as well as in his antecedents, he was well suited to this phase of the agitation. His matter-of-fact speaking style, which gave his listeners the feeling of being brought into his confidence, was even better adapted to small local meetings, as it was to the House of Commons, than to the urban mass meetings where Bright and W. J. Fox were the league's most effective orators. Personal contact between the agriculturalists and their supposed adversary also brought Cobden's best attributes as a popular leader into play. As was increasingly the case with their representatives in Parliament, the farmers, almost against their will, found they liked him. As one close friend who was, however, no political supporter of Cobden's explained it, "Though not good looking, there was something extraordinarily attractive in his countenance which, when he became interested, would light up and almost fascinate one on account of the vivacity and strength of intellect which became clearly displayed."[16] He may not have convinced the farmers, but he certainly disarmed them.

Cobden also thoroughly enjoyed the campaign. He relished doing battle with supporters of the Corn Laws, local or imported, including one confrontation with his old parliamentary enemy, W. B. Ferrand. Although he was frequently heckled and occasionally threatened with worse, on the whole the crowds were attentive, and frequently the meetings ended with a show of hands in favor of free trade. More often than not, of course, this was the result of advance planning, and when that broke down, the consequences could be embarrassing. All the same, the rural campaign was a labor of love for Cobden, who was as convinced as ever of its value. In announcing the campaign, the *Anti–Bread Tax Circular* reiterated Cobden's conviction that "information is all that they [the tenant farmers] have wanted"[17] in order to understand their economic interests, and he ventured into the provinces confident that the "agricultural districts of the south will carry our question."[18]

These exaggerated expectations were neither so outlandish nor so potentially dangerous to the repeal movement as in the rural campaigns of 1839 and 1840. The league had more eggs in other baskets in 1843, and besides, the political and economic circumstances had indeed become more favorable. Thus, while the number of actual converts may have been small, the campaign did serve the league and Cobden well. His often too theoretical approach to the problems of rural England was leavened by contact with innovative and liberal-minded farmers and landowners, many of whom became personal friends as well as advisors to the league. This, in turn, brought support for the agitation from a surprising quarter, the ranks of the landed aristocracy. There had always been a few repealers among the peerage, but most of them had held aloof from the league itself. Beginning in 1843, however, an impressive roster of Whig lords— Ducie, Westminster, Fitzwilliam, Morpeth, and Radnor among them—publicly threw in their lot with the league and in some cases agreed to share a platform with its leaders.

The case of Lord Radnor, one of the most radical of peers, is especially revealing. Twice, first in 1839, at the start of the agitation, and again late in 1842, when the league once more was in need of respectability, Cobden had made overtures to him. On both occasions, although Radnor expressed his private support for the league, he declined to do so publicly, primarily, it seems, because he believed that association with the movement might diminish his influence. Yet, early in 1844, he agreed to chair one of the league's weekly London mass meetings, which presumably now met the standard he had set in rejecting Cobden's earlier approaches, that "your meeting . . . be so grand a one, and so comprehensive of persons connected with other interests, as well as those of manufacturers, that it could be fairly looked upon as an example of the different classes and parties, all now agreeing on this subject."[19]

Clearly, this accommodation between the league and Lord Radnor, let alone more cautious peers, could not have taken place had not the league already become as much a pressure group as a mass agitation; nor is the changed relationship conceivable apart from Cobden's rural campaign and his growing sympathy with the problems of English agriculture. Another, although negative, measure of the effectiveness of the rural campaign was the enemy's response: nothing else the league ever did so riled up the protectionists. The Tory press lamented the absence of equally effective speakers favorable to the Corn Laws, and Cobden's sorties into the countryside were more or less directly responsible for the formation of the so-called Anti-League, a federation of county agricultural protection societies, which was the only attempt at a national level to mobilize opposition to the repealers.

On the propaganda level, then, the 1843 campaign had been a success. Three hundred workers had been employed in assembling and another five hundred in distributing five million packets of anti–Corn Law tracts to electors, as well as more than three and a half million to nonelectors all over the country. There had been twenty-five meetings in connection with the rural campaign, in addition to

140 in towns visited by deputations from the league council. For almost three months the league had staged a series of well-publicized rallies in London. Yet almost all the problems the 1843 campaign had been designed to overcome remained. To too great an extent, Manchester was still the league, the source of most of its support. The newly created regional organization and in particular the work of local canvassers in enrolling new members and working the electoral registers had been disappointing. As for Parliament, the situation there was as intractable as ever. Villiers' motion had picked up support since 1842 but the majority against it remained overwhelming. A number of anti–Corn Law associations had lobbied the waverers among their M.P.s, but with limited success and sometimes counterproductively. As for the front benches, both had all but conceded the theoretical case for free trade but each remained committed to its own policy: Russell to a fixed duty, Peel to his sliding scale. For all its propaganda successes, the league was little nearer translating its popular support into political power than when it first adopted an electoral policy three years before.

Cobden did not attempt to minimize these problems when he outlined the league's plans for the upcoming year in a speech in London—not Manchester—in September 1843. Where necessary, he was prepared to make a virtue of necessity. Because the present Parliament was beyond reach, he declared, the league council had decided to turn its back on Parliament. There were to be no more petitions in support of Villiers' annual motion. Because most repealers were sick of petitioning in any case, this was wise tactically. But Cobden was not merely being expedient. He was as frustrated by the parliamentary situation as any of his followers, and in 1844 he went even further than he had the year before in cutting back his participation in the House of Commons; it was to be the least active year of his entire parliamentary career.

If the constituencies rather than Westminster were again to be the major field of operations, however, the errors of 1843 would have to be corrected. Success in the propaganda campaign, in raising the £50,000 fund, in proselytizing the countryside, and in the organization of London had all come only through direct intervention by the league council. The same techniques were now to be applied to working the constituencies. After a careful analysis of the electoral registers the league offices in London would prepare lists of safe, doubtful, and hopeless boroughs. The league would then correspond with the estimated 300,000 electors in the doubtful boroughs, sending them tracts and personal letters once a week. Following this correspondence, Cobden explained, "we intend to visit every borough in the kingdom [to meet with the electors], not by agents—we will go ourselves because we want the thing well done."[20] The goal in every case was to found a nonparty free trade political organization capable, with assistance from league headquarters, of purifying the electoral roles by adding qualified free traders or challenging the qualifications of protectionists. In addition, if the number of electors at these local meetings was large enough, Cobden hoped to persuade them to memorialize their present M.P.s to support Villiers' motion and, in the longer run, to adopt free trade candidates where none existed.

Cobden's notion of in effect transforming the league into something approaching a political party did not sit well with many rank-and-file leaguers. The defensive tone of his introductory remarks when he announced the new policy is good evidence that an electoral policy was still a sensitive issue within the league. Cobden, of course, regarded direct intervention in the boroughs as the natural outgrowth of the campaign to reach the electorate in 1843 (or, for that matter, of the electoral policy pioneered back in 1840). But many repealers still thought of the league as primarily a propaganda organization; others had all but despaired of influencing the present Parliament or even the present political system. Cobden carried the day with ease, however, partly because he was now indisputably the leader of the movement (and had the support of its most active members), but also because there really was no alternative.

The league had carried the propaganda effort as far as it could go. Cobden preferred to say that propaganda had done its job in preparing the ground for an electoral policy, but that came to much the same thing. As for any hopes for parliamentary reform, they had been dashed by the near collapse of the Complete Suffrage Union after a stormy confrontation between Chartists and middle-class delegates at a conference early in 1843. Cobden did not mention this; he only noted that the league had to work within the system as it was, which, again, came to much the same thing. Finally, and perhaps most important of all, the league faced a new and unprecedented problem, the return of partial prosperity. Already the gradual economic recovery of 1843 had cooled the political temperature. At the least this meant that agitation of the traditional sort was likely to be less effective; at worst it threatened the existence of a movement founded on urban discontents in a time of industrial depression and high food prices. Once again, and for obvious reasons, Cobden avoided public discussion of the league's future in these terms, but there was no doubt in his mind that the consolidation of the league's gains through electoral organization was the best means of ensuring the movement's survival into a period of relative social peace.

The danger in committing the league so heavily to an electoral policy was that the political system might prove to be so heavily weighted in the monopolists' favor that it could not be brought into balance. But Cobden had never believed that. Although he claimed publicly that their aim was to win a majority of the constituencies to free trade, he did not think that would be necessary. It was the front benches Cobden was after. All that was really required to bring one or the other around was success in the larger boroughs, substantial gains in the smaller ones, and the threat of more to come. This would so frighten the political managers of both parties and so demoralize their followers that the protectionist majority in Parliament would begin to disintegrate. In addition, as with his repeated efforts to reach the English farmer, whatever doubts Cobden may have had tended to be overridden by his personal commitment to an electoral policy, which dated back almost to the beginning of the anti–Corn Law movement.

In other respects, the 1843–44 winter campaign was modeled on the league's acknowledged successes of the preceding year. Once the harvest season was over, the rural campaign was renewed by Cobden and Bright traveling together in the far north of England and southern Scotland. Hoping to repeat the league's financial and public relations coup in raising £50,000, the council established a new goal of £100,000. Since petitions to Parliament were no longer to be part of league policy, the winter season of anti–Corn Law meetings was again devoted to fund raising. More than ever before, Cobden and Bright dominated the campaign; the dual cult of personality was firmly established. Increasingly often they shared a platform and quickly developed a pattern for such meetings, which became almost invariable in the later years of the league: Cobden normally spoke first, informing his audience of the latest doings of the league or explaining a new line of argument in the case against protection; to Bright fell the task of bringing the meeting to an emotional climax. Their styles were almost perfectly complementary.

Although the winter campaign lasted until just before the opening of Parliament in February, the greatest propaganda dividend came near the beginning. In mid-November, shortly after £12,000 had been pledged in an hour and a half at the opening meeting of the fund-raising campaign in Manchester, *The Times* observed editorially:

> THE LEAGUE IS A GREAT FACT . . . It is a great fact that there should have been created in the homesteads of our manufacturers a confederacy devoted to the agitation of one political question, persevering in it year after year, shrinking from no trouble, dismayed by no danger, making light of every obstacle . . . These are facts important and worthy of consideration. No moralist can disregard them; no politician can sneer at them; no statesman can undervalue them. He who collects opinions must chronicle them. He who frames laws must to some extent consult them . . . A NEW POWER HAS ARISEN IN THE STATE.[21]

Cobden was having lunch with a small group of leaguers, when the mail from London, including copies of this issue of *The Times*, arrived. Sidney Smith was the first to see the leading article. "I called for silence," he recollected, "and read it aloud. When I had finished, Cobden said, 'Is it Smith's fine reading that deceives us? I move that he read it again.' I did so and all cheered and danced about the room."[22]

This little celebration took place, not in Manchester or London, but, of all unlikely places, in Salisbury, where the league had put forward its own candidate in a by-election. But although *The Times* editorial was a milestone in the league's campaign to gain public recognition, the Salisbury by-election was the first in a series of defeats and the worst example of an ambitious league policy gone wrong since the early days of the rural campaign. In formulating its policy in the autumn of 1843, the league council had not been content with tightening up the electoral organization of its supporters in the marginal boroughs. In addition, Cobden announced that "the League will pledge itself, where a borough constituency finds itself at a loss for a candidate, to furnish it with one, and to give to every borough in which a vacancy occurs an opportunity for its electors to record their votes in favor of Free-trade principles."[23]

The league had fought no by-elections since Walsall in 1841, but by early 1843 Cobden had become convinced that "a stirring League election to rouse up the deadness of the members" was urgently needed and that Bright was the man to provide it.[24] Urban distress was still a major issue at the time, and, as Cobden's attack on Peel demonstrated, he believed that the government could be badly shaken by election losses and by the peculiar talents Bright would bring to parliamentary debate. No immediate vacancy occurred, however, and by the time one did, circumstances had changed. After Cobden's confrontation with Peel and with the gradual improvement in the economy, the focus of league activity had shifted away from Parliament and from the cities to rural England. But to Cobden the case for intervening in by-elections, although different later in 1843, was no less cogent. League intervention would keep the Whigs on their toes and appeal to the "moderate and honest Tories."[25] In April, when a vacancy occurred at Durham, Bright agreed to stand. He lost, but the result was voided on account of corruption, and in a second try in July he won. Two months later there was a vacancy in the City of London and the official Liberal candidate, a free trader who had lost in the general election, was endorsed by the league and won.

It was at this point that the league committed itself to fighting all future by-elections, and for a time the decision seemed justified. Victory in London was followed by an equally clear-cut win in Kendal. Then came Salisbury and after Salisbury a string of setbacks throughout 1844 and into 1845. There were isolated victories and some of the defeats were viewed as victories of a sort. In at least one case league intervention contributed to the defeat of a protectionist Whig by a Tory. This infuriated the Whigs, of course, but that was part of the purpose. "We are at war to the knife with the Whig politicians," Cobden wrote to Wilson in April, "and they hate us as cordially as the Tories do and more thoroughly than they do each other."[26] Some of the league's losses could be ascribed in part to bribery or to deals between Whigs and Tories to shut out the league, but on the whole this sort of activity worked to the propaganda advantage of the league.

By and large, however, the power of local patrons was sufficient to carry the day without either bribery or political deals. Intervention by the league was simply ignored, and what had begun as a brave attempt to force the issue of repeal to the forefront ended in face-saving gestures and bitter recrimination within the league. Inevitably it proved increasingly difficult to find qualified men willing to serve as sacrificial candidates. The league could and did draft members of its own staff but that was hardly satisfactory. Running an outsider antagonized local interests and made the league look as desperate as it frequently was. "We are in a most awkward predicament with the approaching vacancies," Cobden wrote to Wilson, "We can't find candidates—that's certain—and our only course is to let some of them go by default, and get out of the dilemma afterwards with the best excuse in our power."[27] Often local repealers asked the league not to intervene at all, either to avoid a humiliating defeat or because, as Liberals as well as repealers, they did not wish to divide the reform interest. The league warned its provincial supporters that this only played into the hands of its enemies, but it dared not ignore their requests.

Officially the league never abandoned its by-election pledge. After the first few defeats it adopted the argument that its principal goal was to educate the electorate and that victories would come the next time round, as they had in Stockport, Walsall, and Durham. As early as April 1844, however, Cobden had resigned himself to the inadvisability of fighting every by-election, and he took no personal part in any of the contests after Salisbury. Instead, he began a fundamental rethinking of the league's plans and political priorities. "The agitation must be of a different kind to what we have hitherto pursued," he informed his brother Fred. "In fact we must merely have just as many demonstrations as will be necessary to keep hold of public attention and the work must go on in the way of registration labours in the large constituencies . . . The little pocket boroughs must be absolutely given over . . . Time alone can effect the business. It cannot be carried by storm. We were wrong in thinking of it."[28]

From then on he dismissed the by-election strategy as an ill-conceived experiment born of political naiveté, and he welcomed any excuse for not intervening in unwinnable constituencies. Thus, early in 1845, when a number of zealots on the league council (evidently including Wilson) pressed him to find a candidate for a hopeless contest at Leominster, Cobden reacted with an unusual burst of temper. "I presume you decided to contest the borough with a view to win," he wrote to Wilson,

> and had you found a candidate in Manchester, however much I might have doubted the wisdom of the step, I should not have presumed to interfere. But when a messenger comes to London to ask me to find a

candidate for a borough, I am bound in duty to myself and to the party I may solicit to inquire into the prospects of success. I went to Coppock and Parkes to learn the facts on which to form an opinion. The Council seems to be of the opinion that we ought not to consult them. I am on the contrary sorry that I did not consult them about the state of the little rotten boroughs before we committed ourselves to the ridiculous pledge of 1843.[29]

Having changed his own view, he was, as usual, impatient with those who did not immediately see things in the new light. Equally typical was Cobden's refusal to stop at half measures once he had decided that a change was necessary. His alternative strategy, hammered out with Bright in the spring of 1844, repudiated not only the by-election pledge but much of what the league had done over the preceding year, including his own rural campaign. As he put it to Wilson, conveying the substance of his conversations with Bright: "We must now concentrate our efforts upon those boroughs that may be won—Abandon the counties and the farmers as hopeless. I should not be sorry if the whole Council of the League were to resolve itself into a Borough Registration Society. Depend on it we must work more to a point and upon a system."[30]

Even the conduct of the registration campaign, which he now regarded as the key to rebuilding the fortunes of the league, was affected by Cobden's mood of slightly pessimistic realism. Back in September 1843, when he first announced the league's intention of organizing the constituencies, he implied that it would be another of the public campaigns that the league council had conducted since late 1842. In the event it was nothing of the sort. With the end of the parliamentary session of 1844, the league all but ceased to hold public meetings. Formal deputations did not fan out from Manchester; Cobden and Bright were not unleashed on the constituencies. Instead, the league newspaper, normally filled with accounts of meetings and speeches, was largely transformed into a registration manual, and the central league offices reverted to the task of management and control. The real work of organizing the constituencies was placed in the hands of trusted political agents skilled in the technicalities of voter registration. Concerned above all that the work be done well and anxious not to appear partisan or dictatorial, the leadership deliberately kept itself in the background. Indeed, the league as a public agitation was less visible that summer and autumn than at any time since 1840.

The near-absence of league meetings after August, together with the failure of its by-election strategy, led some of its critics to hope that the movement was dying. The vehemence with which the *League* denied such reports suggests that even some repealers shared the same belief. In fact there was no chance the league would go under. To a degree that even Cobden and Wilson may not have fully realized, the league had freed itself from the normal life cycle of earlier agitations. Repeated parliamentary setbacks, tactical errors such as the by-election campaign, and even economic recovery could no longer kill the movement. It was not simply that they could always raise sufficient funds; that had been true since 1840. But by making fund raising the central activity of the agitation, as they had since the autumn of 1842, the leaders of the league had established goals and a justification for agitation independent of Parliament, of public opinion, and, for that matter, of the fate of the Corn Laws. The scope of the league's activities and the mechanics of its operations were increasingly touted and accepted as the measure of its success. The process of raising fifty or 100,000 pounds, the ability to distribute five million propaganda packets, the stage managing of its great public events from the bazaars to the weekly London meetings to the annual gatherings at Free Trade Hall, the seeming ubiquity of Cobden and Bright at meetings all over the country, and even the audacity of the by-election effort were in the end more important to the league than the often meager political benefits they won. Economic prosperity might have killed an agitation less well organized and directed only toward its ostensible goal; as it was, the return of better times may have diminished the ardor of many repealers, but it filled the league's coffers to overflowing, and that was the main point. The agitation had become its own raison d'être.

The mere fact of the league's survival in good health in itself went far toward solving another of its perennial problems, the rivalry of other movements. The Complete Suffrage Union had managed to limp along somehow, even after bitter internal quarrels, but it no longer posed a threat. As for Chartism itself, the association with the Plug Plot strikes followed by the end of the worst of the economic depression had crippled the movement. Disillusioned with militancy and with the politics of class cooperation and undermined by fac-

tional dissension, the dominant O'Connorite wing of Chartism retreated into visions of working-class self-help through the Chartist
Land Plan. Perhaps the best measure of how drastically the relative
positions of Chartism and the league altered in the two years following the Plug Plot strikes was Cobden's agreement to meet Feargus
O'Connor in public debate in August 1844, in what turned out to be
the last important confrontation between the two movements. Heretofore, Cobden had favored avoiding direct contact with the rival
agitation and especially a debate, because such an event would inevitably be viewed as a discussion of the relative merits of the two issues
rather than an exposition of the case for the single issue to which the
league was committed. Besides, there was always the danger in any
joint appearance with a Chartist spokesman of humiliation by a
Chartist-dominated crowd.

By the summer of 1844 Cobden was so confident of the strength of
the league that he discounted these risks. Free trade was in the
ascendent as an issue, the ability of the league's advance planners to
ensure an open and peaceful meeting was proven, and Cobden himself had two seasons of provincial agitation under his belt. Far from
holding out any dangers, a confrontation with O'Connor appeared to
offer the opportunity at the very least to squelch the Chartist accusation that the league dared not debate its rival and perhaps an opportunity to squelch Chartism itself. Thus, when various groups in
Northamptonshire requisitioned Cobden, O'Connor, and a local M.P.
who was also an official of the Agricultural Protection Society to
address a public meeting on the Corn Laws, the first two (although
not the third) accepted. There was a good deal of to-ing and fro-ing
about the preparations for the meeting, but the event itself went off
without incident. Cobden and O'Connor were not the only speakers;
Bright seconded his chief, and there was another Chartist as well. But
then, and since, all attention was rightly placed on the clash between
the leaders of the two movements.

Cobden spoke first, in familiar terms, making the case for repeal as
beneficial to all the productive classes of the country, rural as well as
urban. O'Connor answered with an impassioned but discursive ora-
tion, which failed to answer most of Cobden's points and led to none
of its own. Confused and disheartened, the Chartists in the crowd,
probably the majority, were unable to rekindle their enthusiasm, and
in the show of hands at the end of the meeting, Cobden appeared to

have carried the day. All observers not personally committed to O'Connor concurred in that reading of the day's events, and even O'Connor, writing in his own newspaper, the *Northern Star*, implicitly acknowledged that Cobden had dominated the meeting. "Cobden has not been over rated," he told his readers. "He is decidedly a man of genius, of reflection, of talent and of tact . . . Cobden's voice is above the general standard; his thoughts are clearly arranged; his self possession is remarkable . . . I am not then astonished that a wily party should have selected so apt and cunning a leader."[31] O'Connor clearly had not prepared himself to deal with such an opponent. The first historian of Chartism, himself a Chartist (but no O'Connorite), R. G. Gammage, summed up the result bluntly: "Thus did O'Connor on the 5th of August, 1844, give the league the greatest victory they ever obtained."[32]

Gammage was exaggerating, blinded by his dislike of O'Connor. The debate simply gave an official—and personal—character to what had been happening for a year and a half. Indeed, with Chartism in retreat and the question of the link between wages and agricultural protection settled, the way was open for the league to appeal directly to working-class audiences over the heads of the Chartists. Yet it did not. "After 1842," Lucy Brown noted in her study of relations between the two movements, the repealers showed "little interest in working class needs in general. The movement became, far more than previously, a middle class agitation." This, she argued, was as much due to changes in league strategy as to the decline of the rival agitation: "their campaign was switched from the towns to the rural districts, and from the population as a whole to the electors." That was certainly the case but was not the only reason for the loss of "interest in working class politics."[33]

The league had never based its strategy on winning the active support of the working classes. Cobden, in particular, had always looked to an electoral strategy, in which the support of the unenfranchised masses was a peripheral consideration. In the early, hungry forties the league had wooed the working classes because their hostility, of which Chartism was only the most disruptive expression, undermined the claim of the league to represent urban England. Yet even in that critical time, Cobden never envisaged the league as taking the lead in organizing working-class discontent, let alone of assuming the task himself. "I have not the physical force," he told Edward Watkin, "and the tone of my mind is opposed to such an undertaking . . . My exertions are calculated to bring out the middle class and that will pave the way for a junction with the masses if they can be brought to act under rational and honest leaders."[34]

Inevitably therefore, as the temperature cooled in 1843, the leaders of the league were content to settle for nominal working-class support, which is all they had ever really needed. The movements to which the working classes turned increasingly in the middle 1840s— trade unionism, cooperation, factory reform—did not seek to rival the league and, if anything, because they were nonpolitical, served to reinforce the league's control of radical politics. In the event of a new economic crisis on the lines of 1842, more active support would of course be needed to press the issue of repeal home, but by 1844 Cobden was certain of the league's ability to channel any new discontent whenever it might arise and without serious rivalry from other groups, as had not been the case in 1842. For the first time in its history the league could afford to turn its back on the cities.

If only by default, then, the repeal of the Corn Laws had become the most important domestic issue and the league itself the arbiter of popular politics. As its leaders were fond of pointing out, British radicals no longer needed to debate which cause was to be preferred. The practical question was which had the better prospects of success, and to that question there was, of course, only one answer. This was fortunate for the league, because in reality it had little more chance of immediate victory than the Chartists. Which is not to say that the working of the electoral registers, the cornerstone of league policy in 1844, was a failure. Wilson had targeted 160 boroughs as winnable, and when all the returns were in early in 1845, he estimated that substantial gains had been made in 112. But even if his figures were correct, this was less than he and Cobden had counted on originally. Cobden had not perhaps believed all he had claimed when he first announced the registration campaign late in 1843, but, as in his rural campaign, he did assume that there was a large body of free trade opinion waiting to be tapped in the smaller boroughs. That it had lain dormant heretofore was due to patronage—usually, he assumed, coercive in nature—or to corruption. "Lay Manchester and Birmingham alongside St. Albans and Sudbury," he assumed, "and you will give them a moral influence and support, and . . . you will beat down the influence of the local monopolist squire who has hitherto been able to domineer over the inhabitants of those small boroughs."[35]

In addition Cobden hoped to take advantage of recent election laws designed to nullify the effects of corruption. By the time the league began its registration drive in earnest in August, however, the disastrous by-election results had reduced Cobden's expectations. Manchester had been laid alongside a succession of southern boroughs, many of them neither especially small nor corrupt, but the hoped-for surge of free trade sentiment had failed to materialize. And the registration drive confirmed what the by-election losses had indicated: that for every potentially winnable borough there were at least a couple of others that, either because of local influences or the small size of the electorate, were hopelessly beyond reach. Cobden's notion of using the power of the greater boroughs to counter the influence of the borough patrons was based on a false premise, for the patrons had direct access to the boroughs while the great cities did not. Wilson's 160 boroughs, rather than being the first field of battle, seemed likely to be the last. Although that did not invalidate the registration campaign, it did invalidate the strategy behind it. The league had failed once again to raise the electoral costs of maintaining protection high enough to frighten the leadership of either party into further concessions.

CHAPTER 12

The Key to Victory?

The league's dilemma in the summer of 1844 was depressingly familiar. At the end of every parliamentary year since its formation the league had been faced with the same sense of political impotence. Apart from the actual survival of the movement, now no longer in question, this had always been Cobden's main concern, and routinely every autumn he had somehow managed to come up with a new approach to the problem. In 1840 he had led the league into a limited electoral policy; a year later he had flirted with Sturge's Complete Suffrage movement; as the temperature cooled following the failure of the Plug Plot strikes, he and Wilson committed the league to an unprecedented propaganda campaign aimed at the electorate in marginal constituencies; and finally, in 1843 he had proposed transforming the league into something approaching a political party. Depending as much on his mood as on circumstances, he had thrown himself into these efforts with a constantly changing mix of grim desperation, cold calculation, and naive enthusiasm. Sometimes he had expected little, sometimes a great deal; always he had been disappointed.

But in late 1844 Cobden hit upon a wholly new approach which promised to undermine the political power of the governing class more directly than anything any mass movement had tried before. Stymied in the lesser boroughs, he proposed that the league should turn to the counties, hitherto all but written off as enemy territory. Furthermore, far from limiting itself to enrolling qualified voters, the league, Cobden believed, should seek to create a vast new electorate by persuading its supporters to buy sufficient freehold property to qualify for a vote in the counties. The idea of working at least the urbanized counties appears to have resulted directly from one of the most embarrassing of the league's by-election defeats in 1844, the loss in May of the county division of South Lancashire. There, if anywhere, the number of townsmen possessing qualifications for the county franchise should have been decisive, and almost immediately after the election the league political agents began the hunt for the necessary missing voters. Some were holders of large leases but most of them were small property owners whose modest holdings were nonetheless sufficient to give them the vote under a centuries-old qualification, the forty-shilling freehold. At some point in the process of unearthing these urban freeholders, it occurred, probably to a number of the league's now thoroughly experienced political agents, that this was the easiest and cheapest county voting qualification to obtain and, moreover, that the number of forty-shilling freeholders could be expanded almost infinitely.

Some years later Cobden credited Charles Walker of Rochdale with the idea of mass-producing freehold votes, but whatever the case, from the moment Cobden became aware of the possibility, he seized on it with an enthusiasm he had not shown since embarking on his rural campaign early in 1843. In expounding this new move to the great gatherings of the league in the autumn of 1844, he displayed none of the caution that had characterized his speeches outlining the campaign in the lesser boroughs the year before. This, he believed, was the Achilles heel of oligarchic political power. "From the moment that the plan devised was put forward at a great meeting in Manchester," he recalled some years later, "I never doubted of the ultimate repeal of the Corn Laws; although until then I could never conscientiously say that I saw a method by which we could legally and constitutionally secure their abolition."[1]

The monopolists might continue to control the lesser boroughs and the lesser boroughs might continue unfairly to outweigh the greater, but the counties were vulnerable. Success would no longer depend on the limited ability of the league to rouse and organize supporters beyond its power base; its sure supporters in its urban strongholds could by themselves redress the rural bias of the 1832 reform bill simply by buying freehold property. Towns that had hitherto been overwhelmed in their counties could hope to control these counties. The forty-shilling freehold vote had been retained in the reform bill but balanced, so the landowners thought, by enfranchising fifty-pound tenants at will. Not so, Cobden argued. The landlords had gone as far as they could in creating tenant votes; the middle and even the working classes could go further in creating freehold votes. In some counties he estimated that as little as £35 would buy property sufficient to qualify a voter; even many artisans could afford that. For the middle class buying a freehold property was as good a means of saving as putting money in the bank—or better, since it brought the added dividend of a vote.

There were problems, of course—the legal costs and inconvenience of buying freeholds, the danger that the monopolists might retaliate in kind, objections on principle to buying votes—but Cobden brushed these aside, at least in public. Privately, he was concerned that some of what they were up to—in particular sharing out the ownership of a property with the express purpose of manufacturing votes—bordered on illegality. Much of his correspondence that winter was concerned with ensuring that nothing of that sort should trip them up, for the more he learned about the new possibilities for this old qualification, the more he was certain, as he told an enthusiastic crowd in London in December, that "we have struck the right nail on the head."[2]

From then until the end of the anti–Corn Law agitation, the freehold campaign was at the center of league activity. The tried-and-true techniques of agitation were not abandoned. The league continued to set and meet huge fund-raising goals, and the lecture circuit and the distribution of propaganda were maintained at nearly peak levels; the biggest of the anti–Corn Law bazaars was held in May 1845, this time in London not Manchester; the business of working the electoral registers in the traditional way received almost as much attention in 1845 as it had the year before; the league even fought some by-elections. But the leadership could afford to be more selective. Registration drives were concentrated in the clearly winnable boroughs, and by-elections in most of the lesser boroughs were disdained. The counties were the league's new obsession. Initially, five county divisions—North and South Lancashire, Middlesex, the West Riding of Yorkshire, and North Cheshire—were selected as most vulnerable; a sixth, South Staffordshire, was added to the list a few months later. The league concentrated most of its resources in these areas during the winter campaign of 1844-45. All subscribers to league funds and to the *League* newspaper were circularized, to urge them to buy qualifications; league agents visited local anti–Corn Law associations to help them find property to buy and individuals and groups to buy it; Cobden and Bright devoted the whole of their speaking tour that winter to pushing the new move in the northern heartland of the league (and Cobden himself purchased a qualification in his native Sussex).

The response was enormous, better apparently than Cobden had dared hope for, and by the time he went up to London to address the first league meeting of the new year in Covent Garden, he was so confident of the future of the movement that he felt free to talk of his hitherto unspoken doubts: "We have passed through that trying ordeal which I had always dreaded as the real and difficult test of this agitation; I mean the period when the manufactures of this country regained a temporary prosperity. We are proof against that trial; we have had larger, more enthusiastic, and more influential meetings than ever we had before; and I am happy to tell you, that ... the present state of prosperity in business is merely having the effect of recruiting the funds of the Anti–Corn Law League."[3]

For the first time since the election of Peel's Parliament, he felt able to talk of victory as close: not in 1845, to be sure—"We have begun a new year, and it will not finish our work"—but soon thereafter. At long last he saw the way to power, and not only for the repeal of the Corn Laws:

> Recollect what it is we ask you to do: to take into your own hands the power of doing justice to twenty-seven millions of people! ... We must have not merely the boroughs belonging to the people; but give the counties to the towns, which are their right ... I say, without being revolutionary ... that the sooner the power of this country is transferred from the landed oligarchy, which has so misused it, and is placed absolutely—mind, I say "Absolutely"—in the hands of the intelligent middle and industrious classes, the better for the condition and destinies of this country.

More than ever before, Cobden was convinced that the battle would be won in the constituencies, not in Parliament. Nonetheless, for the first time in two years and largely because of what he hoped for from the freehold campaign, he planned a new approach to the role of the movement in Parliament in 1845. As he explained it when the session was nearly over, "Last year we made a little mistake at the beginning of the session; we laid our heads together, and came to the conclusion that we could employ ourselves better out of doors . . . this year we have changed our tactics, and we thought that Parliament, after all, was the best place for agitating. You speak with a loud voice when talking on the floor of that House."[4]

Cobden, who had all but turned his back on Parliament the year before, was more active in the House of Commons during 1845 than at any time since his first full parliamentary session three years earlier. There were many reasons for this new emphasis on Parliament. The league had gone as far as it could in saturating the country with propaganda, and lecture tours by the leaders of the league were likely to bring diminishing returns at a time when returning prosperity was lowering the political temperature. Cobden was tired of them in any case. Something new was needed and Parliament, having been ignored for some time, was once again a new challenge.

More than anything else, however, it was the freehold movement that made a new parliamentary campaign seem worth waging. Armed, finally, with the means of reaching directly from the constituencies into the House of Commons, Cobden was determined to make the league as visible as possible at Westminster. His calculation that progress in the boroughs would shake the confidence of the major parties had fallen short. Backed by the freehold campaign, however, he was certain that a majority in Parliament could be panicked into repeal. "It will not be necessary to gain the whole of the more populous districts," he explained. "If we obtain North and South Lancashire, the West Riding of Yorkshire, and Middlesex, the landed monopolists will give up corn in order to save a great deal more."[5]

The league's parliamentary strategy was to keep the issue of free trade in the forefront of debate and systematically to demolish what remained of the protectionist case. In addition to making as much as possible of obvious opportunities such as the debates on the queen's speech and the budget, the league planned a series of motions, culminating in Villiers' annual motion for repeal, on various aspects of the rural economy—always, of course, in relation to the central question of protection. Cobden moved for a committee of inquiry into the distressed state of agriculture and its relationship to the Corn Laws; Milner Gibson proposed equalizing the duties on foreign grown and colonial sugar; Bright for the first time rode out to do battle with the aristocracy on what was to become one of his favorite hobby horses, the game laws; and Henry Ward, a Liberal M.P. sympathetic to the cause, moved an inquiry into the special burdens supposedly borne by the land and often used as a justification for agricultural protection. Even the opposition front bench joined in. Lord John Russell proposed a series of resolutions aimed at improving the condition of the working classes, the most important of which called for freer trade.

Russell's participation in the hunt was proof that the government was on the defensive. Both front benches had long since conceded much of the league's case. Whig and Tory leaders alike now openly acknowledged that wages were not linked to the price of food, except perhaps inversely. The Whigs explicitly and many Tories implicitly had accepted the repealers' argument that protection, far from encouraging agriculture to modernize, actually hindered the process. Nor, in view of low agricultural prices, did anyone any longer claim that the Corn Laws could maintain a given price level. The protectionists were reduced to arguing that the Corn Laws were a necessary safeguard against a further fall in prices, which would wipe out many farmers and create high unemployment among agricultural laborers. Furthermore, the protectionists pointed out, the land was subject to special burdens in the form of tithes, the poor rates, and other taxes, which justified giving it special consideration—hence Ward's motion, which the repealers used to demonstrate that the land bore no burdens not shared equally by other interests in society. As for the effects of the Corn Laws in helping or undermining rural prosperity, that had been one of Cobden's main themes for almost two years, ever since agricultural prices began to fall, and was the only subject of his most important speech that session, made in support of his motion for a parliamentary inquiry.

Cobden was unusually on edge in anticipation of this speech. "You will think it very strange in an old hack demagogue like me," he admitted to his wife, "if I confess that I am as nervous as a maid the day before her wedding."[6] As the opening move in the league's parliamentary strategy, much depended on it, and in his final preparations Cobden turned for advice to C. H. Lattimore, a progressive Hertfordshire farmer he had met during his rural campaign. There was nothing novel in the content of the speech. He again denounced the Corn Laws as a fraud, perpetrated for political reasons on the farmers, and advised the landlords on the back benches opposite that only security of tenure, the infusion of capital into the land that long leases would bring, and the resulting improvement in the techniques of agriculture could secure lasting prosperity for rural England. He made effective use of illustrative material drawn from all parts of the country to support his argument and, in particular, to demonstrate that one farmer's or region's cash crop might be another's raw material and that Parliament in protecting the former only raised the cost of production for the latter.

Neither his detailed knowledge of local agricultural conditions nor this technique of using it were new, even to Parliament; Cobden had developed both during his rural campaign and had employed a similar approach in support of a similar motion in 1844. What was new was the tone of the speech. He did not hector or threaten; he talked not so much at as to the Tory back benches. He carefully drew distinctions between the better sort of landlords, interested in the welfare of the countryside, and the political landlords, for whom he reserved his barbs. Even the wording of his motion displayed a sensitivity to his audience. In 1844 he had proposed a committee of inquiry into the effects of protective duties on the interests of tenant farmers and laborers. In 1845 he sought an inquiry into agricultural distress and only secondarily into the effects of protection.

Cynically, one might suggest that, with Bright now in charge of the heavy weapons, Cobden was enabled to take a higher road. Certainly he was not averse to using the landlords in general as whipping boys when that suited his needs. Reporting the reaction to Bright's speech on the game laws to Wilson, Cobden gleefully noted, "His speech took the squires quite aback . . . They seem to feel that we had put them in a false position towards their tenants, and the blockheads could not conceal their spite towards the League."[7] But whatever his private sentiments, Cobden's public moderation was an effective weapon in discomfiting the enemy and even in winning his respect. After the speech "several county members asked me where my land lay, thinking I must be an experienced proprietor and farmer."[8] Allies and enemies alike acknowledged it as his best parliamentary effort, and although at the time he was far from satisfied, in later years, in a letter to Lattimore, he recognized it as "the most successful speech I ever made."

The speech was a milestone, and not only in Cobden's parliamentary career. As Cobden spoke, Peel took notes for a time, but at some point he stopped, crumpled up his paper, turned to Sidney Herbert and, so the story goes, said: "You must answer this for I cannot."[9]

No one would any longer suggest that this marked Peel's conversion to repeal; he had long since ceased to support the Corn Laws except as a political necessity. It has been suggested by D. C. Moore that Peel's reluctance to answer, far from being the result of his inability to counter Cobden's increasingly effective exposition of the traditional arguments against the Corn Laws, was due to the fact that "in 1845 Cobden was using a new argument," one that Peel substantially accepted but had not expected from Cobden. According to Moore,

> Before 1845, Cobden's arguments against the Corn Laws were the standard repealers' arguments . . . [that], while they were a benefit to the landlords, they were an onerous burden on all other groups in the kingdom. But in 1845 he criticised the corn laws not for raising domestic prices but for deterring domestic agriculturalists from investing in agricultural improvements . . . [since the corn laws] had come to symbolize the hope that rural prosperity might be restored on the basis of price at a time when these prices themselves were being reduced by increments of production.[10]

Moore overstated his case. Cobden had been talking of agricultural improvements as the salvation of rural England and citing individual examples of agricultural productivity and prosperity ever since industrial recovery and falling agricultural prices had shifted distress from the towns to the countryside. The overriding importance of modernization to all segments of rural society, including the landlord, was a major theme of his speeches in support of a commission of inquiry in 1844, as in 1845.

Nonetheless, there had been a marked and steady shift in the emphasis, if not in the substance, of Cobden's arguments. Before 1845 he had spoken to the landed interest, often in quite patronizing terms, representing himself as the spokesman for urban and industrial England, which, in effect, he equated with the national interest. The solution to the problems of rural England, he had argued, lay not in protection but in the ability of urban society to absorb the excess population and, over and above imports, the produce of rural England. Agricultural improvements were an important part of the process, but Cobden had always heretofore placed them in the context of urban demand. In 1845, however, he hardly mentioned the cities; instead he stressed the ability of rural England to solve its own problems. The productive capacity of English agriculture, not the size of the urban marketplace, was his central theme. The English farmer, freed from the false promises of protection and given the security of tenure and capital he needed, could, Cobden argued, compete on equal terms with any foreign supplier and in the process give employment to all who now lived on the land. Indeed, at one point he went so far as to declare that "if you had abundance of capital employed on your farms, and cultivated your soil with the same skill that the manufacturers conduct their business, you would not have population enough to cultivate the land."[11]

The extent to which Cobden had come to see things in this way, and still more his readiness to discuss the problems of agriculture in these terms, marked an important shift in his thinking. In this sense, his growing circle of friends and correspondents among farmers, his association with many free trade aristocrats, his day-to-day contact with rural M.P.s in the House of Commons, and his speaking tours in the counties had paid off handsomely. Through his increased knowledge of what some farmers and landowners were already doing, he had become as impressed with the possibilities open to English agriculture as with the backward state of much of it. He had, in addition, become sensitive to the need to appeal to the landed classes on their own terms. It was as much this change in the tone and perspective of Cobden's speeches as in their actual content that made his views at once more acceptable to Peel, and much more difficult to answer.

Between Peel's thinking and Cobden's there remained, in fact, only one major issue, timing. The Tory back-benchers, sensing this, were growing restive; and Disraeli, always alive to any change in the political wind, launched his first attack on Peel during the 1845 session. "For my part," he commented during the debate on Cobden's motion, "if we are to have free trade, I, who honor genius, prefer that such measures should be proposed by the member for Stockport, than by one, who through skillful parliamentary manoevres, has tampered with the generous confidence of a great people and a great party . . . Dissolve if you please the Parliament you have betrayed," he concluded, "and appeal to the people who, I believe, mistrust you. For me there remains this at least—the opportunity of expressing thus publicly my belief that a Conservative Government is an Organised Hypocrisy."[12]

In his concern with timing, Peel was, however, very far from being hypocritical. Total repeal was one thing, immediate repeal quite another. And if it was difficult any longer to accuse Cobden of being dogmatic and intemperate in either the manner or the substance of his arguments for repeal, it was still easy to attack him as rash in proposing the sudden removal of a system of protection that had been in operation for thirty years. Economically as well as politically, great interests were involved and precipitate action could well be dangerous, especially at a time when agriculture was far from prosperous. That was the substance of Peel's answer to Villiers' annual motion, but Cobden, in reply, neatly turned this argument against the government: "The right honorable gentlemen talked of the Free Traders being rash . . . Was it rashness to propose the change now? Were they not rather the rash men, who were blindly passing over this opportunity of effecting it?. . . The time would yet come when they would have a recurrence of those scenes which had been witnessed within the memory of the youngest of them. When that time did arrive, who then would be regarded as the rash men?"[13]

CHAPTER 13

Victory

In referring back to the anguished early years of the decade as a justification for immediate action on the Corn Laws in 1845, Cobden could hardly have been more prescient. Even before Parliament was prorogued in August there was speculation that the three-year string of bountiful harvests was about to end. Two months later the government was faced with the still more ominous certainty of a failure of the Irish potato crop. At that point, it is fair to say, the Corn Laws were doomed, but it was a long way from a situation in which the existing system of protection was no longer tenable to the passage of repeal by a government of either party, and until the last minute Cobden feared that something might go wrong. In May 1845, months before there was a hint of political crisis but when he was already confident that the issue might be decided within a year, Cobden had foretold accurately both the final outcome and the role of the league in bringing it about. "The only position the Whigs can take up is a vanishing duty," he told J. B. Smith, "and in this way the question will be ultimately disposed of by one or the other party. But," he warned, "the League must not invite this. On the contrary I shall try to show that the wisest course for all parties would be the total and immediate repeal. The more stiffly we stick to *our shibboleth* the easier it will be for a minister to pass a vanishing duty."[1]

That, in essence, was Cobden's strategy during the eight suspenseful months from October 1845 to June 1846, but he had no illusions that it would be an easy course to steer or that the league could dictate the outcome. His worst fear was that the repealers would be cheated of their goal by the machinations of the professional politicians or by a falling off in the unity of the agitation as it approached success. He distrusted Russell as unsound on economic issues, as isolated from public opinion by the closed circle of Whiggery, and as a trimmer. Although Russell had paid a much publicized visit to the league's London bazaar and was unusually cordial to Cobden throughout the parliamentary session of 1845, Cobden had not been able to shake him from his commitment to a fixed duty. Not until late November, with the crisis under way and Peel's cabinet on the verge of unraveling, did Russell come out for repeal. That eased Cobden's mind somewhat, but not entirely. Most Whigs resented the league and many still hankered after a fixed duty; a deal with the Tories to dish the radicals could not be ruled out.

Peel was a different matter. Ever since Russell's refusal to abandon a fixed duty in May, Cobden had been certain that "Peel is the man to give us free trade."[2] Cobden never doubted the soundness of Peel's economic views or, from the moment he took up the cause of repeal, his determination. Peel was preferable on practical political grounds as well. Only a Tory backed by Liberals could carry an essentially Liberal measure through a Tory-dominated House of Commons, let alone the House of Lords, short of a repetition of the constitutional crisis of 1832. But such a calculation assumed that Peel would be able to keep a substantial proportion of his erstwhile followers in line. In fact there was always the danger that the Tory majority might throw him over and do a deal with the Whigs. Beyond that, even should Peel somehow manage to pilot repeal through the House of Commons, the Lords might still exercise their veto.

During the early stages of the crisis, from October to January, with Parliament out of session, there was little the league could do directly to influence the course of events at Westminister. From Peel's resignation following a split in his cabinet a few days after Russell's conversion to repeal, through Russell's failed attempt to form a government, to the formation of a new Peel government committed to total but not immediate repeal, high politics developed according to a logic of its own. What happened out of doors happened, so to speak, off stage, but Cobden was convinced that the presence of the league in the wings could be crucial to the final outcome. Its only but vital function was to impress on the leaders of both parties, the back-bench Tories, and the House of Lords that repeal was preferable to what would happen in the country if repeal was not passed. That required, in effect, reversing the two-year-long transformation of the league into something between a pressure group and a political party and reverting to the techniques of mass agitation.

In October, the league began a series of meetings up and down the country demanding that the ports be opened immediately. In November it announced the second phase of its county registration campaign; having won, so it claimed, four of the six counties targeted for 1845, the league published a list of twenty-two additional counties where registration coupled with the purchase of freehold votes might tip the scales. In December the league urged its members to petition Parliament once again, for the first time since 1843, and also in December it launched a new fund-raising campaign, for the extraordinary sum of one quarter of a million pounds. Much of the burden in all these campaigns fell on Cobden and Bright. For three months they did almost nothing but travel from meeting to meeting. Besides the inevitable gatherings in major cities, they visited thirteen of the counties they hoped to win; at the height of the campaign seven widely separate meetings in ten days was not an uncommon schedule. Making maximum use of the railways, they gave the appearance, designedly, of being everywhere. "I like the railways," Cobden said in October 1845, at the start of the league's last great campaign. "They are carrying common sense . . . into the agricultural districts . . . they are drawing us more together; they are teaching the landowner to feel for the manufacturer, and placing the manufacturer on better terms with the landowner."[3] By the end of January 1846, however, feeling more a victim than a pioneer in the political use of the railway age, Cobden was sick of the sight of trains.

Quite apart from the killing pace of that winter's agitation, Cobden was exhausted by the time Parliament convened in January. The 1845 session had been unusually taxing. In addition to leading the league's campaign in the Commons, he had spent much of the session on the time-consuming railway committee. This, in turn, had led him to move—successfully—for a commission of inquiry into railway gauges, a subject on which he acquired far more information than he wanted. He recognized the value of such work—"It is well to do something practical in the House occasionally, as it gives one the standing of a man of business"[4]—but he resented the drain on his time and energy. Often, he complained to his wife, he found it hard to work himself up to speak at the league's Covent Garden meetings, where, of course, he was expected to put in frequent appearances. Worse still, throughout the session he had to deal with a personal financial crisis which reached a climax at the time the potato crop failed in Ireland.

Like the economy as a whole, Cobden's business had had a very uneven career since its reorganization as a family firm in 1839. There had been some bad seasons, the summer of 1842 in particular, but there seemed no doubt that the firm would survive. Cobden had therefore left its management in the hands of his brothers, except for a brief period each autumn between the prorogation of Parliament and the beginning of the league's winter campaign, when he devoted much of his time to selecting the patterns and preparing the manufacture of the coming season's line of printed goods. The first signs that the business was in more than ordinary difficulties came in 1844. Cobden devoted as much time as he could that autumn to putting its affairs in order, but it was plain that the firm lacked proper management, and one of the friends Cobden called on for advice predicted accurately that it was bound to fail unless Cobden quit politics for business. With the league about to make a major breakthrough with the freehold campaign, Cobden did not even consider that possibility. As he had done ever since committing himself full time to the agitation late in 1840, he shut his mind to private matters and threw himself into the work of the league.

Somehow the business survived the winter, but by the summer of 1845 it was clear that intermittent attention to his private affairs would no longer suffice. The spring line of goods was a failure, inventories were high, and the machinery was not being worked full time. Cobden's first reaction to the gloomy reports from Manchester was irritation. "It is of no use your writing bad news to me," he told his brother Fred in early April, "I can't help it while here."[5] Nor, he explained, could he get away; his parliamentary duties would not allow it. Certainly he did not wish to get away, at least not for that reason, or yet believe it was necessary. "I do not see any difficulty in giving adequate attention to the business," he wrote, also in April, "and still retaining, ostensibly at all events, the same public position as before."[6]

Two months later, however, Cobden could no longer think in terms simply of adjusting the balance between public and private obligations. The firm was on the verge of collapse and needed an infusion of cash. Only his personal intervention in the management of the business and money raised from his friends could retrieve the situation. "I have turned the subject over in every way," he confided to Fred in June, "and I see no other solution of it than in absolutely withdrawing myself from public life, first having secured such a promise of support from some of my friends as shall secure me from the effects of the shock."[7] Whether or not Cobden really believed in June that it would be necessary to go that far, firsthand experience of the firm's condition during the next two months convinced him. In September he sent Bright a letter, which he asked him to destroy after reading it, setting forth the details of his financial condition and declaring his intention of resigning from the leadership of the league. Bright (replying in a letter that has survived) was dumbfounded. Hardly able to find words to express his feelings and clearly at a loss to know what to do, he could only urge delay: "I am of the opinion that your retirement would be tantamount to a dissolution of the League; its mainspring would be gone. I can in no degree take your place . . . Do not think I wish to add to your troubles in writing thus; but I am most anxious that some delay should take place . . . and that if the shock cannot be avoided, it should be given only after the weightiest consideration, and in such a way as to produce the least evil."[8]

Bright was on vacation in Scotland with his sisters at the time and told Cobden that he did not see how he could get away without an adequate explanation. After at most a day's reflection, however, he fully realized the seriousness of the situation and rushed south to Manchester. Together with one or two other friends he pressed Cobden to accept a private loan to tide him over the next few months, which, in any case, all of them had begun to suspect might now suffice to win repeal. Cobden could hardly refuse. Personally and as a public man he had little choice. For him to have abandoned the league at that moment, as he had in effect abandoned his own affairs for the sake of the league, might indeed have crippled the movement and rendered his earlier sacrifice meaningless. But although Cobden had been saved for the league's last great campaign, he could not, as he had done in the past, put his private affairs out of mind. He was acutely conscious of the falsity of his position and of his helplessness. To the world at large he was a symbol as well as the leader of a movement, a Manchester manufacturer marching at the head of his order. It was an appearance that had to be maintained, no doubt, but it was purchased at the cost of constant awareness that he was living a lie and deferring the interests of his wife and children to sustain it.

Their welfare was now wholly dependent on the generosity of his friends and was certain to remain so at least until free trade was won.

The accumulated pressures of the winter were bound to take their toll, and early in the new year Cobden fell ill. The illness, an ordinary head cold, was not in itself serious at first but complications prostrated him for nearly a month. This was worrisome enough for a man whose health had never been robust, but reading between the lines of his reassuring references to his health at the time, it is clear that only with this illness did he realize how close he was to nervous exhaustion. As if he needed it, here was another reason for him to turn from politics to concern for his own future. His doctors advised him to limit his participation in Parliament and, once the issue of repeal was decided, to get away from public life for at least a year, perhaps by going abroad. Cobden readily acceded to their advice. He did not speak in the House until more than a month into the session and thereafter he spoke rarely and only once at length. The previous year, 1845, not 1846, marked the height of Cobden's parliamentary efforts on behalf of free trade.

The role that the league M.P.s could play in Parliament had, in any case, been diminished by events. With the leaders of both parties committed to repeal before Parliament met and a repeal bill before the House as a government measure from the outset, Cobden and his colleagues had been superseded in most of their traditional functions by the two front benches. He was, however, not yet ready to relax his vigilance or take the outcome for granted. He remained skeptical, perhaps unnecessarily so, until mid-June, less than two weeks before the Lords passed Peel's bill. Concerned with his health and personal future, he tended, as he recognized, to scan the horizon too anxiously for signs of anything that might delay his escape from the political treadmill. "I feel quite unstrung—like a clock that requires winding up," he confessed to J. B. Smith in March. "Perhaps it is owing to the loss of elasticity that I feel nervous and anxious about the fate of Peel's measure. Everybody views it as quite safe. I can't see it in so sanguine a light."[9]

Yet even if he exaggerated the danger, it was prudent of Cobden to plan for the worst; a protectionist revolt in the Commons, a junction of Tories and compromise-minded Whigs, and, almost to the end, a veto in the Lords were all possible. The league's winter campaign had done what it could to prevent all three, and Cobden saw it as his function to remind Parliament constantly of the significance of what the league was about. In his most important speech in support of Peel's bill he was content to sum up the philosophical case for repeal in the broadest terms; the task of persuasion had, after all, become Peel's. The bulk of Cobden's speech—as of his private conversations with doubtful Whigs—was devoted to warning the protectionists of both Houses of the consequences of forcing a dissolution of Parliament. He denied what most protectionists perhaps still believed, that they could win a majority in a new House of Commons. "Your party is broken up," he warned, now that its best and most popular leaders had abandoned the Corn Laws.[10] Moreover, even if the protectionists could win a majority, it would be a majority without moral weight, for it would include no representatives of the larger boroughs or urban counties. The "amount of public opinion as now exists in favor of the repeal of the Corn Laws," he declared, "is sufficient to change the constitution of this country; to alter your forms of government; to do anything in short that public opinion is determined to effect."[11] If not in the next election, then surely in the one that followed, those that attempted to stand in the way of such a tide would be swept away.

If such warnings were to have their intended effect, it was vital that the league remain united, but that was not easy to achieve. Peel's measure, after all, was not the league's. In addition to delaying total repeal for three years, it provided, in Cobden's view, for a needlessly complicated transition period. When the bill was first published, Cobden carefully reserved judgment. "I abstained from saying a word in the House," he informed his wife, "because I did not wish to commit myself, and I dissuaded Villiers and the rest of the leaguers from speaking. It was too good a measure to be denounced, and not quite good enough for unqualified approbation, and therefore I thought it best to be quiet."[12] Cobden kept in close touch with the leaders of the opposition—he attended a meeting at Russell's house on January 28, the day after Peel announced his measure—and, like Russell, Cobden briefly considered holding out for immediate repeal. But when it became clear that public opinion, including most of the important leaguers (as reported to Cobden by J. B. Smith in a letter of January 29), supported Peel, Cobden, again like Russell, decided to back the prime minister.

Some of the more doctrinaire free traders, including Archibald

Prentice, wanted to oppose Peel, and many rank-and-file leaguers were seized with a kind of Peel mania. Cobden was equally contemptuous of both groups, the former as unrealistic, the latter as endangering the leverage of the league. In order to maintain the unity of the movement and to put maximum pressure on Parliament, he believed that the league had to be firm in its commitment to immediate repeal and at the same time flexible in its approach to Peel's bill. Thus, Villiers performed the now largely symbolic act of moving his annual motion for the last time; yet he, Cobden, and Bright continued to support Peel's bill insofar as it was a measure of total repeal. The rationale for this approach was so obvious to Cobden that he was furious when a number of repealers, thinking they were aiding Peel, voted against Villiers' motion. Cobden claimed he had good reason to know that Peel had wanted a large minority in favor of total and immediate repeal as a means of putting pressure on the protectionists. That certainly is how Cobden saw it. To what extent his handling of the situation contributed to the smooth passage of repeal is, in the final analysis, a question of interpretation, but there can be no doubt that tactically he was correct.

Physical and mental exhaustion and the imminent prospect of having to deal with a host of personal problems reduced the satisfaction that Cobden felt at achieving victory after a seven-year struggle. But there was compensation for that of a very personal nature, although expressed publicly, in the closing moments. The day the Lords passed repeal Cobden spoke against a coercion bill for Ireland, the defeat of which, moments later, brought about the fall of Peel's government. Although Cobden was about to vote against the government, he used the occasion to pay a final tribute to the prime minister:

> He carries with him the esteem and gratitude of a larger number of the population of this Empire than ever followed any Minister that was ever hurled from power . . . I am not misinterpreting the opinion of the people . . . when I tender the right hon. Baronet in my own name, as I might do in theirs, my heartfelt thanks for the unwearied perseverence, the unswerving firmness, and the great ability with which he has during the last six months conducted one of the most magnificent reforms ever carried in any country, through the House of Commons.[13]

Four days later, in a speech announcing his resignation, Peel returned the compliment. "The name which ought to be, and will be, associated with these measures," he said of the passage of repeal, "is the name of one who, acting, I believe, from pure and disinterested motives, has, with untiring energy, made appeals to our reason, and has enforced those appeals with an eloquence, the more to be admired because it was unaffected and unadorned: the name which ought to be chiefly associated with the success of these measures, is the name of Richard Cobden."[14]

Neither Peel nor Cobden would have spoken these words six months before. Close as they had become philosophically during the preceding year, they remained divided personally by their bitter parliamentary exchange in February 1843. Cobden, in particular, had never forgiven Peel for his ungracious acceptance of Cobden's explanation of his words. Thereafter he tended to center his attacks on the government in the person of its leader, although of the incident itself he said little or nothing. In the late months of 1845 that changed. Again and again he referred back to it in his speeches, at first mockingly but with increasing venom, until his attacks on Peel became unreasoned.

"I need not tell you that the word responsibility has an ugly and sinister sound in the ear of the Prime Minister," he reminded a Manchester audience in October.[15] In Birmingham a month later, he added, "I see many attempts made to shirk that responsibility, and sometimes in a very shabby manner, by trying to make it appear that we who cry out against this responsibility mean to do him some personal violence."[16] In December, at Covent Garden, he spoke more subjectively: "I have no reason, and I think you will all admit it, to feel any great respect for Sir Robert Peel; he is the only man in the House of Commons that I can never speak a word to in private without forfeiting my own respect."[17] But Cobden's most savage comment was made a week earlier in Stockport, immediately after the resignation of Peel's government:

> Sir Robert Peel, although sprung from amongst them, had placed himself at the head of the present gang of plunderers and monopolists . . . knowing that the cause of the misery and destitution which then prevailed was the cause which he came into power to uphold . . . Although in March 1842 Sir Robert Peel was much moved by the statement of distress in the manufacturing districts, still no credit can be given to him for feelings of remorse, on account of the injury his policy had inflicted on his countrymen. Sir Robert Peel felt for Sir Robert Peel, but not for the people.[18]

That these assaults on Peel came in the painful aftermath of Cobden's revelation of his financial condition to Bright was surely no coincidence. Whether he was aware of it or not, everything Cobden said of Peel in Stockport can be read both as an indictment of his own failings and as an attempt to justify those failings to himself. After all, had Peel performed what Cobden claimed Peel knew to be his duty to the nation, then Cobden would have long since been free to perform his duty to family and business. Had Peel not maintained a false position for three years, Cobden would not have been forced into a false position at the end of the struggle. Had Peel felt genuine remorse in 1842, Cobden would not have had the occasion to feel remorse in 1845. Had Peel not clung selfishly to power, Cobden would not have been placed in the position of choosing power over his personal obligations.

Apart from Bright, none of Cobden's political allies were as yet aware of the pressures he was working under that winter, and although everyone close to him knew how bitterly the 1843 incident still rankled, the sudden escalation of his attacks on Peel came as a shock. Immediately after the Stockport speech a number of Cobden's friends intervened, urging him to desist. Cobden immediately recognized that he had gone too far. Yet, although he admitted to George Combe that he was wrong to exult in Peel's fall, he attempted to explain away his actions as largely a consequence of the debasing effects of years of agitation on the agitator, and he did not back away from his equally savage remarks at Covent Garden. As late as February 1846 he still felt "that I should forfeit my own respect and that of my friends if I ever exchanged a word with that man in private."[19] Nonetheless, there were no more public attacks on the prime minister.

That was not enough, however, for one of his correspondents and confidants at this time, Harriet Martineau. She wrote a second time to Cobden, sympathizing with his personal indignation over the 1843 incident but also attempting to explain Peel's behavior. Realizing from his replies that nothing short of a public apology would satisfy Cobden, she then decided to contact Peel. She had never met the prime minister and first tried to reach him through an intermediary; when that failed she wrote him directly to inform him of Cobden's feelings. To her surprise, he answered immediately. He had, as she suspected, thought the incident closed and was willing to make amends if possible. The stage was now set for the final act in her successful little intrigue. She wrote again to both men. To Peel she suggested that he find some opportunity in Parliament of adding to his comments of three years before and assured him that such a gesture would not be wasted; to Cobden she predicted some move on Peel's part to which he should be ready to respond.

The occasion was not long in coming. Late in February Bright and Roebuck attacked Ferrand in the House of Commons for slandering George Wilson, and Disraeli added to the mischief by defending Ferrand on the grounds that worse things had been imputed to the leaders of the league three years before by none other than the prime minister. That gave Peel the opportunity he was looking for.[20] "I am sorry certainly," he said, "that the hon. Member for Shrewsbury has thought fit to revive the subject, or, at least, I should have been so if his reference to it had not given me an opportunity of fully and unequivocally withdrawing an imputation on the hon. Member for Stockport, which was thrown out in the heat of debate under an erroneous impression of his meaning."

Cobden rose immediately to reply in kind: "[He] took the present ample and distinct disavowal of the right hon. Gentleman as entirely satisfactory . . . [and] was glad the right hon. Baronet had made it; for it had given him an opportunity quite as pleasant to his feelings of stating that he too felt regret for the terms in which he had alluded to the right hon. Baronet." That put the incident to rest, and late that night an exhausted Cobden wrote a warm letter of thanks to Harriet Martineau. By the same post she also received from Peel an autographed copy of the *Times* containing the report of their parliamentary exchange.

The last stage of Martineau's little plot had not perhaps been necessary. By that time Cobden was probably ready to respond unprompted to any overture from Peel. Since Cobden's remarks in Stockport, after all, Peel had put his own political future at risk by adopting the substance of league policy. Only the 1843 incident remained to diminish Cobden's growing conviction that Peel towered above all his political contemporaries. Once that was out of the way, Cobden was free unambiguously to look to Peel as the man who best embodied the "idea of the age," at least as Cobden interpreted it. "Peel ought to be the leader of the middle class," he commented to Combe in March, "and I am not sure that he is not destined to be so before the end of his career."[21] Two days before the final vote on

Peel's bill in the House of Lords, Cobden acted to give Peel—and destiny—a push in the right direction; in one of the most extraordinary letters in the annals of nineteenth-century politics, he urged Peel to use his unique position to recast the political face of the country.

Specifically, he proposed that Peel seek a dissolution of Parliament, using as a justification the advisability of what amounted to a referendum on Peel's new course. This, Cobden believed, would complete the breakup of the old party system, already under way as a result of Peel's adoption of repeal, and lead to the creation of a coalition of Peelites, Liberals, Radicals, and moderate Whigs, all of them committed to the implementation of the economic reforms implicit in repeal. "You, and no other," he advised Peel, could form and lead a party and a government based on these principles, for "You embody in your own person the idea of the age."[22] Not even the Whigs in 1832 had possessed that degree of power or with it, as Cobden reminded Peel, that degree of responsibility. "Are you justified toward the Queen, the people, and the great questions of our generation, in abandoning this grand and glorious position?" he asked the prime minister. "Will you yourself stand the test of an impartial historian?"

Hoping to anticipate Peel's objections, Cobden claimed that most of the opposition would eagerly transfer its allegiance to Peel. The Whigs by comparison were bankrupt: "the leaders of the Opposition personate no idea." Nor, Cobden claimed, would Peel be forced to associate himself with measures that he did not support, such as parliamentary reform; "questions of organic reform have no vitality in the country, nor are they likely to have any force in the House until your work is done." There was indeed only one issue, Peel's issue: "The Condition of England Question—there is your mission!" As to any sense of obligation Peel might feel toward his old followers, that, Cobden believed, was no longer appropriate. The old-line Tories had turned on Peel long before he turned on them, and in any case the best of the landed classes would go with him. That the social base of Peel's power would nonetheless be changed, Cobden did not deny: "Do you shrink from governing through the bona fide representatives of the middle class? Look at the facts, and can the country be otherwise ruled at all? There must be an end of the juggle of parties, the mere representatives of traditions, and some man must of necessity rule the State through its governing class. The Reform Bill decreed it; the passing of the Corn Bill has realised it."

In asking—indeed tempting—Peel to preside over the political revolution he had always sought in conjunction with repeal, Cobden, for all his enthusiasm, was not naive. He knew his former adversary well enough to recognize that Peel was a conservative out of conviction; but Cobden not unreasonably hoped that the bitter experience of presiding over the Tory party might have altered Peel's view of how best to effect his principles. Peel, however, was not to be drawn. In his reply to Cobden, written in the House of Commons during the debate on the Irish coercion bill, which was to bring about his fall the next day, Peel avoided following Cobden into the realm of political speculation. It was a friendly letter, so far as it went, but it kept carefully to immediate practical considerations. A dissolution was not advisable, he argued. It had proved unnecessary as a means of obtaining repeal. It might not result in the kind of parliamentary majority Cobden anticipated, and even if it did, such a majority, elected in the heat of a political crisis, might prove an uncertain basis for stable government. Only once did Peel address himself to the heart of Cobden's argument, and then only to circumscribe it: "If you say that I individually at this moment embody or personify an idea, be it so. Then I must be very careful that . . . I do not sully that which I represent by warranting the suspicion even, that I am using the power it confers for any personal object."[23]

Peel closed his letter with an apology. Because he had written it in the House during a debate, he noted, "I may therefore have very imperfectly explained my views and feelings." In fact, nothing could have been clearer. Never openly stated but implicit in every sentence was a view of the implications of repeal directly opposed to Cobden's. Where Cobden saw repeal as a beginning, Peel viewed it as an end. Where Cobden hoped to maximize its effects, Peel sought to contain them. Where Cobden hoped that repeal would be the occasion of a better, because more fundamental, version of the reform bill crisis, Peel sought to abolish the Corn Laws as a means of averting such a crisis. Where Cobden hoped to destroy the political power of the landed aristocracy, Peel sought to preserve it. Where Cobden envisioned repeal as likely to produce "a mixed progressive party,"[24] Peel wished to disturb the existing political landscape as little as possible. In this sense Peel's means of passing repeal represented a defeat for Cobden, whose ulterior motives would have been better served by a protectionist revolt or House of Lords veto and the political crisis that would inevitably have followed. Which leaves us to wonder: had Cobden known more of Peel's thinking at the beginning of 1846 and had he himself been in better health and free from financial anxieties, would he have courted a crisis rather than acting as Peel's unofficial political lieutenant?

Possibly so, but probably not. In the first place, circumstances were against it. Although it was widely believed that the only alternative to repeal under Peel's auspices was repeal by a Liberal government dominated by Cobden and the radicals, that prospect served to strengthen not so much Cobden's influence as Peel's ability to win over conservatives who might otherwise have opposed him, including the Duke of Wellington. Cobden, indeed, had little room for maneuver. Once Peel and Russell had adopted repeal and a repeal bill was before Parliament, the league had no choice but to support it. Anything less could only have split the movement, as Cobden recognized. Quite apart from such practical considerations, however, Cobden's views of the purpose of the anti–Corn Law movement had altered significantly in its later years. As the economic crisis in which the league had been born receded and the league, alone among early nineteenth-century popular agitations, learned to survive in prosperous times, Cobden was less and less inclined to see repeal as necessarily or even preferably dependent on some great upheaval in national life. "I really hardly regret . . . that the agitation has lasted so long," he told an audience at Covent Garden in the summer of 1845:

> If we had carried the repeal of the Corn Laws by a multitudinous shout in 1839, 1840, and 1841, it would have been something like yielding to brute force and clamor; but now, besides the advantage of repealing the Corn Laws—our agitation will have been attended with many other advantages . . . We have taught the farmers, I trust, to begin to think for themselves; we have made landlords and farmers think of improving their lands; we have taught the middle classes, I hope, that they have a moral power . . . and a power of applying it as great as the monopolists . . . but I hope in addition that we have set an example of truth to the working classes, showing them that these questions can be carried by moral means.[25]

These were not simply the words of a popular leader attempting to put the best possible interpretation on the history of a six-year-old movement that had not yet achieved its object. Nor were his sentiments as idealistic as they sounded. Although Cobden was never inclined to belittle the power of ideas, he much preferred ideas backed by power. That is precisely what the league had lacked throughout the greater part of its existence, which is why he usually assumed that some catalytic event—a crop failure or a new economic depression—would be necessary to bring about repeal. But by the summer of 1845 this was no longer true. In discovering the forty-shilling freehold, Cobden believed that he had discovered the means of translating middle-class opinion directly into political power. Not only did that vindicate the league's earlier concentration on propaganda, which at times had seemed frustratingly irrelevant, but it also served to reduce the importance of the circumstances and immediate consequences of repeal itself. The work the league had begun, although not the league itself, could survive repeal.

Viewed in this light, the repeal of the Corn Laws in 1846 came at an awkward time. The league was not yet ready to flex its new political muscles; the registration and freehold purchase campaigns in the counties had only just begun and were aimed at an election that most people assumed would not be held until 1847. The league could not force the issue of the Corn Laws to the forefront; as Cobden had so often predicted, that impetus was the result of "some incident of an extraneous nature," in this case the harvest of 1845. Nor could the league claim credit for the adoption of repeal as the official policy of both major parties; that was the work of Russell and Peel. Cobden was acutely conscious of all this in 1846, and to say that the league did not carry repeal is to deny a claim he never made. When, as he often did in later years, he talked of the league's having carried repeal, he did not mean that it had done so directly. Rather, he believed that the league had created the conditions that made repeal inevitable under certain circumstances.

The task he had set for the league in its early days, that of "preparing the public mind," had been accomplished. By keeping the issue alive for seven years and gradually undermining the theoretical foundations of protection, the league had altered the balance of opinion. The league had not converted Peel or Russell or the nation at large, but it had shifted the weight of doubt from repeal to protectionism and the heavy burden of being considered a narrow special interest from the league to the landed interest. For political reasons, the claims of that interest could not be ignored and were generally tolerated, at least in good times. The league did not, even in 1846, yet have the power to do very much about that. But once the claims of the landed interest were seen as coming into conflict with those of the mass of the population, as happened late in 1845, the Corn Laws were finished; the public would not quietly have accepted their continuance. That Cobden believed, with good reason, was the work of the league.

Had that been all, Cobden would have been less sanguine about the fact that the issue was settled on Peel's terms. Just as he was aware that the league by itself had not been able to force the issue, so he did not make the mistake of assuming that repeal would automatically usher in a new era politically. He was therefore greatly encouraged when the process of the passage of repeal appeared to demonstrate something more lasting than the extent—and limits—of the influence the league had gained; it also seemed to provide evidence for his belief that the potential power of the free trade movement was greater than anything the league had yet achieved. In the end, he believed, it was the threat of league penetration of the counties that had allowed Peel's bill to pass smoothly through the protectionist majorities in both houses of Parliament. From their point of view, it was preferable to accept repeal on Peel's terms and hope that the league's political machine would die away than risk political immolation in the counties, which would end in their having to accept repeal—and much besides—on league terms. Whether Cobden was correct or not in this assessment of the motives of the landed interest, the circumstantial evidence appeared to support him. The leaders of the Conservative party had become genuinely alarmed at the league's progress in the counties, and only two days after the introduction of Peel's bill their one remaining hope of thwarting the freehold movement, a challenge to its legality, had been struck down by the Court of Appeals.

To Cobden this was almost as important a victory as repeal itself, for it secured the fruits of repeal, to which, even before repeal was passed, he had begun to turn his attention. Throughout the first half of 1846 he tended, with growing impatience, to look to the time beyond repeal. Politically and personally, he was anxious to move on, and although his personal prospects seemed uncertain, politically he grew increasingly optimistic. The freehold movement would continue in the service of other causes, for the productive classes had been awakened, largely by the league, to their real interests. And although Peel had declined the opportunity to govern through the representatives of the middle class, he might yet be compelled to do so, since, as Cobden had asked him, "can the country be otherwise ruled at all?" In 1846, as ten years earlier, Cobden was sure of the answer, but in 1846 he believed the time had finally come.

PART III

Schoolmaster
1846–1856

CHAPTER 14

Transitions

Personally as well as politically, Cobden led a curiously suspended life during the nine months preceding the repeal of the Corn Laws. Powerless to do anything substantive to retrieve his financial condition until the political crisis was past, he could also only marginally influence the development of that crisis. In the most important matters affecting his future, he could do little more than weigh alternatives and wait; planning was all but impossible. Looking ahead to the time beyond repeal, only one thing was clear: his health and his finances required that he drop out of public life for a time. He had decided to leave England for a rest in warmer climes, perhaps Egypt or the Near East. Beyond that nothing was certain. In the early months of 1846 he was inclined to believe that his entire life would have to be changed, and he considered retiring permanently from politics in order to devote himself to rebuilding his family fortunes. Indeed he often felt he had no right to do anything else.

"I am in a false position," he wrote in March to one of the friends who had bailed him out six months before, "and every day increases its difficulty. My prominent position before the world leads the public to expect that I shall take a leading part in future political affairs, for which I do not feel in health or spirits to be equal, and which private considerations render altogether impossible."[1] To those who did not yet know the full story, he pleaded his health, his growing distaste for politics, and, not very convincingly, his dispensability. "The truth is," he told George Combe, "I have gradually and unexpectedly been forced upwards, by the accident of my position in connection with a great principle . . . Besides . . . I am less and less in love with what is generally called political life, and am not sure I could play a successful part as a general politician."[2]

But the common theme of all his letters was his need to resume his family ties. "During the last five years," he explained, again to Combe, "so much have I been involved in the vortex of public agitation, that I have almost forgotten my own identity and completely lost sight of the comforts and interests of my wife and children." Or as he put it more unguardedly to another correspondent: "My only boy is five years old. At the age of four he did not positively know me as his father, so incessantly was I upon the tramp."[3]

As the time for hard decisions grew nearer, however, Cobden backed away from this stark view of the alternatives open to him. The idea of returning to business full time was intolerable to him and, as he surely expected, to many of his friends, who begged him to stay on in public life after a rest in much the same terms he had used in urging Peel to take his case to the people. "You belong to the nation," Joseph Parkes wrote, "and you cannot return to the treadmill of a Manchester manufacturer."[4] More concretely, many of these same friends were busily engaged in providing him with an alternative in the form of a large sum of money to be given as a testimonial for his efforts on behalf of free trade. Cobden was uncomfortable with this project at first. Concerned that other leaguers might resent his being singled out for reward, he also feared public embarrassment, first from the revelation of his financial plight and subsequently from the probability that the funds raised would not be sufficient. Yet, given his circumstances, he dared not refuse the offer; he only asked that announcement of the testimonial be delayed until he was safely away from Parliament. As the months passed and the fund mounted to a respectable £75,000 and more, Cobden became resigned, if never entirely reconciled, to the need for the testimonial. Whatever it may have cost him in pride, it did at least give him some options, which he began to exercise even before the passage of repeal.

All talk of permanently retiring from public life ceased, and sometime in the spring his friends, led apparently by Coppock, the Liberal election agent of Stockport, persuaded him to keep his seat in Parliament. For the moment, however, his short-run plans remained unchanged. After the fall of Peel's government, Cobden left for Manchester, where he officiated at the dissolution of the league on 2 July. There had been talk of keeping it going until repeal went into effect three years later, but (as Cobden had predicted) that proved impractical. His last duties to the league performed, Cobden retreated to Wales for a month's rest with his wife's family prior to going abroad. But even at the moment of release his mind was full of new schemes. The morning of his first full day in Wales, he wrote to Henry Ashworth to announce a change in his travel plans:

> I have given up all ideas of burying myself in Egypt or Italy. I am going on a private agitating tour through the continent of Europe. The other day I got an intimation from Sir Roderick Murchison, the geologist—a friend and confidant of the Emperor of Russia—that I should have great influence with him if I went to St. Petersburg. Today I get a letter from the Mayor of Bordeaux . . . conveying a suggestion . . . that I should . . . visit the King of the French at his Chateau of Eu, where he would be glad to receive me between the 4th and 14th of August. I have had similar hints respecting Madrid, Vienna and Berlin. Well, I will, with God's assistance, during the next twelvemonth visit all the large states of Europe, see their potentates or statesmen, and endeavor to enforce those truths which have been irresistible at home.[5]

Looking still further ahead, he wrote on the same day to an ally from an earlier agitation, James Simpson: "Education is the only public matter upon which I should be disposed to put on my armour for another 'seven years war.' "[6] Not that Cobden was contemplating another round of agitation; his letter to Simpson involved a moral and long-term, not immediate and practical, commitment to the education movement. Even so, like his letter to Ashworth, it betrayed a restlessness that troubled Cobden. The contradiction between these new plans and his earlier resolution to retire from public life at least for a time was too obvious to be ignored. As he said to Paulton, the first league lecturer, in another letter written that morning:

> I am going into the wilderness to pray for a return to the taste I once possessed for nature and the simple quiet life . . . I feel how much I have lost in winning public fame. The rough tempest has spoilt me for the quiet haven . . . On Thursday I thought as I went to the meeting [to dissolve the league], that I should next day be a happy and quiet man. Next day brings me a suggestion . . . that if instead of going to Italy and Egypt, I would take a trip to St. Petersburg, I could exercise an important influence upon the mind of Nicholas. Here I am at Llangollen, blind to the loveliness of nature, and only eager to be on the road to Russia, taking Madrid, Vienna, Berlin and Paris by the way! Let me see

my boy tomorrow, who waits my coming at Machynlleth, and if he do not wean me, I am quite gone past recovery.[7]

A few days with his family in Wales served, apparently, to ease Cobden's mind, but not his determination to pursue his plans. From the instant the journey to Russia was suggested, he was certain that this was the right thing to do. It was the logical next step beyond the repeal campaign, for it would put the achievements of the league in the wider context of his work stretching back to the economic internationalism of his early pamphlets. Even Cobden had often lost sight of these goals during seven years of agitation; here was an opportunity to correct the balance and begin the process of educating people to the full meaning of repeal, as it touched on political change, economic policy, and relations between peoples. Already, in the final phase of the agitation, Cobden had returned to these wider concerns. To Peel on the eve of repeal he had suggested nothing less than a revolution in domestic politics; to league audiences he presented a vision of the promise of free trade in promoting peace. "I have been accused of looking too much to material interests," he told a meeting in Manchester six months before the passage of repeal:

> [Yet] I believe that the physical gain will be the smallest gain to humanity from the success of this principle. I look further; I see in the free trade principle that which shall act on the moral world as the principle of gravitation in the universe,—drawing men together, thrusting aside the antagonism of race, and creed, and language, and uniting us in the bonds of eternal peace. I have looked even further . . . I believe the effect will be to change the face of the world, so as to introduce a system of government entirely distinct from that which now prevails. I believe the desire and the motive for large and mighty empires, for gigantic armies and great navies . . . will die away; I believe that such things will cease to be necessary, or to be used, when man becomes one family, and freely exchanges the fruits of his labor with his brother man.[8]

The unsolicited invitations from Russia and France opened up an unexpected and unique opportunity to begin the process of realizing these goals. It was a chance Cobden dared not turn down; to travel for no better purpose than to rest was now unthinkable. "Why should I rust in inactivity?" he asked Ashworth. "If the public spirit of my countrymen affords me the means of travelling as their missionary, I will be the first ambassador from the People of this country to the nations of the continent." In any case, he added characteristically, "I am impelled to this step by an instinctive emotion such as has never deceived me."⁹

In other respects as well, a missionary tour of the continent was more to his taste than anything he could do at home. Already he was being importuned by well-meaning friends and lesser agitators for help in various worthy causes. Furthermore, the postrepeal period was bound to be one of political intrigue and uncertainty. Cobden wanted no part of either, and a long journey to the capitals of Europe provided an honorable escape from both. Indeed, he was almost as pleased with what he was getting away from as with what he was setting out to do. "Is it likely," he wrote playfully to Joseph Parkes,

> that I should turn my thoughts from the charms of nature to the intrigues of a party man—from waterfalls, lakes and wooded mountains to your den in George St., or the fetid lobbies of the House? No— I scarcely condescend to recognise the existence of such blots on the face of creation! I "alliterate" you, as Mrs. Malaprop would say, from my memory. Or if you do sometimes flit across my mind's eye, it is in the shape of a troubled spirit, haunting the Reform Club at midnight, holding converse with certain self sufficient elves, or flitting to and fro in cabs, and lingering about the purlieus of the Treasury, chuckling over the ghost of Toryism, tormenting your good wife, the only good belonging to you, by keeping her from dinner, and going to bed at two o'clock with cold feet, all your blood having flowed to that center of Whiggery your heart! Confess—is not this a true picture of Joseph Parkes, during a change of ministry, painted by Richard Cobden, late an agitator, now of Llangollen.¹⁰

If nothing else, Cobden's escape to the quiet of Wales had restored his sense of humor, but Wales was not, as it turned out, far enough from Manchester to ensure him against the political pressures he was so anxious to avoid. One of the sitting members for Manchester had announced his intention of retiring, and in the search for a replacement Cobden's name inevitably was at or near the top of everyone's list of potential reform candidates. Indeed, he could have had the nomination for the asking, and his candidacy would undoubtedly have served to heal the old divisions among the city's Liberals, divisions that had reopened during the last year of the anti–Corn Law agitation. At the annual general meeting of the Manchester Chamber of Commerce in 1845, the leaguers had instigated a purge of one of the directors of the chamber, reminiscent of the purge of 1839 but even more overtly political in intent. The victim in this case, although himself a free trader, had chaired the committee of the protectionist candidate in the recent South Lancashire by-election. Nothing had followed from the 1839 purge, but in 1845 the minority broke away to form a rival body, the Manchester Commercial Association. Most of its members were Conservatives but there were a few prominent moderate Liberals, backed by the *Guardian* and led by Cobden's colleague in the education and incorporation campaigns, William Nield.

Although Cobden had supported the purge, he had not taken a public role in it, as he had in 1839. Hence Liberals on both sides of the issue tended to look to him as a unifying force, and as much because of this as because of his prestige as the leader of the league, the pressure on him to run as the Liberal candidate in Manchester was intense. A few years earlier—or later—in his career he might have succumbed, but in 1845 and 1846 he appears never to have seriously considered it. When the possibility of a vacancy in Manchester first arose, he was on the verge of bankruptcy and contemplating retiring from politics. For him to have taken on the demanding constituency of Manchester would have been unthinkable; quiet and pliant Stockport was much more to his taste, even assuming that he would stay in Parliament at all. All the same, he found it difficult to turn his Manchester friends down flat; although he made his preference clear, he would not say no in unequivocal terms. Instead, largely to relieve pressure on himself, he suggested to his supporters that they recruit Bright, and to Bright that he seek the nomination. For his part, Bright was eager for the honor and began to pursue it vigorously as soon as he was satisfied that Cobden did not want it. To many of the moderate Liberals of Manchester, however, Bright was unacceptable; his manner as much as his ideas was far too radical. Thus, his potential candidacy, rather than healing the breach among local reformers, threatened to widen it further, and the pressure on Cobden was redoubled.

It reached its peak in the summer of 1846, while Cobden was in Wales, and by late July he was sick of the whole business. He admitted to Coppock that he might be the stronger candidate but insisted that Bright had as good a claim as he did to represent Manchester and dismissed much of his own support as born of misguided antipathy to

Bright. With his mind increasingly on his European plans, his determination not to leave Stockport for Manchester was greater than ever, and he asked Coppock and Wilson to do what they could to deter his supporters. "Both on Bright's account and my own," he told Coppock, "I should regret being placed in a situation to be in a manner forced to accept the seat."[11] Bright was equally frustrated, but his irritation was directed almost as much at Cobden as at the more tepid Liberals of Manchester. Late in July he wrote to Cobden, offering to step aside if Cobden wanted the seat, reminding him that it was he who had first suggested Bright seek the nomination and, whatever the case, urging him to make his position clear. The implication that Cobden might be playing a political waiting game was as clear as Bright's ambition to win the nomination. That, at any rate, was how Cobden read the letter, and in a frosty reply he suggested that his earlier letter to Coppock (which had not been intended for Bright's eyes) should suffice to allay any doubts Bright might have. A few days later Bright and Cobden met and cleared up most of their misunderstanding—most, but apparently not all, for shortly thereafter Cobden asked Coppock to show the letter Cobden had written him to Bright.

Cobden's supporters in Manchester proved equally difficult to convince. Despite the behind-the-scenes influence of Coppock and Wilson and a discouraging (but still not unambiguous) response to a delegation from the Manchester Reform Association, the leaders of the association continued to hope he might change his mind or accept a draft. Even after Cobden left England, they did not give up. A petition calling on him to run and signed by fifteen of the city's most influential Liberals followed him to France, and only an unmistakably negative reply finally put the matter to rest. At long last Bright had a clear field, and he won the nomination with ease, although not with the support of the *Guardian*, Nield, and many other moderate Liberals. In the personal relationship between Cobden and Bright, however, this incident marked a low ebb, and it was some time before the easy intimacy of their friendship during the league years was restored.

Four months later, for example, Bright sent to Cobden, then in Spain, a long account of political doings in Manchester. Bright was no longer worried about the nomination; he had that. But he was concerned about the lack of Whig-Liberal support and the persistent rumors in Manchester concerning Cobden's role in the whole business. The *Guardian* claimed that Cobden's earlier decision not to run had changed after the success of the testimonial, that he had been prepared to accept the nomination in the summer of 1846, and that Bright had pressed him to keep to their earlier agreement. Although far from the truth, this account had enough of the truth in it (and was close enough to Bright's own suspicions in July) that Bright asked Cobden "to write Wilson something . . . exonerating me from the foul charges endeavored to be brought against me and expressing your opinion of the propriety of the whole Liberal Party supporting me."[12] Cobden refused, and rather curtly, on the grounds that interference in the politics of Manchester from such a distance would be inappropriate and would not, in any case, still the gossip.

It is easy, in assessing responsibility for this strain in their relationship, to picture Bright as the villain (as Donald Read has done).[13] In his impatience to gain the nomination in Manchester, Bright was insensitive to Cobden's feelings and misread Cobden's actions. But Cobden was hardly less at fault. If Bright had paid too much attention to political developments in Manchester, Cobden had paid too little; he had ignored the problem when it arose and delayed too long in handling it. He had, moreover, confused the issue by suggesting a Bright candidacy in the first place and then not clearly backing out himself. Had he taken a firm stand at the outset, there would have been no room for misunderstanding by Cobden's supporters in Manchester or by Bright, who felt quite as aggrieved as Cobden.

Unfortunately for their relationship at this time, Cobden and Bright had different views of how best to capitalize on the repeal of the Corn Laws. Both wished to take maximum advantage of their newfound prestige, but whereas Bright looked primarily to the political arena at home, Cobden was relatively indifferent to that (at least after his abortive overture to Peel), as compared with the opportunity he saw to influence international economic relations. The strain in their relationship in 1846, which seems at first sight to have been the product of misunderstanding, in fact reflected a wide divergence of views on the significance of the free trade movement. This did not affect the substance of their friendship or alter their habit of constant communication. But over the next few years they disagreed almost as often as they agreed on their priorities in public life.

Cobden's immediate priority was his missionary tour of Europe. During the month between his decision to undertake the project and his departure for France in August, it assumed formidable proportions. In the event, he was absent from England for fourteen months and traversed Europe from Andalusia to the Volga basin. After three weeks in Paris, he and Kate traveled south with the autumn to Spain, where they spent almost three months. Then, by way of the Mediterranean coast of France, they went to Italy at the beginning of the new year and stayed until well into June. With the coming of summer weather, they traveled north through Austria and Saxony to Prussia. From Berlin, Kate went home, while he journeyed east for a month-long visit to Russia. He sailed for home in September, stopping at the Hanseatic ports of northern Germany, and arrived back in England in October 1847.

Little remained of his original plans to travel for his health and to escape the pressures of public life. Virtually everywhere he went, he was wined and dined, interviewed and written up, called upon, expected to return calls, and granted audiences. Even in Rome, where they stayed longest and hoped to have a good deal of time to themselves, there was no escape. Yet, although he found the many banquets in his honor a bit trying, especially in Italy, he generally enjoyed the fuss. For him, if not for his hosts, after all, these occasions were more social than political. After seven years at the head of the league he could relish the excitement of agitation without having to carry any of the responsibility. Quite apart from the doors that were now open to him, simply to travel as a celebrity was a gratifying experience.

Between engagements the Cobdens did some more or less private sightseeing and managed to work in a few brief periods of undisturbed rest. They spent nearly three weeks by the Mediterranean at Nice and Genoa, and still more time in the company of mountains at Pau in the French Pyrenees. Cobden avoided popular festivals, however, and, disliking crowds, did not enjoy those he was caught up in. He was revolted by bullfighting and objected particularly to the indulgent attitude of the Spanish church toward it (a point he later raised in his audience with the pope). Much of their time in Rome coincided with carnival, which he thought a tiresome affair, since it appeared to consist primarily of people pelting one another with sugar plums. He was impressed with the amiability of the revelers, however. "It is quite certain," he noted, "that a carnival in England would not pass over so peaceably as here—people would begin with sugar plums and go on to apples and oranges and then proceed to potatoes and probably end with stones."[14] Only Venice at her most beguiling could break down his aversion to being caught up in a celebratory throng. After a dinner in his honor,

> the party entered their gondolas . . . and, accompanied by the excellent band of musicians which had played during the dinner, we proceeded in procession down the Grand Canal to the Rialto bridge. The music and the gay liveries of some of our boatmen soon attracted a great number of gondolas—the sight and sound also brought every body out on their balconies. As we returned, the moon which had risen gave a fresh charm to the picturesque scene, which was sufficiently romantic to excite poetical emotions even in the mind of a political economist.[15]

Although he had little use for local color, Cobden was fascinated by local customs, especially the methods of farming and the patterns of landholding. Even in areas of great natural beauty, he paid as close attention to these mundane matters as to the look of the landscape itself. This same concern for the practical colored his response to art and architecture. Although impressed, indeed overwhelmed, by the acres of ancient sculpture in the Vatican museum, he was clearly more interested in the everyday items from Pompeii on display in Naples. He was, however, inclined to fault the greater works of ancient Rome, as much on moral as on practical grounds. "These stately and graceful aqueducts," he noted after passing through the Roman Campagna, "are nearly the only ruins which excite feelings of regret, being perhaps the sole buildings which do not merit destruction by the crimes, the folly, and the injustice which attended their construction, or the purposes to which they were devoted."[16]

As for more recent works, Cobden, perhaps predictably, found the interior of St. Peter's as well as much of Spanish architecture too busy for his taste, and he longed for the simple solemnity of York Minster. But he was not merely the archetypal provincial Englishman abroad. The entries in his travel diary on art were often self-conscious and unduly deferential, but when he spoke for himself, his observations were lively and refreshingly iconoclastic. He regarded the Laocoon as the finest thing in the Vatican museum but thought the Apollo Belvedere forbiddingly cold. As to the great masters of the high Renaissance, Cobden approached them with more respect than enthusiasm. Although he admired the execution of Raphael's frescoes in the

Vatican, he was disappointed by what he felt was their too limited emotional range. He confessed to being so irritated by the discomfort involved in viewing the ceiling of the Sistine chapel that it was almost impossible to appreciate the paintings. Indeed, to his surprise, he was disappointed with most of Michelangelo's work in Rome. That, he acknowledged, was a matter of taste, but he was not timid about deflating a reputation he thought overblown. After seeing the tomb of Maria Christina in the Augustinerkircke in Vienna, he judged, correctly, that Canova would never again be as highly regarded as he was during his lifetime. If high classicism of whatever century left him a bit cold, Hellenistic and Baroque art almost never failed to move him. He discovered Murillo in Madrid, immediately adopted him as his favorite painter, and had a copy made of the artist's Moses Striking the Rock in Seville. He was equally drawn to a number of Greek and Roman sculptures and commissioned a copy of one of these as well, a head of Demosthenes in the Vatican museum.

Although Cobden's comments on art, and on places of great natural beauty for that matter, were sometimes stilted, the same was never true of his day-to-day record of their travels. As in his earlier trips abroad, he wrote well-observed accounts of the countryside through which they traveled, the towns they visited, the people they met. And although he indulged in stereotypes—the austere Spaniard, the facetious Frenchman, the voluble Italian, the stolid German, the fatalistic Russian—he did so with humor and an awareness that individuals tend to violate categories. He was particularly fascinated by Russia, for which nothing in his earlier experience of Europe had prepared him. He was surprised by the almost oriental character of Moscow and hypnotized by the vast monotony of the Russian plain. He interviewed prisoners on their way from Moscow to Siberia, and at Nishni Novgorod, the easternmost point of his journey, merchants in a caravan from Bokhara. The exotic character of the country aside, what impressed him most about Russia was its backwardness. He met many competent and educated men in and out of government but sensed that they formed a thin layer at the top of a too widely dispersed, undeveloped, priest-ridden, and often corrupt society. Firsthand experience of the country, far from changing his earlier views, only served to confirm them. He still regarded Russia, for all its faults, as an indispensable force for modernization on the outer fringes of European civilization, but he was more than ever convinced that it posed no threat to that civilization. Even if it possessed the will, which he doubted, it lacked the ability to do so.

There were other echoes of familiar themes from his early travels and writings in the travel diaries of 1846–47. He commented frequently on the advantages of peasant proprietorship over large-scale landholding and was delighted whenever anyone he met criticized English land law. He recorded, without comment, some savage criticisms of the Poles as compared with the Russians. Even his old weakness for enlightened autocratic government reappeared. When the Belgian minister to Prussia informed him that the Belgian Parliament was likely to vote new and higher tariffs, Cobden was not surprised, for, he noted, "the enlightened ministers of Prussia are overruled by the clamors of the chambers of Wurtemberg, Bavaria, and Baden, the majorities of which are protectionist."[17] As the Belgian minister said and Cobden quoted with added emphasis, "An absolute government may represent an idea, but elective legislatures represent interests."

Cobden's main concern was, of course, free trade. It provided the standard by which he judged everything else, and he spent much of his time collecting evidence of the evils and anomalies of protectionism. In Germany, for example, he argued that the agricultural economy and exports of the Baltic provinces had been sacrificed to the protection of Rhineland interests. Almost everywhere he encountered similar contradictions, and not a few absurdities as well. Even in the midst of nature at her most sublime, at the Cirque du Gavarnie in the Pyrenees, the alert free trader "saw with my glass a dozen smugglers wending their way a thousand feet above us loaded with sacks full of goods from Spain."[18] But he was especially taken with the merchants of Nice, who imported woollens made cheap by an export bounty from France and then smuggled them back into France for a handsome profit. On the positive side, he singled out Tuscany, a pioneer among the nations of Europe in applying the doctrines of free trade.

Although the themes and even the language of his travel diaries had changed little over a decade, his purpose and his status as a traveler had. No longer merely an observer, he had access to the governments of Europe and, so he hoped, the ability to influence their policies. Along the way, he had audiences with the kings of Naples and Piedmont, of France and Prussia, and with Pope Pius IX, as well as with leading ministers of all the states he visited. He was not much impressed with most of these men, especially the rulers. He felt most comfortable in the comparatively informal Prussian court, where intellectuals were welcome and the king, although "said to be . . . impulsive and not practical," had "a thoroughly good natured, unaffected German face."[19] Cobden's opinion of Louis Phillipe was more typical: "he is a clever actor, and perhaps that is all we can say of the ablest sovereigns of this or any other country."[20] Cobden had not expected much else in any case; rather, he looked to their ministers and bureaucrats, especially the younger ones or those responsible for trade or finance, many of whom did indeed appear to share his views. Not so the older generation, including most of the first ministers. With few exceptions they seemed appallingly ignorant on economic questions and, as he said of Count Nesselrode, adept only "at finesse and diplomacy."[21] Metternich was the supreme example. "His conversation is more subtle than profound," Cobden observed:

> He talks incessantly, perhaps in order to choose his own topics . . . He seems to speak on the defensive, like a man conscious that public opinion in Europe was not favorable to his policy . . . He is probably the last of those state physicians who, looking only to the symptoms of a nation, content themselves with superficial remedies from day to day, and never attempt to probe beneath the surface, to discover the source of the evils which afflict the social system. This order of statesmen will pass away with him, because too much light has been shed upon the laboratory of governments, to allow them to impose upon mankind with the old formulas.[22]

That was written in July 1847; nine months later Metternich fled to England from revolutionary Vienna. Indeed, a good proportion of the kings and ministers Cobden met during his year abroad were swept from power at least temporarily by the revolutions of 1848. Few would have guessed in the summer of 1847 that the passing of the old guard would come so soon or so dramatically, but Cobden did meet a few of the men of 1848 on his travels and was well aware of the unrest on the continent—and was quite prepared to take full advantage of it—when he crossed the channel in 1846. His mission was free trade, not liberalism or nationalism, and he scrupulously avoided public comments on these questions. To have done otherwise would have alienated the governments he hoped to influence. All the same, there was no question where his sympathies lay. For all his fondness for enlightened autocracies, he knew perfectly well that most of the autocracies of Europe were not especially enlightened. At one point, citing Peter the Great, Cromwell, Frederick the Great, Louis XIV, Napoleon, and Mehmet Ali, he remarked that "warriors and despots are generally bad economists, and that they instinctively carry their ideas of force and violence into the civil policies of their governments. Free trade," he concluded, "is a principle which recognizes the paramount importance of individual action."[23]

He was, he believed, uniquely placed to take that message to the governments of Europe, when they would listen, and beyond that to attempt to awaken the middle classes of the continent to an awareness of their own economic interests. What he had done for Manchester and Birmingham he hoped to do for Milan and Berlin, and when he left England he was optimistic about his chances. "I feel," he told Henry Ashworth, "that I could succeed in making out a stronger case for the prohibitive nations of Europe to compel them to adopt a freer system, than I had here to overturn our protective policy."[24] For one thing, most of the states of Europe were self-sufficient in food; they did not have a landed class interested in protection. As to the middle classes, in countries where industry and trade were often still subject to a maze of internal tolls, tariffs, and regulations, he hoped that they might be peculiarly receptive to the doctrines of Adam Smith.

Not that Cobden was blind to the obstacles in his path. He knew his motives might be questioned. As an Englishman he was open to the accusation that he sought to extend free trade as a means of extending English domination of the world economy. He hoped that his work in winning the repeal of the Corn Laws against the wishes of the English governing class might help allay such fears, but he remained cautious. Even before leaving England he recognized that "it is necessary that my design should not be made public, for that would create suspicion abroad," and during the trip he continually emphasized that he spoke as an individual, free of official ties. The warmth with which he was generally received was reassuring, but he knew that this did not necessarily indicate any great degree of trust, let alone of support for his views. He might travel as an apostle of free trade, but he was greeted, as often as not, as a representative of English radical liberalism or simply as offering an excuse to hold a political meeting thinly disguised as a banquet in his honor. Occasionally the disguise wore very thin indeed, as when an after-dinner speaker, carried away by wine or enthusiasm, stumbled into the forbidden topics of nationalism or political reform. Cobden did not mind being used in this manner; as he told George Combe, "the Italian Liberals have seized upon my presence as an excuse for holding a meeting on a public question . . . often for the first time. They consider this a step gained, and so it is."[25] But while he recognized that his presence was not the reason for the popularity of these banquets, it was the occasion for them, and if he was being used, he in turn could use them for his purposes. It seemed a fair enough trade at the time.

What Cobden seems not to have realized fully, however, was that he and many of his middle-class European hosts were separated from one another by something more than their differing orders of priority. He accepted that questions of national self-determination and constitutional government were bound to take precedence in central and southern Europe. But Cobden himself was relatively indifferent to the form as compared with the economic policies of government, and as an internationalist and a free trader he was suspicious of nationalism. As far as he was concerned, tariffs were tariffs, whatever the current rationalization for them might be and regardless of the nature of the government that adopted them. He had no sympathy with the many advocates he met of the doctrine of protecting the infant industries of Europe; he was inclined to discount them as either naive or self-interested.

In particular, he dismissed the program of planned national economic development, recently propounded by Friedrich List, as merely old-fashioned mercantilism in a new guise, and he noted with satisfaction whatever he heard that might undermine List's reputation. In Leipzig, for example, Cobden recorded at length the views of one informant who spoke "disparagingly of him as a man of business and also of his moral principles, but attributed to his exertions much of the prejudice against free trade which exists in Germany . . . He put forth protectionist doctrines in the most specious form and mixed up the sophisms of the monopolists with appeals to German nationality."[26]

That List's ideas could be seen as the economic counterpart to the national political identity the European middle classes were striving to achieve dismayed and disturbed Cobden. That many who supported List's ideas did so with a disinterested zeal equal to Cobden's in promoting free trade seems hardly to have occurred to him. From first to last, and not only on this trip but throughout his career, he tended to underestimate the force of nationalist sentiment.

That, by itself, did not mean that his trip was a failure, although its significance was certainly greater at home than abroad. It put his free trade labors firmly in the context of internationalism; it prepared the ground for what was to be his most important work over the next few years, his contribution to the nascent European peace movement; it enhanced his credentials as an informed critic of the traditional practice of British foreign policy. The journey also served more personal purposes as well. To his relief, it saved him from having to play any part in the political maneuvering that followed the fall of Peel's government. At the end of 1845, when Russell had attempted and failed to form a government, he had offered Cobden the vice-presidency of the Board of Trade, which Cobden declined on the ground that his work was with the league. The offer was not repeated when Russell formed his government in 1846, nor did Cobden wish it to be. His financial condition was now public knowledge, and he had already announced his intention of retiring temporarily from politics and going abroad for his health. Government office was unthinkable under the circumstances.

Russell was greatly relieved at having this excuse for not offering Cobden a post in his new government. Peel's parliamentary tribute to Cobden (which shocked the establishment of both parties) combined with Cobden's political standing in the country to make "it very difficult for Lord John not to offer office to Mr. Cobden," according to Prince Albert's account of an interview with the prospective prime minister.[27] Yet as the leader of a popular agitation not yet dissolved Cobden was anathema to most Whigs and to the queen. Thus, even had Russell so desired, he could not have offered Cobden a position commensurate with his popularity out of doors. A way out of this dilemma was suggested by the elder brother of Charles Villiers, Lord Clarendon, who wanted to include Cobden in the government as a means of broadening the base of Whiggism. Finding himself alone in wishing to go this far, Clarendon fell back on a compromise proposal: that Russell use Cobden's personal plans as a reason for making not "immediate, but . . . prospective cabinet offers" to him.[28] This formula proved satisfactory to the handful of Whigs consulted, and Russell wrote to Cobden on the same day the league was dissolved, in as friendly a tone as the news he had to convey would allow, to express the hope that "on your return to this country you will join a liberal administration."[29]

The Whig establishment made more of this whole matter than they need have. Even if Cobden's personal concerns had not presented insuperable obstacles, he would have turned down an offer of government office. As always, he valued his independence too highly to play the role of party loyalist, let alone that of spokesman for a government with which he was bound to disagree often. He did not criticize those among his friends, led by Milner Gibson, who accepted office under the Whigs, but he was certain that his own interests would be better served by remaining an outsider. Of course, Russell could not have known in 1846 how strongly Cobden felt about his status as an independent M.P. Moreover, in fairness to Russell, it should be noted that, whatever his crustier Whig colleagues may have wished, he fully intended to make good on his promise of office to Cobden, if only as a means of enlisting radical support.

In the autumn of 1847, Russell proposed to the queen that Cobden be appointed head of the newly reorganized Poor Law administration and given cabinet rank. Although Victoria did not question Cobden's qualifications as summed up by Russell—"his ability, his popularity with the working class, and his knowledge of sound principles of political economy"[30]—she strongly objected to the appointment. "The elevation to the cabinet directly from Covent Garden strikes her as a very sudden step," she advised her prime minister, since it was likely to set "a dangerous example to agitators in general."[31] She therefore suggested that Cobden should serve for some time in appointive office before being brought into the cabinet, but since this was unrealistic politically, Russell allowed the matter to drop. Cobden remained what he would have chosen to be in any case, a private member.

He did not, however, remain the member for Stockport. His trip abroad may have spared him some political bother, but it prevented him from putting a stop to the ill-advised schemes of some well-meaning supporters. Had he been out of the country in July 1846, the Liberals of Manchester would probably have drafted him as their parliamentary candidate; a year later, in his absence and without prior consultation, the Liberals of the West Riding of Yorkshire did just that (with some prodding and considerable assistance from Cobden's Manchester friends). Apart from Lancashire, the West

Riding had been the most successful field of league political operations. Through a methodical working of the electoral registers and the extensive purchase of freehold votes, it had been turned into a safe Liberal seat, and Cobden was returned unopposed at the general election of 1847. He would have preferred to remain at undemanding Stockport, which had also returned him, but the West Riding was the largest constituency in the country; to represent it was an honor Cobden did not feel he could refuse. Moreover, his election represented "a revolt of the town liberals" against the cautious Whig leadership in Yorkshire.[32] Since that was precisely what Cobden had hoped for from the freehold campaign, he could not afford to turn his back on the consequences just because they inconvenienced him. Reluctantly, and with misgivings that were to prove well founded, he abandoned his old constituency.

By itself, Cobden's political passage across the Pennines would not have changed very much in the short run. His problems as a representative of Yorkshire did not emerge for some time. So far as the political world was concerned, his status had been enhanced, not altered: he remained a northerner representing a northern constituency. But the move from Stockport to the West Riding was not an isolated event; it coincided with an even greater change in his personal life. Ever since Cobden's financial collapse in 1845, his friends had urged him to quit the family business. He was certainly inclined to do so but could see no way out that would not damage his family, his employees, and his public reputation. The success of the testimonial fund-raising campaign changed everything, however, and during his trip to Europe the small group of friends and relations who had managed his affairs for nearly a year made the final arrangements. A substantial portion of the fund was used to pay off his debts, and the business was reorganized with Cobden having no part in it.

Since there was no longer anything holding him to Lancashire, Cobden sold his Manchester house and took up permanent residence in the south of England. For the next few years that meant Westbourne Terrace in London, but the seeds of an even greater change in his way of life were also planted at this time. Although he and his brother Fred had talked of buying back the old family house—Dunford—in Sussex ever since their early years in business together, Cobden had all but lost sight of this ambition during the restless league years. By the time repeal was passed, regaining Dunford was more Fred's dream than his, yet when the property became available during his absence in Europe, he authorized its purchase with money from the testimonial fund. At first Cobden thought of it as a temporary residence only, to be used on weekends or short vacations. But Kate and the children came to love it, and gradually Cobden himself was drawn back to the old place, particularly after some of his postrepeal plans ended in disappointment. In 1853 he built a large new house, into which was incorporated most of his birthplace, and thereafter Dunford became his principal residence. Westbourne Terrace was given up and Cobden stayed with friends or rented accommodations during the parliamentary session.

The final move to Dunford was simply the last act in a gradual process of change, but the beginning of that process, Cobden's departure from Manchester, was both abrupt and largely accidental. When he bought Dunford he did not think of it as an alternative to Manchester, to which his ties were as strong as ever when he embarked on his European journey. Yet during the next few years all these ties were weakened or broken by chance developments: his refusal to run for Parliament from Manchester, the end of his connection with the family business, his unexpected election from the West Riding. Thus, although he remained a parliamentary representative of northern constituencies for the rest of his life, he never lived in the North again and visited it less and less frequently. Indeed, his political ties to Yorkshire weakened more than they sustained his personal connections with Lancashire. Increasingly he complained that he could not go to Lancashire as a private citizen to visit his friends without being pressed to put in an appearance before his Yorkshire constituents; and to avoid the latter he therefore often did without the former. In perhaps the most ironic development of Cobden's career, the acknowledged leader of the Manchester School—a term that was only just then entering the political language—was, after sixteen years, no longer of Manchester.

CHAPTER 15

The Manchester School and Post-Repeal Politics

Cobden's return to England in the autumn of 1847 coincided with the beginning of a short but sharp depression, not only in Britain but throughout the western world. Following two years of bad harvests and high food prices, this development was more than sufficient to trigger a dramatic resurgence of political unrest at home and abroad. Early in the new year most of the nations that Cobden had recently visited were swept by revolution, while in England the Chartist movement reemerged as militant as ever. The postrepeal political lull had ended, giving way to conditions similar to those in which the league and Chartism had been born a decade earlier. The opportunity to build on the triumphs of the league appeared suddenly to be at hand.

Unfortunately, conditions in 1848 were also similar to those of 1838 in other, less favorable, respects. As then, there was little agreement on what should be done. Some middle-class reformers, Cobden among them, were more interested in economical than political questions, although most of the better-known leaders were primarily concerned with parliamentary reform. Yet few of them were prepared to contemplate cooperation with Chartism. With the collapse and repression of the Chartist movement during the spring and summer, however, the chances of an alliance across class lines in favor of some compromise measure of reform improved dramatically—or so it seemed. Only three days after the threat of a Chartist march on Parliament evaporated on 10 April, about fifty radical M.P.s met under the leadership of Joseph Hume to adopt a program and a plan of agitation. The program, the so-called Little Charter, was like that of the Leeds Household Suffrage Association in 1840: it called for household suffrage, the secret ballot, triennial parliaments, and more equal electoral districts. The plan of agitation, as might be expected, looked to the repeal movement as its model.

Cobden took a prominent part in all this. He was elected deputy chairman by the meeting of M.P.s and went north to Manchester a few days later to sound out the views of the league leadership. Their response was cautiously encouraging, and Wilson agreed to circularize the faithful supporters of the league to ascertain their opinion of the Little Charter and test their willingness to back a new move. As the replies, mostly favorable, poured into Manchester over the next few weeks and reform meetings and petitions in support of the Little Charter were organized in the league's former strongholds, it appeared that a new round of agitation on the scale of the repeal movement might be in the making. "It is evident," Cobden advised Wilson in May, "that there is a strong current setting in for a reform bill."[1]

That certainly was the impression Cobden hoped to convey when he spoke in Parliament in support of Hume's motion for the Little Charter in July. The House of Commons had a clear choice, he argued: reform the system of representation or face an endless series of agitations. "Since Manchester cannot have its fair representation in this House, it was obliged to organize a League . . . and in this indirect manner . . . make itself felt in this House. Well, do you want to get rid of this system of agitation?" he asked. "Then you must bring this House into harmony with the opinions of the people."[2] Hume's motion was defeated, as expected, by a huge margin. But so too had Villiers' motion on the Corn Laws been defeated, and like Villiers Hume intended to make his an annual motion. This, Cobden emphasized, was no temporary thing. The demand for reform had arisen spontaneously and was not directed from a single source, as, he admitted, the repeal movement had largely been at the beginning. Therefore, he contended, "I have no hesitation in frankly acknowledging that we were five years agitating for a repeal of the Corn Laws before we reached so advanced a point as that which the friends of the present question now occupy."[3]

Whether or not Cobden really believed this, he certainly had no intention of assuming the leadership of the movement himself. As he often said to those who pressed him to take up this or that cause during these years, one seven-year-long agitation was quite enough in a lifetime. Besides, in spite of the agreement to launch a movement in support of the Little Charter, there remained important differences between Cobden and most of his radical parliamentary colleagues. They tended to concentrate on the extension of the suffrage, but he was more interested in the ballot, which would secure the individual elector from corrupt influences, and in a redistribution of seats, to give the urban middle class a political influence commensurate with its economic power. This was not simply a question of emphasis, however, although that is how Cobden treated it in his parliamentary speech; he had begun to have doubts about the efficacy of an extension of the suffrage. Shortly after the Corn Laws were repealed he confessed to Joseph Sturge, "Upon the universal suffrage question, I find I have gone back . . . I dare not oppose the principle of giving men control over their own affairs. I must confess however that I am less sanguine than I used to be about the effects of a wide extension of the suffrage."[4]

Cobden did not, indeed, oppose the principle of universal suffrage; he remained a political democrat all his life. But he was never inclined to pursue political reform as an end in itself. He supported it to the extent that it advanced the causes of peace and retrenchment, the other and to him more important elements in the radical trinity. Hence, when he talked of political reform, his emphasis on the ballot and the redistribution of seats, both of which promised to undermine the power of a bellicose and spendthrift aristocracy. But he saw no evidence that the unenfranchised masses were more enlightened than the present electorate on questions of war and peace and economic policy. On the contrary, his experience in the anti–Corn Law agitation appeared to demonstrate that the bulk of the working classes had been all too successfully misled in these matters by their own demagogic leaders as well as by the governing classes. Cobden did not use this as an argument against an extension of the franchise, for he believed that the best way to ensure that men acted responsibly was to give them responsibility; but he did use it to deflate expectations that parliamentary reform would necessarily lead to an improvement in the quality of government.

Only the unique atmosphere of the spring of 1848 and Cobden's judgment that this might lead to immediate progress toward reform led him to commit himself so fully to the Little Charter in April. It was a commitment that was unlikely to survive the return to political normalcy, at least if there was an alternative more suitable to his tastes. And there was just such an alternative. The Little Charter was not the first cause into which Cobden threw himself after returning from Europe; nor was it the first issue brought to a head by the economic downturn of 1847. The worsening economic situation at home happened to coincide with a foreign policy crisis, and together they forced the government into an uncomfortable dilemma, which seemed likely to provide an opportunity to teach the English people a lesson in the economics of great power diplomacy.

A Franco-Spanish royal marriage (which Cobden, then in Spain, attended), a substantial French naval build-up, and an alarmist analysis of the state of Britain's defenses by the Duke of Wellington, contained in a private letter to the Inspector General of Fortifications, which was leaked to the press late in 1847, combined to produce one of those anti–French invasion panics to which the English were periodically subject during the nineteenth century. The government was faced with intense pressure from the press, Parliament, and the military services for an increase in military spending. At the same time, the sudden downturn in the economy made a budget deficit in the coming year a virtual certainty. Only a substantial increase in taxes could cover the shortfall, let alone pay for new arms.

Cobden could hardly have asked for a clearer illustration of the incompatibility of economical government with an interventionist foreign policy—or for a more promising political opening—and at the turn of the year, two months before revolution on the Continent put political reform back at the top of the radical agenda, he began to speak out in favor of government economy and against additional military spending. He deliberately chose to take a secondary role in the new movement, however: "Don't be alarmed," he reassured Kate, "I am not going to set up any new Leagues."[5] Indeed, anxious to avoid organizational commitments and any suggestion that the economy drive was his creature, he often turned down requests to speak and asked that his name be used sparingly. Instead, he urged Wilson to take up the issue, which "really belongs to the free trade party whose headquarters are in Manchester,"[6] and he kept in close touch with Joseph Sturge, the unofficial leader of the London Peace Society, giving him advice on how to run an agitation. Given his prominence as a radical spokesman, however, the few public appearances he did make inevitably received disproportionate and for the most part unfavorable publicity.

In a speech at Stockport and again in nominating the Liberal candidate for a by-election in South Lancashire in December, he intimated that Parliament, far from increasing military spending, should reduce it. His remarks in Stockport were so generally (and often misleadingly) attacked in the press that he was driven to clarify and, to some extent, redefine his position in a speech in Manchester a month later. He did not back down, although he did admit that his desire to reduce armaments was unpopular. "You cannot have a material reduction in your armaments until a great change takes place in this country with regard to our foreign policy . . . Until that time, I am content to be in this question, as I have been on others, in a minority, and in a minority to remain, until I get a majority." But, he noted, "the real and practical question before the country is not the question of a reduction of armaments . . . The real question is, shall we have an increase of the army, navy and ordinance?" And although he admitted "that public opinion does not go with me . . . [on] a great reduction in our armaments," Cobden was nonetheless certain "that, on the question of an increase in our armaments, public opinion is with me," at least in the larger constituencies.[7] Defensive though he was during much of the speech, he did make some good debating points. In particular, he set out to embarrass the Admiralty, while amusing his audience, by detailing the amount of time much of the British Navy spent uselessly but comfortably at anchor in the salubrious ports of southern Europe. Yet he all but spoiled the effect of that by indulging in a nasty attack on the aged—and, Cobden suggested, senile—Duke of Wellington for his part in generating the anti-French scare.

If Cobden misread public sentiment in his attack on the military—a mistake he was careful not to repeat—he was closer to the mark on the financial side of the question. Early in the new session of Parliament, Russell introduced a budget calling for increases in the naval estimates together with an extended and higher income tax. The result was a near-revolt by the radicals, with Cobden quickly emerging as no less a critic of the government than the official opposition. Apart from his speeches in favor of political reform, he spent most of his time during the 1848 session of Parliament attacking the budget or questioning the military estimates. Fearing a radical-protectionist coalition to bring down the government, Russell quickly capitulated. The naval building program was dropped—revolutionary chaos in France being given as an excuse for ending the scare—and the tax proposals were scaled down. With that, the government began to recover its control of the House of Commons, aided in part by the sudden resurgence of political radicalism out of doors, which diverted attention from the financial situation.

Like everything else, Cobden's plans were overwhelmed by the political issues that dominated the spring and summer of 1848, but there was no question where his priorities still lay. "I consider nine-tenths of all our future dangers to be financial," he wrote in May, "and when I came home from the continent, it was with a determination to go on with fiscal reform and economy as a sequence to Free Trade . . . But when the series of political revolutions broke out on the Continent . . . it was no longer possible to avoid discussing organic questions. But I had no share in forcing forward the subject. I abstained from assisting in forming a party in the House for organic reforms, though I was much urged by a great number of members to head such a party."[8]

Furthermore, to the extent that he did take a role in the Little Charter movement, he sought to ensure that it was broadly based. Cobden's hand is evident in the statement issued by the meeting of radical M.P.s in April, which was more than simply a suffrage meeting: "a more cordial understanding and cooperation are urgently required among such members of Parliament as are favorable to the extension of the suffrage, an equitable arrangement of taxation, a redistribution of expenditure and the general advance of reform principles."[9] Two months later, in his parliamentary speech in support of Hume's motion, Cobden closed by citing the growth of popular sentiment in favor of economical government as yet another demonstration of the need to make Parliament more representative of opinion out of doors.

Specifically Cobden mentioned one group, the Liverpool Financial Reform Association. Like the Little Charter movement, it had sprung up in the overheated political atmosphere of April 1848, but unlike the coalition of parliamentary reformers it was single-minded in its program, and its leaders were not professional politicians or agitators. The president of the association, Robertson Gladstone, the brother of the future prime minister, was a former Tory, now a Liberal, and although most of the founder members were active in local politics or had been subscribers to the league, they were, as a group, not identified with any particular faction. This was precisely the sort of spontaneous local body Cobden had hoped for earlier in the year, and as the tide of agitation ebbed in the summer of 1848, he increasingly looked to the Liverpool financial reformers as the core of a new popular movement. As early as June he was talking of the parliamentary reform movement much as he had back in 1842, as a means of frightening the aristocracy into conceding other things, in this case economy in government. By September his correspondence was almost as exclusively concerned with financial reform as it had been in January. Parliamentary reform was hardly mentioned.

If, as Cobden now believed, the rise of the Little Charter movement had been a false dawn, then the walls of Parliament would have to be breached by other means. To his delight, therefore, at just this time he stumbled across the existence of yet another spontaneous local movement, which had been working for nearly a year at a cause very dear to him, the Birmingham Freehold Land Society. It had been founded after the 1847 general election by a Birmingham working man, James Taylor, who was recommended to Cobden by William Scholefield, an M.P. for the city. Taylor hoped to use the purchase of freeholds on the model of the league campaign as a means of giving the working classes a stake in the land as well as in politics. Cobden, once he was assured of Taylor's abilities, had even larger visions. The more he pondered the political future, "the more I am convinced that our only way of taking another step in the advance against oligarchy is by beginning with the instrument which the League resorted to at the end of our struggle, viz. the 40/-freehold qualification."[10] If a national network of freehold land societies, modeled on Birmingham's, could be linked with a series of financial reform associations, modeled on Liverpool's, each could draw strength from the other. The financial reformers could bankroll the political penetration of the counties, and the presence of the freehold movement behind the financial reformers would give them an influence beyond their actual numbers in Parliament.

A year after his return from Europe, Cobden was at last certain of how he wished to proceed politically, and he immediately set about the task of building the new movement. He spent much of November concocting a specific set of financial proposals, the People's Budget as he was to call it, "to serve for an object for financial reformers to work up to, and to prevent them losing their time upon vague generalities."[11] On the spending side, his goal was a reduction of nearly

20 percent from the present national budget, to bring it down to the level of 1835, the lowest thus far (and, as things turned out, ever) in the nineteenth century. He hoped to use the more than £11 million this would save to accelerate the process of lightening the burden of indirect taxes on raw materials and on the necessities of life. Most of his proposed spending cuts were aimed at the military estimates, which he wished to reduce almost by half.

Aware that this was far too radical to be generally acceptable, he chose his candidates for tax relief with great care, so as "to enlist the sympathy and support of every class and interest in the country."[12] He proposed a sharp reduction in the import duty on tea and the abolition of duties on timber, wool, dairy products, and many lesser items. Only some twenty articles would remain subject to import duties under his plan. The window and advertising taxes would go, as would the traditionally unpopular excise taxes on malt, hops, soap, and paper. "There are other duties I should prefer to remove, instead of one or two of them," he explained to Bright, "but I have been guided materially by a desire to bring all interests to sympathize with the scheme. Thus the tea is to catch the merchants and all the old women in the country—the wood and timber, the shipbuilders—the malt and hops, the farmers—paper and soap, the Scotch anti-excise people—the window tax, the shopocracy of London, Bath, etc.—the advertisements, the press."[13]

Early in December, budget in hand, Cobden went to Liverpool to meet the leaders of the Financial Reform Association, most of them for the first time. He was much impressed with their character, but less so with their potential as agitators. Still, they warmly welcomed his budget, and a few days after his visit Cobden published it for the first time in an open letter to the Liverpool Financial Reform Association, which immediately adopted it as its own. Cobden then turned to London and Manchester, where he hoped the political deficiencies of the Liverpuddlians could be made good. Immediately, he ran into trouble. In London, the most active exponent of a new reform movement was Sir Joshua Walmsley, M.P. for Leicester and secretary of the group of radical M.P.s who had met in London in April. Like Cobden, Walmsley had been to Liverpool, but with the purpose of persuading the financial reformers of his native city to join a movement for the Little Charter. Financial reform was all very well, he argued, but neither it nor any other worthwhile objects could be secured without a measure of parliamentary reform. In Manchester, Bright and Wilson agreed. Cobden "is for one thing at a time," Bright commented to Wilson, "and so am I if it be a thing well defined, which I think financial reform is not."[14] The country was ready for a political reform movement, he believed, and in the long run would accept nothing less. At the least they would have to create a "general registration and qualification society, for without that any attempt at agitation is a farce."

Cobden was all for that, but no more than that, and only in the service of financial reform. In a flurry of letters—four in five days near the end of December—he used every argument he could think of to win Bright over, and even secretly enlisted Henry Ashworth's assistance in putting pressure on Bright and Wilson. Parliamentary reform, he claimed, was dead for the time being and could only be revived by a vast effort none of them was willing to undertake. Their commitment to the Little Charter, appropriate in April, was so no longer. The middle classes would not support it and the working classes would not settle for it. Financial reform was now the live issue, with the Liverpool group already commanding "far more hold on the public mind than we in the League had after three years agitation."[15] Not only the middle class, Cobden went so far as to claim a month later, but the better sort of working man as well had been disillusioned by the excesses of Chartism and was ready temporarily to forsake political for economical reform. If, as they all agreed, only one issue could be agitated successfully at a time, then financial reform was clearly the issue of the day. The threat of a political reform movement might, Cobden conceded, be useful in support of financial reform, but that was as far as he was willing to go.

Much of Cobden's argument was beside the point as far as Bright was concerned. They did not differ only in their views of what was practicable, although that was all they talked of openly in their correspondence. The circumstances in which they operated were now so different that they were bound to disagree. While Cobden was abroad, Bright and Wilson had transformed the machinery of the league into a political caucus operating throughout the cotton districts. Inevitably they were more concerned than Cobden with the practicalities of political power. Had Cobden maintained his roots in Manchester, these differences might have been less, although not perhaps much less. To Cobden, after all, political reform was only one of many possible issues, and given the legacy of the free trade movement and his own predilections, not the most important of these. Bright, however, once repeal had been passed, always maintained that the extension of the suffrage was a precondition of other reforms. In other words, beneath all the discussion of what was feasible lay fundamental differences about what was important, although their friendship and their agreement on most other matters prevented them from recognizing—or perhaps wishing to recognize—the extent to which they disagreed.

In later years, after Cobden's death, Bright went to the opposite extreme and tended to exaggerate their differences at this time. According to G. M. Trevelyan:

> There was . . . one matter of supreme importance in which Bright knew what he wanted better than Cobden, and that was the extension of the franchise to the working men. "Why, Cobden, you haven't got faith in the working people," he said to his friend one day. After Cobden's death there were two stories which Bright used to tell to a young Liberal Member of whom he was fond; the first was how, when his first wife died, Cobden came to him, and how they agreed to work together till the Corn Laws were repealed; and the other was how after the Corn Laws were repealed he wished to make a similar compact about the Franchise, and how Cobden refused.[16]

Like his account of what happened at Leamington, Bright's memory of Cobden's views on political reform is misleading, but there is an important fragment of the truth in Bright's highly colored recollections. In theory Cobden was as thorough a political reformer as Bright—indeed more so, since he accepted, as Bright did not, the principle of universal suffrage. But Bright always believed in the efficacy as well as the primacy of political reform, whereas Cobden remained skeptical.

For the time being, however, in December 1848, they managed to work out a compromise, which, perhaps because of Cobden's greater prestige, was closer to his wishes than to Bright's. They agreed to hold a reform meeting in Manchester early in the new year, at which, after general remarks on the need for unity from Wilson, Cobden would talk of financial reform and cooperation with Liverpool, Gibson would speak in general terms of political reform, and Bright would propose the creation of a registration and freehold land society. In London, meanwhile, a similar debate over priorities ended in similar results. Cobden and Walmsley recruited the grand old man of metropolitan radicalism, Francis Place, to compose an address for a new London-based movement. Place complied with a rough draft emphasizing the five points of Hume's Little Charter and headed "The Great Reform League."[17] Cobden objected both to the heading and to the emphasis on political reform and evidently managed to persuade Place and Hume, although not Walmsley, of the need to keep close to Liverpool. In the end, the reform meeting held in London in January 1849 followed closely the proceedings of the Manchester meeting two weeks earlier. Cobden appeared to have gotten his way.

It was a short-lived victory. Within a few weeks the political reformers in London took control of the movement there and gradually changed its emphasis. The Metropolitan Financial Reform Association, founded in January, had by the end of the year become the National Parliamentary and Financial Reform Association. A similar transformation took place in Manchester, although later and more slowly, partly because of the greater caution of the politically experienced leaguers and partly perhaps out of deference to Cobden. Walmsley was delighted, of course; this was the movement he had wanted all along. Wilson and Bright were also pleased, but more guardedly so, for Cobden was disappointed. Although he remained a member of the council of the London association, he was conspicuously absent from its meetings for more than a year. He admitted that Walmsley was doing much to bring the middle and working classes together but remained convinced that the NPFRA could not succeed even if it were superbly led, which, he believed, it was not. He welcomed the political reform movement insofar as it helped to keep alive the financial reform and freehold movements, to both of which the London and Manchester associations remained officially committed. But as with the suffrage movements that had sprung up in the early years of the league, he feared that the NPFRA might fragment the beleaguered forces of radicalism.

As often as not, therefore, Cobden acted almost as if the London and Manchester associations did not exist; after 1848 he took no part in the debate on Hume's annual motion for the Little Charter. Instead he introduced an annual motion of his own—first proposed in 1849—calling for a reduction of government expenditure to the level of 1835. He knew this would be denounced as irresponsible, but far

from fearing such criticism, he welcomed it. Like the league's uncompromising demand for total and immediate repeal, the sweeping character of his budget proposals "would arrest public interest in a way
which no nibbling at details would do."[18] Not that he neglected the
details. He spent most of the 1849 and 1850 sessions of Parliament
picking away at the army and navy estimates, the costs of colonial
administration, and the salaries of government officials. In addition,
through service on select committees charged with investigating military management and official salaries, Cobden sought to enhance his
standing as a watchdog over public spending and accumulate evidence of the need for financial reform.

He got more than he bargained for. The life of the various army,
navy, and ordinance committees extended over three parliamentary
sessions and into a fourth, from 1848 to 1851, and during the course
of the nearly one-hundred meetings he attended (80 percent of those
held), he heard evidence of waste and inefficiency that exceeded his
need for weapons against the military estimates as surely as the ma-
teriel piled up in government depots exceeded the peacetime needs of
the military establishment. Nonetheless, he enjoyed passing on to
audiences in and out of Parliament some of the committees' more
outlandish discoveries, such as that the army had in store in 1849 a
twenty-four years' supply of haversacks, forty-seven years' worth of
pikes, eight years' worth of kettles, and 1,200,000 sandbags, enough
to supply its annual needs thirty-four times over. The serious side of
this ludicrous situation was best illustrated by the example of rifles.
When the percussion rifle replaced the flintlock, the British army had
nearly 450,000 of the newly obsolete weapons in stock. As late as
1849, 165,000 remained.

Other targets to which Cobden returned repeatedly in the House of
Commons, relying on information generated in the select committees,
included the manufacture and repair of weapons in government ar-
senals and shipyards (of which, in any case, there were too many),
even when contracting out to private firms would be cheaper; the
deployment of naval forces to protect commerce in areas where British trade was small and in no danger; the reluctance of successive
governments to close installations made redundant by the growth of
modern means of communication; the building of fortifications in
remote colonial territories and the tendency to overman these bases
and territories with both military and civilian personnel, of which the

latter were often overpaid. Cobden regarded civilian salaries as an especially vulnerable target, perhaps because, unlike the military and some aspects of colonial administration, they could rarely be defended on grounds of national prestige or security. Having erred in attacking the military directly in 1847, he was determined to make his case as much as possible in terms of efficiency and economy in government.

Moreover, he did not expect immediate results, especially in Parliament, although the military service select committees did suggest to the government a number of reforms in administration, procurement, and promotion, and in the official salaries committee Cobden and Bright moved, often successfully, to cap or reduce several categories of salaries. But the House of Commons almost never reduced the estimates once they were proposed by the government. That being the case, he asked his fellow members rhetorically, "With what hope did independent members discuss them? With the hope," he answered his own question, "that they might bring public opinion to bear upon them."[19] That was his purpose throughout (apart from embarrassing the government): to establish in the public and in the parliamentary mind the possibility of an alternative system of national finance. If that could be achieved, he believed, the rest would follow. "In less than five years," he predicted to George Combe, "all that I propose, and a great deal more, will be accomplished."[20]

Cobden backed up his parliamentary efforts with frequent appearances at financial reform meetings, but he did not embark on anything remotely comparable to the speaking tours of the later league years. He had no wish to usurp the leadership of the financial reform associations or take on the responsibility for running them. The freehold movement was another matter. Except in Birmingham, it had not emerged so spontaneously as the financial reform associations, and apart from the old league leaders virtually no one had any experience with the technicalities of purchasing and distributing freehold property. Necessarily, therefore, Cobden took a large role in the movement. He was a founder and active member of the Metropolitan Freehold Land Society, which had been organized in conjunction with the London Financial Reform Association; he promoted new freehold land societies wherever possible; and, working through James Taylor, he did what he could to make it a national movement. It was largely at Cobden's suggestion that the movement started its own journal,

The Freeholder, and held the first in a series of annual meetings of delegates from freehold land societies in Birmingham in October 1849. When five months later Cobden finally put in an appearance at a conference of the NPFRA, he did so primarily to support the freehold campaign as the only sure foundation on which a parliamentary reform movement could be built.

To most radical leaders Cobden's absorption with his own particular mix of causes was a source of worry, even anger, for without his full participation in what Bright, Walmsley, and others regarded as the mainstream of postrepeal radicalism, the movement was bound to lack unity and a sense of direction. In July 1849, for example, there was "a dinner at Sir Joshua Walmsley's, with the leading radicals. . .Hume, Milner Gibson, Charles Villiers (a fish out of water), Cobden, Bright, Rev. W. J. Fox . . . The object was to see if any combined system of action could be devised." Yet, as one of those present, J. A. Roebuck, reported, "it soon became plain that, amongst these men, a leader or system was impossible. Villiers came there to prevent any such result, ditto Milner Gibson. Cobden is a poor creature, with one idea— the making of county voters. He is daunted by the country squires, and hopes to conquer them by means of these votes. Little Fox . . . was about as fit for a political chief as I am for a ballet dancer. The only man of metal and pluck was Bright."[21]

"The pugnacious Quaker," as Roebuck called Bright, was scarcely less critical of Cobden and was enabled by their friendship to tell him so quite bluntly. The financial reformers and Cobden himself, not the political reformers, Bright believed, were the main obstacles to progress. "I think you have been wrong, as I have often told you," he stated flatly in December 1849.[22] Looking back over the preceding eighteen months, Bright regretted that Manchester had not taken the lead in a parliamentary reform campaign in the spring of 1848. That error could not be undone, but Bright was certain that Cobden's adherence to the financial reform and freehold campaigns only compounded the problem. The financial reformers (as Cobden had to admit) lacked the toughness necessary to sustain a national agitation, and as for the freehold movement, Bright was certain that could never achieve what Cobden appeared to expect from it: "The forty-shilling scheme *alone* will not do the work, and *alone* it will not work extensively . . . It would have been more above board and I think more effectual to have started for Parliamentary Reform, and *for this*, to have set in motion the forty shilling freeholds . . . I think you exaggerate the extent to which people will adopt the system, especially as no definite object or battle is before them."

As far as Bright was concerned, a freehold campaign could only work as it had worked before, in conjunction with a powerful popular movement, and there was only one issue capable of enlisting that kind of enthusiasm, parliamentary reform. That the parliamentary reform associations were in trouble he could not deny. The NPFRA was undeniably deficient in leadership and organization, but that, he argued, was all the more reason for Manchester to take a lead. "You will find," he warned Cobden, "that your indisposition to go with a Manchester organization will end in disappointment as regards a metropolitan party. Lancashire and Yorkshire may be made to move the nation . . . You appear to think otherwise and time will show who is right."

Cobden did indeed think otherwise. "You seem to have fallen into the idea that I am looking to the freehold plan as a substitute for a thorough reform," he replied to Bright. "I look to it as a means to do something, and not as an end. I wish to abate the power of the aristocracy in their strongholds."[23] A weak movement for parliamentary reform, which was all Cobden believed possible, would be worse than useless; the aristocracy would laugh at it. As to his role in Manchester, Cobden was equally unequivocal: "You seem to speak as if I were the obstacle to the movement being carried out in Manchester last year. My own fear was lest the public elsewhere should be deceived as to what we should do for them in Manchester . . . It is not in human nature that, after the exhaustion of one great effort, the same men should begin another of an equally arduous character. I am also of the opinion that we have not the same elements in Lancashire for a Democratic Reform movement, as we had for Free Trade."

All of Cobden's differences with Bright, implied but kept in check in their correspondence a year earlier, were now out in the open, and they did not repeat their attempt to arrive at a compromise platform on which they could both stand. They did attend meetings together early in the new year, but each spoke in support of his particular causes alone.

Soon thereafter, the distance between Cobden and Bright began to narrow, although not because either of them changed his mind. Instead, the movements to which they were committed began to wither away, leaving them all but stranded politically by the end of 1850. The NPFRA was the first casualty. As the leaders of the most successful agitation of their time, Cobden and Bright could never resist lecturing Walmsley on the shortcomings of his movement. Walmsley, understandably irritated, would have preferred less advice and more assistance, but unfortunately for him and the NPFRA, most of the criticism proved correct. The association concentrated too much on the public aspects of the agitation and too little on the inglorious business of organization. In its haste to build a national movement it often wasted effort in areas where there was no grass roots support; in places where there was such support, it frequently alienated local leaders by moving in without adequate consultation. It set itself impossible fund-raising goals nationally, before it had secured its financial base in London. And hoping to attract both middle-class radicals and ex-Chartists, it wavered in its program and political rhetoric to such an extent that it alienated elements in both groups. The league had made similar mistakes in its early years, but Cobden and Bright agreed that there could be no excuse for the NPFRA repeating them. In any case, by the summer of 1850 the movement was in trouble, and in the autumn even Bright was ready to give up in disgust. "I have requested my name to be withdrawn from the Council of the Association," he informed Cobden, "as I cannot do anything in the movement."[24]

By a very different route Bright had arrived at an opinion of the NPFRA little different from Cobden's, but although Cobden may have interpreted this as a vindication of his view that a successful parliamentary reform movement was not yet possible, Bright did not see it that way. The conduct of the agitation, not the concept behind it, was at fault, he believed, and he remained convinced that intervention from Manchester might have saved the day as late as the end of 1849. Cobden, not Bright, was probably correct. Class divisions were still too great and memories of Chartism too fresh on both sides for a coalition across class lines to work. Only a crisis sufficient to push the middle classes into political radicalism could have overcome this lack of trust, which bordered still on fear. Such a crisis was, of course, what Bright and Walmsley expected from the economic recession of 1848 and the frustrations of the financial reform movement. Far from the recession deepening, however, the economy recovered in 1849. By the end of the year England had entered the long era of mid-Victorian prosperity. Good times by themselves did not necessarily signal the end of successful reform movements; the league had managed to survive into the relatively prosperous mid-1840s by transforming itself into a pressure group working within the system. But the league had had four years as a popular agitation in hard times during which to build the necessary base. The postrepeal parliamentary reform movement had scarcely as many months. Certainly by the beginning of 1850 Bright should have realized that the cause was lost.

Even more clearly a victim of prosperity was the financial reform movement. Bright was correct in thinking that the movement inherently lacked a sufficiently definable object, such as repeal had been for the league. Cobden tried to give it one by talking of reducing spending to the level of 1835 and singling out the rise in military spending for criticism. But the level of government spending was not the real irritant. The financial reform campaign was fueled by the budget deficits of 1847 and 1848 and by the threat of new taxes to cover them during a period of economic distress. The financial reformers played a role in forcing the government to abandon its tax proposals in 1848 and to cut the budget to bring it near balance in 1849. But that in itself took much of the fire out of the movement, and subsequent prosperity finished the process. Revenue from existing taxes rose, and the government found itself in the happy position of being able to reduce taxes, increase spending, and still end up with a surplus. The underlying assumption of Cobden's argument, that national prosperity was threatened by a voracious government, appeared to have been disproved; guns and butter might be compatible goals after all. The financial reform movement did not collapse like the NPFRA; it simply withered away as economic conditions improved. Cobden continued to spend much of his time in Parliament questioning the budget, but he did not introduce his annual motion for the reduction of government expenditure after 1850, and financial reform as a movement rather than a goal all but disappeared from his correspondence.

Only one of the agitations spawned in the recession of 1847-48 still thrived, the freehold land campaign, but that too was changing. It had necessarily always been almost as much a business operation as a mass movement, and as the number of freehold societies and properties grew, the balance shifted away from the political aim of creating voting qualifications toward an emphasis on efficient management. The decline of the reform agitations with which the movement had originally been linked reinforced this tendency. The more the freehold movement became an end in itself, the easier it was to think of the purchase of freeholds as an investment or, to the extent it remained political in purpose, as an alternative rather than a prelude to further reforms. As early as 1849 Cobden pointed out to Bright that the constituency created by the purchase of freeholds

> would give you at the present moment a more reliable support for thorough practical reforms than universal suffrage. May I predict that if we should succeed . . . [in vastly increasing the number of freehold votes], there would not be wanting shrewd members of the Tory aristocracy who would be found advocating universal suffrage, to take their chances on an appeal to the ignorance and vice of the country against the opinions of the teetotallers, nonconformists and rational Radicals, who would constitute nine-tenths of our phalanx of forty shilling freeholders.[25]

This emphasis on respectability loomed larger and larger in the propaganda and meetings of the freehold movement as time passed, much to the dismay of Bright and Walmsley and of the moderate ex-Chartists who had always suspected that it was antidemocratic. The continued vitality of the freehold movement, far from indicating that there was life still in the reform movement of the 1840s, was a sign that it was dying away.

It was at this point that Cobden began for the first time to fear that the Corn Laws had been repealed too soon, before the work of the original freehold campaign was complete. His calculation that that campaign could be sustained in the service of causes other than repeal, or perhaps for its own sake, had been wrong and was abandoned. It would be unfair, however, with the advantage of hindsight, to condemn Cobden and Bright for wishful thinking in continuing to pursue these movements after their moment had passed. They believed, understandably, that repeal was a beginning, not an end, and given their background in the league, they were perhaps overly ready to read favorably any signs of unrest and to assume a leading role in any promising agitation. But also in view of their experience in the league, it would have been almost impossible for them to have refused to do so. In any case, conditions seemed ripe in 1847 and 1848, at least as promising as those from which the league and Chartism had emerged a decade earlier. No one could have predicted in April 1848 that the economy would recover so quickly, let alone that the era of mass movement politics was drawing to a close. As late as the end of 1849 both Cobden and Bright were still inclined to blame chance and, to a degree, each other for the failing fortunes of the movements they supported. A year later both were resigned to the situation and largely ready to accept that it had been inevitable.

In the normal course of events the postrepeal era of political agitation would have ended quietly in 1851. But Lord John Russell, for his own good political reasons, had been toying with the notion of a further measure of parliamentary reform for some time, and early in the new year he announced that the government would introduce a reform bill in 1852. Heretofore Russell had upheld the finality of 1832 as firmly as any other Whig, and his conversion to reform, like his abandonment of the Corn Laws in favor of a low fixed duty in 1841, permanently altered the context in which the issue was debated. It was no longer a question of whether but of when and how much, and the all-but-moribund NPFRA revived overnight, supported by Bright and Wilson in Manchester. Even Cobden was swept along, at least temporarily. At a May meeting of the NPFRA, he admitted: "I have taken no very prominent or active part in the agitation . . . But I come before you here tonight . . . because I wish to show that I consider . . . this question which you have in hand is the most practical question politicians can have to deal with . . . Therefore, I do not care from this moment if you leave out of your program the words "financial reform.' Give me Parliamentary Reform, and I will take my chance of getting all the rest."[26]

If nothing else, this proved how far the financial reform movement had fallen, but that did not mean that Cobden was now ready to throw himself unreservedly into the battle for parliamentary reform. In September he and Bright resumed their annual year-end debate on tactics, and Cobden again argued that they should act only as individuals and not attempt to enlist Manchester, which they could not deliver, in support of a movement that hardly existed. "I have been looking out for signs and omens of the political future," he wrote Bright in September, "but cannot say I see any indications of a breeze in the direction of Reform. People are too well to do in the world to agitate for anything."[27] Bright read the signs differently. He detected popular stirrings where Cobden saw none, and besides, he argued, Russell's promise of a bill had changed everything. It gave the radicals an unexpected opportunity to put the reform movement on the track it should have taken in 1848. A lead from Manchester, which he admitted would have been foolhardy a year earlier, had suddenly become indispensable if there was to be a reform bill worth having.

Cobden was not persuaded. But for all his doubts and with a warning to his effervescent colleague that "I have not another agitation left in me," he agreed to help.[28] Intent on giving the movement a coherence it had never had under the NPFRA, Bright planned a series of meetings in Manchester for the autumn. The first, of the Manchester Reform Association council in late September, was designed to set the stage for negotiations between the radicals of Lancashire and their more cautious Yorkshire counterparts, who finally agreed to a compromise proposal. This differed slightly from the Little Charter, and the leaders of the NPFRA, who met with the northerners at a conference in December, were understandably suspicious. Here Cobden's detachment from Manchester proved to be an asset, and he played a critical role at the conference, reassuring his Yorkshire constituents that the final proposal was still sufficiently moderate and mollifying the NPFRA delegates, who feared that the old league machine might be trying to displace them. Although a few Birmingham radicals who had not been invited to the conference denounced its program as insufficient, the parliamentary reform movement emerged from these meetings better united than at any time in more than two years. Indeed, when Russell announced the details of his modest reform bill in February, both Bright and Walmsley (with Cobden's blessing) were sufficiently confident to denounce it as unacceptable.

Neither this newfound unity of the radicals nor their ability to influence Russell's bill was put to the test, however. After the introduction of its reform proposals, the government went down to defeat at the hands of one of those coalitions of incompatible elements that plagued parliamentary politics in the 1850s. So far as Cobden was concerned, that was the end of the parliamentary reform movement. On balance, he was relieved that it was over, for his commitment to the movement was not even as firm as the patchwork coalition he had helped to create in support of it, a fact that would inevitably have caused renewed friction with his friends. "Walmsley seems to be landed in a mess of Charter and red republicanism," he told J. B.

Smith shortly after the fall of Russell's government. "It is quite clear that the Reform agitation is a failure. The best way would be to take the £5 proposed by Lord John as fait accompli," he suggested, returning to his old order of priorities, "and try to get up a strong party for the ballot."[29] Bright, who never quite gave up hope, would not have agreed with that; but even he had to put the reform issue to one side, because the government that replaced Russell's was a Tory government, ambiguous on the all-important question of the Corn Laws.

Immediately, therefore, Cobden, Bright, and Wilson set about reviving the league and for the duration of the Tory government concentrated on the preservation of free trade to the exclusion of other issues. As Cobden put it to Sturge, who as a leader of the peace movement was dismayed at Cobden's willingness to let everything else drop: "My object is to settle the Free Trade question for ever, and to clear the ground for other questions."[30] His strategy was equally clear. The Tories had to be compelled to abandon protection or, failing that, be driven from office. "If in doing so, I should be instrumental in bringing back the Whigs," he further explained to Sturge, "it would not be my fault." Not that Cobden preferred the Whigs to the Tories; he distrusted both parties and normally preferred the Whigs in opposition, where they tended to be more reform-minded. For the moment, however, the issue was between a possibly protectionist government and a clearly free trade government, and on that there was no room for compromise.

Although Cobden and the radicals saw their way clear, almost no one else did. The free trade majority in the House of Commons agreed on little other than free trade and certainly not on the composition of a future government. Russell and the Whigs, Graham and the Peelites, and Palmerston acting on his own were all jockeying for position. On the other side, Disraeli hoped to jettison protection as painlessly as possible and then reach out to the Peelites, or Palmerston, or even the Manchester School. Apart from the ardent free traders, in short, almost everyone wanted to avoid a confrontation, and after inconclusive negotiations with Russell and Graham early in the new parliamentary session, Cobden resigned himself to waiting for a clarification of the political situation.

That did not come until the autumn. Only after a midsummer general election settled nothing and the government continued to skirt the protection issue did the Whigs and Peelites agree to challenge the

Tories on free trade. When Parliament met in November, Villiers moved an amendment to the queen's speech, terming the repeal of the Corn Laws "wise, just and beneficial,"[31] a deliberately provocative phrase that Cobden insisted on as his price for cooperating with the Whigs and Peelites. The government was saved, however, as it had been saved before, by political maneuvering. Palmerston, still playing for position, concocted a compromise motion, which proved enough to satisfy the moderate free traders and acceptable to the Tories. Villiers' motion was defeated, Palmerston's was passed, and the Tories held onto office until the defeat of Disraeli's budget a month later.

A minority Tory government tainted with protectionism, which had been expected to last only a few weeks, had survived for nearly a year. For the radicals it had been a wasted year. Repeal had been reaffirmed but hardly in ringing terms, and their other interests had been shoved aside for the duration. Bright was especially impatient to pick up where he had left off, and when the new Whig-Peelite coalition renewed Russell's reform bill pledge, he set about reviving the reform movement. Bright was more cautious than he had been the year before. He had no use for Walmsley's National Association; his would be a Manchester move. As for the government's intentions, Bright was skeptical at best. Still, there was no reason not to put pressure on the new ministry; indeed Russell had told him privately that outside pressure would be helpful.

Cobden would have none of it. Russell may have joined Bright in his obsession with parliamentary reform, but that did not make a successful reform bill likely. "I am sick of the everlasting attempt out of doors to give the semblance of an agitation which does not exist," he told Bright in January 1853.[32] And this time Cobden meant it. Always before he had gone along with Bright's plans, if only for the sake of appearances. In 1853 he refused to do so. When Bright suggested the habitual beginning-of-the-year reform meeting in Manchester, Cobden, as habitually, advised against it; when Bright persisted, Cobden—for the first time in their long relationship—declined to share a public platform with him. The February 1853 reform meeting in Manchester was reduced to the status of a local gathering.

Had there been any chance that Russell's new bill would be a sweeping measure, Cobden might have acted differently. But there was no possibility that the government would include the two provisions he regarded as most important: a wide redistribution of seats and the secret ballot. This did not mean that Cobden was indifferent to the progress (or lack of it) of the reform question. He tried to put what pressure he could on the government through its one radical member, William Molesworth. In addition, he privately encouraged the formation of a ballot agitation apart from the NPFRA, to the consternation of Hume and Walmsley. Cobden denied, disingenuously, that he was behind any separate move, but he made no secret of his views. "Don't give in for a moment to the cry that the advocates of secret voting seek to shelve the other points of Hume's program," he advised Walmsley. "The only way to gain our object is by making the ballot the sina qua non."[33] Cobden did not, of course, believe that the government could be compelled to adopt the ballot, which was anathema to most Whigs. But that in a way was just the point. As he had in 1837, Cobden took up the ballot primarily as a means of separating sham from real reformers. In the circumstances of 1853 that was perhaps the most valuable service he could render.

Even that point was lost sight of, however, as the time approached for the introduction of Russell's bill. The attempts of Bright and Walmsley to create some semblance of public enthusiasm were overshadowed by the outbreak of war between Russia and Turkey and the growing threat of a wider conflict. As early as mid-November, three weeks before the Russian naval victory at Sinope, Cobden cautioned Bright that the Turkish question was likely to divert public attention from domestic affairs. By the time Russell introduced his bill England was on the verge of war, and shortly after she joined the conflict in March, the bill was withdrawn. Thus, three years after its real demise, the postrepeal reform movement was officially dead.

As Cobden already believed and Bright came to recognize, it had been an embarrassing, even a disastrous chapter in the history of English radicalism generally and of the Manchester School in particular. Both Cobden and Bright had diminished their political capital. To their allies and their enemies they were no longer the formidable figures they had been in the summer of 1846. Too often they had appeared to be agitating to no purpose, or to too many, or simply for the sake of agitation. However severely he had been attacked as the leader of the league, Cobden had never been open to ridicule. Now he was; the Palmerstonian press contemptuously dismissed him as a "disappointed demagogue." The phrase stung, although he deflected it with humor. "This disappointed demagogue wants no public employment," he told a Manchester audience in 1851. "If he did, he might have had it before now. I want no favor and, as my friend Bright says, no title. I want nothing that any government or any party can give me; and if I am in the House of Commons at all, it is to give my feeble aid to the advancement of certain questions on which I have strong convictions."[34] The damage to his role as an advocate was what Cobden felt most keenly in the vicissitudes of politics in the early 1850s. The long, drawn-out disintegration of the movements he and Bright had been associated with since 1847 diminished his reputation as a skilled politician and with it some of his credibility as a public spokesman.

It would be unfair to dismiss the reform movements of the postrepeal era as entirely barren, however. Although they did not achieve any of their immediate goals, save for a temporary reduction in government expenditure and a modest increase in the forty-shilling freehold vote in the counties, they did lay the groundwork for substantial later achievements. Many of the freehold land societies were the ancestors of modern building societies. Through Robertson Gladstone and the Liverpool Financial Reformers, Cobden influenced the economic thinking of that greatest of all Liberal chancellors of the Exchequer, William Ewart Gladstone. As for the political reform movement, although certainly premature, it initiated processes that led, however indirectly, to the reform act of 1867. In the absence of the agitation for Hume's Little Charter, it is unlikely that Lord John Russell would have abandoned the finality of the 1832 reform act as early as he did. Moreover, the reform movement began the difficult business of building political bridges across class lines. This accomplishment was, however, primarily the work of Walmsley's national association, in which Bright and Wilson played only a secondary role and Cobden almost none at all.

CHAPTER 16

The Manchester School and Educational Reform

As the decline of the postrepeal reform movement became increasingly evident during 1850, Cobden began to look about for more productive issues to pursue, much as he had in the opening years of his political career before he settled on the Corn Laws. In 1850, as fifteen years before, he was particularly drawn to the education question, and for the same reasons. The further the chances of immediate reform receded, the more he was struck by the appalling ignorance of his fellow countrymen on the critical issues of the day. "The extension of the suffrage must and will come," he wrote Bright in 1851, "but it chills my enthusiasm upon the subject when I see so much popular error and prejudice prevailing upon such questions as the Colonies, religious freedom, and the land customs of this country. I do not mean to say that these thoughts make me for an instant falter in my advocacy of the extension of the franchise, but they make me doubt whether I may not be better employed in trying to diffuse sound practical views."[1]

In other words, there being little chance of advance in the short term, reformers therefore had to look to the one sure means of effecting change over the longer run, the education of the people. The education question "underlies all our social and political problems," he wrote two years later, on the eve of the Crimean war. "Our people have not really been prepared for the part which in an industrial and constitutional country they are called on to perform."[2]

That reforms in educational policy might require years to bring about and additional years before they had any tangible effects on the quality of public life did not especially concern Cobden, at least once the chances for immediate reforms in other fields began to disappear.

For one thing, he was used to long delays. As he reminded a meeting of freeholders in 1849, a seven-year struggle—and he promised them nothing less—would put them in distinguished company: not only the league but the American Revolution and the Puritan Revolution in England had taken seven years. "This is a work that cannot be done in a day," he told the freeholders, "and if it could be done in a day it would not be worth doing. I have no faith in anything that is done suddenly."[3] Moreover, Cobden was certain that it would not take as long as most people imagined for national education, like any seminal reform, to begin to affect the temper of national life. Much as the adoption of the freehold movement had, or so Cobden believed, helped to bring about repeal when the league had captured only five counties, so would a system of national education influence the nature of legislation long before the products of that system reached voting age.

That seemed to Cobden a realistic approach to the question of reform in the circumstances of 1850, just as taking an opposite view had seemed appropriate in the early hopeful stages of the postrepeal era. In the spring of 1848, for example, Cobden had justified his inactivity in the cause of education to George Combe on the grounds that an extension of the suffrage would be the best means of compelling the governing class to educate the new electorate. With the decline of the reform movement a year later, that argument was no longer tenable, but Cobden had other reasons for wishing to steer clear of involvement in the education question, quite apart from his immediate interest in the financial reform and freehold campaigns. As always, the major obstacle to a national education policy was the competing claims of England's many Protestant sects. Since Cobden's earlier involvement with the question, the situation had improved in some respects but worsened in others. The Anglicans were less of a problem than they had been in the 1830s. Although some church leaders, most notably his old adversary the Reverend Hugh Stowall, persisted in their demands for a dominant role for the establishment in any system of national education, such extreme claims were made less often after about 1850, at least in Lancashire. A new generation of churchmen, led by Charles Richson, was amenable to compromise.

The Dissenters were another matter. Although they had formed the backbone of the old Manchester Society for Promoting National Education, their support had always been qualified. Should the creation of a nonsectarian school system prove unobtainable, many Dissenters were inclined to abandon a public system altogether in favor of private efforts. This tendency toward voluntarism increased during the 1840s. In 1843 the Conservative government proposed a plan for the education of factory children in which effective control would have been placed in Anglican hands. This produced such a storm of protest from Dissenters, Catholics, and Methodists that the proposal was withdrawn, but not before it had done permanent damage to the cause of national education. The scheme appeared to prove what existing patterns of state aid to religious schools already indicated, that any system of state-supported education in which religious instruction was allowed was bound to be weighted in favor of the established church. Since many Dissenters felt unable in good conscience to support an entirely secular school system, that left only one alternative, voluntarism.

Cobden understood and sympathized with the scruples of the voluntarists but never with their fanaticism. Voluntary efforts had failed to provide an adequate education to the whole of the population. England, as Cobden frequently reminded his audiences, was the worst-educated Protestant nation, and the need for a national system was so urgent that, to get it, he was willing to accept almost any compromise on the religious issue. But although closest in his thinking to the moderate Dissenters, as an Anglican himself Cobden had to move with care. Furthermore, the militant voluntarists were led by one of Cobden's staunchest allies from league days, Edward Baines of Leeds, and centered in the West Riding of Yorkshire, Cobden's new parliamentary constituency. He was, in short, in a delicate position, and well into 1849 he used that to justify his decision to stay clear of the education issue. "Owing to the split in the Liberal party, caused by Baines," he explained to Combe, "it would be impossible for me to make it [education] the leading political subject at this moment . . . All I can promise myself is that any influence I may now derive from my connection with . . . any other movement, shall at the fitting opportunity be all brought to bear in favor of National Education."[4]

When the financial reform movement began to decline in 1850, however, Cobden was drawn into an active role in the education controversy, to which in any case a compromise solution appeared to be emerging. As in the 1830s, the initiative came from Manchester, where the Lancashire Public Schools Association, picking up where the Manchester Society for Promoting National Education left off, had been founded in 1847. Cobden had been one of its vice-presidents since 1848, and although not an active member, he agreed with its aims and most of its specific proposals. The first goal of the association was to seek legislation authorizing the creation of schools managed by locally elected boards of education and funded out of local rates. That in itself went some distance toward resolving the religious issue, since educational policy as well as funding would no longer emanate from London. But working out the details of a religious policy proved next to impossible. Even among those who agreed on the need for a national education system responsive to local needs, there were enormous differences between the advocates of some sort of religious instruction in the curriculum and those who, having tried and failed to find an acceptable formula for nonsectarian religious instruction, had opted for the so-called secular system.

The Lancashire association was inclined toward the latter solution and spent an inordinate amount of time during its first two years seeking a formula satisfactory to moderate Anglicans, Dissenters, and Catholics, without violating the central principle to which it was committed: a rigid separation of religious from secular teaching. By the time Cobden became active in the association, it was more or less agreed on such devices as the use in religious instruction of a collection of mutually acceptable selections from the Bible and the concept of release time during the school week, in which sectarian religious instruction would be allowed, although not paid for out of public funds. The exact terms of these compromises were a matter of indifference to Cobden. He too had come to favor the secular system, but it and the methods used to implement it were merely means to an end. What drew Cobden into an active role in the Lancashire association were not the specifics of its religious policy so much as its efforts to achieve a compromise—that and the decision of its leaders, taken in the summer of 1850, to push its plan in Parliament as a pilot project for national education. As Cobden had feared, however, there was no way he could avoid being dragged into the religious debate, sometimes it seemed almost to the exclusion of the question of education itself.

His role, as he saw it, was to keep the debates as close to the main issue as possible and, so far as religion was concerned, to assume that all parties were acting in good faith; and above all, to be inclusive and permissive, not exclusive and dogmatic. Thus, at the conference that transformed the Lancashire association into a national body late in 1850, Cobden spent much of his time on the substantively minor but symbolically important question of what the title of the new association should be. Originally it was to have been called the national secular schools association, but Cobden objected to this as likely to mislead people into thinking that the association was somehow irreligious. The secular system of education was simply a device, he emphasized, not an end in itself. After a long debate Cobden won his point; the innocuous term *public* was carried over from the original title of the Lancashire association. "Instead of being called secularists," he once said in attempting to define his position, "we ought to be called separatists."[5]

Cobden's sensitivity in handling the religious issue undoubtedly helped to broaden the base of the new association and narrow the gap between it and its critics. But it was far too soon for that gap to disappear entirely. As he said in summarizing the results of the conference to George Combe, "I perceive a difficulty in arguing the case if we profess to exclude the Bible from all schools. I would take the Massachusetts ground, and say that no book shall be admitted into the schools which favors the doctrines of any particular religious sect; but this in a Protestant country could hardly be said to include the Bible . . . Still I do not shut my eyes to the fact that we shall be accused of teaching religion, just as certainly as we should be charged with irreligion if we excluded the Bible."[6]

With such unresolved problems very much in mind, Cobden warned his friends not to expect much from the conference or the new association: "I am not as sanguine as others about the result and regret that so much importance should have been attached to my joining the agitation," he told one enthusiastic supporter shortly after the conference.[7]

Cobden was right to be cautious. Shortly after the formation of the national association, a rival Anglican group, the Manchester and Salford Committee on Education, emerged. It too showed a good deal of flexibility; indeed, its program was similar to the proposals for including religious instruction of all kinds in the schools that Cobden and his friends had tried to work out fifteen years before. Cobden welcomed this and limited his criticism to questions of practicality. As he noted at a meeting of the national association in 1851:

I have really passed beyond the time in which I can offer any opposition to any scheme whatever, come from whatever party it may, which proposes to give the mass of the people of this country a better education than they now receive. I will say more,—that in joining the secular system of education, I have not taken up the plan from any original love for any system of education which . . . separates itself from religion . . . But I have found, after trying it, as I think, in every possible shape, such insuperable difficulties in consequence of the religious discordances of this country,—that I have taken refuge in this, which has been called the remote haven of refuge for the Educationalists,—the secular system,—in sheer despair of carrying out any system in connection with religion.[8]

Cobden never made a better statement of his practical philosophy in approaching the education question nor, as things turned out, a truer assessment of the difficulties ahead. Only repeated failures and years of patient negotiations produced a broad consensus. For the time being, the rival Manchester groups went their separate ways. Each put its proposal before Parliament, and each was defeated or talked out year after year. Cobden expected that, at least initially, and was resigned to it. All that he attempted to do in the first parliamentary debate in the national association program in May 1851 was to emphasize the need to find neutral ground and argue the case that the secular system, as developed in Massachusetts and adopted by the national association, was that neutral ground. Nothing more was possible, he declared, and nothing less was acceptable.

Parliament, Cobden realized, was perhaps the last place in which agreement was possible, at least in the absence of a mass movement out of doors, and his real work in the service of national education over the next few years was in the frustrating process of negotiations. Immediately after the foundation of the national association, Cobden met with educational and religious leaders in major provincial centers, hoping to achieve in private what had eluded the national association in public meetings. He also encouraged, although he took no public part in, a series of conferences between the national association and the Manchester committee. Progress was painfully slow, however. Although each made important concessions, the two organizations remained far apart, in effect holding each other in check for another six years.

The militant Dissenters were even more intractable. At least the

Anglicans were moving in the right direction, however slowly; the voluntarists would not budge. And Cobden, who was willing to bend over backward to accommodate any group that showed signs of a willingness to compromise, had no patience with those who held rigidly aloof. After his private negotiations at the end of 1850 failed to wring any concessions from Baines and his followers, Cobden began to attack them publicly, often in terms of the sort he had reserved in the past for the upholders of agricultural protection. As he told the national association early in 1851:

> we have endeavored to be very accommodating to these gentlemen, and have found it very difficult to please them. When the attempt was for many years to have an education combined with religion, then those same gentlemen told us it was contrary to their consciences either to receive or pay money raised by taxation, for teaching religion. When we offer to separate it, we are told by these same gentlemen, that it is contrary to their conscientious convictions to separate religious from secular teaching.

Cobden concluded this catalogue of contradictions with a warning: "Such a course, if persevered in, will go very far to alienate the feelings of the great mass of the working community, who, I am very much afraid . . . are not in communion with either Dissent or Church."[9]

Eleven months later, although now with as much regret as anger, Cobden reiterated his attack and his warning to the same audience in what amounted to his valedictory address to the education movement. "I shall watch with the utmost interest the local agitation," he had informed the national association privately three months earlier, "but I do not think that I can with advantage or propriety take a part in it, unless it be to act in a mediatorial capacity."[10] That he did for the remainder of his life, whenever there seemed to be any sign of progress, but the sense of movement, which had drawn him into an active role in the education question, had dissipated. The secularists, the Anglicans, and, above all, the voluntarists had staked out their positions and appeared less and less inclined to depart from them. Far from having progressed, Cobden exaggeratedly concluded in 1852, the education question was worse off than it had been a decade and a half before. That was not true, of course, but it had failed to produce the tangible results that he and others had reasonably hoped for in 1850.

As was his wont in such circumstances, Cobden again began to look about for something to fall back on. He found it in the, to him, closely related question of the repeal of the taxes on knowledge, as the newspaper stamp tax, the duty on advertisements, and the paper duty were known collectively in radical terminology. In Cobden's view this was a perfect issue to hold in reserve, to be trotted out in a time of diminishing expectations. Like the secret ballot, to which, as the political reform movement dwindled, he retreated at the same time, it had the advantage of simplicity. Like the ballot but unlike the complex issues of educational, financial, and political reform, it could be used as a test of radicalism at a time when the forces of radicalism were on the defensive.

Cobden was first drawn into the movement for the repeal of the taxes of knowledge in 1849, shortly after the publication of his People's Budget. In January, a Chartist splinter group, the People's Charter Union, dominated by education-minded, moral-force Chartists such as Henry Hetherington, George Jacob Holyoake, and Thomas Cooper, appealed to Cobden to include in his proposed budget the repeal of the newspaper stamp duty. Cobden had initially suggested only an "equitable revision" of the duty, but in their address to him his Chartist petitioners hit upon an argument that was bound to appeal to him—that the working classes should be allowed to seek self-improvement through free trade in ideas: "While Churchmen and Dissenters are quarreling as to how we are to be educated, while government accords but a paltry grant, and while earnest reformers like yourself acknowledge that a considerable time must elapse before any scheme of national education can be adopted—the least that all these parties can do is allow us to educate ourselves."[11]

Cobden hesitated only briefly before adopting their proposal as his own, perhaps to their surprise, certainly to their delight. "This address and Mr. Cobden's reply were the basis of the whole of the subsequent agitation" against the newspaper taxes, according to C. D. Collet, who rapidly emerged as the leader of the fight. "Never did any reformer, filled with enthusiasm for an idea of his own, accept a suggested change in it with such self-sacrificing readiness as that with which Mr. Cobden accepted our appeal . . . He certainly did give his very best support to our cause, both in all he did and all he refrained from doing."[12]

This final compliment is interesting evidence of Cobden's commitment to his belief that the leaders of the Manchester school should encourage the spontaneous development of independent reform groups rather than seek to lead them at the risk of smothering them or having them dismissed as creatures of the league. He never attempted to run the movement for the repeal of the newspaper taxes, as he was urged to do by some. Instead, he chose to act as advisor to Collet, who organized the agitation out of doors, and Milner Gibson, its parliamentary spokesman. Although Cobden's role was secondary, it was both active and visible. When Milner Gibson persuaded Lord John Russell to agree in 1850 to receive a deputation from the Newspaper Stamp Abolition Committee of the People's Charter Union, Cobden was one of the M.P.s who accompanied Collet and his colleagues to Downing Street. A year later he took a prominent role in questioning witnesses, as a member of Milner Gibson's select committee on the newspaper stamp. He warmly supported the cause in Parliament, either for its own sake or as part of his larger scheme for financial reform.

Cobden's most important contribution, however, was in educating the abolition committee in the arts of agitation. It was primarily at his urging that the abolition committee agreed, early in 1851, to dissolve itself into a larger group, the Association for the Repeal of the Taxes on Knowledge, which had an impressive roster of M.P.s and professional men on its committee and which, in imitation of the league, could pursue its single goal free of association with other causes. The metamorphosis did not involve a sellout of or by the Chartist founders of the movement. The officers of the old committee, including the chairman, Richard Moore, Collet, and the ubiquitous Francis Place, retained their posts in the new association; only Milner Gibson was added to the list of officers, as president; Cobden and Bright were content to serve as members of the general committee. The change was designed to add weight and respectability to the agitation.

So was most of Cobden's other advice to the association. Although he occasionally spoke at its public meetings, his greatest contribution was made behind the scenes. He served for a time as chairman of the financial committee of the association and frequently attended the weekly meetings of the general committee, to which, with what

Holyoake called his "instinct of fitness,"[13] he made an especially valuable contribution in advising on the most effective avenues of agitation. Cobden also bombarded Collet with letters offering comments and suggestions. As he said at one point to his ever-patient correspondent, "As an old master in that line, who served his seven years' apprenticeship, I must use the privilege of speaking frankly."[14] And so he did. In addition to giving Collet specific advice on how to go about forming branch societies, the best means of getting publicity, whom to contact in the provinces, and the like, Cobden constantly reminded him of the need to adjust the methods of agitation to the moderating temper of the times and to the tastes and prejudices of the all-important middle class.

He stressed that it was better to have a few reliable sources of funds than a host of small contributors, however democratic one's sympathies might be. And although he encouraged the association to continue to use both the courts and publicity to expose the anomalies in the law as it applied to different types of publication as well as the capriciousness with which it was enforced, he advised strongly against too combative an approach: "Make out your case as strongly as you can on the grounds of justice, education and morality, but don't assume too strongly on the part of the public a sense of grievance of which there is really but little evidence, and, above all, don't breath a syllable of menace or defiance."[15] This was necessary, Cobden believed, not only in order to reach Parliament but for the sake of keeping the association going. "If you had for your client the 'fierce democracy,'" he advised Collet,

> you might then fling saucy phrases at the head of the Chancellor of the Exchequer with consistency. But cast your eye over the subscription list of the 'Association,' and you will see how exclusively, almost, we comprise steady, sober middle-class reformers—free trade, temperance, education, peace advocates—who will stand by you from year to year, and gather about them an increasing moral power, provided you handle them judiciously, and do not place them in a position in which they think they are committed to a *tone* of agitation which does not represent their feelings.[16]

Not that Cobden was averse to pressing the issue, if the time seemed ripe. When the agitation against the stamp duty appeared to be close to a breakthrough in the summer of 1854, he suggested that "one of the best things that can happen is the starting of a good many unstamped papers for special objects . . . The more of them the better, for, as the Inland Revenue Board will not be able to prosecute [since such specialized publications were not considered newspapers in the ordinary sense], the regular stamped newspapers will by and by begin to call out for the removal of the stamp, to put them on a fair footing."[17] As in the struggle against the Corn Laws, the only criterion Cobden applied in choosing between different means of agitation was effectiveness.

The most active phase of Cobden's involvement in the agitation began in 1853, when the other postrepeal reform movements were in ruins, but Gladstone's first budget as chancellor of the Exchequer in the newly formed Aberdeen government opened up the possibility that the least controversial (and least revenue-producing) of the duties, that on advertising, might be reduced or repealed. The association did not expect much from Gladstone, who proposed only a reduction. But the sense of the House of Commons, as indicated by the vote on Milner Gibson's annual motion against the duty, was now against its continuation, and when an amendment reducing the duty to nothing was passed, Gladstone accepted this second verdict of the House.

The association, having won a portion of its objective, was understandably euphoric. Cautious as ever, Cobden attempted to introduce a draft of cold air into the celebratory atmosphere. "I have not much faith in your plan of blending music and logic," he commented on Collet's arrangements for a soiree in honor of Milner Gibson. "Both are good in their way, but in the agitation that I have been used to we have kept them apart. However, as on this occasion you are in a certain sense rejoicing, the harp and timbrel may be deemed not out of place. But you must take a sterner and more business-like tone at the anniversary."[18]

Cobden was certain that the repeal of the stamp duty would be a more difficult task and that "the way, and the only way, to bring a sufficient force of moral power to our aid and to put the education loving Government in a crucible from which they never can escape . . . is by making it an education question."[19] The problem was that established papers had an interest in maintaining the duty as a deterrent to the growth of a cheap popular press, and in addition, in Cobden's view, the governing class was not enthusiastic about affording the masses easy access to enlightenment. "The stamp," he concluded gloomily, "is the toughest question, excepting the ballot, left for solution."[20]

For once in the 1850s Cobden was overly pessimistic, although, ironically, it was largely the war in the Crimea that he opposed so bitterly that opened the way to the repeal of the stamp duty. Hunger for war news produced a spate of hastily published papers, which, because they were devoted to that subject alone, had an uncertain status according to the normal definition of a newspaper. This is precisely what Cobden had hoped would happen as a means of finally exposing the contradictions of the stamp duty and turning existing papers against it (although he had looked to papers dealing with more beneficent subjects such as teetotalism to perform this service). In any case, by the end of 1854, the law had become all but unenforceable, and repeal of the stamp duty was proposed first by Gladstone and then, successfully, early in the following year by his successor at the Exchequer, George Cornwall Lewis. Clearly, circumstances (and Gladstone) had been largely responsible for precipitating these reforms, but the role of the Association for the Repeal of the Taxes on Knowledge was crucial nonetheless. Like the Anti–Corn Law League, this "model agitation,"[21] as Holyoake called it, had created a climate of opinion in which in almost any anomalous situation involving the duties the government would have little choice other than repeal. Collet and his Manchester school allies rightly regarded the elimination of the stamp and advertising duties as a great triumph. In an era of disappointment and defeat for radical reformers, it was almost their only victory.

CHAPTER 17

The Pursuit of Peace

Cobden took up the education question in 1850 in part because it looked more promising than the ailing parliamentary and financial reform movement but also because the decline of that movement appeared to demonstrate that the people had to be educated to a better understanding of their own interests before further progress could be made. His growing pessimism about the immediate outlook for radical reform was also fed by a roughly simultaneous worsening of the prospects for peace, which even more than his disappointment with financial reform altered the course of his public career early in the 1850s. For three years before that, ever since the repeal of the Corn Laws, Cobden had been cautiously hopeful. Certain that repeal was the most important single step England could take in promoting peace, he was encouraged in his optimism by his generally warm reception abroad and the early successes of the financial reform campaign in curbing military spending.

Cobden had never believed, however, that a peace dividend would automatically follow from free trade, let alone that it would come quickly. Time and great effort would be required to bring about the changes in thinking necessary if the potential of free trade for reducing international tension was to be realized. It might take years, for example, for the effects of repeal in increasing international economic interdependence to become evident and still longer before the significance of this change began to be fully understood. Old fears and animosities based on outmoded mercantilist concepts of national economic rivalry would die away only slowly, and until that happened, the general public, like its leaders, was bound to see the dangers of a pacific noninterventionist foreign policy as outweighing its potential benefits. The peace issue, at least pursued for its own sake, was therefore likely to remain politically risky for the forseeable future.

Cobden was well aware of all this. Although he had tried to enlist various peace groups in support of the repeal movement as far back as 1842, he had avoided pressing his views on the intimate connection between the two issues in speaking to other audiences. Just how divisive the peace issue could be was forcefully brought home to him by the often savage criticism of his attack on the military and military spending during the anti-French scare of 1847–48. He recognized that he had made a serious tactical error and was determined not to repeat it, at least to the extent that a promising alternative was open to him. In 1848 the financial reform movement seemed to provide that alternative, and for nearly a year Cobden concentrated on that, almost to the exclusion of direct involvement with questions of war and peace. In much the same way that he had hoped, also in 1848, to avoid participation in the education movement, on the grounds that an extension of the suffrage might force the government to create an adequate school system, so, in approaching the peace issue, he preferred to focus on the enlightened economic self-interest of the British taxpayer as a means both of educating the public in the waste of military spending and of placing financial restraints on the ability of the government to pursue an interventionist foreign policy. As he put it in a letter to Joseph Sturge, the most prominent leader of the London Peace Society, in the autumn of 1848: "It may be objected that I appeal to low motives in thus dwelling upon the pecuniary view of the question. True: but if the New Testament has failed to inspire Christian nations with faith in the principles of peace, I may surely be excused if I demonstrate how costly is their reliance for defense upon the spirit of war."[1]

This indirect approach to the peace question had the additional advantage of putting a little distance between Cobden and the organized peace movement. Indeed, at the height of the invasion panic, late in 1847, he suggested to Sturge that there should be a division of labor between them, with the peace societies addressing themselves directly to issues of war and peace, while he concentrated on the financial aspects of the question. This was not simply a polite way of differentiating himself from a movement that many dismissed as naive. Cobden had reservations about the effectiveness of the peace societies but never about their ultimate value. To him the emergence of an active peace movement was one of the few hopeful developments of the postrepeal era. The London Peace Society had been founded in 1816 and from the first had worked closely with equivalent groups in the United States, but it was not until the late 1840s, spurred on by the repeal of the Corn Laws and the French war scare of 1847, that the society hit its stride, extending operations to the continent and receiving extensive publicity at home. Cobden welcomed the change and tailored his activities to it. The effectiveness of his parliamentary attack on military spending depended in large measure, he believed, on having the peace society at his back, raising fundamental questions about the morality of present policy.

The division of labor between Cobden and the peace movement worked well for both parties, and even when Cobden was most absorbed in the financial reform movement, he was careful to coordinate strategy with the London Peace Society. He reestablished good relations with Sturge after an estrangement during the late league years brought about by Sturge's support of the Complete Suffrage Movement and by his opposition to a reduction in the import duty on slave-grown sugar. Sturge had his weaknesses as a popular leader, however; he was often all but oblivious to the practical obstacles in the way of the many noble causes to which he devoted much of his life. A sounder foundation for the revived peace movement as well as a better working relationship between the movement and Cobden was provided by the Reverend Henry Richard, who was appointed secretary to the London Peace Society and editor of its journal, the *Herald of Peace*, in the spring of 1848. He quickly became Cobden's closest confidant on all questions of war and peace, colonial and foreign policy.

Yet despite his collaboration with Sturge and Richard, Cobden did not join the London Peace Society. He disagreed with a number of points in its program and more generally with its approach to agitating the issue. The Quakers inevitably loomed large in the movement (Sturge was a Quaker, although Richard was not), and the peace society was tinged wih pacifism as well as inclined to take positions on a variety of issues from slavery to capital punishment. Cobden was never an advocate of nonresistance, let alone of mixing more than one issue into an agitation. The peace society also favored the creation of a congress of nations with police powers. Cobden did not, fearing that it might actually increase the level of international violence. But even had he supported the program of the peace society in full, Cobden would have pursued it differently. Like most peace groups, the society tended to deal in generalities, to which its critics could pay lip service while simultaneously dismissing them as naive and impractical. If that rationale for inaction and cynical detachment was to be undermined, the peace question had first to be made a practical question, which under the leadership of the London Peace Society it clearly was not.

That was sufficient reason for Cobden to keep his distance, and for nearly a year after his ill-starred attack on the military in 1847, he addressed himself to the peace issue only as part of the financial reform campaign. But 1848 was not a year in which it was easy or seemed necessary to remain cautious, and by the early winter Cobden had been pulled into an active role in the peace movement. The flood tide of liberal revolution during the spring and summer produced a ground swell of optimism throughout Europe about the prospects for peace. In England, as elsewhere, government leaders spoke platitudi-nously of a new era in international relations, and the London Peace Society was taken aback to find itself riding a wave of popular en-thusiasm. Cobden, who was no more immune to this sense of re-newed possibilities than any other radical, began to look to the peace movement more for its promise than its faults and to see even in its faults a reason to become involved.

After all, the rejuvenated peace society was a spontaneous outgrowth of the peculiar conditions of 1848, and like its contemporary, the Liverpool Financial Reform Association, it opened up unique possibilities, which, if not seized immediately, might be permanently lost. Moreover, again like the financial reformers, the peace society was deficient in precisely those areas—its program and political expertise—where Cobden could make an especially valuable contribution. Furthermore, the peace society appeared to be moving in the right direction, away from generalities toward a specific program and beyond its base in Anglo-American Quakerism to become a cosmopolitan movement. The appointment of Richard as secretary of the society was a good sign, as was the holding of an international peace congress in Brussels four months later. Here was an opportunity Cobden could not resist. "I feel that I have the animus within me to battle successfully with the war spirit if I can be supported out of doors," he told Sturge on the eve of the peace congress.[2] Shortly thereafter, at the same time that he was negotiating the adoption of the People's Budget by the Liverpool Financial Reform Association, he adopted a portion of the peace society's program as his own.

It was a limited commitment, however. In essence Cobden hoped to do for the peace movement what he had done for the league, only in reverse. The repeal movement had at first appeared too materialistic and desperately needed a leavening of moral fervor; a decade later the peace movement seemed all morality and needed to be anchored in mundane practicalities. Specifically, Cobden believed that a peace program could be effected only by proposing a succession of small incremental steps, each of which could be defended as eminently safe and sane. In the process, the peace question would be brought down to the level where it belonged, of a series of debates on concrete issues. That in turn would place the supporters of traditional foreign and military policies rather than the peace advocates on the defensive and, not incidently, educate peace advocates in the proper mode of agitation.

As a first step, near the end of 1848 Cobden announced his intention of introducing in the upcoming session of Parliament a motion calling on the British government to take the initiative in negotiating arbitration agreements with other powers. A plank in the peace society's program since 1841, international arbitration appealed to Cobden because, although a clear step in the right direction, it was also a limited step and one for which there were ample precedents in recent international agreements. Furthermore, shortly before Cobden announced his motion, Lord John Russell had given qualified endorsement to arbitration in response to a representation by delegates from the American Peace Society.

All in all, it seemed unlikely that conditions would soon be again as favorable to the peace question, and at the time he announced his motion Cobden even suggested to Sturge that it might win a majority in the House of Commons if sufficient public interest could be aroused. Even allowing for Cobden's tendency to be overly optimistic when he took up a new cause, it is difficult to believe that he really expected a parliamentary victory. He may simply have hoped to encourage Sturge and the peace society, who were to bear the burden of generating public enthusiasm. In any case, whatever illusions Cobden may have had were quickly dispelled. The announcement of his motion was greeted with derision by much of the press and parliamentary opinion, and by the time of the debate in Parliament his primary concern was that the issue be taken seriously.

In this he was successful. Sturge and the peace society arranged more than a hundred meetings in support of arbitration during the winter, and Parliament was flooded with petitions; whatever individual M.P.s might think, there was no denying the extent of public interest in the question. Cobden's speech in introducing his motion was equally effective. Not only was he able to anticipate all the arguments raised by his opponents, but by limiting his remarks entirely to the practical issues involved, he in effect determined the nature of the ensuing debate. It was a cool speech, almost colorless, and deliberately so. "I might have taken higher ground in my argument with more justice to the subject," he explained to George Combe, "but I had to deal with an audience determined to sneer down the notion as Utopian . . . It was to meet these people on what they conceived to be their strong ground, that I dwelt upon the practical view of my scheme."[3]

Cobden referred only in passing to the horrors of war and never enlisted moral arguments. Although he acknowledged the work of the Quakers and the peace society, he was also careful to point out his differences with them and to emphasize the influence of the financial reform movement. He made much of recent precedents for arbitration but belittled the changes it would bring about. His proposal called for the countries involved in a dispute to appoint the arbitrators, with an umpire to be called in only if they could not reach agreement. The decision of the arbitrators would not be enforceable, he pointed out, nor would any party be prevented from going to war should arbitration fail. The only sanction would be world opinion, although Cobden at least was hardly likely to underestimate the force of that. All he was suggesting, he claimed, was that nations agree to conduct in anticipation of war negotiations of the sort normally held at the conclusion of a war. Should this fail, the participants would be no worse off than they were at present. Should it succeed, they "would in this way and in the course of time establish a kind of common law among nations."[4]

Although his motion garnered only seventy-nine votes, Cobden was cautiously pleased by the result. He had put his public reputation at some risk by associating himself with the peace society, but he had suffered little of the political damage that some of his friends had feared. As for the peace issue, he was encouraged by the fact that most M.P.s had not voted at all; this he interpreted as evidence that many of them, perhaps for the first time, had been compelled to think about arbitration as a real issue. Cobden was especially delighted by the obvious discomfort of the government. "It was some satisfaction to me," he reported to Combe, "to draw from Lord Palmerston a speech full of admissions, which ended by an amendment [to move the previous question] avowedly framed to escape a direct negative of my motion."[5] In the press as well there were signs of progress. The mocking tone of six months before was largely absent in June, and although most papers still dismissed Cobden's scheme as utopian, there were some interesting exceptions, the most unusual being a serious—and entirely laudatory—article in *Punch*. If nothing else, Cobden and the peace society had made it difficult to dismiss arbitration as the hobbyhorse of a few impractical visionaries.

The summer of 1849 was the high-water mark of the peace movement. Two months after the debate on Cobden's motion, the largest meeting of peace advocates in the nineteenth century convened in Paris. This was the second in a series of six midcentury peace congresses and the first to be organized, as far as the British delegation was concerned, by the Peace Congress Committee. The committee was established in late 1848 as a device to broaden the base of the peace movement. Although close to the peace society, the committee was a separate entity, not committed to the essentially pacifist program of the society. Thus it provided a meeting ground for pragmatically minded members of the society and sympathetic nonmembers such as Cobden. Its formation was the first sign of the new approach to agitating the peace question for which Cobden and Henry Richard were largely responsible.

The committee's first act was to help organize the campaign of meetings in support of Cobden's arbitration motion, but its main purpose was to make the peace congress, beginning with the 1849 Paris congress, the centerpiece of the movement and a forum for all sympathetic groups. By contrast, the first congress, held the year before in Brussels, was a parochial affair, made up primarily of delegates from established peace societies inspired by the hope that the revolutions of that spring and summer might open the way to greater international cooperation. Cobden did not attend, although not because of any lack of sympathy with their aims. In a letter to Sturge, written to be read to the delegates, he emphasized his agreement with most of the program of the congress, especially its support for international arbitration. On the other hand, he took care to point out his reservations concerning a congress of nations and his preference for approaching the peace question as a financial issue. In a way this letter represented the opening public move in a process of negotiation between Cobden and the peace society that led rapidly, by way of the formation of the Peace Congress Committee and Cobden's decision to propose an arbitration motion in Parliament, to a close working relationship. By the time arrangements for the Paris Peace Congress were made in the summer of 1849, it would have been unthinkable for Cobden not to have attended.

He arrived in Paris almost a week before the congress convened to assist in the final preparations. As the most important political leader in attendance, Cobden inevitably became one of the stellar attractions of the congress. He spoke to every session of the three-day meeting. He defended his arbitration proposal in answer to some critical questions during the opening session. On the second day he delivered—in French—his major address to the congress, a defense of the practicality of the peace program, as compared with the dangers and crippling costs of traditional policy. He used the third and final session to bring the congress back to the level where he himself felt most comfortable, of specific courses of action. His target, a new one for the peace movement, was war loans: "It is from the savings . . . of the merchant, manufacturer, trader . . . agriculturalist and annuitants of civilised Europe that warlike governments can alone supply their necessities, and to them we will appeal by every motive of self interest and humanity not to lend their support to a barbarous system . . . We will do more—we will in every possible way expose the character and object, and exhibit to the world the true state of the resources of every government which endeavors to contract a loan for warlike purposes.[6]

If only because he was able to raise this issue, Cobden counted the Paris congress as a worthwhile exercise. He was, to be sure, a good deal less satisfied with his major speech on the second day, and many of the other speakers and their speeches he found bad or simply "half crazy."[7] The meetings he arranged with ministers in the French government were equally disappointing. Even those few who appeared to Cobden to talk sensibly on military and economic matters were not willing to risk public utterances. The shaky new republican government in France, however, welcomed the decision of the organizers of the congress to meet in Paris, and the delegates were treated with respect and a good deal of fanfare. On a propaganda level at least the Paris Peace Congress was a success.

In the normal course of events Cobden would have continued his pursuit of the peace issue into 1850 much as he had begun it in 1849. That was his intention. He attended one of a series of meetings in the autumn in England sponsored by the Peace Congress Committee to publicize the work of the Paris congress, and he enthusiastically endorsed the idea of holding another congress the following year. In addition, immediately after the defeat of his arbitration motion, he began to plan for its reintroduction in 1850. To this he proposed to add a similar declaratory motion in favor of the mutual reduction of armaments. Both in turn were to be linked to his second annual motion calling for a reduction in national expenditure. Backed out of doors by the peace society and the financial reform movement and confidant of a steady accretion of radical strength through the forty-shilling freehold campaign, Cobden was more certain of his future course in the autumn of 1849 than at any time since the repeal of the Corn Laws. The only distraction was the increasingly unwelcome pressure from his friends in the parliamentary reform movement.

By the following spring little was left of Cobden's long-range plans. In almost everything touching the peace question, the apparently favorable trends of 1849 were reversed over the winter. In its dealings with two small and defenseless peoples, in Borneo and Greece, the British government, urged on by much of the press and public opinion, condoned or conducted policies that seemed to Cobden mindlessly aggressive, even barbaric. Although neither incident posed as serious a threat to peace as the anti-French scare of 1847—largely because no other great power was directly involved—what they revealed about the national state of mind disturbed Cobden even more profoundly. Under the circumstances it no longer seemed sufficient to seek to impose restraints on the government through pressure for financial reform while sketching in the outlines of an alternative foreign policy through motions in favor of arbitration or disarmament. Cobden did not abandon these motions, let alone his practice of subjecting the army, navy, and colonial estimates to searching criticism, but to them he added increasingly direct and personal attacks on the conduct of British policy, attacks of a sort he had on the whole avoided since the end of the anti-French scare two years earlier; and in his attempts to reach and alter public opinion at large, he more and more often tended to go beyond arguments of practicality and financial responsibility to appeal to his audience on moral grounds. As long as Cobden had believed that immediate progress on the peace issue was possible, he had been willing to suppress his private feelings for tactical reasons. As that prospect receded, he saw little reason to contain his growing sense of outrage. Nor, by early 1850, could he easily have done so.

The change came suddenly. In the autumn of 1849, following his initiative at the Paris Peace Congress, Cobden set out to undermine an attempt by the Austrian government to float a loan in western Europe. In addressing a protest meeting in London in October, he concentrated almost exclusively on the financial aspects of the issue; apart from some closing comments on the immorality of subscribing to a loan that would be used to pay off debts incurred by Austria in the course of suppressing its own people, he devoted the bulk of his speech to proving that the loan was an unsound investment. Three months later, however, in condemning a similar attempt by the Russian government to float a loan, Cobden shifted the balance of his attack. Above all, he declared, this was a moral issue, because those who subscribed to the loan were in effect condoning the recent Russian suppression of the Hungarian revolution, the costs of which, he asserted, the loan was primarily designed to cover. Moreover, should Russia succeed in raising the money, other nations would follow her example. Thus, to lend the money would serve to encourage military adventurism elsewhere and to retard the progress of liberty by propping up the autocracies of eastern and southern Europe. "What shall we say of England," he asked, "if we have to record that, in the year 1850, there were found men in London ready to endorse the desperate wickedness of Russia by lending her money to continue the career of violence she has hitherto maintained?"[8]

Englishmen, whose liberties had been won largely as a result of the financial embarrassment of their rulers, could not in good conscience provide the means of saving other peoples' rulers from a similar fate, Cobden argued. Nor, putting the moral issues to one side, could the loans even be defended as compatible with English national interests, which surely were not served by the perpetuation of autocracy or the financing of potentially antagonistic military establishments. That the

Russian loan also would not be a sound or safe investment, Cobden did not of course fail to point out. "In thus lending your money, you place it upon a volcano," he said. But that was no longer his major theme, and it had never been his major concern. Only his calculation of what would best serve to sink the Austrian loan had led him in October to emphasize the financial risks involved. By January, he was less inclined to make that kind of calculation.

Between Cobden's attacks on the Austrian and Russian loans, word had reached England first of an assault on the Dyaks of Sarawak by Sir James Brooke and then of British pressure on the government of Greece, culminating in a blockade of the port of Piraeus. The subjugation of the peoples of North Borneo by Brooke was perhaps the most extraordinary example of individual imperial freebooting in the nineteenth century. His personal empire and the title of Raja, dating from the early 1840s, were rewards for assistance to the local sultan in bringing order to the coastal regions of North Borneo. With occasional aid from British naval forces, he conducted a decade-long campaign that culminated in an attack on a group of Dyak boatmen and villages—nests of pirates, so it was said—in the summer of 1849.

When word of this reached England, Cobden was appalled and even more appalled by the public reaction at home. Brooke excited that strain in Victorian thought that tended to make heroes of men of force. In an especially virulent expression of muscular Christianity, Charles Kingsley questioned misplaced sympathy for Brooke's victims:

> "Sacrifice of human life?" Prove that it is *human* life. It is beast life. These Dyaks have put on the image of the beast and they must take the consequences . . . Physical death is no evil. It may be a blessing to the survivors. Else, why pestilence, famine, Cromwell and Perrot in Ireland, Charlemagne hanging 4000 Saxons over the Weser Bridge; did not God bless these terrible righteous judgements? Do you believe in the Old Testament? Surely then, say, what does that destruction of the Canaanites mean? If *it* was right, Rajah Brooke was right. If he be wrong, then Moses, Joshua, David, were wrong.[9]

To Cobden events in Sarawak called to mind less reassuring historical precedents:

> Here you have a slaughter unparalleled in its character since the massacre of the feeble Mexicans by the Spaniards in the sixteenth century,

committed upon a race of barbarians upon no other pretence than that they were living in a state of uncivilized warfare with neighboring barbarous tribes. No attack was made or contemplated upon Englishmen or Europeans—no attack was possible; for mark the features of the case: . . . two thousand were blown to atoms, and we do not find that there was . . . the loss of a single life to an Englishmen. This fact constitutes it the most wanton, cruel and cowardly butchery of modern times.[10]

During the winter months Cobden tried to rouse public anger while avoiding taking too prominent a part himself. He wrote (anonymously) or inspired letters and articles in the press; he urged Sturge and Richard for the peace society and, along with Sturge, the Aborigines Protection Society, to hold protest meetings; and early in the new year he joined in parliamentary attacks on Brooke and on the British government for complicity with Brooke. He seconded a motion by Joseph Hume calling for a commission of inquiry.

Throughout this eight-month-long campaign Cobden assumed that what had happened to the Dyaks was an unprovoked massacre. He doubted the allegations of piracy, and even were they true, he questioned the right of Britain to intervene to stop it because British commerce had not been affected. He was even more certain that Brooke was the villain of the piece, intent on suppressing local conflicts for the sake of his own aggrandizement while using the issue of piracy to get the British navy to do his dirty work. As far at least as Brooke was concerned, Cobden was largely mistaken. He relied uncritically on information from personal enemies of Brooke, and in his revulsion at the killing of the Dyaks Cobden was too ready to personalize the evil in the figure of the Raja of Sarawak. Thus, when an inquiry was finally held two years later and Brooke was exonerated—a verdict most later historians have accepted—his critics, especially Hume and Cobden, were to some degree discredited.

Cobden's tactical error in concentrating too much of his fire on Brooke diminished his influence on more than the Borneo question, because the larger issues that he regarded as implicit in what had happened there were lost sight of. Even had Brooke and the British navy acted with the best of intentions, Cobden believed, it was no business of the British to suppress local piracy in coastal Borneo, because in the process of doing so they were bound to become inextricably involved in the fortunes of yet another non-European people.

To Cobden this was madness, yet at that very moment the British government, for the best of reasons and with none of the ambiguities involved in Sarawak, was contemplating an extension of imperial responsibilities in tropical Africa, by purchasing the Danish forts on the Gold Coast.

The cost of these new territories aside (although he regarded that issue as far from incidental), Cobden was particularly disturbed by what he saw as a failure on the part of the government to think through the consequences of such an act. Its stated motives were unexceptionable: to suppress the slave trade, open the area to commerce, and advance Christianity and civilization. But Cobden questioned whether military bases were the best means to any of these ends and, further, whether Britain did not have better economic opportunities in advanced countries, not to mention more immediate moral responsibilities closer to home.

Moreover, there seemed to him insuperable objections to additional territorial expansion into inhabited tropical areas: "There was a great difference between acquiring territory where the race might become indigenous, so as to extend commerce and to spread the principle of self-government over the world, and taking possession of tropical territory, where their own race was not indigenous, where government must be upheld by force, and where there was no prospect of being able to disembarrass themselves of the responsibilities of governing the people."[11] In this view, what had happened in Sarawak was no accident, no chance consequence of the actions of an individual. It was the all-too-likely result of the inequality between governor and governed in tropical territories ruled by Europeans. Dormant in every tropical colony lay the seeds of new Sarawaks.

Important as the Borneo question was to Cobden, it had no long-term impact on the public at large. The same could not be said of the Greek crisis, the Don Pacifico affair. In diplomacy as in domestic politics, it was a watershed event. Despite Palmerston's questionable conduct throughout the crisis, it ended in a triumph for him personally and for his approach to the conduct of foreign affairs, and it was an equally dramatic defeat for his critics, Cobden included. It was the occasion of perhaps the most stellar parliamentary debate on foreign policy in the whole of the Victorian era and established both the terms and the political alignments of future conflict over foreign policy until the deaths of Palmerston and Cobden fifteen years later. And finally, more clearly perhaps than any other single incident, it raised fundamental questions about the appropriate use of British power at a time when Britain occupied a unique position in the world.

Certainly there could have been no more dramatic illustration of the resort to gunboat diplomacy than Palmerston's dispatch of a naval squadron to Greece in support of claims against the Greek government by a number of British subjects, one of whom, Don Pacifico, happened to be British only by the accident of birth in Gibraltar. That many of these claims were questionable and most of the claimants even more so, or that England had acted unilaterally without consulting France or Russia, the other major powers with interests in the area, was almost beside the point so far as Palmerston was concerned. In defending his actions in the House of Commons, he was willing in the end to rest his case on the doctrine that "as the Roman in days of old held himself free from indignity when he could say "Civis Romanus sum,' so also a British subject, in whatever land he may be, shall feel confidant that the watchful eye and the strong arm of England will protect him against injustice."[12]

Cobden was not alone in regarding this as the most alarming passage in a generally alarming speech by the foreign secretary. In the debates in both Houses on the Don Pacifico affair an extraordinary array of distinguished parliamentarians joined in the attack on Palmerston, including four former or future prime ministers. All of them were disturbed by a pattern of interventionism and of disregard for the rights of other peoples, of which the Don Pacifico affair was only the most blatant example. To Palmerston's critics the implications were alarming. Already England had alienated almost every major power in Europe and by its own actions had licensed interventionism by others. Unless this trend was reversed, they feared, the fabric of European diplomacy seemed likely to suffer serious damage, and whatever influence Britain still possessed to check the rule of the weak by the strong would be lost.

Cobden spoke late in the debate, in its fourth and final day, and after most of the leading Peelites (although not yet Peel) had delivered their sweeping indictments of Palmerston. Speaking almost immediately after Gladstone, Cobden was much briefer and ranged less widely; nor was he inclined, as Gladstone was, to couch his argument largely in moral terms. As in all his best parliamentary performances, he kept close to the specifics of the case, employing a mix of factual analysis, ridicule, and contempt to deflate the overblown rhetoric concerning national honor and the rights of Englishmen abroad that had obscured the original issues. He used the same tools to dissect the conduct of British diplomacy: bullying in its handling of a small country (Greece), meek in reply to protests from a major power (Russia), and uncooperative in response to offers of mediation from another great power (France). "It seems as if the system at the Foreign Office is calculated to breed and perpetuate quarrels," he concluded.[13] Cobden was unable to resist pointing out that Britain's differences with Greece could best have been dealt with through his own recommended prescription of arbitration, a device that had indeed been ultimately employed but not before much damage had been done to England's relations with France and Russia or before Lord Palmerston, acting for a Liberal administration, had once again done violence to the Liberal principle of nonintervention in the internal affairs of other nations.

This was the heart of Cobden's objection to the whole trend of Palmerstonian policy, and in proposing nonintervention as an alternative basis for policy, he raised it almost to the level of an absolute principle:

> I maintain this Government has no right . . . to interfere with any other form of government . . . If you want to give a guarantee for peace, and, as I believe, the surest guarantee for progress and freedom, lay down this principle, and act on it, that no foreign state has a right by force to interfere with the concerns of another state, even to confer a benefit on it . . . Let us begin, and set the example to other nations of this nonintervention. I have no doubt that our example and protest would exercise some influence upon the Government of Austria and Russia; but what possible moral influence can this country have with those States when the Government goes abroad to interfere with the domestic affairs of other countries.[14]

Cobden could hardly have drawn the line between himself and Lord Palmerston more clearly. He was certainly well aware of the risks involved. By placing so much trust in the doctrine of nonintervention and the power of example, Cobden opened himself to the charge that he would expose England to dangers at least as great as any that he accused Palmerston of creating. Politically as well the costs seemed likely to be high; he was bound to lose influence in his own party where already he was being accused of disloyalty. But such considerations, of vital importance a year before, no longer mattered much. The peace issue, which Cobden had taken up late in 1848 as an idea to be advanced cautiously and in conjunction with other issues, had suddenly taken on new urgency. In the wake of Raja Brooke and Don Pacifico, Cobden increasingly tended to think of the program of the peace movement as less a cause to be advanced than as a fixed position from which to attempt to beat back those who threatened the peace. That task demanded a toughness and willingness to take risks that Cobden had not thought necessary or desirable in the early optimistic months of his association with the peace movement.

Not only did the peace movement suddenly become a matter of greater urgency as a result of the Don Pacifico affair; it also took on an intensely personal character, developing into a contest between Palmerston and his critics among the Peelites, with Gladstone in the fore, and the Manchester school, led by Cobden. This added another element of danger, so far as the peace advocates were concerned, because as long as Palmerston was in office issues of foreign policy were rarely debated primarily on their merits. In 1850 (and often during the next fifteen years), although Palmerston's critics may have had the better of the argument, Palmerston's supporters had the votes. In large measure this was simply a function of partisan politics. The attempt to unseat Palmerston was doomed from the moment the political world began to contemplate the practical consequences of unseating him. Prime minister, queen, and consort were all inclined at first to dispose of their troublesome foreign secretary. Once the Conservatives decided to make Palmerston's behavior a partisan issue, however, Russell and most elements of the government coalition rallied to his defense. It was unlikely that the government could survive without Palmerston's support, and for the moment the only alternative to a Whig government was a Tory protectionist one. Given that choice, few free traders were willing to risk the future of the government by attacking Palmerston, and Cobden was bitterly assailed for playing into Conservative hands. However impressive they might be in debate, the anti-Palmerston coalition of Peelites, Conservatives, and Manchester radicals offered no reasonable alternative to the political status quo.

Had that been the only reason for the vote of confidence in Palmerston, Cobden would not have been so disturbed by the result, but as Palmerston's critics were forced to acknowledge, it was more a personal than a party victory. Although Palmerston's handling of the Don Pacifico affair was all but indefensible (and his defense of it the weakest part of his speech), his intentions in interfering in Greece commanded general public and parliamentary backing. He and his supporters all but neutralized criticism of the Don Pacifico affair by putting it in the context of Palmerstonian policy stretching back twenty years. Moreover, the characteristics of that policy that commanded the greatest support were often precisely those that most disturbed the Peelites and Cobden: Palmerston's ebullient nationalism, his tendency to go it alone in international affairs, and above all his cavalier attitude toward foreign intervention or, short of that, toward lecturing other nations on their internal affairs. In launching a frontal assault on the foreign secretary, his critics misread the public mood quite as seriously as they misread the political balance of power at Westminster. Palmerston misread neither; the day after his parliamentary vindication, he rightly claimed that he was now perhaps the most popular man ever to hold the office of foreign secretary.

To Cobden that was the worst result of the Don Pacifico affair, because the nearer Palmerston approached to being the most popular man in politics, the closer he was to becoming the most dangerous. Of that Cobden was certain and remained so for the rest of their mutual public lives. Had it been possible to dismiss Palmerston as a deceitful and merely calculating political leader, Cobden would have worried less. But Palmerston seemed the most natural of demagogues, and that was a large part of what made him so threatening. A political leader intent on cynically manipulating popular prejudices could be successfully attacked sooner or later, but one who, like Palmerston, appeared to share those prejudices was all but unassailable, at least until the public mind could be altered. Hence, in part, Cobden's growing indifference to the extension of the suffrage, which appeared less and less likely to make any difference in the character of British policy, given the breadth of popular support for Palmerstonianism. Hence also much of Cobden's growing involvement in the movement for public education, which alone seemed to offer the hope of shaping a sounder public opinion for the future.

CHAPTER 18

Protecting the Peace

Palmerston's rise to power had begun four years before his triumph in the Don Pacifico debate and was not completed for another four years or more, but 1850 was a pivotal year not only in his career but, as many realized at the time, in British public life as well. From then until Palmerston's death, no government could survive without his presence or forbearance. He dominated the politics of the next fifteen years as completely as Peel had dominated those of the preceding fifteen. Indeed, it is perhaps the best measure of how radical the transformation was at midcentury that a man as profoundly different from Peel as Palmerston should have become the central figure in public life within four years of the repeal of the Corn Laws. And as if to emphasize that the change was permanent, at the very moment of Palmerston's ascendency fate intervened to remove Peel from the political scene. Peel's speech in the Don Pacifico debate was the last he ever delivered. The following afternoon he was thrown from his horse while out riding on Constitution Hill, and three days later he died.

Peel's death produced an outpouring of national grief unparalleled in the nineteenth century. Politically, however, the effects were less dramatic. Because the Peelites were more than a personal faction, they survived their leader's death reasonably intact. That, in turn, ensured the perpetuation of the unstable balance of midcentury politics but with the difference that the Peelites were no longer inspired by the hope—nor did their rivals need to fear—that they would return to power under Peel's leadership. The practical consequences of that change could only be guessed at, but to Cobden they seemed certain to be bad. Near the end of 1849, with the country apparently in an increasingly bellicose mood, Cobden had begun once again to look to

Peel as the most important political leader who shared his vision of the long-run implications of free trade. With Peel's death, Cobden felt cut adrift. "Poor Peel," Cobden wrote a few days after his death. "We do not yet know the full extent of our loss ... I had observed his tendencies most attentively during the last few years, and had felt convinced that on questions in which I take a great interest, such as the reduction of armaments, retrenchment of expenditure, the diffusion of peace principles, etc., he had strong sympathies—stronger than he had yet expressed—in favor of my views."[1]

Cobden's expectations of Peel were almost certainly exaggerated. Peel was a cautious leader in opposition. He had no wish to unseat the Whigs and was the last among his own party to join in the attack on Palmerston. As Cobden admitted, Peel had as yet said little on the subjects Cobden thought so vital. Nonetheless, Peel was perhaps the only one in a position to check the rise of Palmerston, and Cobden was confident, at least after Peel's death, that Peel had already come to see the necessity of this. It was almost as if the drama of Corn Law repeal was to be played out again, with Cobden and Peel once more in their historic roles, only this time in the cause of peace. However aware of this vision Cobden may have been before Peel's death, he certainly was afterward, and the timing of that death was surely a factor in his sometimes nearly obsessive preoccupation with Palmerston during the next few years. Gladstone was only just beginning to emerge as an important critic of foreign policy, and Cobden and Bright had to carry the burden of advocating a noninterventionist policy almost alone.

The timing of Palmerston's victory in the Don Pacifico debate and of Peel's death was crucial to Cobden's thinking in another respect. These events coincided with a decline in the postrepeal reform movements that could no longer be overlooked. By midsummer 1850 the entire structure of interlocking agitations for peace, retrenchment, and reform, which had appeared so vital as recently as the previous autumn, had all but totally collapsed. Cobden was suddenly as bereft of a sense of purpose as at any time in his public career. He responded in a number of ways: by falling back on those portions of the reform movement that had survived the rout, most notably the freehold campaign, by diverting his energies in new directions, such as the education campaign, or by grasping at straws, as in his sudden but brief recommitment to the cause of parliamentary reform following the announcement of Russell's conversion to reform early in 1851. In addition, he was fairly constantly concerned with preparations for the Great Exhibition of 1851.

Cobden played only a supporting role in the story of the Great Exhibition. It grew out of the work of the Royal Society of Arts in promoting exhibitions of British industrial design and was the creation of two men above all, Prince Albert and one of the most original of that extraordinary generation of bureaucrats who founded the Victorian state, Henry Cole. Cobden had worked with Cole already in support of the penny postage a decade earlier (and had attempted to recruit him into the league), but even without these connections, Cobden would have been a likely candidate for membership on the royal commission appointed in 1849 to oversee the preparation of the exhibition. Indeed, to the extent that the exhibition was seen as a celebration of economic internationalism and of free-trade-induced prosperity, his appointment was almost inevitable, quite apart from his standing at home and abroad. As Catherine Cobden proudly informed one Manchester friend, "I am told that several lists of names were submitted to the Prince, and that Mr. Cobden's name appeared in them all."[2]

Of Cobden's work on the commission we know little. At least one of his fellow commissioners was not impressed. According to Lord Hatherton, "Peel said that Cobden appeared to be nobody in the commission, [where] he showed no talent for business."[3] Unfortunately, Peel (or at least Hatherton) did not elaborate, but as these comments were made early in the life of the commission, they likely referred to the question of how best to finance the exhibition, a matter that was not resolved until months later. As a member of the finance committee of the commission, Cobden was closely involved with this problem, on which he held strong views. He believed that the project should be funded entirely from private sources, and at one of a series of public meetings held early in 1850 to generate enthusiasm for the exhibition, he declared that "if a grant from Parliament in support of the exhibition . . . should be [proposed] . . . by the Chancellor of the Exchequer, he should give it his strongest opposition."[4] Whether or not it was this issue that occasioned Peel's strictures on Cobden, they were not shared by Cole, who called Cobden "the most laboriously conscientious man he had ever known."[5]

If the nature of Cobden's contribution to the Great Exhibition is open to question, his commitment to the project is not. When Sturge sent him a petition urging that armaments be excluded from the exhibition, Cobden agreed to pass it on to the commission but would not press the issue. "I feel so much for the Prince's difficulties," Cobden told Sturge, "and am in so much love with the project as a whole, that I shall be disposed to deal leniently with him in this matter."[6] Furthermore, Cobden enthusiastically endorsed the proposal to use the proceeds of the exhibition to purchase the tract of land in South Kensington on which were later built the major institutions of Victorian science and culture. And finally, the exhibition inspired Cobden to erect a monument of a more personal character. When he rebuilt his birthplace at Dunford shortly thereafter, he added a solarium designed by Joseph Paxton, the architect of the Crystal Palace.

Although Cobden regarded the Great Exhibition as a "truly magnificent project"[7] and was proud to serve on the commission, he had as little use as ever for the ceremonial aspects of his position. He was the only commissioner, Bright noted approvingly, who did not wear court dress at the opening of the exhibition. Cobden was also immune to the mood of press-induced euphoria that swept the country that summer (and has misled many later commentators as to the benignity of the public mood in 1851). Indeed, he was inclined to take a somewhat perverse view of its possible benefits. Far from being a source of national self-congratulation, the exhibition would, he hoped, serve as a salutary lesson to Englishmen by displaying the progress of other peoples. That was internationalism of a sort and therefore welcome, as was the amiability of the crowds that visited the Crystal Palace.

But in contrast to the notion that the response to the exhibition presaged an era of domestic tranquility and international goodwill, recent events revealed a darker side of the public mind that impressed Cobden far more. During the winter of 1850–51, a papal decision to establish a diocesian structure for Catholicism in England provoked a surge of popular anti-Catholicism. That the English could revert to the old slogans of the church in danger and papal aggression and, led by the prime minister, support an unworkable attempt to prevent the creation of a Catholic hierarchy in England confirmed Cobden in an increasingly pessimistic view of the immediate future. The whole shameful affair was proof that the Whigs were hopeless; it appeared to justify his decision to concentrate on the long-run education of the people; but, above all perhaps, it demonstrated how far the country was from the breadth of vision necessary for further progress in pursuit of peace.

Cobden did not abandon the peace issue. In 1850 and 1851 he continued his practice of closely questioning the military and colonial budget estimates, and his second annual motion, in 1850, for a reduction in national expenditure was, like the first, largely directed at military spending. But Cobden did not repeat his arbitration motion in 1850. In part this was accidental; he had terrible luck in the draw for private members' motions in the House of Commons. Tactical indecision also was a factor; he wanted to renew the arbitration issue and, in addition, raise the issue of disarmament, but he could not decide whether to combine them, make two separate motions, or pursue only one. In the end, he put the matter off until 1851, a decision he justified by maintaining that the Don Pacifico debate had "advanced the question of arbitration very much."[8]

That this was largely a rationalization even Cobden would probably not have denied, but it would be a mistake to conclude that he was considering abandoning the peace issue itself, as he was, for example, backing away from the political reform campaign at just this time. Clearly, in the wake of the Don Pacifico debate it would have been unrealistic to attempt to carry out his plans as if nothing had happened. The peace party was on the defensive, and realism dictated a less structured, more pragmatic approach, which in essence is how Cobden pursued the peace issue over the next two to three years— sometimes attacking, more often defending, but always trying to make the best or avoid the worst of any situation, until, in the dark days just before the outbreak of the Crimean war, his options ran out. During all this time, however, he never suggested that the peace movement draw in its horns or that he should take a lesser role in it. On the contrary, he increased his public identification with the movement. He pursued his parliamentary motions when that seemed appropriate; he appeared prominently at meetings and congresses; he returned to his first public role, that of pamphleteer; and he continued to advise Henry Richard on the contents of the *Herald of Peace*. Inevitably, these years lacked the coherence of his early association with the peace movement, but he was determined to keep the movement alive as a check on the excesses of government, and if that was a less exalted goal than his original one, it was no less important.

As if to emphasize that his commitment to the movement was

unaltered, in August, two months after the Don Pacifico debate, Cobden traveled to Frankfurt for the third international peace congress. The English and American delegates once again dominated the proceedings, but there were sizable French and German contingents, and Cobden was pleased with the progress of the movement. That the congress had become an annual event was encouraging, as was the unanimity of the delegates in support of a set of concrete, if cautiously worded, proposals. This was not always easy to achieve. Before the congress convened, there were sharp differences between the advocates of total disarmament and those, primarily Germans, who were concerned that this would threaten the internal security of nations. According to Henry Richard, Cobden was primarily responsible for finding a wording acceptable to both groups. In other respects as well, it appears that Cobden was the central figure of the congress, the most frequent speaker, and much in demand as interpreter between French- and English-speaking delegates.

Yet for all the harmony of the proceedings and the talk of progress, the Frankfurt congress was undeniably an anticlimax. Frankfurt, particularly in 1850, was hardly to be compared with Paris, especially as Paris had been the year before. In the interim, the tide of political reaction had swept across Europe, and Frankfurt was not a place in which that could be forgotten. The peace congress met in the Paulskircke, where the revolutionary Parliament of 1848, since dispersed, had met. One of the observers of the proceedings was the Austrian general, Haynau, who had recently earned the sobriquet the butcher of Budapest. Cobden, like all the delegates, was conscious of having to choose his words with care. In future, he concluded, peace congresses should be held in "some small and yet independent state like Switzerland, Belgium or Holland where the government has an interest in upholding our peace principles."[9]

In the circumstances of its meeting, if not in its results, the next peace congress was an improvement. It was held in London in the summer of 1851, in order to coincide with the Great Exhibition. Once again, the proceedings went smoothly, largely because they were nearly identical with those of earlier congresses. Indeed, they were perhaps too nearly identical. Although Cobden, in his major speech to the congress, spoke of the need to move beyond appeals to idealism to a program founded on practicalities and backed by political organization, little along these lines was accomplished. Nor was his theme picked up by others. The London congress was largely content to repeat the generalities of earlier congresses. These had served their purpose two or three years earlier, but in not breaking new ground, the peace movement risked losing the ground it had gained since 1848. Yet even had the 1851 congress been more adventurous, London was not the place it should have met. The air was thick with platitudes about international brotherhood that summer; beneath the shadow of the Great Exhibition, the peace congress appeared superfluous.

Just how easily the exhibition could be used to blur distinctions vital to the peace movement had been made clear in the House of Commons only a month before the peace congress met. In June Cobden finally got parliamentary time for his disarmament motion, which he had originally planned to introduce the previous year. As with his arbitration motion, he was cautious in what he proposed. To be acceptable, he realized, any first step had to be small; the important thing was to establish the principle. Leaving aside the army and anxious to avoid the complexity of proposals for multinational negotiations, he suggested that the British government enter into negotiations with France for a bilateral agreement aimed at a mutual reduction of naval forces. Arguing that this could not endanger either country vis-à-vis a third power (since there were no other great naval powers) and that each country built its navy primarily in relation to the naval building program of the other, Cobden believed that Anglo-French naval rivalry offered a virtually risk-free opportunity to test the theory of controlled mutual disarmament.

The speech was vintage Cobden—clear, factual, persuasive in its logic—but, unfortunately for Cobden, he was up against an adversary, Palmerston, also at the top of his form. In a beautifully crafted reply the foreign secretary questioned the basis of Cobden's argument while at the same time identifying himself with the spirit behind it. The British and the French alike, he suggested, had good reasons other than suspicion of one another for maintaining large naval forces, and Cobden, in concentrating exclusively on the navies of these two countries, was dangerously oversimplifying a complex question. Better, he concluded, to leave such matters in experienced hands such as his own and not to tie those hands with resolutions such as Cobden's.

Not content with questioning the practicality of Cobden's motion, Palmerston also set out to show that it was unnecessary. The Great

Exhibition was his prime piece of evidence. After painting a glowing picture of the era of good feelings symbolized by the Crystal Palace, he in effect asked the Commons to trust him to act in its spirit. The response was all he could have hoped for. His sentiments were echoed from all quarters of the House, and Cobden, realizing that he had been outflanked, withdrew his motion. A victory for Palmerston was not necessarily a defeat for Cobden, to be sure. The debate, and even its outcome, had gone a little way toward fulfilling his intention in first proposing his motion: "to see the principle recognised that it is the policy and duty of a Government in these days to discourage the system of rival warlike preparation."[10] All the same, the recognition was so vague and the principle so broadly defined that the value of the exercise was questionable.

Much the same was true of Cobden's part in the only event that rivaled the Great Exhibition for public attention in 1851, the visit of Louis Kossuth to England late in the year. Kossuth had fled from the Russian repression of Hungary in 1849 and was on his way from Turkey to the United States. He did not stay long in England, but his visit was potentially of considerable political importance. He was a great popular hero, and his country had become the symbol of resistance to political reaction throughout Europe. To liberals and radicals everywhere he was an inspiration and, to some, a possible source of political advantage. Palmerston, for example, had originally intended to receive Kossuth personally, despite (or perhaps because of) the reaction that this would have produced in Vienna and St. Petersburg. Russell and the queen managed to dissuade him, which was probably all to the good, since Kossuth had no great regard for Palmerston, who had done nothing to deter the Russians from invading Hungary. Kossuth preferred the company of radicals and spent much of his time in England with Cobden and Bright. Cobden was much impressed with Kossuth and genuinely moved by his plight, but like any seasoned politician he was also well aware of the political opportunities—and risks—of Kossuth's visit.

The Russian repression of Hungary and Kossuth's arrival in England produced a surge of popular Russophobia in England, especially among radicals, exceeding even that which had led Cobden to write his first pamphlet fifteen years before. This threatened to isolate the peace party in England but, in Cobden's view, need not do so. Indeed, the Hungarian question could be made to work to their advantage, for surely there was no better illustration of the value of establishing the principle of nonintervention. That was Cobden's aim during Kossuth's visit and his major theme at a meeting they attended together at Winchester. Kossuth spoke first, and at the end of a long speech he reassured his audience that he asked of England not that it should go to war on behalf of Hungary but only that its leaders should say to Russia in unmistakable terms: "Stop." Cobden picked up Kossuth's phrase and endorsed it but pointed out that no such declaration was possible. Not only was opinion divided on Hungary, but England was itself so tainted by interventionism that its leaders could not convincingly preach nonintervention to others. This was the real lesson of what had happened in Hungary, Cobden believed. Short of threatening or using violence, which Cobden was certainly not prepared to do in this case, the liberal states of the west (France and America as well as Britain) had forfeited much of their ability to influence the warlike acts of others. The solution was for the British and the Americans to commit themselves to noninterventionist policies: "then, I believe," Cobden concluded, "the word Stop applied to Russia would be as conclusive as if we spoke with a thousand cannons."[11]

In its vigorous support of the right of Hungary to self-determination, Cobden's Winchester speech was one of the most combative assertions of the principle of nonintervention he ever made. So much so, in fact, that his critics and even some of his friends felt that he might be open to a charge of inconsistency. *The Times*, an increasingly bitter foe of Cobden ever since his attack on military spending four years earlier, pounced on his stop Russia statement as proof that he was as much an interventionist as anyone else, even while he sought to deprive England of the means of effective intervention. The latter contradiction did not bother Cobden's friends in the peace movement, but the former certainly did, and he was placed in the uncomfortable position of having to defend his speech to Bright and Henry Richard. Cobden was inclined to dismiss the matter as a misunderstanding based on distortion of his views by *The Times*, which in the main it was. But the commentary in *The Times* hit on an essential truth about Cobden's views that potentially set him apart from the peace society. For Cobden nonintervention was emphatically not a policy of passivity or isolationism, any more than was his favored means of dealing with international disputes, arbitration. Indeed, he envisioned both as active principles of foreign policy, to be asserted by the peace movement and ultimately, he hoped, by a rising tide of public sentiment in the great democracies against the inevitable hostility of most governments.

The year before, for example, when a delegation from the Frankfurt Peace Congress attempted to intervene in the dispute between Prussia and Denmark over Schleswig-Holstein, Cobden endorsed this venture in personal shuttle diplomacy designed to bring the parties to arbitration, although he advised against backing it up with public meetings in England or associating it in any way with Palmerston's efforts at mediation. Cobden's reservations were not made out of a cautious concern that the peace movement might be going too far. On the contrary, in order to strengthen the hand of the delegates, he sought (through a mutual friend, the Prussian minister to Britain, Chevalier Bunsen) to enlist the support of Samuel Gurney, a Quaker financier with great influence in the City of London. Furthermore, Cobden had no compunctions about suggesting the use of well-timed letters to the press from the likes of Gurney as a means of isolating the recalcitrant Danes from public sympathy in England and thus, perhaps, of moving them toward concessions. Far from trying to rein in the peace movement, in short, Cobden's aim was to ensure its integrity and independence as a means of furthering its influence.

For the English to preach peace from the public platform to foreigners would be hypocrisy in the year of Raja Brooke and Don Pacifico, Cobden believed, and as for the peace movement's throwing in its lot with anyone else, that would be an error, he advised Sturge and Richard, not only in the case of England's far-from-clean-handed foreign secretary (even if he might for a change be doing the right thing) but on general principles. "I hope our friends will keep aloof from all diplomatists, partisans and political pimps," he wrote Richard in October 1850, "and we may yet live to see the day when the Peace Congress may have a voice potential in the settlement of the squabbles of Europe."[12] Such an ambitious role for the peace movement involved considerable risks, Cobden acknowledged, but this, he believed, was perhaps the only way of regaining the initiative that appeared to be slipping away from the movement. Thus when, in the aftermath of Kossuth's visit, some in the movement began to worry "that others might push our doctrines to the point of physical force," Cobden was not deterred; "even if they do," he told Bright, "that is no reason why we should cease to give moral power its only chance, by boldly proclaiming the right and justice of the Hungarians to settle their own domestic affairs."[13]

Many in the peace movement, and not only among the Quakers, could not endorse such a view. However, as Cobden and Bright were constantly reminded while Kossuth was in England, quite a few radicals were prepared to say stop to Russia in more forceful ways than Cobden was willing to contemplate. That was not yet a serious threat to radical unity but the very different priorities of the peace society were. The *Herald of Peace* used the Kossuth visit as an occasion for preaching not only the lesson of nonintervention but also, to the Hungarians, the wisdom of nonresistance. Cobden was furious, although at first largely on tactical grounds. Now was not the time, nor Hungary the place, he pointed out to Richard, in which to advance the Quaker doctrine; that was bound to alienate the bulk of radical sentiment in England and weaken the peace movement.

The more Cobden thought about the whole mess, the angrier he became. Not only had the peace society placed its non-Quaker allies in a false position, Cobden suggested in a second letter to Richard, but in doing so it had demonstrated that it had learned little about how to agitate the peace question. The prominence of the peace movement since 1848 had been based on an alliance between the society and others, like Cobden, who were not so doctrinally absolute. They had been able to work together, Cobden pointed out, only because they had agreed to differ where they could not agree. "There is a great difficulty in acting together on any great public question, unless we are agreed in principle," he acknowledged to Richard, "but I had hoped the Peace Congress party had hit upon an expedient by which men could combine for measures of alleviation, even if they did not all hope for the total extirpation of a great evil. For this end I have always endeavored to avoid being brought into collision with the 'Friends' principle, and I had thought they were similarly minded towards those who were, like myself, laboring to give practical effect as far as they could to their doctrines."[14]

If the broader peace movement was to continue, Cobden therefore believed, the unwritten basis for cooperation might have to be spelled out in full. Unless that was done, he feared, "the practical agitation carried on latterly, under the auspices of the . . . [Peace Congress Committee], must be seriously injured, and the cause itself resume again the position in which it was placed before the Congress at Brussels was thought of."[15] But Cobden also recognized that any move to clarify the differences between the Peace Congress movement and the peace society might "perhaps lead to a secession of the Quaker party, and if so," he concluded, "I should despair of keeping alive the other movement."[16]

Under the circumstances, the political upheavals of the winter of 1851–52 must have come almost as a relief to the leaders of the peace movement. The fall of the Whigs took the pressure off reformers of all kinds and, by bringing in a Tory government tainted with protectionism, gave them a badly needed source of unity. The price was an almost total lack of political movement during 1852, but since the peace as well as the political reform and education issues were stalled in any case, the brief Tory government was seen as a period of regrouping by Whigs, Peelites, and radicals alike.

Unfortunately for the peace movement, however, free trade was not the only old issue to reemerge in conjunction with that winter's political changes. Louis Napoleon's seizure of power in France in December 1851 and Palmerston's endorsement of the coup gave Russell and the queen the excuse they had both been seeking to get rid of their too independent foreign secretary. Russell also used the invasion scare produced by the sight of a new Napoleon across the channel to revive his scheme for an expanded militia. But Palmerston could play that game far more effectively than Russell. Believing, as he had in 1847, that Russell's militia bill did not go far enough, Palmerston combined with the Tories and dissident Whigs in February 1852 to revenge his own dismissal two months earlier. Thus the Tories came to power in an atmosphere of anti-French panic and growing public demands for an increase in military spending reminiscent of the circumstances six years earlier that had first drawn Cobden into the peace movement. As an article in the *Herald of Peace*, almost certainly written by Cobden, on the "Natural History of Panics" put it: "The symptoms of this distressing disorder are a wild and restless wandering of the eyes across the channel, an irrepressible propensity to write letters to the public journals, a morbid longing for an augmentation of the army and navy estimates, and abuse of Mr. Cobden and the Peace Society so furious and excessive that the poor patient sometimes becomes frothy about the mouth and almost loses the power of articulate and intelligible utterance."[17]

As the tone of this article suggests, Cobden at first believed that the opponents of increased military spending might be able to repeat their earlier success in forcing the government to abandon its proposals. The coup in France could be used as an object lesson in the dangers of large military establishments, and the similarity between the two invasion scares might ultimately lead the people to be more sceptical the second time around. By mid-January, however, it had become clear that public sentiment was moving in the opposite direction. Only the financial burdens of increased defense spending could bring the people to their senses, Cobden concluded; but whereas that had been an immediate issue in the hard times of the late 1840s, it was scarcely felt in the prosperous early 1850s. Other than waiting for the crisis to burn itself out, Cobden had no idea what to do, and even before Russell's replacement by a Tory government subordinated all other issues to free trade for the Manchester radicals, it was evident that 1852 was going to be a poor year for the peace movement.

Just how out of sympathy Cobden was with public opinion was made clear during the first debates on the militia in February. As the leading spokesman for the opposition to the bill, he did what he could to demolish the case for an expanded militia. He ridiculed the notion that the French had the means or the will to invade England. The forces at their disposal were less than in 1848, when, as it turned out, the invasion scare had been illusory. Moreover, far from being a source of greater national security, an expanded militia might, Cobden argued, endanger England by alarming the French and giving to England's diplomatic and military leaders additional means for meddling on the continent. Domestically, too, the consequences seemed likely to be negative, at least once the taxpayer and those subject to service in the militia became fully aware of what was involved. If the British government was truly concerned with an invasion, which Cobden did not believe, that could be met by a redisposition of the fleet. Indeed, much of his speech was devoted to a demonstration of the superiority of the British navy and of how a small addition to the home fleet would secure Britain against invasion.

It was a characteristic parliamentary performance, but to many M.P.s it was also as unwelcome as it was predictable, and Palmerston had the majority of the House with him when he rose to answer Cobden. Given the mood of the country, Cobden surely expected that; what he could not have anticipated was the growing unwillingness to give his views a hearing. As one Liberal M.P. put it, "the services of a highly gifted man were placed in abeyance by the unfortunate monomania to which he was subject."[18] In that atmosphere the most that Cobden, Bright, and Gibson could do was to fight a rear-guard action against the militia bill. They tried to delay its progress in the hope that the peace movement could make its influence felt through meetings and petitions. They attempted to play on the factional divisions in Parliament and the minority status of the Tory government to water down the bill in committee. But public and parliamentary support for an enlarged militia held firm, and the only compensation Cobden could find in the lopsided majorities for the bill was that most M.P.s from the larger constituencies opposed it. "The establishment of the militia was a disastrous defeat sustained by the Peace party, and until we can regain our position of 1851," he told Sturge, "it is useless to think of getting back to 1835."[19]

For the moment, however, the free trade question still had priority, and by the time that was settled and Cobden could turn his attention to the problem of how to regain the lost position of 1851, the conditions that had given rise to the militia bill in the first place had returned with a vengeance. The invasion scare had abated during the spring and summer of 1852, but the chance coincidence of two events in the autumn—the death of the Duke of Wellington and the declaration of Louis Napoleon as Emperor of France—reawakened all the latent fears of Bonapartism in England. By the time Derby's Tory government had been replaced by the Aberdeen coalition in December, the country was under siege, if not by the French then by rumors of their impending descent, and the demand for military spending beyond the militia bill had grown irresistibly.

Cobden was dismayed by this, but not much surprised. The public response to the Duke's death served to confirm his increasingly pessimistic view that although the aristocracy might be the authors and sole beneficiaries of an interventionist foreign policy, they had the support of virtually everyone else in pursuing it. If the peace movement was to survive at all, let alone regain its earlier momentum, it had to adjust itself to that reality. As Cobden put it to one of his Lancashire correspondents shortly after the Duke's death in September:

> Unlike every other people, we have during seven centuries been fighting with foreign enemies everywhere excepting our own soil. Need another word be said to prove us the most aggressive race under the sun? . . .

The moral of all this is that we have to pull against the wind and tide in trying to put down the warlike spirit of our countrymen. It must be done by showing them that their energies have been perverted to a disastrous course, so far as their interests are concerned, by a ruling class which has reaped all the honors and emoluments, while the nation inherits the burdens and responsibilities. Our modern history must be re-written.[20]

Shortly thereafter Cobden decided to undertake a portion of that task himself, and by the end of the year he had half finished a pamphlet on the origins of the war with France in 1793 and the relevance of that to England's situation sixty years later. Surely not coincidentally, Cobden turned to pamphlet writing—for the first time in fifteen years—at a time when everything else appeared to have reached a dead end. It was in October 1852 that he wrote to Combe despairing of the national education movement. It was in January 1853 that Cobden for the first time refused to share a public platform with Bright in support of a failing parliamentary reform movement. The check on military spending formerly provided by the financial reformers had all but disappeared. Cobden still hoped for much from the forty-shilling freehold movement, and in view of the vote on the militia bill, he regarded its work as vitally important. After all, according to his calculations, it was the representatives of the counties that had chiefly overwhelmed the urban opposition to the militia. But Cobden also recognized that the work of the freehold movement would take many years, and in any case public gullibility during periodic invasion scares was ample proof that the problem was as much one of awareness as of the distribution of political power. Hence the pamphlet.

Cobden had first been drawn into looking again at the origins of the revolutionary wars by the response to Wellington's death, in particular by a gushing sermon delivered on the occasion to the effect that the Duke had fought a defensive war against the forces of foreign aggression. When it came time to write the pamphlet, Cobden borrowed his source of inspiration as a central literary device. The pamphlet was written in the form of three letters to a fictitious minister who had delivered just such a sermon. It was an effective approach. The epistolary form allowed Cobden to write informally and indulge to good purpose his penchant for asides. As one half of a dialogue, the pamphlet had a tension it would not have possessed as straightforward exposition. But, above all, by taking the death of Wellington as his starting point, Cobden ensured that his work would be controversial.

He certainly intended it to be so. The purpose of the first letter was to deny the traditionally accepted British view of the origins of the late war with France and to frame the terms of an indictment of British policy. "In the case before us," he wrote, "not only are we constrained by the evidence of facts to confess that we were engaged in an aggressive war, but the multiplied avowals and confessions of its authors and partisans themselves leave no room to doubt that they entered upon it to put down *opinions* by physical force, one of the worst, if not the very worst of motives with which a people can embark on war."[21]

The second letter was devoted to proving this assertion, primarily with evidence culled from diplomatic correspondence or the columns of Hansard. His interest, of course, was not primarily historical. Rather, he hoped to reveal "the true secret of despots, which is to employ one nation in cutting the throats of another, so that neither may have time to reform the abuses in their own domestic government"; and to counter that with "the true secret of the people, [which] is to remain at peace; and not only so, but to be on guard against false alarms about the intended aggressions of their neighbors, which when too credulously believed, give to government all the political advantages of a war, without its risks."

In the third letter, he shifted his attention to the present, drawing on history only to justify his plea for greater understanding of the French or as the starting point for his argument that a similar conflict was highly unlikely to recur, at least at the instigation of France. In his efforts to get his readers to see the world through French eyes, Cobden was deliberately provocative. If England had been the aggressor in 1793, as he believed, then it was the French who had a right to feel aggrieved and fearful. Employing an even larger historical perspective, Cobden asked rhetorically, "If we are so alarmed at the idea of a French invasion, which has not occurred for nearly eight hundred years, may we not excuse the people of France if they are not quite free from a similar apprehension, seeing that not a century has passed since the Norman Conquest in which we have not paid hostile visits to her shores?"

Nor could Cobden resist an oblique attack on favorite domestic targets, even when ostensibly accounting for some misunderstood characteristic of the French. After explaining the French predilection for men on horseback as primarily the result of foreign aggression, Cobden noted that Frenchmen were as protective of their social equality as the English were of their political liberties. To prove his point, Cobden cited, apparently at random, three things that no French government since the revolution would dare attempt to impose on its people: a privileged state church, a hereditary peerage protected in its landed wealth by laws of entail and primogeniture, and taxes on succession applying only to personal not to landed property. Yet these were measures, Cobden noted, lest his readers miss the point, "which are all in full force in England." That was only a suggestion of what Cobden would like to have written on the subject. "A real exposé of the comparative economic status of the two peoples would make ours a discontented lot," he told Henry Richard. "So much the better."[22]

Clearing the air of popular misapprehensions about the French, their revolution, and the most recent of their wars with England might help to undermine the rationale for invasion scares, but it did not necessarily disprove it. Near the end of his pamphlet, therefore, Cobden turned to a different line of argument to demonstrate that, regardless of earlier history, a French attack on England was now all but inconceivable. There were any number of reasons: that the increasingly large armies of Europe were needed "at home to repress the discontent caused in great degree by the burden which their own cost imposes on the people";[23] that the problems of financing a modern war would be almost insuperable; that advances in the technology of warfare were making it ever more expensive. "I have great hopes from the expensiveness of war and the cost of preparation," Cobden concluded after reviewing recent advances in the manufacture of shells, "and should war break out between two great nations I have no doubt that the immense consumption of material and the rapid destruction of property would have the effect of very soon bringing the combatants to reason or exhausting their resources."

All this was only introductory; the heart of Cobden's argument against the likelihood of war was the transformation of the world economy since the end of the eighteenth century. For its raw materials and as a market for its goods France was hostage to its international economic interests. Although governments are preparing for war,

Cobden concluded, "all the tendencies of the age are in the opposite direction . . . It is the gigantic growth which the manufacturing system has attained that deprives former times of any analogy with our own: and is fast depriving of all reality those pedantic displays of diplomacy and those traditional demonstrations of armed force, upon which peace or war formerly depended." This is the closest Cobden ever came to subscribing to the common liberal faith that the nature of the modern economy made a great modern war all but impossible.

As propaganda (and as history) his pamphlet, entitled *1793 and 1853*, was flawed by being perhaps naively uncritical of French intentions in the early stages of the revolutionary wars. But it was a clever political move. In his account of the origins of the war, Cobden was echoing pure Whig doctrine; at the very least, and much to his delight, this placed the Liberal participants in the present anti-French hysteria in an awkward position. "The Liberal press is so taken aback by this slap in their face in the very midst of their anti-French howl, that they hardly know what to say about it," he gleefully reported to his wife.[24] On the whole, Cobden was generally pleased with the response to *1793 and 1853*, which was widely noticed and quoted in the press and rapidly went through a number of editions.

Cobden had hurried the completion of the pamphlet, so that its publication would coincide with a peace conference, the fifth since the revolutions of 1848, held in Manchester in January 1853. Strictly speaking, this meeting was not a continuation of the series of international congresses held in Brussels, Paris, Frankfurt, and London, because the movement that had given rise to them had, like so much else, withered in the bellicose climate of 1852. In the wake of the invasion panic and the militia bill, the peace society decided not to attempt an international congress that year but to sponsor a conference of British peace advocates in the comparatively friendly home territory of the free trade and financial reform movements. But even that modest goal proved unattainable in 1852. At the request of George Wilson, it was delayed until early in 1853, largely because free trade remained the overriding issue in Manchester as long as there was a Tory government but also because he had difficulty mobilizing local support. So much so, in fact, that Cobden worried lest the decision to hold the conference there backfire. "I should be very sorry," he wrote Wilson early in December, "to be the cause of dragging some of my colleagues into the agitation at a moment when the popular tide seems setting in the opposite direction."[25]

From personal conviction as well as loyalty to Cobden, Wilson persevered. The conference was held in January 1853, and the local turnout was impressive after all. In his opening address Wilson argued for the peace movement as the natural extension of the great radical movements with which Lancashire was identified. Cobden was equally positive. After reiterating the arguments of his pamphlet against the invasion scare and outlining and then dismissing as unimportant the differences between himself and the peace society, he announced ambitious propaganda and fund-raising campaigns, modeled on those of the league in its greatest days.

How much of what Cobden and Wilson committed themselves to at the Manchester conference they believed to be possible is questionable. The propaganda campaign appears to have been primarily Sturge's idea; Cobden had been urging caution on him and Henry Richard for months. Not that Cobden favored inaction; but with the movement on the defensive he did not see how they could pursue their agenda at home, let alone abroad, until the war hysteria had subsided. Cobden's response to the early stages of the Eastern crisis which led eventually to the Crimean war was typical of this increasingly deliberate approach to the peace agitation. Rumors of an imminent Russian descent on Constantinople and the possibility that France might seek compensation in Belgium led Cobden to decide, in June 1853, not to "give notice of my disarmament motion; because, if it were met with a continental explosion, it would be alleged against me as proof of want of practical forsight and sagacity."[26]

Cobden was not yet seriously alarmed. "Six months experience of what a war in 1853 is would, I know, bring John Bull to such a state of mind as to induce him to sneak out of the fray in the most ignominious manner," he predicted to Richard. To be sure, he believed that "we must endeavor to open the eyes of Manchester, Liverpool and Glasgow to a sense of what would be the consequence of a rupture of peace with the Continent *before* such an event takes place"; but he was certain that "I could do it in half an hour, if the public mind were in the full prospect of a war." Besides, he reflected philosophically, "whatever course events may take, the Peace Party is sure in the end to gain by it. Being the only true principle, it cannot fail to reap advantage even from the temporary triumph of its opponents."

On balance, in the summer of 1853, other issues appeared more pressing.

As in 1850, so three years later, it was not only in Europe that the situation seemed to Cobden to be deteriorating. There was a colonial crisis as well and one of greater significance than the peripheral events in Borneo. Early in 1852 the government of India invaded the coastal provinces of Burma. The crisis had begun the previous summer, as a result of complaints from British merchants of extortion by the authorities in Rangoon, and had escalated rapidly, through diplomatic misunderstandings and provocations by both parties, into open conflict. The war dragged on for some time, but the outcome was never in doubt, given the disparity in power between the combatants; it ended with the annexation of the coastal province of Pegu by Lord Dalhousie, the most expansionist of early-nineteenth-century viceroys.

From the first, Cobden had not the slightest doubt that the British were at fault. Many of the merchants' complaints appeared frivolous, if not actually spurious; the legitimacy of British intervention on their behalf was questionable and the method of that intervention frequently provocative; the Burmese responses could be characterized as generally conciliatory, except for a few minor incidents; and the outcome of the affair in war and territorial expansion seemed hardly justified even by the most indulgent interpretation of British policy. Almost as disturbing to Cobden was what the affair revealed about the lack of clear lines of responsibility in the direction of Indian policy. The British naval commander at Rangoon had acted largely on his own, exceeding his instructions from the governor general, who had, in any case, no authority over him. What is more, he had no orders from his superiors at the Admiralty; yet his actions as a British naval officer contributed to a war, the cost of which would be borne by the people and government of India, not Britain. No administrative system could be imagined that was more likely in Cobden's view to lead to unchecked abuses.

Although Cobden regarded the Burmese war as a classic illustration of the worst aspects of British imperial policy from the moment news of hostilities reached England in March 1852, he was not in a position to do much about it for fully a year. The pertinent government documents were not published until well into 1852, and in addition a host of more pressing matters occupied his attention that year: the

French invasion scare, the militia bill, and free trade. Henry Richard kept the issue before the public as best he could in a series of articles and then a pamphlet based on official documents. In much of this work he received assistance from Cobden, who himself wrote an article on Burma for the September *Herald of Peace*, but it was not until the spring of 1853 that Cobden brought the issue before a wider public both in Parliament and, for the second time in a year, by writing a pamphlet. Foiled in his attempts to get parliamentary time for a full-scale debate on the annexation of Pegu, he resorted to a variety of parliamentary maneuvers and a debate on the government of India to press at least some of the issues involved, especially the question of responsibility in the conduct of Indian policy.

The rest of his case was reserved for his pamphlet, *How Wars are got up in India*, published in the summer of 1853. Although it too raised questions about the broader issues of Indian government, the bulk of it was devoted to an analysis of the origins of the war, culled entirely from published government documents and intended to demonstrate what Cobden had been told privately by a director of the East India Company—that the crisis had been precipitated by the unauthorized actions of the naval commander on the scene, whose errors were then compounded or glossed over by his superiors through a misguided sense of esprit de corps and concern for national prestige.

Cobden erred (in tactics as well as factually) in exonerating the Burmese of virtually all responsibility for escalating the crisis. Nonetheless, as was not to be the case with his attack on Raja Brooke, most later authorities have concurred in the substance of Cobden's criticisms. Overwhelming as his indictment was, however, he did not expect it to turn the tide of public sentiment. "Public opinion in this country has not hitherto been opposed to an extension of our dominion in the East," he observed at the end of the pamphlet. "On the contrary, it is believed to be profitable to the nation, and all classes are ready to hail with approbation every fresh acquisition of territory, and to reward those conquerors who bring us home title-deeds, no matter, I fear, how obtained, to new Colonial possessions. So long as they are believed to be profitable, this spirit will prevail."[27]

This reading of the political climate did not deter the peace movement from pursuing the Burma question further—it was too clear-cut an example of the pattern of British expansionism to be let drop. In the late summer of 1853 Cobden, Bright, Sturge, Richard, and the secretary of the Indian Reform Association hatched a scheme to bring a Burmese representative secretly to England as a means of embarrassing the government and, if possible, rousing public opinion. Only the worsening crisis in the Balkans led them to abandon the project.

Cobden had resorted to writing a pamphlet about Burma only because he had failed to get sufficient parliamentary time to deal adequately with the issue. But in a way it was just as well. Like his critique of British policy toward France in 1793, Cobden's analysis of the Burma question was too complex for a speech. That he was compelled to fight this particular battle on paper and not in the House of Commons may also have been a relief to Cobden. The increasing parliamentary isolation of the Manchester radicals on the peace issue was beginning to weigh heavily on him and even to affect his parliamentary performance. Of Cobden's major speech on India in the 1853 session, Henry Richard commented: "It was very badly delivered, broken and hesitating to a degree that greatly marred the effect of his reasoning. He told me before he went in that he was exceedingly nervous, and would be as pleased as a schoolboy when it was over. He said also, what I was very sorry to hear, that he becomes more and more nervous every time he addresses the House, which, no doubt, partly accounts for his speaking so rarely."[28] Still hated by some Tories, disliked for his independence by many Whigs, looked upon with some jealousy by not a few of the older radicals (as Richard noted), and regarded even by some of his friends as too obsessively concerned with the peace issue (as Richard did not note), Cobden had forfeited much of his parliamentary influence—and knew he had done so.

In many respects the situation was like that of a decade earlier, when, facing a generally hostile House of Commons, Cobden had turned his back on Westminster and thrown himself into the work of the Anti–Corn Law League. But if the comparison was apt, it was not reassuring, because the peace movement was not and probably never could be the equal of the league. "In this Peace Congress movement," he confessed in September to an old Scottish ally from league days,

we have not the same clear and definable principle on which to take our stand, that we had in our League agitation. There are in our ranks those who oppose all war, even in self defense; those who do not go quite so far, and yet oppose war on religious grounds in all cases but in self defense; and there those who from politico-economical and financial considerations are not only the advocates of peace, but also of a diminution of our costly peace establishments. Amongst the latter class I confess I rank myself . . . In seeking to diminish warlike establishments, we have to encounter as tough an opposition as we had in our attack on the corn monopoly, whilst we look in vain for that powerful nucleus of support which gave us hopes in the latter struggle of an eventual triumph.[29]

A month later, reflecting on these failures in a letter to Henry Richard, Cobden in effect wrote the epitaph not only for the mid-nineteenth-century peace movement but for the entire postrepeal reform effort: "I have never varied from the opinion, ever since the League was dissolved, that the same men who took the lead in that body would never form the most prominent actors in any other out-of-doors agitation. I was always of this opinion, even when, yielding to the wish of a majority of my old colleagues, I joined in the formation of the 'Financial and Parliamentary Reform Association,' which has really ended in nothing. *Fresh men* must be found for each distinct movement."[30]

Although ready to concede that the peace movement was incapable of forward motion and had all along lacked many of the ingredients necessary to a popular agitation, Cobden was still not willing to withdraw to politically safer defensive positions. On the contrary, just as in 1850, following the Don Pacifico debate, he had shifted his emphasis from methodically advancing his peace program to a view of the movement as essentially a check on irresponsible government policy, so, too, when that vision finally faded during the French invasion scare and the passage of the militia bill, he found other justifications for speaking out. The long, drawn-out process of disillusionment with the effectuality of the peace movement had at least the compensation that it freed Cobden from the constraints of political calculation. His practical peace program, which he had undertaken with the genuine expectation of substantial public support and persisted in—or clung to—as much for the record as anything else, was abandoned as counterproductive, at least for the time being. In its place Cobden felt increasingly free to attack the underlying assumptions as well as the conduct of British foreign and imperial policy. He continued to hope that he might reach the British public, but he was more and more inclined to think that they would only learn from disaster, rather than in time to avert it. That being the case, the task of the peace advocates as he conceived it was to make their case as forthrightly as possible, without too much regard for the public and parliamentary reaction, in the certainty that events would ultimately vindicate them.

CHAPTER 19

War

Cobden was already well on the way to an almost fatalistic view of the future of the peace movement even before the Eastern question began to threaten the peace of Europe in the summer of 1853. The development of the crisis thereafter and above all the popular response in England ultimately fed both his unwillingness to lessen the severity of his attacks on English policy and his feeling of personal impotence to alter the course of that policy. At the outset, however, and for as long as he believed that he might be able to influence government thinking or, failing that, Parliament or, failing that, the public, Cobden chose his words with as much care as he had shown in the early optimistic days of the peace movement.

In his first parliamentary comments on the crisis, in August, he did not attempt to hide his well-known views on Turkey, Russia, and nonintervention, but with the government engaged in diplomatic negotiations and the cabinet known to be divided, he did what he could to gloss over the differences between his views and those of the more pacifically minded ministers. Not surprisingly, the speech was not a success. It lacked form as well as fire, and Cobden ended it with an apology for having spoken too long. Palmerston, who answered with an often abusive speech designed to point up the differences Cobden had sought to blur, was justified in accusing Cobden of being less than straightforward. Indeed, the only point that Cobden gained in the exchange was to extract from Palmerston an overblown defense of Turkey: "I assert, without fear of contradiction," he said, "that so far from having gone back [within the last 30 years], Turkey has made greater progress and improvement than any other country in the same period."[1]

As the crisis deepened in the autumn, however, and the weight of public, press, and parliamentary opinion shifted overwhelmingly toward almost unconditional support for Turkey and an equally unquestioning Russophobia, Cobden perforce abandoned the search for points of agreement with anyone outside the narrowing circle of the peace party. All he could do was what he had done during the French invasion scare: question the assumptions underlying the public clamor and government policy and warn of the dangers of war. Yet, although the audience he felt certain of reaching was diminishing daily, Cobden was not temperamentally inclined to accept the role of Cassandra. He preferred the part of a prosecuting attorney. At best, he believed that war might still be averted by appealing if not to the reason then to the skepticism of his fellow countrymen and parliamentary colleagues; at worst, he would have pleaded his case for the record. And if his performance that summer in the unresponsive environment of the House of Commons disappointed, the same was not true of the series of speeches that he delivered to a friendly audience at the peace conference of 1853, the sixth and last of the midcentury peace gatherings.

By the time the conference met in Edinburgh in October, the Russian army was in the Danubian principalities, and the French and British fleets were at Besika Bay; the Turks had just declared war on Russia, and Europe appeared closer to general war than at any time since 1815. Although the conference reendorsed the familiar resolutions calling for arbitration, disarmament, and a variety of lesser reforms, the Eastern question inevitably dominated the proceedings. Cobden talked of almost nothing else. The first of his three speeches to the three-day conference was a magnificent performance; even now it leaps from the printed page. Point by point he set out to demolish not only the case for war with Russia on behalf of Turkey but the public reputations of those who dared suggest such a thing. Turkey in Europe was doomed, he declared: "There are seeds of decay and dissolution, founded on the very nature of things, that you cannot combat by fleets and armies."[2] Britain and France could only delay the inevitable and in the process transform the dreaded Russians into heroes to the oppressed Christian peoples of the Balkans. If Britain was to interfere at all—which Cobden opposed—it should be alongside Russia on behalf of these subject peoples. Instead, Britain's leaders attempted to delude the British public and perhaps deluded themselves into a fantasy version of the situation in the East. Here, as he was to do so often, Cobden delighted in quoting Palmerston's extreme claims for Turkish progress during the last generation.

As for the other side of the equation, the Russian threat, Cobden had, in the recent French invasion scare, a powerful weapon with which to call that recurrent English obsession into question. The fact that many of the same voices that had made most of the French menace were now directed against Russia raised some embarrassing possibilities. Either they had been wrong about France, in which case their judgment about Russia might be equally faulty, or they had been right about France, which called into question the wisdom of siding with the French against Russia. Cobden had a fine time exploiting the ironic possibilities of both lines of argument, especially the latter. "Now suppose a person . . . had left our shores last January," he asked his audience to imagine,

> and had returned again after making the circuit of the globe—what would be his experience? When he left England he saw us preparing a militia, fortifying our coasts . . . He left in the midst of all these prep- arations to meet a French invasion, and then he makes a circuit of the globe, seeing no newspapers . . . he comes back and lands in England in the month of September, and the first thing he reads in the newspapers is, that the French and English fleets are lying side by side . . . in Besika Bay. He immediately says there is going to be a great battle now; but, on turning to the leading articles of the very papers that told him when he left that the French Emperor was a brigand and a pirate, ready to invade us without any declaration of war, the first thing he sees is that France and England are cordially united; that the combined fleets are in Besika Bay under the command of Admiral Dundas; and that we are prepared if necessary to send our army to be put under the command of the French general, and that we are going into action, probably tomor- row, with the Russian fleet.[3]

In sharp contrast to this bit of deadly serious whimsy, Cobden suggested a third, more sinister explanation of the French scare: that its authors knowingly manipulated public opinion in the hope of achieving some ends Cobden deliberately did not spell out, allowing his audience to draw its own conclusions. Similar motives—perhaps of personal, perhaps of political self-interest—might, he suggested, be behind the anti-Russian frenzy. In any case, the effects of the anti- French scare had been disastrous, because by misleading Russia as to English intentions, it had contributed directly to the present crisis. "I speak," he told the conference, "from information short only of information from the first parties acting in these proceedings when I say that that which has been done in the East by the Emperor of Russia was done on the deliberate calculation that it was impossible France and England could unite to oppose him."[4]

As long as he stayed close to his indictment of official thinking and policy, Cobden was on strong ground; but, as he certainly knew, what he had to offer as an alternative was unlikely to be any more popular. Faced with Russian expansion and the imminent collapse of Turkey, he appeared to favor an essentially passive policy of nonintervention. In the hope of putting the peace advocates in a more positive light, he suggested the possibility of economic sanctions as an alternative to war—in particular, making illegal what he had tried to make impractical four years earlier: the sale of Russian government bonds in England. To those who argued that this would be a violation of sound principles of political economy, he replied that that "was not half so bad as going to war" and that, even should it fail, it would at least be "an attempt in the first instance to apply coercion by other means than physical force."[5] Cobden did not pursue this further, however, probably because it went beyond what many members of the peace party were willing to contemplate while falling short of the Russophobes' demands. Nor did it reflect Cobden's own thinking in this crisis. As in his first pamphlet written fifteen years earlier (which he used as the basis of much of his second speech to the Edinburgh conference), Cobden was both unafraid of Russian expansion and resigned to the collapse of Turkey. His critics were largely correct. He did favor a policy of strict nonintervention, regardless of the consequences, a fact that he did not bother to gloss over, despite—or perhaps because of—the mounting war hysteria in England.

At the time of the Edinburgh conference, war with Russia, although it looked likely, was not yet imminent. Even as late as January 1854, a month after the crushing Russian naval victory over the Turks at Sinope, he still believed that English participation in the war might be averted. With the press in full cry against Russia, however, he rested his hopes not on the public but on the House of Commons, especially on the Peelite wing of the government. He may also have hoped to reach the back-bench country gentlemen opposite, who, in large numbers, according to Lord Stanley, "dislike prospective disturbances in Europe, who object to fight where England has nothing to gain: and who in their hearts agree with Cobden."[6] In any case, in his last peacetime speech against the coming war, delivered in the House in late February, he in effect asked his fellow members to use their better judgment if necessary against the weight of public sentiment—an extraordinary reversal, as Cobden was the first to recognize, of his normal practice of attempting to bring outside pressure to bear on the House. For public meetings he no longer had any use. "To hold a meeting now merely to enunciate abstract opinions against war would be simply ridiculous," he told Henry Richard, just before England entered the conflict in March. "If we deal with the question, it must be in reference to existing difficulties and dangers . . . And to be honest, we could not deal fairly with the matter without a due measure of censure on the Czar which would only be adding fuel to the fire . . . Until some new phase in the affair presents itself, it would, I think be not only useless but mischievous to the Peace cause to attempt to hold public meetings. We have done our duty."[7]

That, in essence, was his attitude until the end of the war. He remained active in Parliament, but he was noticeably less so during 1854 and 1855 than at any time since the repeal of the Corn Laws. And although he spoke on a variety of topics from an adultery bill to the naval estimates, he avoided the subject of the war for the remainder of the 1854 session. He did not, in short, embark on an antiwar campaign, at least in the sense that English-speaking nations in the twentieth century have come to understand the term. Nor, in fact, did Bright, although he is often recalled as the man who most effectively attacked the Crimean war. And rightly so, for his eloquence and natural combativeness suited him better than Cobden to the task and made his antiwar speeches, infrequent though they were, memorable events. Bright had serious limitations as a critic of British policy, however. He lacked Cobden's knowledge of foreign affairs and was sometimes too abrasive. "I have often tried in private to persuade our friend to rely less upon attacks on the personnel of the Government, and more on the enforcement of sound principles upon the public," Cobden explained to Richard; but, he added indulgently, "his pugnacity delights in a knockdown blow at something as visible and tangible as a Minister of State."[8] Cobden did what he could to adjust the balance of Bright's antiwar speeches, the best of which combined a rhetorical flair that was pure Bright with well-documented assaults on government policy reminiscent of Cobden's oratory. The resemblance was not coincidental; Cobden constantly supplied Bright with raw material and advice. But Cobden never imagined that he could match Bright's ability to appeal to the conscience of the nation.

Nonetheless, although Bright spoke brilliantly, he did not speak often—and Cobden spoke even less. Bright said nothing during the slide toward war early in 1854, Cobden ceased speaking once the war had begun, and Bright spoke only once in its early stages; both kept silent thereafter until the end of the year. And although they intervened occasionally in parliamentary debates on the war during its second year, they never attempted to rouse the people against the war; both all but disappeared from the public platform for the duration. In this they were realistic; there was no reason to believe that a more active opposition to the war would have had any effect. But they were also fatalistic. Each in his different way felt powerless in the face of actual conflict to do much more than disassociate himself from it: Bright often treated the war as an evil against which, nothing else availing, he must at least bear witness; to Cobden the war hysteria was a fever that only adversity could break. "It is hard to stand still when one feels that the world is going wrong on a question in which one is deeply concerned," he wrote reflectively to Richard in October 1854. "But events are working out the best arguments for our principles, and if there be any truth in them it will be more fully vindicated by the deeds of the Crimea, and their consequences, than anything we could say ... If we take the proper moment there will be in every town and in almost every 'good' family mourners for the loss of friends and relations who will listen to us ... The Time has not yet come, but it may come."[9]

Only at the end of the year—after the indecisive battles of Balaklava and Inkerman, after the allied armies had stalled before Sebastopol, after the first revelations of British military and administrative mismanagement, after the early rumblings of a political crisis at home, after a peace overture from Russia had opened the way to a negotiated settlement—did Cobden feel that it was right for him to speak out again. Not that he expected very much even then. Throughout most of 1854 he had clung to the belief that "amongst the middle class the feeling upon the war is rather that of acquiescence than of enthusiasm," but a trip to the North in December dispelled that illusion. "The war spirit was far rifer than I expected," he informed Henry Richard, "and it pervaded all classes, infecting many from whom I had expected better things."[10] Even so, the chance of promoting a negotiated settlement could not be passed up; and once again it was to the House of Commons not to his normal audience out of doors that he looked for a response when he made his first wartime speech against the war in December 1854.

His theme, the major theme of all his wartime speeches, was the folly—he did not yet publicly call it anything worse—of continuing to fight for unreachable goals, when all that England could realistically hope to achieve was attainable by diplomacy.[11] With the country at war, Cobden could not afford to reiterate the detached view of Russian expansion in the Balkans he had adopted the year before, but he did not deviate much from his prewar position. He accepted the need to contain Russian expansionism, but he was certain that it could best be done—as he believed it could have been done without going to war at all—through concerted diplomatic pressure by the other European powers. Hence, once Russia agreed, as it had in November, to negotiate on terms—the Four Points—proposed by the other powers at Vienna, and once Russia was willing, as it now said it was, to abandon its claim to interfere militarily in the internal affairs of Turkey and to accept some form of restriction or balancing of its naval forces in the Black Sea, then, Cobden believed, it would be irresponsible of the allied leaders not to begin negotiations. And not only because it would put an end to the bloodshed, but also because the Four Points represented the most the allies could get given the limitations imposed on the war by geography and by the nature of the opposing forces.

The decision of the two great Germanic powers to remain neutral had permanently altered the character of the struggle. In Cobden's view this should have sufficed to make the western allies question the wisdom of continuing the war themselves (as, for that matter, should Austro-Prussian support for the Russian peace terms later in the year). But although that was a matter of opinion, some practical consequences of Austrian and Prussian neutrality were not. It meant, for example, that the war would be fought on a smaller scale than many of its proponents had hoped or expected, that the western allies would have to bear the burden of very long lines of supply, and that the battlefields of the war would by default be on the periphery of Russia, in areas like the Crimean peninsula.

No victory that could be won in such a war would inflict a decisive setback to Russian power. Nor could such a victory guarantee the fulfillment of perhaps the most important British war aim, the maintenance of the security and integrity of Turkey. That depended in the end on the capacity of Turkey itself for renewal, which Cobden, as so often before, set out to disprove. And finally, Cobden dismissed almost contemptuously any notion that more lofty ends were involved, such as the protection of European liberties against Russian autocracy or aid for Polish nationalism, as the great delusion and deception of the Crimean war. Urged on by the jingo press, the most ardent supporters of the war within the government—Cobden singled out Palmerston and Russell—might play on Conservative fears and Liberal hatred of Russian power, but no one in a position of responsibility, he noted, argued publicly—whatever their private geopolitical fantasies might be—that Russian influence in eastern Europe could be permanently rolled back. All such talk was empty rhetoric, he concluded, designed to divert attention from the promising path of diplomacy and to gull a misinformed public into supporting the continuation of an unnecessary conflict.

Cobden spoke out even more bluntly a month later in his only appearances before public meetings during the war. At a soiree for Bright and Gibson in Manchester he suggested that some members of the government might actually be deliberately stringing out the peace negotiations in the hope of taking Sebastopol before the terms of peace could be agreed on; and for this reason only, "that the government, having raised the devil of war, had not the courage to announce to the public the terms on which they sought to lay him to rest."[12] Of the war itself, and above all of any attempt to justify it as a matter of principle not power, he spoke even more savagely. "It was a war," he told an audience of his constituents in Leeds two days before the Manchester meeting, "in which we had a despot for an enemy, a despot for an ally, and a despot for a client—and we had been for twelve months endeavoring to make an ally of another despot."[13] Challenging his Liberal listeners to keep to their best traditions, he urged them not to turn their backs on diplomacy in favor of war, if only because of the horrific cost of war against such a vast enemy at such a distance. It was a cost, Cobden believed, that neither the government nor the people in their present mood had stopped to consider; it was a cost, he was certain, that they would refuse to countenance if they were honestly confronted with it.

Clearly, Cobden no longer saw any point in temporizing, even in dealing with his constituents, and for good reason. The circumstances of the Leeds meeting proved that he was out of touch with the Liberals of the North on the war. The Manchester meeting went reasonably well. It was managed by George Wilson with his usual skill. Designed partly as a public vote of confidence by the city in its M.P.s at a time when that relationship was seriously strained, it also was simply another in the series of meetings of reformers, held on the eve of the opening of Parliament, which Wilson had organized every year since the repeal of the Corn Laws and to which Cobden was always invited. The meeting served both purposes as well as could be expected under the circumstances. Many familiar faces were absent, but it was well attended. Although Bright had recently been the subject of personal attacks in the Manchester press, it went off without a hitch.

Leeds was another matter. While Wilson was planning the Manchester meeting, Cobden had to make his own arrangements in Yorkshire. Initially he approached the chairman of his committee at the last election, Francis Carbutt, an alderman and former mayor of Leeds, but Carbutt, after consulting other reformers, refused to have any part in promoting such a meeting because he disagreed with Cobden on the war and felt that a meeting could only further divide the Liberals. Cobden, determined not to be denied a public meeting in his own constituency, then turned—through Henry Richard—to the peace party of the West Riding to make the arrangements. When word of this got out, a prowar coalition of Liberals and Tories announced its intention of moving a resolution in support of the war at the meeting. Cobden's most vocal adversary through all this was Edward Baines, the proprietor of the *Leeds Mercury*, who had once been a close ally but was now—and had been ever since the emergence of the education issue some years back—among Cobden's most persistent critics. Inevitably the meeting was crowded and finally had to adjourn outside to Cloth Hall Yard, where Cobden and Baines addressed the crowd without incident in a cold driving rain. To no one's surprise, Baines carried the day easily. An amendment urging the continuation of the present negotiations was brushed aside, and despite Cobden's pleas that a strong statement in favor of the war might jeopardize the prospects for a negotiated settlement, the original motion was passed overwhelmingly.

Cobden had not perhaps expected so direct a rebuff, although he never had any illusions that the Leeds and Manchester meetings would bring favorable results. He had done his best to disabuse Bright of any notion that the tide of opinion might be turning, and when Sturge raised the possibility of making the Manchester meeting the occasion of a peace demonstration, Cobden was flabbergasted. The support simply wasn't there. All that he hoped to do was show the flag of the peace party in public, demonstrate that they had not been intimidated into silence, and get some public exposure for their views. "What I want," he told Richard, "is to be able to hold such a meeting as will afford an excuse to deliver a speech which will be reported in the London and Yorkshire papers . . . It would certainly be a very desirable thing to be able to speak through *The Times* to the whole world from the West Riding at the present moment."[14] This he certainly got, but although the meetings were in this limited sense a success, Cobden did not speak again in public during the war.

Nor did he say very much in Parliament. With the accession of Palmerston to power in February 1855 and the collapse of the Vienna peace negotiations three months later, an enlarged war appeared unavoidable. Cobden held his tongue in the interim between these events, on the chance that the allies might be seriously pursuing a compromise peace, but he did so more in hope than expectation. The most encouraging sign that spring was that he, Bright, and Gibson were joined in their criticism of the war by two Peelite former ministers, Gladstone and Graham. But it soon turned out that this development had served only to enlarge the closed circle of the peace party, not to end its isolation—an isolation Cobden felt so keenly that in June he was driven to defend his right, although an opponent of the war, to comment on its conduct.

The occasion of these remarks was a debate on the failure of the Vienna negotiations, which hinged in the end on the limiting or balancing of Russian naval forces in the Black Sea. That the difference between peace and the renewal of war had come down to that issue gave Cobden the opportunity to reiterate the arguments of his December speech. He dismissed the differences between the Russian and allied positions as minimal and pointed out that in any case no commitment made by Russia regarding the Black Sea would be trusted or, in the long run, enforceable by the allies. Yet it was for the sake of this illusion of certainty that the government appeared willing to resume the war. This, Cobden argued, was the act of irresponsible men, for it was bound to end either in disillusionment or in a more awful war, and, whichever was the case, in political retribution from a misled public.

Cobden strongly suspected that the government was deliberately holding back information on the Vienna negotiations, that they had come much nearer to agreement than Parliament or the public was being told, that the negotiations collapsed because of the unwillingness of the British government to accept a last-minute compromise, and therefore that Britain, as the main proponent of a renewed war, could no longer hope for support from neutral Austria and might even have strained relations with her major ally, France. At this point Cobden had only fragmentary evidence to support his suspicions and, not surprisingly, had been unable to extract anything from the government, although he and Bright had tried to pin Palmerston down at a meeting of Liberal M.P.s.

Within a month, however, the substance of what Cobden had pieced together was confirmed. There had indeed been a last-minute compromise suggested by the Austrian foreign minister Buol, which Russell, the British plenipotentiary at the conference, had tentatively accepted as a basis for settling the Black Sea issue. Back in London (and Paris), however, the proposal—it involved balancing off Russian forces—was not well received, since both governments were now committed to the neutralization of the Black Sea. Russell nearly resigned and was only dissuaded from doing so by pressure from his cabinet colleagues. Yet he said nothing of all this in recounting the Vienna negotiations to the House of Commons. Indeed, he endorsed renewing the war against Russia in pursuit of war aims he himself had been willing to abandon only a few weeks before.

Russell had good but, because they involved the internal affairs of France, necessarily secret reasons for his actions. It was feared by many that the French army might not peacefully accept nor Napoleon III long survive a negotiated peace made before the fall of Sebastopol. Nonetheless, Russell would have done better to have persisted in his resignation, because he should have known that the full story would come out. The agent of its doing so was Count Buol, who understandably felt that his contribution had not been given its due by Russell. But in correcting the record to his benefit, Buol opened Russell to such bitter recriminations that he was forced to resign from the government. He was almost universally condemned in the press and from all quarters of the House of Commons as having misled Parliament and misrepresented his own views. Cobden went even further. Russell's actions, he suggested, were only the latest episode in a pattern of contradictory policies and less-than-honest dealing with Parliament and the electorate, characteristic of the entire Crimean war period. "I look back with regret on the vote which I gave on the motion which changed Lord Derby's Government," Cobden concluded. "I regret the result of that motion, for it has cost the country 100 millions of treasure and between 20,000 and 30,000 good lives."[15]

Cobden's attack on Russell was his last major speech against the war. Two weeks later, a debate on a proposed loan to Turkey to shore up her finances provided him with an irresistible opportunity to remind the House how often he had predicted it would come to this, but Cobden's parliamentary opposition to the war ended, unfortunately but more revealingly, with a personal exchange between himself and a former ally now a government minister, Sir William Molesworth, each of whom accused the other of misrepresenting his present views and past record. This was, *The Times* noted editorially, a measure of how far Cobden had fallen in the esteem of his colleagues; and although Cobden fired off a letter to *The Times* attacking its interpretation of his words with Molesworth, the fact that he bothered to reply at all is good evidence of how keenly he felt his political isolation. He managed, even so, to end the letter with a ringing defense of his record on the war, distant though he now expected his vindication to be:

> It is true I opposed the war, and would never have allowed my country to draw the sword until Austria and Germany, more nearly concerned in the quarrel than ourselves, were ready to strike the first blow.
>
> It is true I was against the invasion of Russia with a sick army, in ignorance of the strength of the enemy or the place we were going to attack.
>
> It is true I was in favor of peace on the basis of the four points at the Vienna Conference; and I think it not impossible, after the facts of that negotiation shall be known, that the people of this country, when they recover their wonted common sense, may call for the impeachment of the present Ministry as the sole responsible authors of the continuance of the war.[16]

Cobden must have been more than normally relieved to escape from London to Dunford at the end of that parliamentary session (one of the few happy aspects of this period for him was that the rebuilding of Dunford had been completed just in time to provide him with a haven during the war years). Never had he felt so out of step with his countrymen as in the late summer of 1855. The entire nation seemed bent on war, and the fall of Sebastopol in September only seemed to whet the appetite for battle. Powerless even to slow the juggernaut, Cobden kept his distance from the public world and, as he had done twice before in difficult moments for the peace movement, turned to authorship as perhaps the only means of making his views felt. At the end of October he wrote a long letter to the *Leeds Mercury* (reprinted in *The Times*), once again urging his countrymen to face up to the costs and limits of this war. At the close of the year he wrote a pamphlet, *What Next—And Next?* which was published in January.[17]

Cobden wrote the pamphlet at a time of renewed speculation that the war might be ended soon by negotiations, in this case at the instigation of France, which appeared reluctant to fight on after the fall of Sebastopol. Although Cobden welcomed any sign of movement, he was, after the failure of the Vienna negotiations, understandably guarded. No hint of the latest sign of a possible break in the diplomatic deadlock appeared in *What Next—And Next?*; the pamphlet was written on the assumption that the war would continue, and on a larger scale, in the spring. It was therefore devoted primarily to an expanded version of one of his oldest arguments against what he called the war-at-any-price-school, the impossibility of successfully invading Russia. Cobden left no argument unexplored. Russia's size, the nature of her economy, her national character, and even her relative backwardness were used to bolster his case. All in all, he provided his readers with a (perhaps inadvisedly) sympathetic and, under the circumstances, surprisingly leisurely excursion into enemy territory.

Of the effects of an invasion on the invaders, he wrote more briefly and tentatively. A modern industrial society, he suggested, might find war on such a scale surprisingly difficult to fight. England's greater wealth and technological superiority might mean less in practice than her leaders imagined, for many of her resources, human as well as material, were inextricably involved in the running of a sophisticated industrial economy and could not be quickly transferred to the purposes of war without acute social and economic dislocation. All this was merely suggested as a possibility. Cobden had nothing with which to back up his speculations, which were based as much as anything on wishful thinking (and were soon disproved, as he recognized, by the astonishingly successful mobilization of the North in the American Civil War). For the moment, however, his only concern was that something, anything, in his pamphlet might give his readers pause.

What Next—And Next? was Cobden's last act of opposition to the Crimean war, because by the time it was published discussions were already under way that led to the convening of a peace conference in February and ultimately to the Treaty of Paris a month later. But Cobden had been fully justified in writing on the assumption of a wider and longer war. If Palmerston had had his way, the war would have gone on; as Cobden had suspected late in 1855, the main impetus for peace on the allied side came from Napoleon III. Thus the pamphlet, like all his public acts of opposition to the war, at least since the Leeds and Manchester meetings a year earlier, was aimed at building the case against the war in anticipation of the day when the public might turn in exhaustion or anger against such a conflict. Given the public mood in England that winter, it was the most that Cobden could do.

Even had the war dragged on, however, it is unlikely that a majority in Parliament, let alone the country, would ever have come around to Cobden's views. Savage as was the criticism of the conduct of the Crimean war, there does not appear to have been any erosion of the national consensus in favor of the war itself. Thus, when Cobden joined in the criticism of the management of the war—from the choice of battlefield to the care of the wounded at Scutari—he likely did himself more harm than good. Unlike those critics of the government whose credentials in support of the war were impeccable, Cobden's motives were suspect. It was widely assumed that he sought out and welcomed evidence of waste and inefficiency, not as a means of improving the conduct of the war but in order to taint the entire enterprise. At the very least he was charged with demoralizing the country by failing to close ranks once hostilities had begun; at worst he was accused of prolonging the war—and thus of endangering British lives—by encouraging the enemy to fight on in the hope that Britain was divided. (Despite the war hysteria, Cobden was never branded a tool of Russian interests.)

Much of this was nonsense, but, as Cobden himself realized, not

all. It was (and is) absurd to attempt to shift the blame for misman-
aging and prolonging a war onto the shoulders of those who opposed
it in the first place; but like most wartime critics of a war, Cobden was
ambivalent about the fortunes of his country's arms. Although he
dreaded the practical consequences of administrative bungling on the
condition of the soldiers serving in Turkey or the Crimea, he derived
a grim satisfaction from the endless revelations of mismanagement,
which promised to undermine the structure of aristocratic government and call into question the war-making machinery of Great Britain. Moreover, although he could not bring himself to wish defeat on
British troops, he did not wish them to win an easy or decisive victory.
That would only vindicate the warmongers at home. On the whole,
"putting humanity and patriotism aside for the sake of argument,"
Cobden believed, "perhaps the best thing that could happen would be
a long and sanguinary contest without decisive result" from which
both sides would emerge having learned something of the futility of
war.[18] Cobden never doubted the soundness or rightness of this view
of the war, but that did not mean that it was a comfortable view to
live with. Nor was he able, as Bright evidently was, to still his doubts
with the certainty of his rightness. And if as a result his position
personally was agonizingly difficult, his position politically was
thereby rendered all but untenable. It was not only the difficulty of
gaining a hearing for his views that led Cobden to limit his role in
wartime politics; it was also the knowledge that he dared not hint
publicly at many of his most deeply felt convictions.

Cobden was acutely conscious of this dilemma and of its inhibiting
effects almost from the day the war began. What he does not appear
to have seen so clearly was that, even without the Crimean war, his
credibility and effectiveness as a critic of British foreign policy had
eroded. Just as the Manchester school, with Cobden following somewhat reluctantly in the wake of Bright and Wilson, had spent its
political capital in the pursuit of parliamentary reform, so Cobden
had diminished his reputation as a practical politician through his
connection with the peace movement. Aware of the danger of this
from the start, he had done what he could to prevent it, by approaching the issue at first as a financial question and avoiding any suggestion of unilateralism in his proposals for disarmament and arbitration.
With the decline of the financial reform movement, the death of Peel,
and the ascendency of Palmerston, however, Cobden found it difficult

to maintain his dispassionate public stance on the peace issue. And the second French invasion scare, the militia bill, the Burmese war, and the Eastern crisis only served to confirm him in his growing conviction that British policy was itself among the greatest threats to world peace. In the circumstances he felt he had no choice but to put personal political calculations to one side along with his plans to build a broad base for the peace movement over a long period of time. The threat and then the actuality of war made such considerations irrelevant.

Yet even supposing that Cobden's assessment of English policy and of how he could best influence it were correct, he nonetheless made errors in tactics and judgment that seriously damaged the cause he sacrificed so much to serve. Like many persistent critics of their own country's foreign policy, he was often harder on Britain than on its enemies, past, present, or prospective. Indeed, from revolutionary France to the Russia of Czar Nicholas I, adversaries appeared in Cobden's writings and speeches as, if not quite innocent, then certainly misunderstood. To those who dismissed him as naive in this regard, Cobden replied that he was naturally most concerned with the policy of the country whose direction he could influence, his own, and that in any case to elucidate the motives and thinking of foreign governments was not necessarily to condone them. Moreover, there seemed to him to be quite enough criticism of France, Russia, and others without his joining in the chorus. Even so, it would have been politic to have given the appearance of better balance.

More fundamentally, Cobden's tendency to place present crises in a long historical perspective and to see the fate of nations as largely the function of the working out of impersonal economic forces led him to the comforting (but to some disturbing) practical conclusion that less should or could be done than most statesmen imagined. This predisposition toward laissez faire in international politics was reinforced by his revulsion against England's tendency to respond even to minor provocations by throwing its weight around, and it was largely in reaction to this side of Palmerstonianism that Cobden carried his own doctrine of nonintervention to the point where it appeared to critics that he rejected the idea of ever projecting national power abroad.

Cobden always vigorously denied that his was a negative or escapist policy, likely to invite aggression, let alone that it had anything in common with pacifism; a noninterventionist policy, as Cobden understood it, involved not merely a commitment to lead by example but a willingness to press the principle on other nations. Yet Cobden never spelled out how that should be done in practice. His opposition to the floating of Austrian and Russian loans in London and his speech to the Edinburgh Peace Conference on the eve of the Crimean war pointed toward a policy of economic sanctions; his response to Kossuth's visit to England suggested the possibility of a concert of nations, led by the Atlantic powers, to oversee a policy of nonintervention. Beyond these tentative suggestions for alternatives to the use of force Cobden did not go, however. Nor did he discuss what should be done in the event such restraints did not work. Indeed, it is not unfair to say that, apart from his acceptance of the need for Britain to maintain a navy sufficient to protect itself and its sea lanes, on the one hand, and, on the other, his vision of international limitations on the exercise of military power through arbitration treaties and mutual disarmament—that apart from such matters Cobden avoided the issue of the use or threat of force.

Hence in large measure the paradox of Cobden's role in the peace movement of the 1850s: the more accurate he became as critic and prophet, the less he was able to influence the course of British policy. The fault certainly did not lie in any lack of publicity for his views. *The Times*, for example, although hostile toward Cobden, nonetheless scrupulously fulfilled its role as the national newspaper of record by publishing full accounts of his speeches and lengthy excerpts from his pamphlets. The leading newspapers of his former home and of his present constituency, the *Manchester Guardian* and the *Leeds Mercury*, although scarcely less critical of Cobden than *The Times*, were also thorough in their coverage of him. Nor was it only in hindsight that Cobden's vision often seemed clearer than that of those who managed British foreign policy; many of his contemporaries suspected that he might be right. To be sure, by the time England went to war against Russia Cobden no longer commanded the audience he had at the time of his earlier contests with Palmerston. Nonetheless, his reputation as a critic had recently been enhanced by the outcome of the second French invasion scare, which was brought to an end, embarrassingly for its proponents, by the need to close ranks with France against Russia.

As for the Eastern crisis, even some of Cobden's detractors acknowledged in private the force of his arguments against some of the assumptions underlying British policy: that Russian influence could be kept out of the Balkans; that the Islamic minority could successfully rule over the Christian majority in European Turkey; that the Turkish empire could survive at all, let alone as a contributor to the stability of the European state system; that Britain could act in the East in advance of Austria and Prussia, whose interests were more directly affected. Sir James Graham, for one, came away from Cobden's confrontation with Palmerston on the future of Turkey in the summer of 1853 certain that although "both pushed their doctrines to extremes, Cobden in the long run, will have England with him."[19] Yet Graham supported the war until after the formation of Palmerston's government, a year and a half later. For him and his Peelite colleagues, and still more for most other M.P.s, Cobden's ideas might have great merit in the long run or in the abstract, but they seemed almost beside the immediate points at issue in an ongoing crisis and unacceptably risky in the short run.

There was little Cobden could have done to correct this. The political situation was against him. Many M.P.s, including quite a few cabinet ministers, were swept along by the tide of press and public opinion, often, as they later acknowledged, against their better judgment. Moreover, his most likely allies, the Peelites, were in the government, not in opposition, when the war began. That said, however, Cobden made two disastrous errors, one in tactics, one in strategy, in the months leading up to the war. His fatalistic, almost casual, attitude toward Russian expansion during 1853 did him incalculable damage as a critic of government policy and the public temper. Even more importantly, he failed to provide way stations, in the form of concrete alternative proposals, in which potential sympathizers could take shelter, short of his exposed position of nonintervention. Faced with a choice between that and the pursuit of traditional policy, if necessary to the point of war, even many who had grave doubts about the government's course and suspected that Cobden might be largely correct inevitably opted for the government, for traditional policy, and finally for war. As Palmerston said, cruelly but accurately, "The British nation is unanimous in this matter; I say unanimous, for I cannot reckon Cobden, Bright and Co. for anything."[20]

That Palmerston could dismiss his great radical adversaries so contemptuously is perhaps the best measure of how far they had fallen in the years since the repeal of the Corn Laws. Although their status as the leaders of the Manchester school still afforded them an automatic public hearing and, even during the war, a surprisingly respectful one (at least in Parliament), they had by then become leaders almost without followers, teachers without pupils. The war revealed the extent of their isolation and completed it but was far from being the cause of it. As Charles Greville observed, "It seems that they had already ceased to be popular, when they made themselves enormously unpopular . . . by their opposition to the Crimean War."[21] Had this not been so, had they not long since lost much of their reputation and power as the leaders of great interests, they might have enlisted the support of some who concurred in their doubts, if not in their specific recommendations for the conduct of foreign policy; they might even perhaps have given pause to those who fundamentally disagreed with them. As it was, the widely held notion that they were unsufficiently realistic about power in general and Russian power in particular, reinforced by the knowledge that they no longer commanded any great political forces, rendered them ineffectual during the war.

Cobden had long feared just such a falling off of influence. Even at the height of his reputation in the summer of 1846, he was aware of the impermanence of his enormous popular following. The repeal movement in Manchester in the early 1840s represented a unique conjunction of time, place, and issue, and far from assuming that it could be kept in being in the service of other causes, he was inclined to believe that its supporters and its organization were nontransferable. At the same time, he had always seen the Corn Laws as implying a host of other issues and repeal as bound to raise them in new and compelling ways. The upper middle class of Manchester might not take the lead in these new movements, but other groups and other cities in the great repeal coalition would emerge to carry on the work begun in Manchester. As for his own role in this, Cobden had neither the intention nor the desire to manage any new agitations. He always believed that they should be and should be seen to be the spontaneous creations of their own leaders and supporters, not the creatures of the Manchester school. He saw himself in the role of an advisor, uniquely placed to provide day-to-day activists with a sense of perspective and an awareness of the connections between all of the great reform issues.

This was a more modest—and more realistic—view of his own and of the Manchester School's potential in the postrepeal era than that taken by almost any other radical leader. Moreover, when movement after movement failed to fulfill its promise in the late 1840s, Cobden was less inclined to wishful thinking than either Bright or Wilson, let alone comparatively inexperienced leaders such as Sturge, Robertson Gladstone, or Walmsley. He recognized that a nation as prosperous and self-confident as England had become by the early 1850s provided poor ground for agitation at home but a dangerously fertile field for those inclined to flex the national muscles abroad. Indeed, he often noted the great irony of his position: that repeal had removed the one issue on which the middle classes were genuinely radical, thus opening their way to acquiescence in the ascendency of the traditional governing class; and the prosperity that he ascribed largely to free trade all but guaranteed the perpetuation of the politics of social deference. As early as the autumn of 1851, Cobden had come to believe that perhaps only a downturn in the economy could reawaken the middle class to a sense of its real interests.

For all his hard-headed realism, however, Cobden was not immune to wishful thinking. He was slow to come to terms with the lack of support for his own pet projects (as opposed to Bright's pet projects, the weaknesses of which he saw clearly), and he was inclined to misread the causes of the growing ineffectuality of the Manchester school. Like most politicians, especially those who have enjoyed a mass following, he continued to believe that there were huge reserves of popular support ready to be tapped if only the right issues could be developed in the right way. As late as 1852, in the controversy over the militia bill, he clung to the hope that a rising tide of public support might carry the day for the parliamentary radicals; only after nothing of the sort happened did Cobden permanently lower his expectations. Similarly, he was slow to abandon the notion that there might be one issue, comparable to the Corn Laws, around which the forces of radicalism could regroup in the late 1840s, despite the evidence from his dealings with other radical leaders that no such consensus was possible. His attempt to make financial reform backed by the forty-shilling freehold movement the centerpiece of postrepeal radicalism encountered such stiff resistance—or indifference—from other reformers that he had to back down. As early as 1849, he was corresponding with each of his fellow radicals—Bright, Wilson, Robertson Gladstone, Hume, Sturge, Richard, Collet—only about the issues of greatest concern to them. The radical movement had become compartmentalized, a fact that Cobden did not entirely accept until the decline of the financial reform movement led him to devote his time to his own special concerns, education and peace.

Even then Cobden did not entirely abandon his belief that repeal and the method of its passage, especially the freehold movement, had permanently altered the balance of power and opinion in British politics. That this was not evident in government policy or in the composition of the House of Commons and of cabinets was due, he argued, to the effects of the harvest of 1845 and the opportunistic conservatism of Peel in bringing on repeal before its natural time, before the free trade movement had been able to complete its task of reshaping the political system. Had this not happened, Cobden came to believe in the early 1850s, the promise of the reform bill of 1832 could have been realized in 1847 or 1848, rather than aborted once again in 1846. This view of the postrepeal era did little to ease Cobden's frustration, but it did preserve intact his view of the seminal importance of the league in shaping the future of the reform movement in England. The implications of free trade might take longer to work themselves out than he had hoped, but of the ultimate outcome he remained almost as sure in the early 1850s as he had been when he left England on his European tour in the summer of 1846.

Even that vision could not survive the coming of the Crimean war, however. As the fever mounted, as all classes were swept up in it—and as Cobden found himself looking to an aristocratic Parliament as a check on the people, rather than the other way around—he had, finally, to abandon his belief that free trade necessarily pointed British policy in any particular direction he wished it to go. As he put it some months after the end of the war, "Depend on it, the radicals have cut their throats before Sebastopol."[22] This was an especially bitter realization for Cobden, who had spent seven years in the battle for free trade and another seven in vain attempts to cultivate what he thought were the fruits of free trade, and there appeared during the war itself to be no compensations for these failures. He could not see, as we can, that although the years since repeal had been almost barren of measurable achievements, they were full of promise for the future. He—and Bright and Wilson, and the Manchester educational reformers, and the Liverpool financial reformers, and Walmsley's parliamentary reformers, and even Sturge's peace society—were helping to build the programmatic foundations of the late-nineteenth-century Liberal party and even, through their increasingly close association with Gladstone on financial, educational, and peace questions, shaping the future leadership of that party. For the moment, however, Cobden had no such assurance of the value of his work over the past decade; whatever satisfaction he felt was private in nature. What he said of his pamphlet, *What Next—And Next?* might, with little alteration, have served as a comment on the whole of his public career since repeal: "I suppose people won't read it, but my conscience will be at rest."[23]

PART IV

Diplomatist
1856–1865

CHAPTER 20

Postwar Casualties

The end of the Crimean war in March 1856 passed almost unnoticed in Cobden's correspondence. Indeed, although the peace settlement included an important advance in the international law of the sea, its signing was the occasion of only muted celebrations by the leaders of the peace movement. For they, and Cobden especially, had other more personal concerns. Just two months earlier the war had claimed its most important civilian casualty: following a speech to his Manchester constituents on 25 January, John Bright suffered an emotional collapse. That this was no minor episode was soon apparent. He felt totally drained, physically as well as mentally; he could concentrate his thoughts only with difficulty, and even then often at the cost of excruciating headaches. The discussion of politics left him agitated and anxious. He was plagued by insomnia. Inevitably he withdrew completely from public life, and for more than a year his doctors and closest friends doubted that he would ever be able to return to it.

For Cobden that possibility was unthinkable. For himself as for the nation, he believed, it would be calamitous. The strain in their relationship earlier in the decade, which their lonely opposition to the war had healed in any case, was entirely forgotten. Only the length of their close association and the symbiotic nature of that association now seemed important. Cobden thought of himself as bringing to their partnership an intellectual rigor lacking in the impulsive and relatively unreflective character of Bright's mind, but Bright contributed a physical dynamism and emotional intensity that Cobden never claimed to match. In Cobden's view, Bright's breakdown appeared to confirm this reading of his character; it was a case of Bright's boundless energy outrunning the capacity of his mind to sustain the effort. And, just as Cobden, who had the opposite problem, had learned to husband his limited physical resources to sustain his mental activity, so, he felt, Bright would have to learn to rein in his instinct for action and give his brain sufficient rest.

Hence Cobden's campaign, begun shortly after the breakdown and kept up for more than a year, to restore Bright to something more stable than his old condition. Cobden approached his self-appointed task with a disarming combination of tender solicitude and an inventiveness reminiscent of the great days of the league. He inundated Bright with advice. He suggested that Bright be bled and that he eat a less sanguineous diet. More commonsensically, he recommended that Bright treat himself "as much as possible like a child"[1] and spend time in the company of children, that he play games and get plenty of exercise, that he do only light reading. Cobden intervened with friends, urging them not to write to Bright, and with Bright, urging him not to reply. Above all, he believed that Bright should get away, perhaps to America (with a trip to Niagara Falls), or on a walking tour in Switzerland or the south of France, or for a winter in Rome or Egypt. "You have sprained your brain," Cobden advised. "You must lay it on a cushion and afterwards put it in a sling, just as you would your ankle."[2]

Cobden's almost parental concern for Bright's health was rendered all the more important to both men by the death ten weeks after Bright's breakdown of Cobden's oldest child and only son, Richard Brooks Cobden, a month after his fifteenth birthday. Young Dick was not the first of the Cobden children to die. They had lost a daughter, named for her mother, in 1843, and another son, William, seven years later. But neither death had anything like the impact of Dick's. Both children were sickly from the beginning and had died in infancy. Moreover, Catherine Cobden was in her early childbearing years when she lost her first daughter; another girl, also named Kate, was born the following year. By the time of William's death, there was a comparatively large family, four daughters in addition to Dick. All five surviving children were in excellent health (the four girls lived well into the twentieth century).

There were no similar mitigating circumstances surrounding young Dick's death. Both parents doted on their son. Catherine Cobden "loved her boy with," as Cobden put it, "too excessive a fondness,"[3] although the closeness of their ties was understandable. "For the first four years of his life," Cobden explained, "when I was almost incessantly absent from home on my agitating mission, he was nearly her sole companion."[4] Cobden did not develop a close relationship with his boy until some years later, when the vicissitudes of his postrepeal career coincided with Dick's early adolescence to open the way to real companionship between father and son. The growing importance of Dunford, which Dick adored, as a retreat for Cobden from an increasingly hostile political world created a special bond between them; more than once Cobden used the occasion of Dick's school holidays as a welcome excuse to quit London for Sussex. Of all the children, Dick was individually the most precious to both parents. "The dear boy was affectionate beyond any of his sisters," Cobden recalled, "and his truthful and bold character, allied with this more than feminine gentleness of feeling, attached us to him by ties so strong that his death seems too awful to be borne."[5]

As if Dick's death in itself was not painful enough, the occasion of it and the way in which his parents heard of it combined to make the blow even more devastating. He died quite unexpectedly of scarlet fever, and he died far from home, at a boarding school in Germany, to which Cobden, hoping that his son would be more broadly educated there than in England, had taken him the previous autumn. The news of his death reached the Cobdens in a way guaranteed to reinforce their sense of separation from the event, and of the event from reality. As soon as Dick fell ill, his schoolmaster contacted Cobden's closest friend in Germany, Chevalier Bunsen, who had recommended the school to Cobden. Unfortunately, both Bunsen and the schoolmaster assumed that the other would inform the Cobdens, with the result that Cobden heard nothing of his son's illness until informed of his death in a letter of condolence from Bunsen. What is more, Cobden received this letter while in his lodgings in London, nearly a day's journey from the rest of the family at Dunford:

> I had invited Colonel Fitzmayer from the Crimea to breakfast at nine on the Thursday. When I came down from my sleeping room in Grosvener Street, I found him and the breakfast waiting. My letters were lying on the table, and I apologized for opening them before beginning our meal—and the third letter I opened informed me that my dear boy, who by the latest accounts was described as the healthiest and strongest in the school, was dead and in his grave. No one not placed in the same

situation can form the faintest conception of my task in making the journey to this place [Dunford] which took me five hours, bearing a secret which I knew was worse than a sentence of death on my poor wife . . . I found her in the happiest of spirits, having just before been reading to my brother and the family circle a long letter from the dear boy, written a few days previously, and when he was in the best possible state of health. I tried to manage my communication, but the dreadful journey had been too much for me, and I broke down instantly and was obliged to confess all. She did not comprehend the loss, but was only stunned, and for twenty-four hours was actually lavishing attentions on me, and superintending her household as before.[6]

This brief period of denial was followed by something far worse: a refusal by Catherine Cobden to resign herself to what had happened, coupled with and finally overwhelmed by almost total withdrawal into herself. This might not have happened, Cobden realized, "if she could have watched over his deathbed and seen the poor dear boy waste away in spite of all her efforts to relieve him."[7] As it was, her experience of Dick's death was like stumbling "over his corpse as she is passing from room to room."[8] Small wonder that, months afterwards, "she starts with tears, when we walk out, at the sound of the pony's steps or at a whistle in the woods, thinking it must be he coming to meet us as of old."[9] She became obsessed with thoughts of what might have been had something been done differently, and she fueled her imaginings by reading medical books. Incapable of anything but the most fitful rest, she was, despite reservations on Cobden's part, given opiates and, as the desired effects wore off, in increasingly larger doses. Cobden was right to be concerned. By midsummer she had joined the numerous ranks of drug-dependent Victorian women. The still unresolved problem of coming to terms with her son's death had only been confused by the use of opiates, which had now in themselves become quite as serious a problem.

At first Cobden was inclined to blame himself and to play his own version of the dangerous game of "what if." "When I think of it," he concluded an anguished summary of all his questions concerning his son's death, "I wonder how we sent him so far to die."[10] For a month or more, the intensity of his sorrow was quite the equal of his wife's and, to his surprise, little different in character. He was subject to uncontrollable spasms of grief and to a listless indifference to all other matters that he had never experienced before and regarded as more appropriate to a woman's mourning than a man's. "I feel incapable of entering the lists to contend again for anything," he told Sturge, "for I have lost the great prize and everything else seems not worth struggling for."[11]

This mood did not last long, however. Perhaps in part in reaction to the unexpected quality of his own suffering, which clearly disturbed him, and certainly because the worsening condition of his wife demanded attention, Cobden began to pull himself together in May. There was, of course, no question of his resuming his public career immediately, even had he wished to do so; for the foreseeable future his first obligation lay at home. Even discounting his notion that women were constitutionally more vulnerable to sorrows of this kind than men, Cobden recognized, more or less implicitly, that the circumscribed role of women in the nineteenth century made them more vulnerable, and he recognized, quite explicitly, that Catherine Cobden was more vulnerable than most. The demands of his public life had forced her to rely too much on her children as both objects and sources of affection. Although what their son's death had revealed of the emotional cost of this could not be undone, Cobden could at least atone in part by devoting himself entirely to her well-being until the crisis was passed.

And this he did. Apart from two quick trips to London in May to clear up loose ends, Cobden dropped out of public life for nearly a year, during which he never left his wife alone. As with Bright earlier in the year, he busied himself with plans for her recovery. Because Dunford was filled with reminders of the boy, he arranged short trips to the seashore, to the homes of nearby friends and relatives, and finally to London. When all this proved too exhausting and too depressing to her spirits, he hoped that a return to Dunford and her daughters might lift her out of herself. And when that too failed to work, he arranged with Manchester friends to take their house on the north coast of Wales for the autumn and early winter. The Brights visited Llandudno, only twenty miles east of the Cobdens on the Menai Strait, for much of the same season, and Cobden and Bright were able to exchange visits for the first time since their personal disasters.

Even before that, however, as soon as the arrangements for the trip to Wales were settled, Cobden's thoughts had begun to turn back to Bright. Concerned that Bright was not doing enough to ensure his own recovery and that many of their political friends, especially Wilson, did not fully understand the seriousness of Bright's condition, Cobden took matters into his own hands, making certain that the details of Bright's illness reached the right people and urging Bright to consult Sir James Clark, the royal physician. Cobden's meetings with Bright in Wales convinced him that more direct action was required. He contacted Clark on his own and made an appointment for Bright to see him; and when Clark suggested that Combe should be consulted, Cobden arranged that as well. He even vehemently reproached Bright for not taking proper care of himself. For a time Cobden feared that Bright might be "in danger of falling into imbecility."[12] Reassured by Clark and his own observations that this was not likely, Cobden still did not expect much. "All that I saw of him," Cobden reported from Wales to a mutual friend, "convinced me that he may live a happy and cheerful life in the full enjoyment of all his faculties, although not in the fullest use of them. This is a great calamity to the country. But I thank God he is not in danger of outliving his intellect, which is worse a thousand times than the grave."

As for Catherine, after a brief period when Cobden hoped that the responsibility of caring for her daughters in an unfamiliar setting might serve to lead her back to reality, he was finally forced to admit to his brother Fred that "Kate is worse than when we came. She takes less notice of the children, flies more to her own bedroom, and is entirely indebted to her drafts for sleep . . . The truth is she has never yet submitted to her loss, and therefore has not sought the consolation of religion or reason."[13]

Cobden was closer to a sense of utter helplessness than at any time in his adult life. As he told Joseph Parkes, "I try to delude myself with the idea that Bright is not so bad as I believe him to be. Next to the loss of my boy, I have had no sorrow so constant and great as from his illness. The two together make me feel quite unnerved, and I seem to be always feeling about in my mind for an excuse for quitting the public scene."[14]

In practice Cobden did not mean quite what he said. For some time to come he avoided the social side of public life, largely because he dreaded having to deal with questions about his wife's condition. But far from wishing to quit the political scene, he clung to certain aspects of it as perhaps the best way of maintaining his equilibrium. Indeed, there were times during 1856 when he was sure that only his interests outside the home (interests, he recognized, that Catherine did not share), together with "a singular power of diverting and concentrating my attention according to my own will and independent of external circumstances," had kept him from sinking into despair.[15] Cobden's domestic obligations imposed limitations on what he could do, to be sure. He could not participate directly in day-to-day politics. Nor did he wish to. But he could act by proxy, so to speak, and the means of doing so had fortuitously come into being early in the year. In March a new radical newspaper began publication in London. It was designed as the mouthpiece of the Manchester school and the peace movement, and the terms of its establishment included an oversight role for Cobden and Bright. Thus, not only did their brand of radicalism find a voice at a time when their influence was at its lowest ebb, but Cobden was granted a personal outlet when he desperately needed one.

The idea of starting a paper was not a new one to Cobden, who saw the need for it in long-run historical terms. "Twenty years ago," he told Bright in the gloomy autumn of 1855, "I had hoped that having got rid of the boroughmongers, and preserved *their* debt, we should have for ever eschewed their foreign policy. Later when I found that the Whigs had taken to praise Pitt and imitate him up to their little best, I turned to the religious public and thought they would help to keep the peace. But, alas, of all the bitter assailants of the foreign foe, and the unscrupulous traducers of the peace party at home, your religious organs have been the worst. I turn now with very blunted hopes to the cheap press."[16]

More specifically, Cobden had talked of the need for their own paper since the beginning of the decade, when the Manchester radicals had been deserted by former press allies such as the *Daily News* (on the peace issue) and Baines' *Leeds Mercury* (on education). The isolation of the peace party during the Crimean war gave the building of a secure platform for their views renewed urgency; the repeal of the newspaper stamp in 1855 made it possible. Preparations for founding a paper began that summer and bore fruit with the publication of the first issue of the *Morning Star* on 17 March 1856.

From first to last, the process was plagued with even more problems than one might expect to attend the birth of a newspaper. In addition to the half-dozen or so founding fathers, others who were brought in as the money was raised and the editorial staff assembled had their own ideas about how the paper should be run. And although Cobden, Bright, Wilson, Sturge, and Richard were basically agreed, the fact that they were all busily writing to one another about the project inevitably led to confusion. There were also differences on matters of substance. Cobden was most concerned with how such a paper would steer the difficult course between expediency and commitment to principle. On the one hand, it might degenerate into little more than a daily *Herald of Peace*, preaching only to the converted. On the other, the proprietors of the papers might sacrifice editorial integrity for the sake of short-term popularity. In either case the paper would abort its purpose and, in the end, probably its life. The maintenance of a satisfactory balance depended on the quality of those chosen to run the paper and, Cobden believed, on the formula by which authority was shared out among them and the founders of the paper.

Unfortunately for the *Star* it was not well served in either respect. The most pressing problem was raising funds to get the paper started. As the months passed, Sturge and Bright, who were primarily responsible for funding, looked increasingly to Henry Rawson, a Manchester stockbroker and Archibald Prentice's successor as proprietor of the *Manchester Times*. Cobden was not happy with this. He questioned Rawson's conscientiousness in business and feared that he might be willing to sacrifice principle for the sake of immediate profitability. Furthermore, Manchester seemed too great a distance in outlook as well as mileage from which to manage a metropolitan paper. Cobden would have preferred silent and more patient partners among the potential investors from the North, and he also proposed giving the prospective editor a financial stake in the paper as a means of ensuring his dedication and of preventing too sharp a distinction between editorial and financial control.

By the time Cobden raised these matters, late in 1855, it was too late to change course, however. He was reminded—and acknowledged—that he had earlier refused to share in the burden of financing the paper. Moreover, Rawson had been involved from the beginning, was experienced in running a paper, and had promised to give much of his time to the task of getting the *Star* established. Bright sought to reassure Cobden further by suggesting a tightening up of an arrangement agreed to in general terms at the outset, designed to ensure the editorial probity of the *Star*. As Cobden understood it, this called "for

Wilson to be legally invested in the majority of the shares representing Sturge's contribution and for us [Cobden and Bright] to be referees in matters of principle."[17] Short of eliminating Rawson and the money men entirely, this was as much as Cobden could ask for, since it appeared to place a predominant interest in the hands of those who had originated the idea of the paper.

Such an arrangement could have worked perhaps only if it had never been invoked, that is to say if the editor of the *Star* had been a man of great ability and presence, able to fend off outside interference. No such man appeared. The first editor, William Haly, was nobody's first choice and was ultimately agreed to by a process of elimination. Cobden, his major backer, seems to have liked him primarily for his American-inspired ideas about building circulation, which accorded well with Cobden's view of what the new penny dailies should be. But even Cobden had reservations about Haly, and most of them proved well founded. For some weeks after its birth the *Star* was poorly written and sloppily put together, and it lost money at an alarming rate. The look and literary quality of the paper gradually improved thereafter, but the financial hemorrhage continued. Inevitably Rawson intervened and in May, with Wilson's backing, decided to fire Haly. Given the circumstances of his appointment, Haly turned to Cobden for help, and Cobden, convinced that Rawson's laxity and his failure to spend enough on publicity were largely responsible for the *Star*'s anemic condition, gave Haly qualified support in letters to Sturge and Bright. Had Bright been well and active, the situation might never have deteriorated to this point, as Cobden lamented at the time, but Bright's breakdown took place before the *Star* appeared, and there was no one else who could act as a buffer beween Cobden and Rawson.

At this stage nothing could be done to save Haly, even had Cobden unequivocally wanted to; Rawson had the right, as Cobden admitted, to fire the editor. Still, the dispute could be used to limit Rawson's influence and give Haly's successor more authority. First, however, a new editor had to be found. Cobden would have preferred A. W. Paulton, whose friendship with Cobden dated back to his days as an anti–Corn Law lecturer and editor of the league newspaper. But Paulton and Rawson had come to distrust one another during Paulton's years as editor and co-proprietor of the *Manchester Times* (which may have influenced Cobden's negative view of Rawson). For his part, Rawson briefly supported two other candidates, but both were unacceptable to everyone else, and the job was finally given to Henry Richard.

Once again, as with Haly, he was no one's unqualified choice (except perhaps Sturge's). Cobden, for example, was concerned that Richard might be too close in his views on education to Baines, although such reservations were more than balanced off by Richard's soundness on other issues. Moreover, Richard's standing in the peace movement was some insurance against too much meddling from the likes of Rawson. To ensure that that would indeed be the case, Richard was given a financial share in the paper. If there was any danger in his editorship, it appeared to lie in the possibility that he might sacrifice the *Star*'s character as a general paper to its obligations as a propaganda organ. But Cobden was certain that this could be prevented by those like himself who had a clear vision of what the new popular press ought to be. After all, Richard had been amenable to Cobden's advice on the contents of the *Herald of Peace* ever since 1848.

When Cobden first agreed to act as a watchdog over the *Star* at the end of 1855, he likely envisaged his role as akin to his behind-the-scenes contribution to the movement for the repeal of the taxes on knowledge. But the bitter wrangles over the management of the *Star*, the need to train Richard in the requirements of editing a general paper, Bright's indisposition, and Cobden's isolation from other access to public life combined to push him into an active role in the paper. Not that he took a greater public part in it. On the contrary, conscious of his own unpopularity and wishing to avoid having the *Star* dismissed as a factional paper, he asked Richard to keep his name out of it as much as possible. Hidden from view, therefore, Cobden sought to shape the character of the *Star*. For more than a year he inundated Richard with letters—one every three or four days—advising him not only on how the paper should handle the issues of the day but also on any and all aspects of running a newspaper, from the length of articles to how best to increase circulation.

Whatever the recipient may sometimes have thought, Cobden's steady barrage of letters to Richard was like a lifeline to him. By early 1857, however, he needed something more tangible. His constant attendance on Catherine, so necessary to both husband and wife in 1856, began to weigh heavily—perhaps on both of them, certainly on him—soon after they returned from Wales in December. Moreover, the political scene, which had offered few opportunities during 1856, began to look inviting around the turn of the year. The reason was the *Arrow* incident in China. Like the Don Pacifico affair seven years earlier, it was a perfect example of what the English critics of the Palmerstonian style in foreign policy most disliked, and not only radical critics such as Cobden. Again like the Don Pacifico affair, the *Arrow* incident attracted a wide range of opponents, that opened up the alluring prospect of breaking down the coalition that had emerged in support of Palmerston in the wake of the Don Pacifico affair. Cobden would have to have been almost superhuman not to have gotten involved in such an effort.

The facts of the case did not reflect well on British policy, as even most cabinet members agreed in private. The Chinese authorities had boarded a Chinese-owned but British-registered vessel, the *Arrow* (on which, however, the registration had expired), and seized a number of men suspected of piracy. The British consul at Canton, backed by the governor of Hong Kong, Sir John Bowring, who was, ironically, an old ally of Cobden's in the free trade and peace movements, denounced this as a violation of the treaty of 1842 and demanded that the men seized be handed over to the British authorities, along with a note of apology. The Chinese did give up the men but persisted in their claim that the seizure had been legal and was no business of the British. Bowring therefore ordered the British squadron at Hong Kong to attack the fortifications at Canton.

The legal justification for Bowring's actions was questionable at best, and it was difficult to deny that he had acted precipitously, not to mention out of all proportion to the provocation. Yet the government decided to back him, partly because the *Arrow* incident was only one element in a pattern of Chinese provocation, partly so that Britain would not lose face, and also, although this was not admitted publicly, because the incident opened the way to further British penetration of China. The government, in short, hoped to escape censure much as Palmerston and his supporters had blunted criticism of his policies ever since the Don Pacifico affair: by appealing to national pride, by calling, after the fact of action, for unity in the face of a foreign enemy, and, all other arguments failing, by asking for a vote of confidence in Palmerston.

Cobden, who led the opposition attack, was determined not to let

Palmerston escape in this manner again. His parliamentary motion concentrated on the weakest link in government policy, the actions of Bowring, and was careful to criticize the British government only to the extent that it associated itself with these actions. He could hardly have stated the issue in terms more likely to appeal to a disparate coalition of radicals, Peelites, Conservatives, and disillusioned Whigs. In speaking to the motion, Cobden did not limit himself so narrowly, however (and alienated some who had been attracted by the motion but thought his speech "anti-English").[18] Indeed, he reiterated most of the themes he had developed over his years of opposition to Palmerstonian policy.

While condemning Bowring, Cobden suggested that he would likely not have acted as he did without some indication that "it would not be unfavorably regarded at home."[19] He presented a mass of evidence from the Blue Books to support his contention that it was the British, not the Chinese, who had acted provocatively. He condemned Bowring's high- handedness as yet another instance of a disturbing trend in British policy, of bullying weaker nations; he also, if some- what contradictorily, condemned it as part of a pattern of pressing quarrels with almost all nations to the point of crisis (citing a recent boundary dispute with the United States, the French invasion scare, and, of course, the Crimean war). In his one touch of humor, Cobden pointed out that trade could only be won, not enforced. "The Noble Lord inscribes 'Civis Romanus sum' on our passports," he noted, "which may be a very good thing to guard us in our footsteps. But 'Civis Romanus sum' is not a very attractive motto to put over the door of our counting houses abroad."

In his one direct appeal to idealism, he reminded the House that China was the oldest continuing civilization on earth: "There must be something in such a people deserving of respect. If, in speaking of them, we stigmatise them as barbarians, and threaten them with force because we say they are inaccessible to reason, it must be because we do not understand them; because their ways are not ours, nor our ways theirs. Is not so venerable an empire as that deserving of some sympathy—at least of some justice—at the hands of conservative England?"

None of this was new. What made the speech so powerful—and all agreed that it was one of Cobden's strongest parliamentary perfor- mances—was that even his most general reflections were anchored in the facts of the *Arrow* incident. There were few rhetorical flourishes and no gratuitous assaults on the prime minister. Cobden moved with relentless logic from the particular to the general and back again, picking up thread after thread to weave into his overall argument. It was an all-but-unanswerable speech, and Palmerston did not really answer it. Instead he attacked his attackers personally, Cobden especially. "There pervaded the whole of it [Cobden's speech]," Palmerston charged, "an anti-English feeling, an abnegation of all those ties which bind men to their country and to their fellow countrymen . . . Everything that was English was wrong, and everything that was hostile to England was right . . . The hon. gentleman has said that he should not like to have written over his counting house the motto, 'Civis Romanus sum'; if he writes up instead, 'I am a British subject,' that description would be held by those who know him to be untrue in spirit and at heart."[20]

Although this outburst undeniably reflected the sentiments of many members of Parliament, the manner of its delivery embarrassed even some of the prime minister's supporters. Yet despite this, and despite the fact that Cobden had the support of every major political figure not in the cabinet, defeat for Palmerston was far from certain and, when it came, far from crushing. Cobden's motion was carried by only sixteen votes. That Palmerston very nearly won was due in part to the nature of the forces arrayed against him; they were unnatural allies from which no stable government could be constructed. Palmerston also kept his wavering supporters in line through veiled threats of a dissolution in the event of his defeat. But perhaps the main reason for his near-victory was his extraordinary personal ascendency in the House of Commons.

Cobden had only recently begun to appreciate this fully. During the Crimean war he dismissed Palmerston's influence as his only by default and deception:

It is only because all the Parliamentary chiefs shrink from the responsibility of continuing the war that he has been enabled to seize the reins . . . and Lord Palmerston, having had the experience of nearly half a century of Parliamentary life, having continued to persuade the democracy that he was a revolutionist, while the aristocracy knew him to be their safe friend, he became the fittest incarnation of the delusion, bewilderment and deception into which the public mind has been plunged . . . Had it not been for the war, the present ministry could never have been in power, and it will not last two months after the return of peace.[21]

By the end of 1856, after nine months of a peacetime Palmerston government, Cobden had grudgingly to admit that his old adversary's peculiar political characteristics were equally well suited to postwar politics, at least so long as the lines between parties remained poorly defined.

What Cobden, along with virtually every other leading parliamentarian, appears not to have fully understood was that Palmerston's ascendency was not any longer a negative phenomenon. He was not just the leader who divided people least, or whose unique combination of activism in foreign affairs and relative indifference to domestic affairs made him acceptable to Liberals and Conservatives alike. These characteristics had opened the way to his rise to power, but they did not account for it or for his capacity to remain on top. Rather, it was his willingness to assume the management of the Crimean war when that war was going badly and others had failed or refused to carry the burden; it was his eagerness to assert the interests of England, even if necessary at the cost of isolation, and to continue to do so in the wake of the less-than-conclusive end to the Crimean war, when other, less confident leaders might have moved with greater caution; it was, in short, the very qualities that most disturbed Cobden that had, by the time of the *Arrow* incident, brought Palmerston closer to being identified with the nation than any individual political leader since the younger Pitt.

Cobden was not unaware of the danger of this happening. Ever since the Don Pacifico debate he had been concerned at Palmerston's skill at appropriating to himself the role of defender of the national honor and in managing to make his critics look less than patriotic. Nine months before the debate on the *Arrow* incident, for example, when a flare-up between Britain and the United States had ended in the dismissal of the British ambassador in Washington, Cobden was anxious that the peace movement handle the incident carefully. He wrote to Henry Richard: "We must guard ourselves against being thought a party aiming at peace by any means, and at any price, and without any care for national character, or what some people call 'honor' . . . We must show as sensitive regard for our national character as anybody, and I doubt whether we do so in meeting so great an affront as the sending away of our Minister with toleration of the Government, and without saying that they ought to resign in order to place the *country* in an honorable attitude and themselves in a graceful position towards the Americans."[22]

Unfortunately for Cobden, blinded as much by contempt for Palmerston's methods as for the substance of Palmerston's policy, he appears not to have recognized that it was no longer possible to contest Palmerston on that ground. The prime minister might have been vulnerable to a charge of recklessness or incompetence, but when it came to matters of national honor, he was already in undisputed possession of the field and had been at least since the wartime crisis that brought him to power.

That is the lesson that the passage of Cobden's motion condemning the *Arrow* incident obscured. The real significance of that division lay not in Palmerston's defeat but in the narrowness of that defeat and in the wholesale abstention of back-bench Tories. Although Cobden failed to realize this, Palmerston himself did not, and he responded to his defeat by calling for a general election. The election of 1857 was, therefore, among the more unusual of the nineteenth century not only in its circumstances but also in its results. It came closer than any other to being a referendum on the policies of an individual, Palmerston, which he won handily, and it also involved the most clear-cut repudiation of a political faction, the peace or Manchester wing of the Liberal party. No one expected anything quite so dramatic, although Palmerston rightly sensed that a forward policy in China would be popular beyond the walls of Westminster. As for Cobden, his judgment was initially distorted by his parliamentary victory. At the time of the dissolution of Parliament he expected that the election would result in more Tories and more independents but "fewer of that Whig section on which the Palmerston imposture rests for its support."[23] Once he got down to electioneering, however, he quickly sensed that the tide was running against him.

It was an especially trying election for Cobden, who, as well as contesting a new constituency himself, assumed much of the burden of campaigning for the absent Bright. Bright, still far from well, was in Rome and could not return to England for the election. For the Whig-Liberals of Manchester, many of whom had been Bright's political enemies ever since the league purge of the Chamber of Commerce in 1845 or the dispute over the representation of the city a year later, his absence, together with the unpopularity of his views on the Crimean war, provided a unique opportunity to get rid of an M.P. whom they had always regarded as not their own man. Local Conservatives, beaten in every election since the reform bill, were eager to cooperate, and the two groups combined forces in support of a couple of Palmerstonian Liberals. Led by the *Guardian*, they embarked on an often-savage campaign to unseat Bright, and within a few days, as the extent of the erosion of Bright's support became apparent, Wilson wrote Cobden for help.

Despite his own electoral difficulties, Cobden did not hesitate. Twenty years in public life had raised his threshold of personal outrage considerably, but the nature of the campaign against Bright angered him deeply because among its leaders were men who had worked with Cobden in the league and even earlier in the education and incorporation campaigns. Thus, when Cobden appeared in Bright's place before a meeting of the electors of Manchester, his speech, which began as an ordinary political speech, became by turns an indictment of the integrity of some in his audience, a revelation of the quality of his past relationship with Bright, and, in anticipation of electoral disaster, a valedictory address to the city where he had begun his career.

Necessarily he defended himself against charges of disloyalty to his party and conspiracy against the prime minister in proposing his China motion. More generally he defended his and Bright's long record of independence—an independence, he reminded his audience, without which the repeal of the Corn Laws could not have been won. He attacked Palmerston as an enemy of liberal causes at home and a false friend to liberal causes abroad. But the heart of his speech, its most moving and famous passage, dealt inevitably with Bright:

> I have lived with Mr. Bright in the most transparent intimacy of mind that two human beings ever enjoyed together . . . Knowing him, then, I stand here, in all humility, as his representative; for what I have long cherished in my friend Mr. Bright is this, that I have seen in him an ability and an eloquence to which I have had no pretensions, because I am not gifted with the natural eloquence with which he is endowed; and that I have long had the fond consolation of hoping that Mr. Bright, being seven or eight years younger than myself will be advocating principles...when I shall no longer be on the scene of duty. With those feelings, I naturally take the deepest interest in the decision of this

election. I feel humiliated—I feel disgusted to see the daily personal attacks—the diatribes that are made against this man—with his health impaired for the moment . . . Yes; while this man is not able to use those great intellectual powers with which God has gifted him . . . the vermin of your Manchester press, the ghouls of the *Guardian*, are preying upon this splendid being, and trying to make a martyr of him in the midst of his sufferings!

I will deal with you very candidly, men of Manchester, in this respect. I say you have not the character, or the fame, or the destinies of John Bright in your hands; but I will tell you this, that your own character and reputation are at stake.[24]

As for Cobden's own electoral situation, it did not involve any such issues of principle, at least as far as he was concerned. But it was no less difficult for that. He had never been happy as a member for the West Riding, a position into which he had been drafted without his knowledge, and from the moment that his participation in the education campaign brought him into conflict with Edward Baines and the Yorkshire voluntarists, he had decided not to stand for that seat again. In the 1852 election, with the Tories in office and free trade again an issue, the repeal coalition revived in Yorkshire, and Cobden was compelled by circumstances to change his mind. As he explained the situation four years later: "The protectionist cry was revived and the Tory papers had threatened to oust me from the Riding. I went down to Leeds, and without consulting anybody, announced myself again a candidate, but announced that I would not stand again."[25]

Nothing occurred between then and 1857 to change his mind again. On the contrary, Cobden's differences with Baines over the Crimean war made another run for the representation of the West Riding unthinkable. Unfortunately for Cobden, there were no obvious or safe alternatives. Nor, because of the war, followed by family tragedy, had he sought out a new constituency; for a time, at the end of 1856, he had even considered retiring from Parliament, before the *Arrow* incident rekindled his interest. Therefore, when a group of Huddersfield Liberals offered to adopt him as their candidate, he had little choice but to accept, despite serious misgivings. The misgivings were justified. All the factors that had rendered his candidacy in the West Riding impossible were present to some degree in Huddersfield, and his supporters had little organization. Thus, although preoccupied with the situation in Manchester—which was so desperate that he agreed to make a second visit there—Cobden had to spend most of his time in Huddersfield. He spoke almost daily to open-air meetings and was compelled to take an active part in the canvass of voters in a frantic attempt to close the gap with his better-organized opponents. It did him no good in any sense. He was soundly defeated in Huddersfield, and on the day he returned to Manchester to speak again for Bright, he fell ill and had to retire to bed for three days.

Although disappointed by his loss in Huddersfield, Cobden was not surprised by it. The failure of a last-minute candidacy in a constituency where he had no personal connections could not be interpreted as a clear-cut repudiation. Only in the context of other radical losses— Miall in Rochdale, Fox in Oldham, and above all Bright in Manchester—did Cobden's defeat appear to have any broader significance. The Manchester result in particular could not easily be explained away. Bright was defeated so overwhelmingly, by the largest margin of any major candidate since the city was enfranchised in 1832, that it was inevitably read as a repudiation not only of Bright and his opposition to the Crimean war but of his political philosophy and associates, Cobden included. Indeed, the collapse of the Manchester party was so complete that some of its critics, led by *The Times*, were shaken by the result, regretted that it had been so decisive, and began to talk wistfully of the day Cobden and Bright would return to Parliament.

Bright accepted the Manchester result with good humor. "We have taught what is true in our School," he wrote Cobden from Italy, "but the discipline was a little too severe for the scholars."[26] Cobden was less philosophical:

> The only incident of the election which hangs about me with a permanent feeling of irritability, is the atrocious treatment Bright has received from the people at Manchester. They are mainly indebted to him for the prosperity which has converted a majority into little better than Tories, and now the base snobs kick away the ladder. I find my scorn boiling over constantly, and can hardly keep my hands, or rather my pen, off them . . . He was one of themselves . . . He was an honor to his constituents. They had no grievance on account of his peace views, for they knew he was a Quaker when they elected him. To place such a man at the bottom of the poll, when prostrated by excessive labors in the public

service, is the most atrocious specimen of political ingratitude I ever encountered.[27]

For all his anger, however, Cobden had long been sufficiently distant from the politics of Manchester to realize that there were reasons for Bright's defeat beyond the legacy of animosity left over from the Crimean war and the machinations of the league. Manchester was not the ideal home for the school which bore its name. "There is no remedy for what has occurred at Manchester, believe me," he explained to one of his Lancashire correspondents:

> I never concealed from myself, though I might have done from others, that the League movement had its origins in the pocket argument, which pressed more urgently upon the great spinners and manufacturers of Lancashire than any other class . . . But the free trade question being carried, I never was of the opinion that Manchester would be found the headquarters for a reform agitation. Our friends there seemed to act on a different impression, and year after year we met and presented ourselves as the Manchester Party...and so we went on until we were knocked on the head last month. There was perhaps no other way of dying. But we are dead as a Manchester party, and depend on it that place will not in our time become the headquarters of another great public movement of any kind.[28]

Hence, later in the year, when Bright won a by-election in Birmingham, Cobden was delighted, for Birmingham was almost ideally suited to Bright's politics, as Cobden pointed out to Joseph Parkes:

> The honest and independent course taken by the people at Birmingham, their exemption from aristocratic snobbery, and their fair appreciation of a democratic son of the people, confirm me in the opinion I have always had that the social and political state of that town is far more healthy than that of Manchester, and it arises from the fact that the industry of the hardware district is carried on by small manufacturers, employing a few men and boys each, sometimes only an apprentice or two, whilst the great capitalists in Manchester form an aristocracy, individual members of which wield an influence over sometimes two thousand persons. The former state of society is more natural and healthy in a moral and political sense. There is a freer intercourse between all classes than in the Lancashire town, where a great and impassable gulf separates the workman from his employer . . . In my opinion Birmingham will be a better home for him than Manchester.[29]

Cobden's only reservation about Bright's election was that his friend had yet to recover, and still might never recover fully, from his breakdown.

Concerning his own defeat and absence from Parliament, Cobden appears to have been almost indifferent, if not relieved. The demands of his family situation seemed likely to remain as great as ever for some time to come, and apart from his moment of triumph in the *Arrow* incident debate, it had been years since Cobden felt happy or useful in the House of Commons. The prospects for the upcoming session looked even less inviting. Bright's continued absence would have made Westminster a lonely place, and Palmerston's electoral victory ensured that the new Parliament, which Cobden quickly dubbed the "servile Parliament," would be utterly unproductive of reform. The quiet life at Dunford in the company of his pigs, "fulfilling so wisely the purpose of their being," seemed preferable.[30]

Cobden was soon given a more serious reason to be grateful at his absence from public life. In the early summer the first news of the great Indian mutiny reached England, and from the moment the extent of it became evident, Cobden realized that his views, if known, would have been as unacceptable to the country as during the Crimean war. In certain respects, to be sure, he shared the concerns and prejudices of his fellow countrymen. Like many Englishmen, he was very nearly obsessed with events in India following the mutiny. He also almost unquestioningly assumed the inferiority of Indian to European civilization and by and large accepted the reports of Indian atrocities as proof of that inferiority. Moreover, he never doubted the need to put the mutiny down by whatever means were necessary. At the same time, Cobden saw the mutiny as a confirmation of his conviction that Britain had no business being in India at all, and not only because of his well- known views on the uselessness of nonsettlement colonies in the age of free trade. The mutiny, like the conquest of Borneo and the Burmese war, raised questions that went beyond the analysis in terms of costs and benefits that Cobden usually applied to peaceful acts of imperial expansion or to the civil and military estimates for colonial administration. More than any other event in his lifetime, the mutiny appeared to Cobden to expose the evils inherent in any colonial relationship, evils that tended toward the corruption of ruler and ruled alike.

The savagery of the mutiny was in itself, he believed, a damning indictment of a century of British rule, which not only had failed to civilize its subjects but perhaps had contributed to the ferocity of the revolt. The retribution he had predicted at the time of the subjugation of Borneo had been swift in coming. The arrogance of the British in India, although it could not justify the atrocities committed by the mutineers, was, he concluded, sufficient justification for rebellion. "If I were one of the natives, I would be one of the rebels," he admitted to Sturge.[31] The conclusion was inescapable: "Hindustan must be ruled by those who live on that side of the globe. Its people will prefer to be ruled badly, *according to our notions*, by its own color, kith and kin, than to submit to the humiliation of being better governed by a succession of transient intruders."[32]

Finding some means of getting his countrymen out of India was no theoretical matter to Cobden. The ferocity with which the British put down the mutiny was frightening evidence to him of how far they had been debased by exposure to the worst aspects of an alien society and by the arbitrary nature of their power over that society. Nor did there seem any reason to expect that the situation would improve once the mutiny was quelled. Surely India could only be governed in the future by force and at enormously increased cost, with what consequences to the liberties of Englishmen at home could only be imagined. Already England had exhausted the reservoir of international moral authority that it had accumulated through its leadership in the abolition of the slave trade. "This is the great loss we have sustained by our Eastern policy," he reflected sadly after the mutiny had been put down but while the war in China dragged on, "the loss of moral power, which is in fact the loss of all permanent power."[33]

All of these views Cobden kept carefully within the circle of his closest friends. The accident of his being out of Parliament saved him from having to comment publicly on the mutiny. With his Crimean war experience only just behind him and the electoral repudiation of the Manchester school still very fresh, he welcomed the opportunity to say nothing. The notion that he might be able to influence government policy or public opinion did not enter into his calculations. More than ever he was convinced that only a calamity could bring the nation to its senses. As he put it to Paulton early in 1858: "When I look back on the last seven years, and reflect on the political fruits of that prosperity which you and I labored with some success to produce

. . . I am I confess sometimes tempted to doubt whether the success of our free trade labors has been an advantage to the country . . . So convinced am I of this, that I confess to you I can never again take my old interest in the material progress of the nation . . . For I am convinced that it would, in the present state of the public mind, lead to nothing but outrage and folly of some kind."[34]

Even before the mutiny reinforced Cobden's decision to remain in self-imposed political exile, he found himself again overwhelmed by personal tragedy. His elder brother, Fred, was dying. For years he had suffered shooting pains in his legs; in the spring of 1857 his legs gave way completely, becoming, as Cobden put it, "quite useless excepting as a vehicle for almost constant pain."[35] Unfortunately for the whole family, Fred lingered on for a year, during which his doctors could do no more than dull the pain and sometimes not even that. Death, it seemed, was destined to visit the Cobdens in the most cruel ways. Whereas two years earlier they had been devastated by the suddenness and remoteness of young Dick's death, Frederick Cobden died in the spring of 1858 only after a protracted death watch and without a moment's tranquility in the final weeks. Stunned by the first loss, Kate and Richard were numbed by the second. "Even now," Cobden wrote to Bright the day of Fred's death, "although the poor body has been at rest for many hours, I still find his cries and groans sounding in my ears."[36]

Even had Fred passed on peacefully, his death would have been especially difficult for Richard Cobden to come to terms with. They had been close throughout their adult lives in a way that was bound to stir up more than the normal regrets in the surviving brother's mind. Fred, although the elder, had lived half his life in the shadow of his famous younger brother. Having unsuccessfully tried to run the family business after Richard entered politics, he spent his last years managing the estate at Dunford. Yet even there this gentle man proved insufficiently assertive. As had happened often during the years of Richard Cobden's transition from business to politics, so also in the difficult 1850s, he lost patience with Fred's indecisiveness. It was a pattern in their relationship that Richard was to regret bitterly during and after his brother's long illness, and especially so since Fred's most irritating characteristics may have been linked to the disease that killed him. When his doctor suggested that Fred might have had spinal problems all his life, Richard wondered if that might account in part "for his lethargic inactive temperament, about which I sometimes reproach myself for not having been sufficiently considerate."[37]

Cobden was plagued by more cosmic doubts as well. Fred's death, and especially the manner of his death, coming so soon after the loss of young Dick, tested his religious faith almost to the breaking point. Normally he was not given to such speculations or for that matter to the discussion of questions of religious belief. As a young man, at the time of the death of his brother Miles, he referred to himself as not "possessing the slightest hint of superstition or even enthusiasm in my religion,"[38] and so it remained for the rest of his life. As an adult he was a devout Anglican, regular in church attendance and family observance. He distrusted anyone who lacked a firm religious foundation to his life. Yet he equally strongly disliked public displays of religiosity. The missionary impulse was especially distasteful to him; individuals, like societies, had enough to do in their own lives without attempting to Christianize others. To Cobden religion was an essentially private matter.

The death of his son threatened to break apart that world of largely habitual beliefs and practices. "I feel the words, 'you know not all', constantly rising to my tongue," he confided to Sturge, "to answer the doubts and check the rebellious thoughts which would obtrude upon my mind, sometimes, when I think of the bright and beautiful being who has been torn from us at the time when he was more dear to us than ever in our lives—But I must not pursue the subject."[39]

Cobden could not help but pursue it after Fred's death, which appeared as inexplicable in its manner as Dick's had been in its timing. A few days afterwards he wrote, again to Sturge: "My poor harmless amiable brother suffered for years the most acute pain, until life became a burden to him, and the last fortnight of his existence was one continued paroxysm of agony. I should have despaired the very existence of God if I had not been consoled with the belief in a future life where all that is now a mystery will be made clear."[40] Whether that formulation served to still Cobden's doubts we do not know. He did not return to the subject.

In any case, Frederick's death raised more immediate problems. In the summer of 1857, after Fred fell ill but nearly a year before he died, Cobden commented: "When I wound up my affairs in Manchester and came here to live, my brother became my *locum tenens* in the out door life of a rural residence. How I am to leave home when he is no longer able to take my place is more than I can tell. I don't like to talk of my wife's morbid state of grief. It is very painful to me to be obliged to dwell on what I cannot justify. But she is very helpless and equally unfit for solitude or society."[41]

Cobden's feeling of being trapped intensified in the months that followed. It was his brother and his wife who kept him tied to Dunford initially, but even before Frederick's death he was hemmed in by more mundane concerns. Explaining his unwillingness even to consider running for Parliament again, Cobden wrote Bright early in 1858: "Now if I could bring my wife and my brother up to London and could live there for six months, whilst my little girls were here in the charge of governesses, it would suit me very well, for it would give me the opportunity of consulting a first rate doctor for my brother and of finding distractions for my wife's mind . . . To transfer one's whole household to London must be very agreeable to those who have 5 or £6000 a year. To me it is an impossibility."[42] In fact Cobden was understating his problem. For the second time in his adult life he was on the verge of financial disaster.

Cobden was always ready to back his political and economic beliefs with money and, unfortunately, to commit too much of his resources too far into the future. In the 1830s he had invested heavily in real estate near Manchester in anticipation of the city's growth. Twenty years later that land remained "more than the old man of the mountains astride my shoulders . . . It is liable to a ground rent of nearly 1000 a year, and I have never to this day disposed of a yard of it."[43] In the middle of the 1850s he repeated the same pattern, only this time on an even larger scale and in an area that he did not know personally. He decided to invest in America's future. Specifically he bought stock in the Illinois Central Railroad. The company, organized in 1851, had from the first looked to Europe for capital, and a temporary fall in the price of its stock in 1854 made it attractive to English investors, including Cobden. He did not regard this as a speculative investment in the ordinary sense. The company was backed by a land grant from the state, and it was the value of this land, some of the richest in America, that attracted him. "It is not a railroad speculation," he informed George Moffat, M.P., a wealthy tea merchant and Cobden's closest financial advisor, "but the acquisition of a landed estate more than double the area of Lancashire, on the very terms of making it accessible to eager purchasers and cultivators."[44] Indeed, so certain was Cobden of the ultimate value of the stock that he "sold everything I had to sell and borrowed all I could and secured upwards of 2000 old shares and options, which with the new shares will give me 3000."[45]

But it took years for Cobden's optimism to prove justified, and in the gap between his short-term expectations and their long-term fulfillment lay financial disaster. He knew the risks involved. The similarities between his Manchester and Illinois ventures could hardly be overlooked, and the railway speculation held out peculiar dangers to someone in Cobden's position. His stock was not fully paid up, and although the company directors assured prospective investors that assessments on the stock to raise capital were not likely, the stock was subject to calls at any time. In effect, Cobden was gambling that there would be no such calls or, if there were, that the value of the stock would have appreciated enough to cover them. The few friends who knew what he was up to—and for that matter the president of the railroad, William Osborn—warned him that this was a dangerous assumption for a man who had no reserves and needed a steady income from his investments.

Although he persistently ignored such advice, Cobden listened to it with good humor, even after it had proved accurate. When Osborn visited Cobden in England in 1858, Cobden regaled Moffat with a self-perceptive account of their conversation:

> Osborn was so candid with me, so disinterested and friendly in his advice, that I could not help suspecting that a very good friend of mine had whispered into his ear something to this effect. "Say nothing to feed his sanguine views. He has already become *Tête monté* about the Illinois; but rather throw in a word of caution about putting too many eggs in one basket. He is a worn out agitator, out of business, with a young family. As a rule your public men, and especially your revolutionary leaders, make unsuccessful men of business. They look too high and too far, and others who fire at a shorter range beat them in the field. Besides, they look at things too much in the gross, neglect details, and disregard the element of time, which in speculation is everything. Here is Cobden dealing with Illinois Central as if they were going to yield him a profit next quarter-day. Warn him that it will take many years to realize all his expectations." Am I not right in my surmise?[46]

By this time, however, it was too late. After a promising year in 1856, Illinois Central stock dropped more than 40 percent in the panic of

1857, and the company's directors had no choice but to resort to assessments on the stock. As early as September Cobden confessed to Moffat that he was in trouble: "The terrible collapse of the New York money market has robbed me of all my pretty margin of profit and premiums."[47]

Yet Cobden refused to turn his back on the Illinois Central. His faith in the ultimate value of his investment remained unshaken, as did his confidence in the management of the company, apart from a moment of near-panic occasioned by rumors put about by some of Osborn's rivals. Osborn's visit to England and an investigation of the company's finances by a committee of English investors permanently dispelled Cobden's doubts on that score. Thus, when Moffat advised him to sell out in the spring of 1858, Cobden resisted. "If it had been a mere piece of by play of speculation," he explained, "and I had other things in hand, I should have parted with it long ago, but it has been the most serious private business of my life." Therefore, he concluded, "I would prefer to borrow 4000 for six months than sell." Yet he was quick to add, "I do not wish it to be got from friends or as a friendly act."[48]

That was a point of pride that soon proved impossible to maintain. As Cobden admitted a few months later, "Nothing but an increase in net earnings will raise the price of the shares—of which I fear there is not much prospect."[49] Thus, even Cobden and certainly his friends could hardly avoid recognizing for what it was the financial salvage operation they embarked on in 1858. Admittedly, it did not—yet—involve a fund-raising campaign, such as had been necessary a decade earlier. Instead a small group of friends and colleagues (including the speaker of the House of Commons) paid the calls on his shares of stock, thus maintaining the fiction that this was a loan to tide Cobden over until his investments recovered their value. That this was a fiction was reconfirmed that summer by a bad harvest in Illinois, the second in two years, followed by a drop in freight and land-sale revenues to the railroad. Cobden had, finally, to accept that it might be a long time before he regained financial independence.

Perhaps in the hope of speeding up that process, some time late in the year Cobden decided to visit America himself. There was no particular need for him to do so. His doubts about the management of the company had been largely resolved some months before. At most, he explained to Henry Ashworth, "I have gradually yielded to some of my colleagues' and friends' wishes to go with a view to infusing some new blood into the management of our affairs."[50] In particular he hoped to use his influence to get the center of decision making shifted from New York to Chicago and, once he was satisfied with the quality of the management and had collected sufficient evidence to back up his confidence, to help relieve the company of some of the pressure from its worried European stockholders. He may even have hoped that the publicity surrounding his visit would serve to restore the English public's interest in the Illinois Central as a sound investment.

Beyond all these practical justifications for crossing the Atlantic was the lure of America itself. Almost a quarter century had passed since Cobden's first visit, and although he now took a less roseate view of the United States in light of its tariff policy, its often aggressive pursuit of manifest destiny, and increasing sectional strife, he still looked to it as both a beacon and a challenge to the old world. On the eve of his trip he confessed to Joseph Parkes "the desire . . . to take another peep at that people before I go hence, and judge for myself as to the progress, moral and material, they have made."[51] To Bright as well as Parkes he promised a full accounting of "what the 'hellish' thing they call a Republic is really like (to quote old Cobbett)."[52] That a trip to America, even one undertaken to retrieve his financial situation, also provided needed escape from his personal trials, he did not mention. But he did note that Catherine and their daughters would be absent from Dunford—in Paris—while he was away, and on the whole he was inclined to "think the complete change and throwing her on her own resources will also be of service to my wife."[53]

Cobden's two trips to America could hardly have been more different. In 1835 he was absent from England for three-and-a-half months but spent less than six weeks in the United States; regular steamship service was still three years away, and a one-way passage occupied a month or more. In 1859 the crossing took only two weeks, and Cobden was able to spend almost four months in America. Travel within the United States had been even more dramatically transformed. Railways were a novelty in 1835, and Cobden spent more time getting from place to place than he could devote to the places themselves. Yet he went no further west than Lake Erie, no further south than Washington, D.C. In 1859 he traveled rapidly from city to city and was able to spend a month in New York, more than two weeks in Chicago, and a few days each in Boston, Washington, Albany, and

Philadelphia. He traveled west to Illinois and the Mississippi Valley twice and went as far south as Memphis.

Cobden's status as a traveler had altered little less. The successful young businessman with political ambitions had become an international political celebrity with serious financial troubles. Half the trip was devoted to investigating the affairs of the Illinois Central Railroad. He met with investors and railway executives in New York and Chicago and with interested political leaders in Washington and Springfield, Illinois. He talked to farmers, merchants, and the heads of planned settlements on the prairie. He traveled every mile of Illinois Central track and took riverboats on the Mississippi from the company's railheads at Cairo and Dunleith. On the whole Cobden was impressed by what he saw. He was generally satisfied with the quality of those at the head of the railroad's affairs, the vastness of the prairie exceeded his most optimistic imaginings (although he eventually became bored by its "monotonous richness"),[54] and the future of the Illinois Central as the conduit for the bounty of the cornbelt south to the port of New Orleans appeared unlimited. The crash of 1857, followed by two bad harvests, had dealt Illinois and its railroads a devastating blow, but it seemed bound to be temporary.

Throughout his trip Cobden was accorded the courtesies of a visiting minister of state. While in the middle west he was given the use of the private railway cars of the directors, and not only on the Illinois Central. In many of the cities he visited he was entertained in the clubs or homes of local business or political leaders, the proprietors or editors of major papers, or now and then a literary figure; on his second visit to Washington he stayed in the White House as the guest of President Buchanan, whom Cobden had met while Buchanan was American ambassador in London. He was allowed the privileges of the floor by two state legislatures and both houses of Congress. Quite by chance, he met both Abraham Lincoln (in Springfield, Illinois) and Jefferson Davis (on the boat to Memphis); on the whole, he recollected after the Civil War broke out, he was more impressed with Davis. He was photographed by Mathew Brady.

Cobden was almost as concerned with reconfirming earlier impressions as with exploring the new lands of mid-America. He revisited the two areas he had found most inspiring on his first trip, Niagara Falls and the Hudson valley (and he met the most famous painter of Niagara, Frederic Edwin Church). In most cities and in a few frontier communities, Cobden investigated the local schools. As in 1835, he was favorably impressed, particularly with those things that set American schools apart: the democratic character of the student body, the mixing of sexes in the classroom, and the predominance of women among the teachers. He was surprised by the competence of these young women but not, at least on reflection, by the respect they commanded; for, as in 1835, he was struck by the greater deference and status accorded to women in America (although he felt they took unfair advantage of this). He was also pleased to note how much less liquor was consumed in America than in England. Commenting on the good manners of his fellow passengers on the Mississippi river boat, he suggested that "the superior education in America will be thought by some, and the concealed bowie knife and revolver will be said by others, to account for the courtesy and forebearance of my fellow passengers, but I think the absence of stimulants to be the one great preserver of peace."[55]

The good public manners he encountered almost everywhere were a subject he often returned to in looking for clues to the American character, and like much else he admired—the high level of public political discussion and the adaptability of American business—it appeared to him to stem largely from what he had always regarded as the finest traits of the country, its egalitarianism and the individual optimism of its people. That this analysis contradicted the views of many other European visitors, Cobden explained with an interesting argument:

> Writers and travellers fall into a great unfairness in comparing the middle and upper classes with whom alone the tourists and the book writing class associate in Europe with the *whole people* with whom they meet at the table d'hotes and in the railway cars in the United States. There are no second or third class railway carriages. The American mechanic or day laborer puts on his broad cloth coat and steps into the same car as that which the richest merchant or the governor of the State occupies, and where his manners are quite as sedate and orderly as are those of what we in England should call his "betters".[56]

Perhaps because he rarely played the ordinary tourist during this trip, and in any case knew the United States well, Cobden did not often indulge in such reflections, let alone in the humorous asides that enlivened his earlier travel diaries. He had not lost his touch, however. After a visit to Plymouth to see the relics of the Pilgrim fathers, he observed: "Like the pieces of the 'true cross' which are every where to be seen by the devout believers in those relics, these memorials of the Pilgrims seem capable of indefinite multiplication to meet the demands of the faithful."[57]

Like most of the chattier entries in his travel diary, this was written late in the journey, after his lingering doubts about the Illinois Central had been dispelled, and he felt able to give himself over completely to the pleasure of travel. In that sense his second American journey provided a passage out of the private anxieties that had consumed almost all his time during the preceding three years. America was, at once, healingly distant and different from the world in which he had been confined for so long and reassuringly familiar. And if revisiting America was in part an exercise in nostalgia for Cobden, it was also a way of measuring how far he, as well as America, had come since his first journey. Nor was it solely in relation to his own past, his beginnings in public life, that Cobden felt personally involved with the United States. In 1859 he sought out not only direct evidence of the future he had predicted a quarter century before but the raw material of even more glowing visions of a future he would never see. Money was the least of what Cobden had invested in America.

Under the circumstances he could be forgiven for taking a selective view of America. There was hardly a word of criticism in his diaries or letters home. Although he was concerned with stories of corruption in America and raised the subject with many of the public men he met, he clearly wanted to hear only the evidence that would allow him to render a favorable verdict. Even more extraordinary was what he failed to mention at all: nothing in either his diaries or his letters home indicated that the country was in the midst of a crisis that would lead in less than two years to the tragedy of civil war. Similarly with his own interests in the United States, Cobden returned to England convinced that one good harvest and the completion of the rail link to New Orleans would recreate the boom of the mid-1850s. In making this judgment he overlooked some important factors, chief among them a worldwide increase in grain production, which would have undermined his calculations, even had local conditions proved all he hoped for. As it was, in the same month he left America, frost badly damaged the corn crop in Illinois. The wheat harvest was also poor, and Cobden's hopes for a quick recovery from the troubles of 1857 and 1858 were finally dashed. Shortly after his return to England he was forced to acknowledge what some of his friends had known for months, that he could no longer be kept afloat financially through the disguised charity of friends willing to pay the calls on his railway stock. Nothing less than a direct bail-out would suffice.

This did not, as it had in 1846, take the form of a public fund drive but was handled in private by a few of Cobden's Lancashire friends. When he first approached them August 1859, there was some talk of their buying his property in Manchester at the value he anticipated for it. Cobden had no illusions that this would be anything other than a face-saving device, however. "I have some hope," he informed one of his American correspondents, "of getting rid of all my land and etc. here through the intervention of some rich friends, who will disguise an act of friendship with the mask of business."[58] When these negotiations fell through, the mask of business was finally dropped; Henry Ashworth, Thomas Bazley, and John Slagg, three of Cobden's colleagues from league days or before, set about the delicate task of soliciting contributions to a private relief fund, which ultimately amounted to just over £40,000, half the amount that had been raised by public subscription fourteen years earlier.

Among the more than one hundred contributors, by far the most generous was Thomas Thomasson, one of the richest cotton manufacturers in England and a rarity among them in his support for Cobden's peace efforts as well as for the league. He gave £5000 to the fund, solicited more than £1000 from others, reimbursed a number of those who had earlier paid the calls on Cobden's stock, and gave Catherine Cobden an additional sum—as much as £20,000, if Bright's account was correct—apart from what he gave her husband. Cobden knew nothing of these acts of generosity or for that matter of the identity of his benefactors apart from Ashworth, Bazley, and Slagg. He did ask Ashworth "to favor him with a list, under seal, of the names of the subscribers to this fund, observing that at some future time, perhaps after his decease, his widow and his children might be desirous to know from whom they had derived so substantial a benefit. I therefore prepared and gave him the list of names," Ashworth recalled, "and after his decease his executors found the paper in his desk, with the seal still unbroken."[59]

Even this large new fund did not end Cobden's financial difficulties. The late stages of the American Civil War benefited his investments in Illinois by increasing the demand for grain. But the coming of the war simply extended the troubles of the late 1850s into the early 1860s, by cutting off the Illinois Central from its southern outlet and drying up the flow of European immigration to the prairies. The management of the railroad had to make further calls on the stock, and Cobden, as determined as ever to hold on to it, was severely pressed. He never had to be bailed out on a large scale again, but there were intimations of a new public subscription in 1861, a proposal that he scotched as both unnecessary and humiliating. There was also a suggestion, first from Cobden's parliamentary friends and later from within the government, of offering him a parliamentary pension or sinecure post, but Cobden wanted none of that either.

Above all, there was talk, often nasty talk. News of Cobden's financial condition and of the steps taken or proposed to remedy it leaked out, and old adversaries drew discomforting conclusions. Palmerston, in a letter to Russell supporting the proposal of a parliamentary pension for Cobden, referred to him as "having mismanaged his own affairs, just as he would, if he could, the affairs of the nation."[60] Not content to be condescending, *The Times* suggested editorially: "The drawback in his nature is that he cannot take care of himself . . . Mr. Cobden ought not only to be subscribed for but taken care of. As he cannot be made a ward in Chancery, he ought to be placed in the hands of a responsible committee, not to regulate his expenditures, which no doubt are modest enough, but to secure him from 'good' investments . . . We hope that he will be treated as a woman or a boy, and put under trust."[61]

Cobden could not very well object to the substance of such remarks; he had been grossly irresponsible in the management of his affairs, and he had, in effect, been put under trust. As to the waspish tone of *The Times*, Cobden did his best to ignore it. That was the price a public man paid for private failure. But as with the less tangible emotional burdens heaped upon him since 1856, he had to carry the weight of fresh dependency and all that followed from it for the rest of his life.

CHAPTER 21

Negotiating a Treaty

The circumstances of Cobden's return to England from America in the summer of 1859 are a gift to the biographer or historian. The day he left Boston for Canada and his journey home, Lord Derby's government was defeated in the House of Commons and resigned. When Cobden's ship docked at Liverpool almost three weeks later, he heard for the first time that the drama of making a ministry was in its last act and that he was being called upon to play an important role. Even before he stepped ashore "a packet of letters was put into my hand, containing one from Lord Palmerston, offering me a seat in the cabinet as President of the Board of Trade, and another from Lord John Russell, urging me in the strongest terms to accept it."[1] Moments later, certainly before he got his land legs (Cobden was a terrible sailor), he was in his hotel, besieged by friends and allies, clamoring for him to join the government. The same scene was repeated in Manchester the following day. "Indeed, almost without exception," he informed Catherine, "everybody, Radicals, peace men and all, are trying to pursuade me to it."

The case for going into the cabinet was compelling. The Liberal majority in the House of Commons was small. If the new government was to stay in office and remain committed to Liberal principles, it would need not only radical support in the House of Commons but a strong radical presence in its innermost councils. More than any other radical leader, Cobden could guarantee both. Moreover, as Russell pointed out, by joining a cabinet that already included all the major Whig, Liberal, and Peelite leaders, Cobden would significantly improve the chances of blending all the non-Tory factions in the Commons into a coherent reform party. "If you refuse," Russell concluded,

"I do not see a prospect of amalgamating the Liberal party during my life-time."[2] Beguiling as that argument was, Cobden never allowed this to overcome his aversion on principle to serving in a government headed by Lord Palmerston. Commenting to Catherine on his friends who had pressed him to go in, he wrote:

> Now it really seems to me that they must all have gone mad, for with my recorded opinion of Lord Palmerston's public conduct during the last dozen years, in which opinions I have experienced no change, were I suddenly to jump at the offer of a place under him, I should ruin myself in my own self-respect, and ultimately lose the confidence of the very men who are in this moment of excitement urging me to enter his Cabinet. So great is the pressure put on me, that if it were Lord Granville, or even Lord John, at the head of affairs, I should be obliged, greatly against my will, to be a Right Honorable . . . I listen to all my friends and say nothing, but my mind is made up.[3]

And so it was. A few days later Cobden went up to London to convey his views personally to Lord Palmerston, who proceeded to press Cobden as hard as any of his friends had done. The prime minister dwelt "particularly on the fact that as questions of foreign policy were now uppermost, and as those questions were in the hands of the Executive, it was only by joining the Government I could influence them . . . This was the argument I found it most difficult to answer, and therefore he pressed it most strongly."[4]

But Cobden was not to be moved. He had begun the interview with characteristic bluntness. After a few opening pleasantries, "I broke the ice in this way," as he recalled the conversation:

> "You have acted in so manly and magnanimous a manner in pressing me to take office in your Cabinet, that I feel bound to come and talk to you without reserve upon the subject. My case is this. For the last twelve years I have been the systematic and constant assailant of the principle on which your foreign policy has been carried on. I believed you to be warlike, intermeddling and quarrelsome, and that your policy was calculated to embroil us with foreign nations. At the same time I have expressed a general want of confidence in your domestic politics. Now I may have been altogether wrong in my views; it is possible I may have been, but I put it candidly to you whether it ought to be in your Cabinet, whilst holding a post of high honour and emolument derived from you, that I should make the first avowal of a change of opinion respecting your public policy? Should I not expose myself to severe suspicions, and

deservedly so, if I were under these circumstances to step from an Atlantic steamer into your Cabinet?"

With the lines thus firmly drawn, the interview proceeded surprisingly amicably. Palmerston continued to press Cobden; Cobden reiterated his determination to stay out, although he did pledge conditional support for the government. Both men disclaimed any personal animosity and probably genuinely so, for the moment. Each certainly had good reason to hope that their antagonism was a thing of the past, and each was ready to make the necessary gestures of personal accommodation. "As I left the room," Cobden told his brother-in-law, William Sale, Lord Palmerston said:

> "Lady Palmerston receives tomorrow at ten?" To which I instantly replied, "I shall be happy to be allowed to present myself to her." "I shall be glad if you will," was his answer, and so we parted.
>
> The next evening I was at Cambridge House for the first time . . . and was the lion of the party. The women came and stared with their glasses at me, and then brought their friends to stare also. As I came away, Jacob Omnium and I were squeezed into a corner together, and he remarked, "You are the greatest political monster that ever was seen in this house. There never was before seen such a curiosity as a man who refused a Cabinet office from Lord Palmerston, and then came to visit him here."

Altogether these were an extraordinary few days for Cobden, but exciting and flattering to him as the whole episode was, he was able to enjoy little of it. "I never had before so much annoyance to my feelings as in this matter," he complained to Sale. "To be pressed by nearly all my friends to take a course which I felt from the first moment to be impossible, was a most painful ordeal to go through . . . However, I hope my friends will on reflection do me justice, and believe that I acted conscientiously." On the whole they did, and quickly too. Moreover, all later commentators have agreed that Cobden made the right decision. Some have even suggested that he would have made a poor minister in any case. That is probably true. Having spent his whole public career as an outsider and critic and accustomed to hold himself aloof from any government and from the social life of the political establishment, Cobden would have found it next to impossible to subordinate his individuality to the collective responsibility of membership in a government.

Moreover, Cobden was undeniably correct in thinking that service in a Palmerston government would have imposed unbearable strains. Within months of its formation, deteriorating relations with France led to yet another invasion scare in England and to proposals from Palmerston for increased military spending. Under these circumstances Cobden would have begun to quarrel with his colleagues almost from the moment he entered the government and would probably have resigned before the end of 1859. The question of how good a minister he would have been is therefore beside the important point, which is that, because he did not live long enough to see Gladstone become prime minister, there was no government formed in his lifetime in which Cobden could comfortably have served. Only the ministry that would likely have emerged had Peel followed Cobden's advice at the time repeal was passed would have offered him the chance to take both his ideals and his ambitions with him into office.

Such speculations on the might-have-beens of political history tend to obscure what is perhaps a more interesting way of assessing Cobden's career at this stage. He occupied a unique position in 1859. He had ceased to be merely the leading radical politican of the day and had become the elder statesman of radicalism. The rancour of the league years had been largely forgotten, and even the bitter controversies surrounding the Crimean war had lost much of their sting. His three-year-long semiretirement had ensured that and won for him much personal sympathy as well. Even the circumstances of his return to Parliament contributed to his special status. The general election of 1859 took place while he was returning from the United States, as did the maneuvering that led up to the formation of Palmerston's government. Cobden's adoption as the reform candidate for Bright's home town of Rochdale was arranged without his participation; it was Bright's repayment for Cobden's efforts on Bright's behalf in Manchester two years earlier. But it ended far more happily: Cobden was returned unopposed by a constituency that was to prove as supportive as Stockport had been. Thus Cobden returned to England in the summer of 1859 as a newly minted M.P., free from political debts and from association with the commitments recently made by the leaders and factions of Liberalism in order to put Palmerston in office with a working parliamentary majority.

Cobden also had the good luck not to have played a part in the most recent attempt to revive popular radicalism out of doors, Bright's abortive campaign to launch a new reform movement late in 1858. Cobden had sufficient personal reasons for remaining aloof from public political activity, but these aside, his differences with Bright on this issue were almost identical with what they had been seven or eight years before. Admittedly, Bright now claimed far less for his efforts than he had back in the days of the Parliamentary and Financial Reform Association. He had to, given the fragmented state of radicalism. What he hoped to do was resuscitate parliamentary reform as a major issue in British politics and make it again the focus for a revived radical movement. Cobden refused to take any part in this campaign, however; so much so, indeed, that Bright ultimately complained to him that his silence was damaging the cause. But Cobden was adamant. He doubted that British radicalism was capable of revival so soon after selling its soul in the Crimean war. He also had no intention of ever leading a mass movement again and questioned the wisdom of the old league leadership once more attempting to set itself up at the head of a new agitation.

Cobden's disagreement with Bright involved more than timing and tactics, however. As Cobden finally admitted, he did not share Bright's assumption that enlarging the electorate would necessarily further the cause of radicalism: "You seem to assume that a wiser policy in taxation or other matters will necessarily follow from a democratic reform," he wrote. "I am always willing to take my chance of the consequences of such a change . . . But I do not feel so confident as yourself that a great extension of the franchise would necessarily lead to a wiser system of taxation."[5]

As he had a decade earlier, Cobden regarded peace and retrenchment as more important and, on the whole, as separate goals from political reform. Bright was even less inclined to accept this argument than he had been in earlier years, and in the long run he was proved right in practice: his campaign in the late 1850s was an important part of the process that led to the formation of the Gladstonian Liberal party in the following decade. In the short run, however, the campaign hurt as much as helped Bright. He did not get the popular support he expected, and at the same time he managed to alienate both the working-class radicals who wanted more and the moderate leaders of the Whig-Liberal coalition, who were alarmed by the rhetoric of class conflict that he often employed. That left Cobden in an extraordinary position. Alone among radical leaders, he had the prestige of a national political figure, together with the respectability that allowed him access to the inner circles of government.

Under the circumstances, for Cobden simply to have resumed his role as back-bench critic and head of the Manchester school was unthinkable. To most observers and all his friends and supporters, the right next step in his career was ministerial office. That was the logic of the situation, as Cobden recognized and others reminded him, and his refusal of office did not therefore end the questioning about how he was to use his newfound status. Even Palmerston, in the interview in early July, raised the issue. "Finding me still firm in my objections," Cobden reported, Palmerston, "observed laughingly, 'Why are you in the House of Commons?' I answered also with a laugh, 'Upon my word I hardly know.' 'But why did you enter public life?' said he. 'I hardly know,' was my answer; 'it was by mere accident, and for a special purpose, and probably it would have been better for me and my family if I had kept my private station.' Upon which he threw out both his hands, and, with a laugh louder than before, he exclaimed, 'Well, but being in it, why not go on?' "[6]

That question Cobden himself was at a loss to answer in the summer of 1859. Only once before in his public career, in the summer of 1846, had he been so uncertain of how best to go on. The circumstances were similar. As in 1846, he was in deep financial trouble, and he was finally compelled to throw himself on the generosity of friends, much to his embarrassment but also with the result of freeing him for other things. Also as in 1846, he had agreed to spend some time abroad, away from politics. Then, his health appeared to require a long stay in a warmer climate; in 1859, he planned to spend the autumn and winter in Paris in order to get his wife away from Dunford. But, again as in 1846, as the time for his departure from England approached, Cobden grew restless at the thought of doing nothing useful with his sojourn abroad. In 1846 he had seized on suggestions that he might be able to influence the commercial policy of other governments as a justification for undertaking a tour of Europe on behalf of free trade; in 1859 much the same thing happened. A letter from the French political economist, Michel Chevalier, led to an equally dramatic shift in Cobden's plans and ultimately to the second great triumph of his public career, the negotiation of the Anglo-French Commercial Treaty of 1860.

Chevalier, the leading free trader in France and a friend and frequent correspondent of Cobden's ever since they had first met in Paris in 1846, had long advocated such a treaty as the only means of weaning his countrymen away from protectionism. Reductions in French tariffs would only be politically palatable in France, he believed, if made in conjunction with France's trading partners; furthermore, according to the imperial constitution, a treaty, even one including sweeping tariff reductions, could be implemented by the French government without consulting the protectionist legislature. Chevalier first proposed such a treaty to Cobden at the time of the peace negotiations to end the Crimean war. Although Cobden responded by easing Chevalier's access to Lord Clarendon, the foreign secretary, he did not take up the cause himself. Bright had just suffered his nervous breakdown, Cobden's political influence was at its lowest ebb, and besides, he had reservations about pursuing free trade through a treaty, since bilateral arrangements violated the principle of the uniform application of tariff reductions to all nations. Chevalier's proposal did not get far in any case; Palmerston refused to consider reductions in the duties on luxury goods such as wine.

When Chevalier renewed his proposal three years later, however, the circumstances were more favorable. Not only was Cobden free and, for personal reasons, tempted to take up such a suggestion, but his political standing was now as strong as it had been weak at the end of the Crimean war. Furthermore, Chevalier now had a ready answer to Cobden's reservations on principle: any reductions in British duties on French goods could be applied by Britain equally to all other nations. This cleared the way for Cobden (although not for some more orthodox free traders). There was, to be sure, another liberal objection to proceeding by treaty. Since one of its principal purposes was to circumvent a popularly elected legislature, "we thus," as one of Cobden's most admiring followers later commented, "for a commercial object, became accomplices in absolutist encroachment."[7] But Cobden, ready as ever to give economics primacy over politics, was apparently untroubled by that criticism, which he never bothered to answer.

Well disposed and well placed to undertake another mission on behalf of freer trade, Cobden was also encouraged by favorable political signs in both countries. Gladstone, the new chancellor of the Exchequer, was faced with the pleasant prospect of a budget surplus and was casting about for taxes and duties to reduce. In addition, he shared Cobden's disquiet at the anti-French tone of Palmerston's rhetoric and was anxious to preserve what critics of the Crimean war regarded as the one good thing to come out of it, the entente cordial between Britain and France. Palmerston and Russell could not oppose the idea of such a treaty because they had need of the radical wing of the party. Across the channel the situation was no less encouraging: Napoleon III, deeply embroiled in Italy, wished to ensure the benevolent neutrality of England.

Thus, when Bright suggested in July in the House of Commons that Britain unilaterally reduce some of its duties on French goods in order to ease tensions, Chevalier wrote to Cobden in the hope of resuscitating his treaty proposal. This time Cobden took it up with enthusiasm and wrote to Gladstone requesting "a little talk with you about the trade with France."[8] Gladstone replied with an invitation to Cobden to visit him at his country estate at Hawarden, where, after "several hours walk and talk,"[9] on September 12 and 13, Gladstone noted that he and Cobden were "closely and warmly agreed."[10] From then on events moved swiftly. Chevalier came to England early in October, ostensibly to meet with English advocates of the metric system but really for a series of meetings with Cobden and, through Cobden, with Bright, J. B. Smith, and Gladstone. At the same time Cobden saw the French ambassador, Persigny, as well as Russell and Palmerston, both of whom agreed—although not, as Cobden noted, with great enthusiasm—that informal overtures should be made to the French government.

On 18 October, little more than a month after his visit to Hawarden, Cobden left for Paris, where Chevalier arranged secret meetings with government officials and ultimately with the emperor. Cobden went to Paris with few illusions. He had no official status in or from the British government and was suspicious of the ulterior motives of the leaders of both countries, who might at any moment have dropped the treaty proposal if it no longer suited their purposes. Only Gladstone, among leading English ministers, and Rouher, the minister of commerce, among the French officials he dealt with, were deeply interested in the idea of a treaty for its own sake and as a vehicle for transforming Anglo-French relations.

But that in a way made Cobden's task all the more exciting. Working against time, he was attempting to turn the opportunism and political necessities of Palmerston and Napoleon III to his own advantage. If he could use the opening he had been given to get a treaty, then, he believed, the increase in commercial contacts between the two peoples would go far toward undoing the national animosities kept alive by professional diplomats and military men. That, Cobden maintained from first to last, was why he undertook the job at all, for at a time when British capital and labor were stretched to the limit the country hardly needed additional markets; 1859 was not 1839 and Cobden never pursued the commercial treaty, as he had Corn Law repeal, for its economic benefits. "I would not step across the street, just now," he wrote Gladstone from France, "to increase our trade, for the mere sake of material gain. *We have about as much prosperity as we can bear.* But to improve the moral and political relations of France and England, by bringing them into greater intercourse and increased commercial dependence, I would walk barefoot from Calais to Paris."[11]

As well as hoping that he might be able to use for his own purposes the men who were trying to use him for theirs, Cobden soon found that he rather enjoyed the game of diplomacy (although this was a pleasure that wore off quickly). He was amused by the air of intrigue surrounding the negotiations, which, because of the strength of protectionist sentiment in France, were initially kept secret even from most of Napoleon's ministers. Only the emperor, Chevalier, Rouher, Foreign Minister Baroche, and Minister of State Fould knew what was going on until the negotiations were an accomplished fact. Cobden took advantage of this climate of suspicion and of the French fear of diplomatic isolation and was especially pleased with his handling of his first meeting with Fould:

> Before parting I alluded to the state of uneasiness not only in England but on the Continent, and reminded him of the great increase of warlike preparations that had been going on; and I expressed an opinion that a Bonaparte being on the throne of France, who had last spring invaded Italy and fought great battles, was the cause of the present feelings of mistrust . . . I remarked that . . . so far as I was acquainted with the state of public opinion in England, nothing would instantaneously convince the people there of the Emperor's pacific intentions as his entering boldly upon a policy of commercial reform.[12]

And so, on and on. After some days of this sort of thing, Cobden concluded: "The droll part of these interviews, besides the timidity of the parties, is that here is a government having so little faith or confidence in one another, that some of its members tie me down, a perfect stranger, to secrecy, as against their most elevated colleagues." Cobden used similar arguments in talking to the emperor, although presumably his tone was somewhat more deferential. Somewhat, but not much, for Cobden had never been particularly respectful of crowned heads of state, and Napoleon III was no exception (at least at first). Cobden confessed to Palmerston that he may have talked too much in his audience with the emperor, whom, in any case, he found "short in stature and very undignified."[13] Moreover, although Cobden judged Napoleon a good listener and well disposed toward free trade, he also thought him poorly informed and lacking in the courage of his convictions. Thus Cobden felt called upon to instruct the emperor, not only in economics but in tactics. "He asked me how I should go to work if I were in his place," Cobden told Palmerston:

> I told him I would act precisely as I did in England, by dealing first with one article which was the keystone of the whole system; in England that article was corn, in France it was iron; that I should abolish totally and at once the duty on pig iron, and leave only a very small revenue duty, if any, on bars, etc. . . . This would render it much easier to deal with all the other industries, whose general complaint is that they cannot compete wih England owing to the high price of iron and coal . . . He made me repeat to him these last remarks . . . I was struck with his repeated allusion to the opposition he had to encounter, and his evident fear of a handful of monopolists . . . The result of my interview is a conviction that, if left to himself, the Emperor would at once enter upon a free trade policy, but I am by no means certain that he will do so.[14]

The condescending tone of Cobden's remarks on Napoleon III and his ministers is surprising from a man who knew France and its language well and had a reputation at home for seeing the French side of an issue all too clearly. That Cobden did not take the French protectionists seriously at first is also odd in view of his own seven-year struggle in England. Furthermore, as he was later to admit, he initially underestimated the strength of purpose and quality of mind of Fould, Rouher, and the emperor. All three were briefed by Chevalier before Cobden met them, and they may have allowed him to do so much of the talking as a way of sizing up this Englishman who had come to them as something between a private citizen and an official envoy—a possibility that was not lost on Cobden. Of his peculiar status, he wrote to Gladstone: "One of the difficulties I find is the suspicion everybody has that I seek some selfish object for England. Certainly I stand in a better position to remove that feeling than if I were an accredited representative. The only other category they will put me in, if I am not to be considered an interested agent, is that I am a fanatic, to which I have no objection."[15] All in all, it was an odd position from which to conduct delicate negotiations, and Cobden may have adopted a somewhat patronizing approach, so unlike the optimistic enthusiasm with which he ordinarily undertook a new venture, as a way of guarding himself against the possibility that the whole thing might collapse before it was properly begun.

This was a legitimate concern. As Cobden was told any number of times by his French hosts and as subsequent events were to remind him again and again, everything depended on the emperor. Only four days after his apparently successful interview with Napoleon, Cobden learned unofficially from Fould that the emperor was having second thoughts (and Fould and Rouher a concomitant attack of cold feet). Confused and exasperated, Cobden complained to Chevalier that he did not know how to proceed. Yet a week later Cobden was informed—again by Fould but this time officially—that Napoleon "did not require to be convinced of the truth of my commercial principles; that he was satisfied of their soundness and, both on economic and political grounds, was anxious to carry out my views."[16] Napoleon never backed away from that commitment during the two-and-a-half months of negotiations that followed before the Commercial Treaty was signed in January 1860, but there were a number of occasions when it seemed that he might be about to abandon the project, and Cobden had no way of knowing whether this reflected a change in the emperor's thinking, concessions to political pressure, or simply a ploy in the game of French diplomacy or domestic politics.

In mid-December, when the negotiations had gone far enough that the entire Council of Ministers had to be informed, there were rumors that Napoleon was beginning to regret his earlier decision. Urged on by Rouher and Fould, Cobden requested and was granted a second audience with the emperor, whose questions, it turned out, far from being a sign of slackening resolve, were designed to elicit arguments in support of a treaty, preparatory to what Napoleon knew would to be a stormy session with his ministers. Still, because a majority of them opposed the treaty, even the emperor's determination did not end their attempts to pressure him into changing his mind. In response, he reluctantly agreed to hold an inquiry into the state of French industry and more than once was said to be on the verge of abandoning the negotiations.

Cobden was less and less concerned about domestic opposition as time went by, however, partly because he knew he could gain access to the emperor, of whose determination he was increasingly confident, but primarily because the confrontation between Napoleon and his ministers was decisive: it led to the opening of official negotiations. Thereafter, turning back would have been at least as difficult for Napoleon as going on. This, indeed, was confirmed in the final stages of the negotiations, when the emperor, severely pressed by his protectionist ministers, toyed with the idea of submitting the treaty to the legislature after all. However, Cobden, on being asked his views, reminded Rouher in the strongest terms that this would constitute a violation of their original understanding. The proposal was immediately withdrawn by the French, and the negotiations proceeded as before.

At the same time, there was a potentially greater threat to the treaty from the emperor's ulterior motives in Italian policy. If he could have extracted a pledge of support in Italy from Britain, he would, at the least, have needed the Commercial Treaty less. Once during the period of unofficial treaty negotiations Napoleon made approaches to London for just such an understanding on Italy. The results were unsatisfactory, and it has been suggested that this was one of the reasons Napoleon moved to official negotiations on the treaty when he did.[17] In any event, shortly thereafter, Cobden heard (from Persigny by way of Chevalier) that the emperor was considering an even broader scheme for linking—and possibly superseding—the Commercial Treaty with an agreement for Anglo-French cooperation in Italy. Frantically Cobden tried to track down these rumors, at first through Persigny, who, however, had already returned to England, and then through Fould and Rouher, who assured him that the negotiations would proceed as planned. But news of a sudden visit to London by Lord Cowley, the British ambassador to France, seemed to confirm Cobden's fears, and he wrote to Gladstone, informing him of all the recent goings-on in Paris and suggesting in the bluntest terms what Persigny had apparently already told the emperor, that any delay in the treaty or attempt to tie it to other schemes would be considered a breach of faith and undermine the credibility of the imperial regime.

In the event, no broad Napoleonic scheme was proposed, although exactly when and why he dropped it—if indeed it had ever been fully formed—is not certain. The final threat to the treaty had passed, and the emperor proved at the end, as he had been from the beginning, a dedicated supporter of it. Yet there is no question that his maneuvering had delayed the signing of the treaty and was largely responsible for the "almost incessant nervous irritation and excitement" that Cobden complained had been his lot ever since coming to France.[18]

In comparison, his own government could hardly have been more cooperative. Coincidentally, Cobden had to return to England on railway business a few days after Napoleon committed himself to the negotiation of a treaty. Cobden took advantage of this to report personally to Palmerston and Gladstone, both of whom reiterated their support. A month later, when the negotiations reached the point at which both sides felt they should take on an official character, Cobden understandably thought he might be superseded or placed in harness with a diplomat. Instead, he was given plenipotentiary powers and continued the negotiations on his own. Cobden was concerned that this might be resented by Lord Cowley, on whose turf he was undeniably poaching, but nothing of the sort happened. Cowley readily deferred to Cobden on economic matters, and the two got along personally as well as professionally.

This support made the negotiations less difficult for Cobden than for his French counterparts. Dependent on the whim of the emperor and fearful of their protectionist colleagues, they were as concerned for their jobs as for the treaty. The stakes were not nearly so high for Cobden. And even had they been so, his approach would have been little different. Coming immediately after three years of personal tragedy and near-retirement, which in turn succeeded two years of political isolation during the Crimean war, the treaty negotiations were a convalescent phase in Cobden's public life. Of a piece with his earlier work for peace and free trade, they were not, as that earlier work had been, part of a grand design. He undertook the negotiations as "a labor of love" and took a remarkably detached view of the difficulties he might encounter.[19] "My time is of little value," he remarked to Palmerston, concerning the possibility that the negotiations might end in nothing, "and therefore no harm can come of it."[20] This was not false modesty, to which Cobden was not given in any case. He did not know what he would do next.

Nor, for that matter, was it certain there would be a next. Cobden fell seriously ill during the negotiations. He had enjoyed reasonably good health for some years. His weakest link physically, his respiratory system, had failed him now and then, most recently during the 1857 election campaign, but then, as during most of the preceding two decades, a few days of bed rest had restored his strength. In November 1859, however, during his brief visit to England from Paris, Cobden's health gave way alarmingly. On the evening of his interview with Palmerston, November 14, London was choked by fog. Walking away from Number 10 Downing Street Cobden suddenly found that he could hardly breathe and nearly collapsed. He struggled through his remaining days in England, took to his bed immediately after returning to Paris, did not go out of doors for three weeks, and was a semi-invalid for another two months. This was far more serious than his only other protracted illness during his years in public life, the cold that incapacitated him for a month in the winter of 1845. Indeed, not since the early 1830s had Cobden had so much reason to be concerned about his health.

Yet he all but ignored his illness, at least in his diary and in letters to friends. Or rather he accepted it almost as one might accept a natural phenomenon of the winter season. And far from letting his illness slow down the treaty negotiations, he used his condition as a ploy in dealing with the French. He pleaded illness as a justification for keeping discussions as long as possible where he preferred them, on general principles rather than specifics. He also used his confinement to establish the mechanics of the negotiations: instead of meeting personally with Rouher, Cobden worked in his hotel and Rouher in his office, with Chevalier acting as courier. This arrangement was equally satisfactory to the French, particularly during the early stages when they wished to keep everything secret.

Next to secrecy, Rouher's greatest concern was to establish a framework for the negotiations that would make it appear that the English were conceding more than the French. Cobden and Gladstone were quite willing to play along. To this end Chevalier concocted "a written document drawn up by himself, but which purported to be my [Cobden's] original proposal for the basis of a Commercial Treaty. He had contrived without any direct falsification to leave the door open for M. Rouher to propose some alterations which might appear to give him an advantage in the negotiations."[21] Appearances aside, the French most wanted a specific British commitment to substantially lower duties on French wines written into the treaty. Britain's offer to eliminate tariffs on most manufactures, coupled with general assurances regarding wine, the details to be announced later in Gladstone's budget, would not suffice to neutralize the protectionist party in France, Rouher and Fould argued, and Cobden was increasingly inclined to agree with them, as he became more impressed with the determination of both sides in the free trade controversy in France.

For his part, Cobden was particularly interested in persuading the French to accept two basic principles: that prohibitions on imports should be abandoned and that tariff rates should be low enough so as not in themselves to constitute de facto prohibition. Not surprisingly, therefore, it was his idea to negotiate the treaty in two stages. The first, the treaty itself, would set forth the broad guidelines governing trade; the second, consisting of supplementary conventions, would establish actual French tariff rates. As well as expediting the completion of the basic treaty (and thus protecting it from the vagaries of politics on both sides of the channel), this division would emphasize the fundamental principles involved. More specifically, Cobden hoped the French would agree to the unfettered importation of raw materials and to rates of between 6 and 20 percent on manufactures. The French countered with a proposal for a maximum of 30 percent, and Cobden spent most of his time and energy trying to get this reduced. He appealed to Rouher on every conceivable ground, including, finally, patriotism. Pointing out that England was to eliminate most tariffs, Cobden commented that "my only difficulty was in seeing how the French government could reconcile it with the sense of national pride to accept even such humiliating terms."[22] Compared with this matter Cobden was all but indifferent to the timetable for implementing the new tariff schedules.

That, together with the problem of how to handle the duties on French wines, brought him into conflict with his own government. Throughout the negotiations, even after they took on an official character, Cobden did not communicate through normal channels. He reported back directly to members of the cabinet. At first he wrote to Palmerston as well as Gladstone, largely, as he explained to the latter, "because I wish to interest him, knowing *your* heart was in the business. Besides, a man has a right to feel that the child he has to father is his own."[23] Well before the negotiations entered the official stage, however, Cobden was reporting only to Gladstone. They exchanged letters at least once a week and, as the treaty approached completion, almost on a daily basis. Because their views on the benefits of the treaty were nearly identical, on the whole they worked well together, but their approaches to certain practical issues diverged sharply as time went by, primarily owing to the different circumstances in which they operated.

Like many diplomatic representatives sent abroad to negotiate with a foreign power, Cobden became increasingly sympathetic with the problems of his French counterparts. This was particularly true when it came to the matter of including the wine duties in the treaty itself, whereas Gladstone's objections to doing so were based on financial considerations. The wine importers of Britain had earlier been promised compensation for duties paid on wines imported but not sold at the time new duties were established by treaty. Because similar drawbacks would not be required if the reductions were made in a budget, Gladstone obviously preferred the latter approach. However, when it became clear that the French might abandon the negotiations if the duties on wine were not spelled out in the treaty itself, the chancellor of the Exchequer gave way. The French, backed by Cobden, won out.

Similar considerations of domestic politics worked in the opposite direction when it came to the issue of the timetable for implementing the treaty by the French. On the surface the terms of the proposed treaty appeared highly unequal. Britain was to abolish most duties, but the French only reduced theirs or replaced prohibitions with tariffs of up to 25 or 30 percent. Furthermore, although the British reductions were to be contained in Gladstone's next budget, the French, owing to earlier pledges by Napoleon, were to spread theirs over a number of years. Gladstone, whose budget would be the primary instrument of implementing the treaty in Britain, feared an adverse parliamentary reaction and at the end of December began to press for some immediate reductions by the French and for a commitment to the earliest possible date for all tariff reductions.

Cobden never took this issue seriously. Away from England and out of touch with the English press and public opinion, he was not in any case likely to see the treaty as others saw it. Like Gladstone, he would have been happy to make reductions in British tariffs unilaterally. Moreover, for Cobden the treaty was more a political than an economic issue, and even in economic terms his concern was with persuading the French to adopt basic principles, which, once established, would have their own momentum. The initial inequalities in the treaty were therefore a matter of indifference to Cobden, and it was Cowley who ultimately negotiated the French concessions that Gladstone rightly felt were politically necessary in England.

That said, however, the negotiation of the Commercial Treaty was undeniably a testimony to Cobden's political vision. As with the repeal of the Corn Laws, he pursued it not as an end in itself but as a means of transforming fundamental economic and political relationships. In February 1860, two weeks after the treaty was signed, he wrote of its significance:

> We only do what we ought to have done for consistency long ago, whereas the other side enters on a new policy, and is going to do as much in favor of free trade principles in eighteen months as it took Huskisson and Deacon Hume ten years to accomplish . . . The effect of the treaty will be felt all over the world. It will raise the topic of "international tariffs" into practical importance with all the Governments of Europe . . . All the chancelleries of the embassies of Paris will be studying political economy from this moment, which will certainly be an improvement on their old studies.[24]

The long-term influence of the treaty did not come close to matching the stunning success of Corn Law repeal, which ushered in the eighty-five-year reign of free trade in England, but it was followed, as Cobden predicted, by a tide of tariff reductions throughout Europe, which was only swept back by the flood of American grain into world markets twenty years later.

Cobden was far from alone, of course, in looking beyond the treaty to its effects on world trade, and the tendency at the time to label it simply the Cobden treaty was misleading and unfair. Chevalier and Gladstone had no less broad a view of its significance, and Gladstone at least understood the immediate politics of the treaty better than Cobden. So too, in his way, did Napoleon III. But if Chevalier was the J. B. Smith of the Commercial Treaty, and Gladstone and Napoleon III in 1860 shared between them the role of Peel in 1846, Cobden was again what he had been in the repeal movement, the catalyst. With his position at but not of the inner circle of British partisan politics, his considerable but unofficial status internationally, his dedication to free trade beyond short-term considerations of national self-interest, and his fair-minded, even affectionate, view of France, Cobden was uniquely placed to seize the opportunity opened up by Chevalier. And as had been the case two decades earlier at the beginning of the anti–Corn Law agitation, he did not hesitate once he recognized the significance of that opportunity, as indeed he did from the moment it was laid before him. In the final analysis that quality of mind was Cobden's greatest asset in realizing both of his great concrete accomplishments.

Cobden paid a high price for his success in negotiating the Commercial Treaty, however. The killer fog of 14 November put him to bed for three weeks; during the following two months he negotiated the treaty as a semi-invalid; and five days after the treaty was signed he traveled south to spend the rest of the winter on the French Riviera. Cobden tried to make light of all this, explaining to his friends that his doctors' main concern was that he might lose his voice. Apart from that, he assured everyone, he was almost as well as ever. In fact, he was no such thing. The sickliness of his youth, which he had once feared would put a premature end to his public career, had returned permanently. And although it did not end the career to which he had so recently returned, it did curtail it. For the rest of his life Cobden retreated into semi-invalidism every winter. He dared not go to London until spring weather arrived and therefore rarely attended the opening weeks of parliament. He spent the coldest months sequestered at Dunford or, as in early 1860, near the Mediterranean. He rarely spoke to public meetings, preferring to make his case in the House of Commons or through private contacts or correspondence.

That degree of withdrawal from the old pattern of his political life did not come about all at once, however, and in 1860 Cobden felt obliged to throw himself into the arduous task of translating the general principles of the Commercial Treaty into specifics. He need not have volunteered for this time-consuming job, which certainly was not expected of him. Ordinarily, this would have been the work of a team of civil servants from the Foreign Office and the Board of Trade. Indeed, "it had been thought in the Cabinet," Cobden learned, "that it would be *infra dig* to take the part of Chief Commissioner after minister plenipotentiary. But," he advised Lord Cowley, "if you do not feel shocked at such a breach of etiquette on the part of your late colleague, I shall not be horrified myself."[25]

Joking aside, Cobden very much wanted the job. Despite his health, he was certain he would best be able to ensure that the promise of the treaty was fulfilled. The treaty encountered a good deal of criticism in Parliament and the press, far more than Cobden (although not Gladstone) had expected. A provision that forbade England from prohibiting the export of coal or levying duties on its export was denounced as possibly mortgaging the future security of the country in the event of war. To many the treaty seemed one-sided in that it committed Britain to reducing her tariffs both more and sooner than France. As *The Times* put it the day the treaty was signed, "England pays ready money and receives in exchange a bill at eighteen months without interest and without any extra benefit to England to compensate for the lack of interest."[26] Because he was resting in the south of France, there was little Cobden could do to counter such criticism. He thought briefly of returning to England to answer his parliamentary critics, but his health would not allow it. He was therefore reduced to writing to friends urging them to get up petitions in favor of the treaty from local chambers of commerce and the like. Petitions from the provinces did indeed pour into the House of Commons and, together with a brilliant defense of the treaty by Gladstone in his budget speech, helped disarm the opposition. By the time Cobden returned to Paris in March, the treaty was safe.

Nonetheless, he was determined to vindicate the treaty from its critics. Those who objected to the treaty as unfair to England failed to understand that the document signed on January 23 was provisional in nature, at least so far as the tariff rates to be charged by France were concerned. The maximum rates set out in the treaty—30 percent for four years, 25 percent thereafter—were just that, maximums. To speed up the initial negotiations and disarm French protectionist opinion, Cobden and the British government had agreed to leave the setting of specific rates to later negotiations, on the basis of assurances given privately by the French that most rates would be far lower than the maximum. Cobden had no doubt of the sincerity of Rouher and Fould in this, but he understandably thought that he might be able to strike a better bargain than negotiators new to the job, and in any case he wanted to have a hand in what he regarded as an integral part of the treaty. His French counterparts were equally anxious that he should head the British team.

Cobden had an even more deeply felt reason for wishing to complete the negotiations himself. The signing of the treaty, far from leading to an easing of tensions between France and Britain, was followed by a deterioration in relations, largely as a result of the announced intention of France to annex Nice and Savoy. Critics of the treaty in England found that they had a new argument: that the French had entered into the negotiations as a diversion behind which to carry out their territorial ambitions. Cobden was determined to rescue the treaty from that imputation, to separate it from the bitter tone of diplomatic relations between the two countries, and to salvage what he could of his original goal of better Anglo-French understanding.

Early in April therefore Cobden returned to England to receive instructions and map out strategy for the negotiations with his two newly appointed colleagues, one from customs, the other from the Board of Trade (the latter, Louis Mallet, quickly became a disciple of Cobden and later negotiated similar treaties with other European countries). Also in preparation for the negotiations Cobden hoped to enlist advice from representatives of the British industries to be affected by the new French tariffs as a means not only of strengthening the hand of the British negotiators but also of providing information with which to counteract the fears of French industrialists. This suggestion was immediately agreed to, and Cobden contacted a number of manufacturers he knew personally, although most of this task was handled by his fellow commissioners, working through local chambers of commerce. Thereafter, Cobden stayed in London only long enough to hold a few meetings with industrial representatives, explain the nature of the negotiations to them, and draft them to come to Paris to give evidence before the full commission if needed.

By the end of the month Cobden was back in Paris, only to find that the work of the joint Anglo-French commission would be delayed. To quiet domestic opposition, the French government had agreed to hold hearings and take evidence regarding the French industries concerned. This turned out to be so time-consuming that the date on which the new tariff schedules were scheduled to come into effect had to be put off. During all this time Cobden was kept informed of the proceedings, but there was nothing he could do to expedite the business. It was not until late August, four months and far too many receptions and dinner parties after Cobden had returned to Paris, that the commission actually got down to work.

On the whole, the negotiations went smoothly, at least as long as Cobden and Rouher were left to their own devices. They liked and trusted each other well by this time and had been given full authority by their governments to determine the specifc figures. Moreover, at Cobden's suggestion, the commission proceeded informally, by discussion rather than the exchange of memoranda, which also speeded up matters. Where there were problems, they arose as a result of outside interference, either from French industrial interests or from the Foreign Office at home. Both sources of intervention were at their most insistent early on, when the tariffs on iron manufactures were at stake. There was no more powerful lobby in France than the iron industry, which was all but unanimous in seeking to delay or reduce concessions to the British; the Foreign Office, concerned that tariffs negotiated in Paris might be unfavorable to English interests, wanted to review everything agreed to by the joint commission.

Cobden held out against the pressure from both quarters, realizing that even at this late date the spirit of the treaty was at risk. When Rouher suggested placating the French iron industry by making smaller reductions at the outset with the promise of more to come, Cobden objected, in words suspiciously like those *The Times* had used to attack the treaty: "if I were now to agree to accept payment for the most part in a bill at three years date, and to receive but a trifle in ready money, everybody would say I had been imposed on and that the debt would not be paid."[27] And when Cowley informed Cobden of the proposed interference from the Foreign Office, he immediately pointed out "the impossibility of the task of revising in London the details of the tariff which we had arranged."[28] French tariffs, he noted drily, could only be set in Paris.

Cobden's obstinacy paid off. Rouher, who agreed with Cobden in principle, dropped the proposal for granting special treatment to the iron industry, and although the first supplementary convention, which dealt with metal products and machinery, did not go as far as Cobden hoped, it did involve substantial and immediate French concessions. Interference from London proved harder to deal with. After registering his objections unsuccessfully through Cowley, Cobden enlisted the aid of his friends in the Cabinet, Milner Gibson, president of the Board of Trade, and Gladstone. Cobden also encouraged the French to publish the completed but unapproved text of the first convention, possibly as a means of putting pressure on the "circumlocution office at home,"[29] an action that infuriated Cowley. Despite or, very likely in part because of, Cobden's utter disregard for the niceties of dealing with the departments to which he was ostensibly responsible, he won a complete victory. Supported by Gladstone and the Board of Trade, he was granted what, as a plenipotentiary, he had returned to Paris thinking he already had, final authority to negotiate the conventions implementing the treaty.

By the time this was settled, a month after the issue first arose, Cobden's personal indignation and his latent suspicions of the motives of the government at home were aroused. "When the post of plenipotentiary was conferred on me, without my solicitation, I little thought that it would subject me to feelings of humiliation,"[30] he noted in his diary, comparing his situation unfavorably with the degree of independence he had enjoyed as a young commercial traveler. As for the attempted interference, he ascribed much of it to bureaucratic infighting and professional jealousy of an interloper such as himself, but he also suspected that elements within the Foreign Office, the services, and even the cabinet deliberately sought to undermine him and the treaty. "There is an intuitive feeling on the part of our aristocratic politicians," he concluded, "that if the Treaty should prove successful . . . it would produce a state of feeling which might lead to a material limitation of armaments, and thus cut down the expenditure for warlike services on which our aristocratic system flourishes."[31]

That the system finally lost this round was due, Cobden was certain, entirely to his own prestige, Gladstone's active intervention, and the need of Palmerston and Russell to retain radical support. Neither prime minister nor foreign secretary had been of any help to Cobden in his difficulties with the Foreign Office, and left to themselves, Cobden believed, they would have been content to see the treaty crippled. Cobden's conviction that his old enemies were enemies still was the one lasting legacy from this final hitch in the negotiation of the Commercial Treaty. Neither his position as a negotiator nor the treaty itself was weakened, but he never again was willing to suspend his critical judgment of Palmerston's last government, as he had for the better part of a year after his return from the United States.

Once these impediments were out of the way, the negotiations moved along without further delay. The parade of industrial representatives from England proved invaluable to the negotiators, and their informal method of proceeding allowed them at last to progress as rapidly as Cobden had hoped. It was an exhausting business, nonetheless. Cobden began each working day as he normally did at home, with his personal correspondence, to which was now added the constant flow of advice and questions from concerned businessmen in England. Interviews with business representatives were followed by a late-morning strategy session at which the three commissioners reviewed their evidence preparatory to the actual negotiations with the French. The negotiations took up the whole of the afternoon and were sometimes stormy, particularly in the beginning, before each side had taken the measure of the other. The French normally opened by proposing the maximum rate for whatever item was under discussion, the English countering with the minimum; each side presented evidence on prices, costs of production, and the likely effects of various tariffs and then did its best to expose the weaknesses or misrepresentations in the other's case. After the day's negotiations and dinner the English commissioners returned to the business of conducting interviews and compiling evidence, preparatory to starting the whole process over again the following day. "The labor is very tedious," Cobden reflected near the end, "and after all, what a barbarous system of raising a revenue this is, by placing obstacles in the way of trade and impeding men in the natural operations of commercial exchange! The only consolation is in the faith I feel that this is only a step in the path which by a natural progress leads eventually to perfect freedom of trade."[32]

His faith was certainly justified. Despite the number of items involved, the negotiations moved rapidly and flexibly once the negotiators established a good working routine. Because of this, Cobden later regretted that the most contentious category of goods, iron products, had been dealt with first. On balance, however, Cobden had reason to be pleased. Napoleon and Rouher lived up to their promise not to hold out for high rates. The first supplementary convention took a month to complete, but the second convention, covering everything other than metal products, also was negotiated in only a month and established tariff schedules that Cobden thought reasonable and, in some cases, politically courageous on the part of the French. He paid Rouher the compliment of comparing his achievement with that of Huskisson in England, but with the difference that it had taken England two decades to carry through what France was doing in as many years.

There was only one aspect of the treaty with which Cobden was disappointed, and that was a result of English policy, not French. The problem was the wine duties, and once again Cobden found himself in conflict with his closest ally in the government, Gladstone. Cobden had always favored a low uniform duty on all wines, but Gladstone, for the sake of revenue, had successfully insisted on a scale of rates tied to alcohol content. By the time the second supplementary convention was being negotiated a year later, however, an unforeseen problem had arisen. The light wines of Bordeaux entered England at a lower rate than the slightly stronger wines of Burgundy or, absurdly, the cheap *vins ordinaires* of the Midi. Supported by Cobden, who all but promised that the system would be changed, the French again raised the possibility of a uniform duty. When Gladstone refused to budge and suggested that the British government was not bound by Cobden's private promises, Cobden reacted almost irrationally. His and England's honor were at stake, he asserted, and if all else failed he declared himself ready to take his case to the higher court of public opinion. "Now as vanity is not my besetting sin," he reminded Gladstone,

> I am not afraid to avow that no one not occupying my peculiar position could or would have been allowed or enabled to do what I have effected here. With all *your* good will in the matter, there were influences at work which would have tripped any person up engaged in my irregular diplomacy, who had not the power I retained to right myself, and *punish wrongdoers at home* . . . I shall give, if necessary, all the health and strength I possess, even to the extent of another League agitation, to carry out faithfully that part of my original programme . . . The greatest trouble which such an agitation would give me would be to find myself in opposition to you.[33]

It was an extraordinary outburst, unprecedented in Cobden's entire public career. Gladstone had the good sense to reply to Cobden as if he had said none of this, and Cobden, clearly aware that he had gone too far with Gladstone as well as with his promises to the French, let the matter drop. Exhausted though he was by the negotiations and keenly as he must have felt the difficult position he had placed himself in, Cobden would surely not have reacted as he did had he not felt constantly undercut by his own government. The attempted interference of the Foreign Office two months before and the increasingly anti-French tone of Palmerston's defense policies left him isolated and vulnerable in Paris.

It is also unlikely that any issue other than the duty on wine would have set Cobden off so explosively. Not only was it of prime importance to the French, but he had a special interest in it. Cobden looked to the importation of inexpensive French wine as an important means of improving the "social habits and morals of the country" through a change in its drinking habits.[34] Cobden was no fanatic on the subject of alcohol. As a young man he drank moderately but his health and the demands of public life led him to give up spirits, then port and sherry, and finally all alcohol except on social occasions. He became an advocate of temperance out of experience rather than principle, but he was nonetheless dedicated for that. In his late life he ascribed the generally good health of his middle years primarily to abstinence. From the late 1840s onwards he was, unusually for a national political figure, a vocal supporter of the temperance work of Joseph Livesay, who, like many in that movement, had earlier been a free trader. While in Paris to negotiate the Commercial Treaty, Cobden drank and enjoyed the light table wines of France and became convinced that used in moderation they might be a healthy alternative to the stronger wines of Spain and Portugal traditionally drunk in England. It has also been suggested, not without reason, that Cobden's class prejudices played a role here, for madeira, port, and sherry were unmistakably the wines of the aristocracy and its imitators.

The second convention—with the wine duties unaltered—was signed on 16 November 1860, one day short of a year after Cobden had returned to Paris from London authorized to open negotiations toward a commercial treaty. A week later Bright joined him for a few days in Paris, and they had a joint audience with Napoleon to exchange congratulations on the success of the negotiations. That should have ended Cobden's business in Paris. The negotiation of the conventions had taken longer than anyone expected and winter was approaching. Cobden, who had not fully recovered his health, had been ordered by his doctors to go south for a long period of recuperation. He would not leave, however, before taking care of two other matters that were linked to the treaty in spirit if not in substance. Two days after the second convention was signed he suggested to Rouher that contact between the peoples of France and England should be facilitated by raising the weight of letters that could be sent across the channel for the minimum postage and by eliminating passport requirements. He pressed the passport question at his and Bright's audience with the emperor, and early in December he approached Count Persigny, recently returned from England to become interior minister, over dinner at Chevalier's.

Persigny was cautious at first but Cobden followed up their conversation with a written proposal, and in mid-December the French government announced the elimination of passports as a requirement for British subjects traveling in France. The change in postal regulations was an easier matter. Approaches were made to the chief of the French postal system, who endorsed the proposal subject to equivalent action in England. Cobden then wrote Rowland Hill, the chief secretary to the postmaster general, whom Cobden had known ever since he joined in support of Hill's agitation for the penny postage back in 1838. With the success of Cobden's two proposals assured, he wrote delightedly to Bright, "Thus in the same year we have the tariff, abolition of passports, and a postal facility. The question arises naturally, why should not our Foreign Office accomplish some good of this kind?"[35]

This letter was written from Algiers, to which Cobden had rushed as soon as he was satisfied that his passport and postal initiatives were on their way to success. There was no question in the minds of his doctors or, apparently after a good deal of persuasion, in his that the trip was necessary. When the possibility was raised of his returning even briefly to England after the treaty was concluded, he informed a few of his more intimate correspondents that such a journey undertaken during the winter might cost him his life. Cobden chose Algeria because there he could be assured of warm weather; the previous winter on the Riviera had been bitterly cold. There was no question this time of his changing the purpose of his journey, as when he went to Paris in 1859, let alone of changing both purpose and place, as he had in 1846. Rest and recuperation were the sole objects of a four-month stay, first in the city of Algiers, then in a country hotel where Bright had stayed while recovering from his breakdown and briefly on trips into the interior. The climate and its recuperative powers were as advertised, and Cobden returned to Paris in April and to England in May 1861 with his throat and voice back to normal. By the time he left Algeria, however, he was almost as restless as he was healthy. He had quickly satisfied his curiosity about the economy and government of Algeria and the more exotic aspects of its society and desert regions. Local European society, although pleasant, was provincial and dull. He disliked being so far from his friends, and he returned to England determined never to spend another winter season vegetating in the sun.

Cobden's only compensation for his enforced absence from England following the completion of the Commercial Treaty was that he had an unanswerable excuse for not attending any of the testimonials, banquets, and meetings held in his honor by chambers of commerce and city governments throughout the industrial districts of Britain. Other more tangible rewards for his services were rumored or offered, to Cobden's even greater discomfort. When he heard there was talk of Parliament voting him a pension or gift, he wrote to Bright to put a stop to it: "It is bad enough to have neglected one's affairs till I am obliged to see something of this sort done privately for my family. But the *two* processes would be intolerable."[36] Two months later, in March 1861, Palmerston offered Cobden a baronetcy or a place on the Privy Council. Without hesitation Cobden refused, as he had before and was again to refuse any government honor or office. "An indisposition to accept a title being in my case rather an affair of feeling than of reason," he explained to the prime minister, "I will not dwell further on the subject." Moreover, he noted, "it would not be agreeable to me to accept a recompense in any form for my recent labors in Paris. The only reward I desire is to live to witness an improvement in the relations of the two great neighboring nations which have been brought into more intimate connection by the Treaty of Commerce."[37]

Cobden had other, less exalted motives for declining Palmerston's offer. Not only had Palmerston and Russell failed in Cobden's estimation to give him their full support at critical junctures during the treaty negotiations, but at the same time that Cobden was desperately trying to improve Anglo-French relations through the treaty Palmerston appeared to be moving in the opposite direction. Far from cooling the overheated rhetoric of the invasion scare of 1859 or reserving judgment pending the outcome of the treaty negotiations, the prime minister had pursued a policy founded on a suspicious interpretation of French motives and actions, which culminated during the summer of 1860 in proposals for vast new coastal fortifications and an enlarged naval building program. "The conduct of the head of the Government during my negotiations was so outrageously inconsistent," Cobden commented privately to Bright, "so insulting to myself in the position in which I was placed, so calculated to impede the work I had in hand, and to render it almost impossible for the French Government to fulfill its intentions, that, as I told Lord Cowley, if my heart had not been in my work, I should have thrown up my powers and gone home."[38]

Once the treaty was completed Cobden no longer had any reason to act so circumspectly and a very good reason "not . . . to allow the Government to be my paymaster." He had already tried, through the treaty, and still hoped, through its effects, to undermine Palmerstonian policy, much as Palmerston had very nearly and, Cobden suspected, intentionally undermined him. "The whole affair is so shockingly gross and offensive to serious minds," he concluded, "that, unless we are to degenerate to a nation of political mountebanks, it cannot be much longer tolerated that we are to be governed and represented by such persons."

CHAPTER 22

The Third French Invasion Panic

From the moment Michel Chevalier suggested the possibility of an Anglo-French commercial treaty in the summer of 1859, Cobden thought of it only secondarily as a means of enhancing the economic well-being of the two countries. England at least seemed perhaps too prosperous for its own good, and if that, ironically, was in large part the result of the free-trade-induced prosperity that he had helped bring about, then it was incumbent on him to seize any opportunity to revive the promise of economic internationalism, which he had always regarded as implicit in the repeal of the Corn Laws, but which had been lost sight of in the postrepeal boom. That, at any rate, was his long-run ambition for the treaty; more immediately, he intended to use the negotiations and the treaty itself as a counterbalance to the growing clamor of Francophobia in England, which appeared to him to be dragging the two countries dangerously close to open conflict.

That was perhaps an exaggerated fear, but it was not an irrational one. Three times in little more than a decade the specter of a French invasion had been raised before the English people, and although the first two crises had passed without serious repercussions and the third might reasonably be expected to have a similar history, the cumulative effects of these panics could not easily be dismissed. Each was worse than the one before, and together they accustomed the people of both countries to think of each other as perpetual enemies. Of all Cobden's disappointments in the postrepeal era, this recurring nightmare of a possible Anglo-French conflict was, next to the outbreak of the Crimean war, the most dispiriting, because the most senseless. In his view France and England were close to being natural allies. Their economies, like their strategic interests, were rarely in direct conflict and often complementary; whatever their past differences, they had more in common with one another than either had with the other major European states. Working together, they were capable of ensuring a peaceful and liberal Europe; yet by perpetuating ancient hostilities, they emboldened the reactionary forces they professed to abhor, while setting an example of belligerency that even the military despotisms of eastern Europe could hardly exceed.

With the stakes as Cobden accounted them so high, it is hardly surprising that each of the three panics marked a turning point in his postrepeal career. The first, in 1847, drove him into association with the organized peace movement; the second, in 1851, led him ultimately to return to authorship for the first time since he entered politics; the third, in 1859, was the most important factor in inducing him to attempt the negotiation of a commercial treaty with France. In such circumstances he was understandably inclined to exaggerate the influence of the negotiation process and of the treaty on public and official opinion. In the early stages, while the whole matter was still secret, Cobden was convinced that a simple announcement that a treaty was being considered would serve to abate the hysteria. And even after this failed to happen, he continued to believe not only in the pacifying effects of the treaty but in the tendency of the negotiations themselves to moderate the climate on both sides of the channel. "If the peace of Europe is preserved," he told Chevalier in September 1860, "it will be our doing."[1]

Gladstone, who was Cobden's most frequent correspondent on all matters connected with the treaty, did what he could to reduce Cobden's expectations. Not that Gladstone thought much less than Cobden of the ultimate significance of the treaty, for which, after all, he could claim a large share of the credit. Reflecting on this period many years later, Gladstone wrote, "It was and is my opinion that the choice lay between the Cobden treaty and not the certainty but the high probability of a war with France."[2] He did not, however, share Cobden's hope that the mere prospect of a treaty would relieve Anglo-French tensions. Gladstone recognized that the current of anti-French sentiment in England ran deeper and wider than Cobden was willing to acknowledge. Cobden tended to dismiss it as a temporary hysteria got up by Palmerston, Russell, the service chiefs, the aristocracy, and elements in the press for a variety of reactionary purposes. Hence, once the general public and the business community saw that the traditional enemy across the channel was interested in accommodation with England, Cobden was sure that popular Francophobia would peter out.

Gladstone, who was in closer touch with public opinion as well as with the government, read the situation more accurately. Not only was Cobden absent from England for almost the whole of 1859 and 1860, but he had been largely out of public life for three years before that. This situation, along with a good deal of wishful thinking, distorted his understanding of the popular mood at home. Even when it became clear that the treaty negotiations were having little impact on English public opinion, and in later years as well, Cobden fell back on the argument that the wave of anti-French hysteria did not emanate from the people and that they shared in the blame for it only to the extent that they had allowed themselves to be deceived by their leaders and by the press. Yet even before the treaty was signed at the beginning of 1860, Cobden had reluctantly to admit that, if nothing worse, the campaign to deceive the English people had been carried out with remarkable efficiency, because far from reducing Anglo-French misunderstanding, the negotiation of the treaty coincided with a deterioration in Anglo-French relations.

To the apprehensions of Englishmen at the thought of a second Napoleonic regime in France had been added growing suspicion of French intentions in Italy and increasing alarm at the level of French military spending, particularly on the navy, which appeared to be aimed at rivaling the British fleet. Much of this bill of indictment was based on innuendo and debatable military statistics, but that did not suffice to prevent the invasion panic of 1859 and with it a dramatic increase in British naval spending and the formation of citizen-soldier volunteer units all over the country. Early in the following year Napoleon gave his critics a piece of concrete evidence in the form of his annexation of Nice and Savoy to France. Even those who had earlier been inclined, however cautiously, to support Napoleon's Italian adventures as a means of furthering the cause of Italian unity had now to face the possibility that he might be bent on a policy of territorial expansion and had taken up the Italian cause and the Commercial Treaty only as a means of diverting England's attention and separating her from the other powers of Europe.

Prudence seemed to demand that England make a demonstration—diplomatic certainly and perhaps military—of her resolve not to allow

France to alter the European status quo. Inevitably, therefore, the direction of British policy fell entirely into the hands of those, like Palmerston and Russell, who, although willing to cooperate with France when that suited English interests, had always viewed the Second Empire as a potential danger. Thus Palmerston, who had encountered considerable resistance from within the cabinet late in 1859 to further increases in naval spending and, above all, to his plans for strengthening coastal defenses, was able to carry these proposals easily the following spring. With only Gladstone still unalterably opposed, Palmerston had to make only token concessions, and in July he introduced his long-delayed pet project for a new generation of fortifications to the House of Commons in a provocative anti-French speech.

As English policy moved toward this climax, Cobden became increasingly alarmed and angry. Personally he felt betrayed by the governments on both sides of the channel. Although he had always dismissed the worst suspicions of Napoleon as born of English paranoia and therefore refused to consider the annexation of Nice and Savoy as more than an isolated event, even Cobden had to acknowledge that the French had handled the matter stupidly. Moreover, the timing of Napoleon's move—between the signing of the Commercial Treaty and the negotiation of specific tariffs—raised questions about his sincerity in pursuing the treaty and thus, potentially, about the worth of the treaty itself and possibly even about the sagacity of its chief English negotiator.

Angered and humiliated as Cobden felt by the actions of the French government, he reserved his special fury for his own political leaders. Here, as with Napoleon, the timing of their actions was critical and, to Cobden, inexplicable on any rational grounds. Because he never accepted the view that the British government was responding to public sentiment in acting on the invasion scare, it appeared to him that Palmerston and Russell were willing to risk the ruin of the Commercial Treaty, not to mention the prospects for cooperation with France in other spheres. Of their motives he was certain only that they had to be reprehensible. Perhaps Palmerston and Russell simply hoped to neutralize Conservative opposition; perhaps they saw the invasion scare as a means of sneaking their rearmament plans past their radical supporters; or, worst of all, perhaps they genuinely shared the prejudices of those who had a pecuniary or professional interest in perpetuating hostility toward France.

Wherever the truth lay, all of Cobden's old animosity toward aristocratic government was reawakened, along with his distrust of Palmerston personally. The prime minister had betrayed him in the midst of his great work in Paris, perhaps deliberately, perhaps simply through indifference. In either case, by that act Palmerston had broken the agreement among the factions of Liberalism that had allowed him to form a government in 1859, and Cobden therefore regarded himself as freed from the pledge of support for that government he had made at the time of his interview with Palmerston. Hence a noticeable shift took place in Cobden's thinking about the long-run significance of the Commercial Treaty in the early months of 1860: gradually he came to see it not simply as a counterweight to Francophobia but as the basis of an alternative, even of a rival, to the foreign policy of Russell and Palmerston.

Specifically, he hoped to use the contacts and leverage that he had established in negotiating the treaty to revive his ten-year-old scheme for a mutual reduction of naval armaments, but with the difference that he would now be in a position to approach the French as well as the British government. In December 1859, just three weeks before the treaty was signed, Cobden suggested something of his future plans to Bright: "One great object which I should like to force our rulers, much against their will, to accomplish is the limitation of our armed forces in relation to that of France. And that I will endeavor to promote . . . by an appeal to the French government in the same unofficial way as I am now at work."[3]

Exactly a month later, with the treaty, his major weapon, in hand, Cobden wrote even more confidently to Gladstone:

> I do not think it impossible to range such an amount of opinion in favor of my views as to effect a great reduction in our respective armaments . . . Is it certain that I could not succeed in inducing the emperor's government to allow me, even this year, to be the bearer of a qualified or conditional offer of mutual reduction of armaments to our government? And though I am illiberal enough to suspect that such a proposal would be less acceptable to our governing class than to any other in Europe, yet, with such an offer, I could become a very troublesome person in the evenly balanced state of political parties at home.[4]

All such schemes were predicated on the successful completion of the second phase of the treaty negotiations, however, and news of the fortification plan therefore came as a double blow to Cobden. Not only did it threaten to undermine the treaty negotiations, but it pushed him prematurely into opposition to Palmerston and Russell, at a time when he was still representing their government and under circumstances disadvantageous to him. Even so, there was no doubt in his mind that he had to oppose the fortification scheme, which he regarded as the most irresponsible single act of the British government since the Crimean war, if only because of the threat that it posed to the treaty. Yet precisely because he was in the midst of negotiations, he dared not act publicly. Whatever he did, he had to do in secret and from a distance of 200 miles, in Paris. Above all, he had to act in such a manner as not himself to endanger the treaty.

Not surprisingly, this was also the major theme of his increasingly frantic letters home. That he should be allowed to complete the treaty and the treaty be allowed to fulfill its promise before the government committed itself to any policy directed against France was the common ground from which he both appealed to his friends for help and sought to check his enemies. For more than a month before Palmerston announced the fortification scheme Cobden spent much of his time ringing the changes on this theme in a steady stream of letters to a widening circle of correspondents back in England. To Palmerston and Russell he wrote with extraordinary restraint, considering the depth of his feelings, asking only that they delay their plans for a few months in order not to "weaken my position here...and discredit by anticipation the political value of the Treaty."[5] (Since Cobden still believed that the completed treaty would have an instant impact on public opinion and make the reintroduction of the fortification scheme all but impossible, this was less of a concession on his part than it seemed.) From Palmerston by this time Cobden expected nothing positive and got what he expected; he wrote the prime minister mostly as a matter of form.

Russell was a different matter. Cobden regarded him as the key figure, whose decision one way or another could carry the cabinet, and as a party leader who, unlike Palmerston, was susceptible to pressure from the Liberal rank-and-file. Therefore, many of Cobden's often outspoken letters written to third parties were clearly intended to filter back to Russell or to others in the government. Thus, on a number of occasions Cobden reminded Gladstone of his earlier speculations on the damage the radicals could do in opposition, and he hoped, correctly, that Gladstone would pass this none-too-subtle threat on to his more moderate cabinet colleagues. With Bright Cobden could conspire more directly, and he suggested to Bright that Bright suggest to Russell that Russell's future leadership of the party might be at stake, despite the foreign secretary's identification with parliamentary reform. It is a "delusion," Cobden argued, "that any reform bill . . . will ever give him the power to hold office apart from the strength which is to be derived from the advocacy of such measures as Gladstone and Gibson are prepared to support in the cabinet."[6]

Like Gladstone, however, Russell interpreted the political implications of the fortification scheme differently from Cobden—and more accurately. Nor did Russell think that there was anything incongruous in simultaneously offering a leader as unpredictable as Napoleon III both the carrot of a commercial treaty and the stick of increased military expenditures. Indeed, in his reply to Cobden's letter he supported both in adjoining paragraphs, a juxtaposition that horrified Cobden and left him perplexed as to how to proceed. With Gladstone alone among the major ministers in opposition to the fortification scheme, it went ahead substantially as Palmerston had intended. Cobden, who had exerted all the influence he could muster on a personal level, had suffered his worst political setback since the electoral annihilation of the Manchester school in 1857.

Anticipating this outcome almost from the moment the fortification scheme was mooted, Cobden initially seemed more determined than ever to lead open opposition to the government, at least once he was free from his responsibilities in Paris. "I shall on my return to public life at home," he declared to Bright, "go into a determined opposition to the party at present in power."[7] No doubt this was in part a bluff, designed to impress Bright—and through Bright others—with Cobden's determination (although he asked Bright not to reveal his plans, surely that was disingenuous in view of what he was writing to Gladstone). Still, it would be a disservice to Cobden to read these letters only as moves in a game of political calculation. At the moment he wrote them Cobden meant every word, at least emotionally. He felt betrayed and would have loved nothing better than to return to England to do public battle against Palmerstonianism. But for his unfinished treaty, he might well have done so.

It was not only the treaty that gave Cobden pause, however. Even before the passion engendered by the fortification issue had cooled, he had to acknowledge that he did not command the ingredients of a successful agitation to change the direction of foreign policy. The middle class might support the treaty enthusiastically, but that did not mean that the business community accepted Cobden's corollary to the treaty—that it all but guaranteed a lessening of Anglo-French tension and eliminated the need for increased military preparedness. Indeed, in view of his failure to win widespread support for the peace movement a decade earlier and his differences with former allies over the Crimean war, Cobden would have been foolish to count on a ground swell of support. Moreover, even had such support been waiting to be mobilized, the means of doing so did not exist. The vehicles of the early 1850s, let alone any organization like the league, were no longer in place. The peace society had been all but demolished by the Crimean war and the financial reform movement crippled by prosperity. If the foreign policy of Palmerston and Russell was to be attacked successfully, Cobden was inclined to believe that the arena would have to be Parliament, not the public platform.

Cobden had serious reservations about his own role in that battle, however. He neither wanted nor felt able to lead a long fight in or out of Parliament. He was fifty-six years old and felt older. More than twenty years had passed since the founding of the league, ten since the height of his earlier parliamentary peace campaign, and five since he had last been active in the House of Commons. There was some question as to whether he could ever address large public meetings again, and no question at all that his health would not stand up to the rigors of a full parliamentary session, let alone survive the demands of a campaign out of doors. If there was to be a campaign of opposition to the anti-French policies of Palmerston and Russell, then Bright, not Cobden, would have to lead it.

Yet Cobden was far from certain that Bright knew how best to operate in the political circumstances of the early 1860s. To be a great radical leader out of doors was not a good route to power or influence. By attempting during 1859 to rouse the masses for political reform (without effectively arousing them), Bright, Cobden believed, had only succeeded in throwing the middle class into the arms of the aristocracy, which, in turn, was more irritated than intimidated by Bright. As more than one member of the cabinet had told Cobden privately, Bright's immoderation had excluded him from consideration for office and reduced his influence on government policy. Given the moderate temper of the times, Cobden concluded, "we are comparatively powerless if we can be assumed to be excluded from the government by either our own will or that of the ruling class, owing to our entertaining revolutionary or fundamentally subversive doctrines."[8] Throughout the winter of 1859–60 Cobden peppered his letters to Bright with bits of advice, urging him to forsake the stump for the House of Commons, to learn to live with the power of the governing class, and so forth. Such letters were a clear signal that Cobden had irrevocably decided to pass the leadership of the Manchester school into Bright's hands. Yet even had this not been so, even had Cobden had unbounded energy and been sure that his old lieutenant would listen to his advice, he would have hesitated to expose either of them to a public campaign, because, as he told Bright early in 1860, "You and I have comparatively little weight in these matters on account of our peace principles."[9]

Although the case against a public agitation in opposition to government policy was overwhelming, the same arguments did not weigh so heavily against risking his future career in an attempt to bring private pressure to bear. There was, in fact, one respect, although only one, in which Cobden felt better positioned to pursue the peace issue than he had been a decade before: he had closer personal relations with the inner circle of government. Not only had he been strongly pressed at the highest level to accept cabinet office and successfully negotiated the Commercial Treaty as the representative of that government, but he had in the process developed a close relationship with the third most powerful member of the government, Gladstone. Indeed, by the summer of 1860 Cobden had come to pin much of his hope for the future on Gladstone, whom he now saw as the rightful heir to Peel and the likely future leader of radical Liberalism.

This had not always been so. As recently as the early months of 1857 Cobden had viewed Gladstone with suspicion: for his protectionist past, for his support of the Crimean war, and more fundamentally, for being perhaps too clever for his own good. "What right have we to reckon on his aid to carry out our views of foreign policy?" Cobden asked Richard in January 1857:

> He was a party to the invasion of Russia, and to this day defends the policy of sending a British army to the Crimea . . . I have the highest opinion of Gladstone's powers. He is the most eloquent and impressive

speaker we have . . . But his conscience has not yet taken him in our direction . . . And indeed I fear he sometimes entangles his conscience with his intellect. I have heard him defend "protection" with such sophistical arguments that I have doubted whether he was more than a reasoning machine for the moment, with his moral sense put in abeyance. I am afraid he is not even yet committed to any broad and intelligible principles.[10]

This harsh verdict was somewhat softened a few months later, when Gladstone backed Cobden's motion on the *Arrow* incident and followed up his parliamentary support with a letter of praise for Cobden's efforts. The real turning point in their relationship came with the negotiation of the French treaty, however. From the moment Cobden told Gladstone of Chevalier's proposal, Gladstone adopted it with an enthusiasm and a dedication to the idea of the treaty as an instrument of pacification little different from Cobden's. In addition, for the first four months of the treaty negotiations, Gladstone was the only one with whom Cobden dared to communicate freely; until his mission was given an official character, Cobden withheld the details even from close friends such as Bright and Ashworth.

During these same months Gladstone came to value their correspondence almost as much. As friction within the cabinet over military spending mounted and Gladstone found himself almost alone in opposition to it, he more and more frequently turned to Cobden as one of the few men in public life to whom he could safely vent his frustration and be certain of a sympathetic response. By the time Cobden's treaty had been shepherded through Parliament by Gladstone and the battle over the fortification scheme had been lost by them, their enforced political camaraderie and the frequent letters that cemented it had become as habitual as they were valuable to both men. They remained important influences on one another and constant correspondents—with one important interruption—until Cobden's death in 1865.

Their correspondence was and is fascinating. From the outset Cobden wrote characteristically long and chatty letters. Gladstone, equally characteristically but also presumably because of his official position, was more cautious—and not infrequently delphic—at first. But that changed rapidly. Drawn by the warmth of Cobden's letters, which contrasted so sharply with the growing sense of isolation he felt from his cabinet colleagues, Gladstone gradually opened up, revealing more and more of his thinking and finally of his emotions. The process culminated in an extraordinary cri de coeur written in January 1860:

> It has been a great happiness of my public life heretofore never to have wanted . . . [the opportunity] to seek advice from persons in the same situation, of the same habits of mind and political training and connections . . . but at the present moment for the first time it fails me, I mean within the narrow circle of those who are equally with myself aware of the course of affairs; and I seek and find most of concurrence in quarters where I am politically a stranger. It is with reference to this subject, and to my belief that gross extravagance constitutes a public danger, that I have often to you and otherwise peculiarly expressed my regret that the proposal made to you in the summer could not take effect.[11]

This served to remove whatever doubts remained in Cobden's mind concerning Gladstone. Two weeks later he commented to Bright that Gladstone "has more in common with you and me than any other man of his power in Britain."[12] This increasing identity of outlook had its limits, however. They agreed in their opposition to extravagance, especially in military spending, but Gladstone did not go as far as Cobden in seeking retrenchment or alterations in the system of taxation. More immediately, they disagreed on tactics. Their growing respect for one another kept this from getting out of hand, as did their mutual recognition (sometimes reluctantly given on Cobden's part) that each was valuable to the other politically precisely because of the different positions they occupied: Gladstone as a member of the cabinet and Cobden as an independent yet sympathetic critic. Thus, although Gladstone often thought that Cobden's criticisms of Palmerston, Russell, and himself were impolitic and inflexible, he tended to answer Cobden by trying to put the errors of the government in the broader context of its achievements or, when that proved difficult, by defending his own role or, if worst came to worst, by not answering Cobden's more extreme comments at all, as if they had never been written.

As for Cobden, he often accused the government of betraying its principles and Gladstone of compromising his integrity (and perhaps his political future) by remaining part of that government, but he readily acknowledged that Gladstone, by staying at his post and pressing his views, was displaying a kind of political fortitude of which he, Cobden, a perennial independent, was incapable. "For myself, I would never be tempted by any consideration to enter upon official life," Cobden told Gladstone. "To lose my individuality would to me be a moral death . . . Yet," he conceded, "I am fair to confess the world can't go on upon my theory. I admit that men must cooperate in bodies and that there must be a compromise of opinions."[13] In light of that, Cobden often felt reluctant to comment on Gladstone's official conduct. That was only one of the normally undefined restraints that both Cobden and Gladstone imposed on the tone and subject matter of their correspondence. Whereas one was an insider and the other an outsider and each occupied his position by choice, they did not conspire, gossip, or leak information.

Although Cobden naturally felt less constrained than Gladstone in such matters, he took care not to go too far. Once, for example, after savagely attacking Palmerston for putting Gladstone in an awkward position, Cobden took the edge off his remarks by concluding, "You see I always talk treason in this way the moment I take up my pen to write to you."[14] In fact, Cobden rarely talked treason, at least directly. He sought to influence Gladstone and, through Gladstone, the direction of government policy and was not averse to attacking the government or threatening to go into opposition to make his point. But in the end Cobden was committed to supporting Gladstone as a means of enhancing the influence of both of them, just as Gladstone, for the same reason, was intent on keeping Cobden's support, even at the price of swallowing some criticism.

Yet even when they saw eye to eye, there was often little they could do. Until the Commercial Treaty was completed their hands were tied. Indeed, the great irony of the politics of the summer of 1860 was that the treaty negotiations, undertaken partly in the hope of inhibiting such things as the fortification scheme, acted instead as an inhibition on its opponents. Gladstone often contemplated resignation but only once, at the height of the fortification controversy, did Cobden even half hope Gladstone might go through with it. At other times he urged Gladstone to stay on, if only for the sake of the treaty. Once that was no longer a consideration, Cobden became more outspoken. He stepped up his pressure on Gladstone to disassociate himself from some of the government's policies and perhaps from the government itself, and more than once he suggested that a Tory government under Lord Derby would be preferable to a pseudo-Liberal government under Lord Palmerston. This was not idle talk. Late in 1860 Bright—directly and in specific terms—and Cobden—indirectly (through Ambassador Persigny) and apparently in a more general way—approached the Conservative leadership with the suggestion that they join forces to oust the government.

It was only in moments of extreme frustration, however, that Cobden contemplated a Tory government as an acceptable alternative rather than as a stick with which to beat the Liberals into being more liberal. As he well knew, no Tory government would have sponsored the treaty negotiations, and as Gladstone often reminded him, each of the anti-French panics and the demands for increased military spending they spawned were bipartisan in character. As proof of that, Derby and Disraeli, far from being tempted by Cobden's and Bright's overtures, were so desirous of "strengthening the hands of the government in a patriotic sense" that they gave the prime minister assurances of support against the Manchester radicals and his own chancellor of the Exchequer.[15] A tactical alliance between radicals and Tories, a desperate option at best, was out of the question until well after the French panic had passed.

Necessarily therefore Cobden returned to Gladstone's preferred means of fighting the battle of the budget, as a holding action by the chancellor of the Exchequer within the cabinet, while Cobden did what he could from outside to provide Gladstone with support from the radicals and ammunition in the form of hard information on French policy. That essentially is how they had begun their work together on the issue of military spending a year before. Cobden first approached Gladstone about armaments as an issue distinct from the treaty early in 1860. In January, with the treaty about to be signed and in the hope of influencing cabinet deliberations on the budget, he sent the chancellor, unsolicited, a summary of French naval expenditure since 1845, designed, of course, to demonstrate the greater strength of the British navy as well as the absurdity of the invasion scare. Six months later Cobden provided even more detailed figures, this time in answer to a request from Gladstone, who was then engaged in the climactic cabinet battle over the fortification scheme. This was to be the normal pattern of their joint effort to check arms spending over the next couple of years. Gladstone might inform Cobden of a rumor concerning French policy or ask him a specific question about French naval plans, and Cobden, usually through Chevalier, would seek out the information.

In the process Cobden was compelled to become something of an expert on the subject, all the while he was involved with the negotiation of the second stage of the Commercial Treaty. In February 1860, while he was in the south of France for his health, he visited the naval base at Toulon to see for himself the extent of new shipbuilding. In July, in addition to providing London with the most up-to-date available figures on French naval spending, Cobden met Admiral Fourichon of the French navy (through the admiral's brother-in-law, an Englishman with interests in the Illinois Central Railroad) and had him, together with the British naval attaché in Paris, Captain Hore, to dinner. Much to Hore's surprise and Cobden's satisfaction, Fourichon provided them with a detailed breakdown of the French fleet according to type of vessel and the like. After the final tariff convention was signed in November 1860, Cobden paid a brief visit to the Loire valley, in part to inspect a recently built fleet of barges that had done much to excite the invasion scare the year before but which the French claimed were designed to carry coal.

As Cobden learned more, the nature of his concern changed subtly but importantly. As late as the early months of 1860, he was anxious first of all to avert a possible Anglo-French conflict and, beyond that, to prevent a large increase in spending and taxation, which might neutralize the benefits of the treaty or even, should such increases and the implementation of the treaty coincide, make the treaty unpopular in England. Well before the end of 1860, however, with the treaty and its favorable reception in England secure and the immediate issue of the fortification scheme out of the way, Cobden began to see the question of Anglo-French naval rivalry in a new light. He was one of the early laymen to recognize that the nature of the arms race was changing. It was no longer merely a matter of adding to the number of ships, costly and dangerous as that might be. Gone permanently were the days when a vessel, built for one war, could be refitted to do service in another, as H.M.S. *Victory*, triumphant at Trafalgar, had survived from the Seven Years' War.

The application of industrial technology to naval armament was opening up new and terrifying possibilities for the entire western world. A major advance in methods of propulsion, in the building of ironclad or iron-hulled ships, or in naval artillery could render entire fleets obsolete almost overnight. This process had begun a generation before with the application of steam power, but Cobden was right in thinking that they were only just now entering the truly dangerous and expensive phase of naval rivalry. "The success of the inventions by which a vessel could be rendered impervious to shot without impairing her traversing qualities," he wrote in September 1860, "marked a complete revolution in nautical warfare and threatened to be the birth of a gigantic folly on the part of the governments of Britain and France."[16]

Unless checked, Cobden believed, the ability of one great power to leapfrog another would lead to endless arms races at unprecedented cost, to ever greater instability in the relations between states, and to an increased likelihood that nations would resort to war if only to escape the anxieties and ruinous burdens of peace. Although Cobden underestimated the ability of nations to bear the emotional and financial burdens of the modern arms race, he was remarkably prescient in identifying its chief characteristics and above all, perhaps, in appreciating its greatest irony—that each advance in the technology of warfare, far from enhancing the security of those it was intended to protect, has served only to diminish it further.

On the whole, Cobden believed that his own country was primarily responsible for tipping the delicate naval balance of the late 1850s toward a full-scale arms race and pushing it out of control, if only because the British government reacted in panic to what the French were doing and began to build up the navy out of all proportion to any foreign threat. Nonetheless, Cobden did not exonerate the French or hesitate to lecture them on their share of the blame. It was France that first sought systematically to apply the lessons of the new technology to its navy by replacing its sailing and wooden-hulled ships with a steam-powered ironclad fleet. Although the French could hardly be blamed for wishing to modernize their navy and there was no evidence that it was being done with hostile intentions toward England—given that the French naval building program was neither secret nor rapid—the context in which the new navy was emerging was nonetheless alarming. Coming as it did in conjunction with French intervention in Italy, war with Austria, the annexation of Nice and Savoy, and an expansion of the army, the modernization of the French navy appeared to threaten England and certainly explained, even if it did not justify, the invasion panic.

Increasingly disturbed at a situation that he saw as getting out of hand on both sides of the channel, Cobden embarked on a personal campaign to convince the French of their folly, first in the spring of 1860, after his return to Paris from the south of France, and again in the fall, after the furor over the fortification scheme had died down. In conversations with Fould, Rouher, Persigny, Chevalier, the Prince Napoleon, and even in an audience, his third, with the emperor, Cobden bluntly pointed out the degree of French responsibility for the deterioration of European relations generally and for the naval race with Britain in particular. In addition he warned his French contacts repeatedly of the novel dangers of the world they were so blithely entering in deciding to build a new navy and urged them to propose a naval holiday immediately as the only means of preventing Britain from matching and soon exceeding any innovation or number of vessels the French might undertake. Indeed he went further, at least with friends such as Chevalier. The French, Cobden argued, were not merely foolhardy in competing with British seapower, they were wrong to do so. History and geography justified Britain in her determination to maintain naval supremacy. Her economy and her security as a nation depended on her navy, as France's did not. "We islanders," he reminded Chevalier, "are justly jealous of the naval preparations of a great military power like France, whom we do not pretend to rival on land and whose rivalry on sea we shall not, coute que coute, tolerate."[17]

Had Palmerston known that Cobden was using such arguments with the French, the prime minister would have been much surprised, because he always thought of Cobden as Cobden thought of him, as irresponsible to the point of recklessness on anything to do with defense. Cobden can certainly be faulted for not making his views on the necessary superiority of the British navy as clear to his own countrymen as he did to Chevalier, for Palmerston was far from alone in thinking Cobden almost un-English in his constant criticism of British military policy. To that extent Cobden was himself responsible for his failure to translate the prestige he had won in negotiating the Commercial Treaty into influence on the wider course of Anglo-French relations, a failure that had become cruelly apparent well before his return to England in the spring of 1861.

During Cobden's absence in Algeria on the eve of the 1861 session of Parliament, efforts were made to galvanize the radicals in the House of Commons behind Gladstone and a reduction in the military budget. Hoping to build on this as well as capitalize on the more sympathetic attitude toward France that seemed bound to follow the completion of the treaty, Cobden asked Samuel Morley, a wealthy hosiery manufacturer and a power in the City of London, to get up a memorial among the leading bankers and merchants of the city in favor of arms limitation talks with the French. Simultaneously he sounded out a few French friends on the feasibility of a similar move in Paris business circles. Morley, although an old ally of Cobden's in the league and a leader of the nonconformist movement, refused even to consider Cobden's suggestion. Anti-French sentiment might have diminished, but there was no sign that public support for Palmerston or his policies was waning. A memorial from the city simply was not practicable. Cobden, on hearing this, at first cast about for alternative ways of bringing public pressure to bear on the government but shortly before leaving Algeria he gave up. Thus ended his only attempt to cash in directly on the peace dividend he had always believed would follow the Commercial Treaty.

The more modest scheme for parliamentary action got little further. A round-robin letter from the radicals to Palmerston calling for budget cuts had exactly the opposite of the effect intended. It served primarily to strengthen the informal understanding by which the Conservatives agreed to back Palmerston's military spending plans, thus not only emasculating the radicals but also reducing Gladstone's influence on policy either from within the cabinet or through threats of resignation. As long as the bulk of the Liberals were willing to live with this, Palmerston and his policies were all but unassailable. That was the political climate to which Cobden returned in May 1861.

In his growing frustration during the months that followed, although Cobden now and then suggested to Bright the possibility of going into open opposition to the government, he did so with little conviction. Recognizing that there was not much he could do, he simply absented himself from day-to-day politics. He spoke in the House of commons only once in 1861.

As the prospects of deflecting the government from its course through normal political channels decreased, in the fall Cobden turned back to the tactics that he had proposed using two years earlier, of trying to repeat his success in negotiating the Commercial Treaty in the area of arms control. In October he sent a memorandum to Palmerston and, translated by Chevalier and delivered through Persigny, to Napoleon III. It was deliberately moderate in tone and in its proposals. Specifically he suggested that Britain and France negotiate a mutual reduction of forces only in the field of wooden ships of the line, a category of naval vessel that all experts agreed was outmoded, which Britain and France had both stopped building and of which no third power possessed significant numbers. An agreement to reduce or eliminate such ships could therefore be undertaken in safety and would serve, Cobden argued, not only to reduce tension and save both countries significant sums of money but also to open the way "for an amicable arrangement for putting some limit to those armaments which are springing out of the present transition state of the two navies."[18] As had become increasingly the case in his recent private correspondence, Cobden stressed the unprecedented dangers inherent in the application of industrial technology to the naval arms race:

> The application of iron plates to shipbuilding, which has rendered the reconstruction of the navies necessary, must be regarded as the commencement of an indefinite series of changes; and looking to the great variety of experiments now making, both in ships and artillery, and to the new projects which the inventors are almost daily forcing upon the attention of the governments, it is not improbable that, a few years hence, when England and France have renewed their naval armaments, they will again be rendered obsolete by new scientific discoveries.

Cobden never made the case for the urgency of immediate negotiations on arms reduction more eloquently or more succinctly (the memorandum was barely 2000 words long), yet he wrote it with only the slimmest hope that it would have any effect at all. He expected nothing from Palmerston, who, in a reply not sent until three months later, predictably dismissed the proposal as impractical. Moreover, so as not to make Gladstone and Milner Gibson any more uncomfortable within the government, Cobden told them nothing of his memo. His hopes, such as they were, rested on Napoleon, who, he believed, might take up the issue out of self-interest. Should that happen, Cobden was certain that Palmerston would have to respond or risk alienating moderate opinion at home. In either case, the hand of the British government would have been forced, much as, Cobden had come to believe, its hand had been forced on the Commercial Treaty.

When the French responded in sympathetic but noncommittal terms, however, Cobden finally had to admit that his plans to drive or lure the British government onto the defensive on the issues of arms control and arms spending had failed. He therefore fell back on a position that he had already begun to prepare in anticipation of just such a failure: he turned author once again, as he had in similar circumstances three times before. The resulting pamphlet, *The Three*

Panics: An Historical Episode, was the longest of his political writings, but like the shortest, *How Wars Are Got Up in India*, it consisted primarily of a close analysis of official documents and parliamentary speeches. By comparing one with the other, earlier documents with later ones, and statements from present and former ministers when in office and when in opposition, Cobden was able to demonstrate a pattern of misrepresentation by successive British governments and a small circle of self-appointed experts that more than sufficed to show to Cobden's satisfaction not only why there had been a panic but that it had been groundless.

From start to finish, all the official estimates of comparative naval strength had overestimated French forces (by listing only ships afloat but not ships being built, in which France lagged behind) while underestimating the British (by comparing only ships of the line and frigates, regardless of age and tonnage, and leaving out smaller vessels, in which Britain was overwhelmingly superior). That the French navy was nonetheless equal or nearly equal to the British in the number of capital ships afloat at the end of the 1850s Cobden could not deny, but he did deny that this was or was intended to be a threat to Britain. France had moved to near-parity in such vessels, he argued, only because she had committed herself to a modern navy earlier and more thoroughly than Britain, which continued to build sailing as well as steam ships longer than the French. "It is hardly reasonable," Cobden noted acidly, "to hold the French government responsible for a state of things which arose out of the maladministration of our own affairs, and which the Minister of Marine could have no power of remedying, except by lowering his own management to the level of that of our Admiralty."[19]

Cobden was here being less than fair. Britain had a huge investment in its fleet of wooden sailing vessels. As the greatest naval power, it had to move cautiously into the new technology and could not afford to take the risks that were so inviting to a lesser naval power trying to stay in the race with more limited resources. That said, there was and is no denying Cobden's central assertions regarding the panic: that the French navy was being modernized according to a plan published for all the world to see in 1857; that there was no hard evidence to support the belief this was being done to challenge British naval supremacy; that French parity in capital ships at the time the panic began came about accidentally, not by design, and was in any case a temporary situation. By the time Cobden wrote his pamphlet Britain was once again supreme in all categories of traditional naval vessels.

Indeed, well before this the concern with French parity in ships of the line and frigates—the original justification for the invasion scare—had been replaced with a new source of alarm: the supposed French superiority in ironclads. That the great wooden ships built so hurriedly as a result of the first phase of the panic would be rendered obsolete by the ironclads that occasioned its second phase was an irony that Cobden made good use of in his pamphlet. But his purpose was not primarily to point up the irrationality or gullibility of his fellow parliamentarians or even to demonstrate the incompetence of the Admiralty. Once again he set out, through analysis of official and readily available sources, to prove that the perception of French superiority was a myth, based on a misreading—indeed, a misrepresentation—of the facts.

That being the case, it followed that the measures taken in response to the French threat—the crash naval building program, the formation of volunteer corps, and, above all, the fortification scheme—were unnecessary and dangerously provocative acts. Furthermore, he argued, they were militarily unsound. This was obviously the case with the building of wooden-hulled ships after virtually every authority condemned them as useless, but Cobden also cited a number of experts to call into question the wisdom of defending England with fixed fortifications. Even Palmerston's often repeated but rarely challenged dictum that "steam had bridged the Channel"[20] did not go unanswered. The introduction of steam power benefited the defense as much, some said more, than the offense, Cobden noted.

Although such conclusions were undeniably matters of opinion, Cobden's critique of the invasion panic was not, and he not unreasonably hoped that the pamphlet might influence the future disposition of measures undertaken during the panic, now that the panic had subsided. In this he was disappointed. The pamphlet was largely ignored, a fact that Cobden attributed to a conspiracy of silence among those who were embarrassed in retrospect that they had succumbed to panic. That may well have been true, but Cobden was also unlucky in his timing. He finished the pamphlet just as the deterioration of Anglo-American relations arising out of the American Civil War was shifting the focus of British foreign policy concerns away from Europe. In view of that, he considered delaying or even abandoning publication of the pamphlet, but in the end he decided to meet the problem head on, if somewhat awkwardly, by incorporating a few comments on America into the final pages of the pamphlet.

Bad luck and a hostile audience were not the only factors working against the success of *The Three Panics*, however. In many respects it was the least good of Cobden's pamphlets. It was self-defeatingly one-sided: Cobden did not include in it any of the criticisms of French policy that he had made privately to his French friends. Moreover, it lacked the historical or theoretical framework that distinguished his earlier writings. This is puzzling, since the obvious unifying theme, the revolutionary consequences of the application of industrial technology to the weapons of war, appeared repeatedly in his correspondence and was the core of his memorandum to Palmerston and Napoleon (which was tacked on to the pamphlet as an appendix). The technological revolution in weaponry occupied only four of 160 pages, and too much of the remainder was taken up with extracts or summaries of parliamentary debates. In *The Three Panics* Cobden expertly accomplished the demolition job he set out to do; but he missed the opportunity he may have had to influence the terms of debate on military policy.

Although Cobden continued to do battle with Palmerston and warmed to the task during the 1862 session of parliament, the writing of *The Three Panics* marked the end of his campaign to alter the course of British rearmament. His attacks on the prime minister were different in tone from what they had been in 1860 or 1861; they were no longer so urgent, so desperate. The great battles on specific policies had been won or lost, after all; Cobden had his treaty, Palmerston his ships and forts. The struggle now was for no less important stakes—the character of the Liberal party, even of parliamentary government, as Cobden saw it—but these were not matters that could or perhaps should be settled quickly. A temporary victory such as he had won in the House of Commons over the *Arrow* incident might again count for nothing. Nor was even such a victory likely. In June Palmerston was able to defeat a motion concocted by some of the younger radicals in favor of economy in government, through a combination of personal popularity and the threat of an appeal to the electorate on the pattern of 1857.

There was some room for hope, however, in the fact that the Conservative front bench had briefly joined in the attack, a sign perhaps that Palmerston's immunity from serious partisan opposition might be about to end. That, together with the renewed vigor of the radicals, sufficed to bring Cobden back to an active role in the House of Commons for the first time in five years—since his Pyrrhic victory over the *Arrow* incident, in fact—but the skill and force with which Palmerston was able to deflect the radical and Tory challenge of June 1862 demonstrated that no amount of parliamentary maneuvering could bring the prime minister down. The tide could only be turned by a sustained assault on the roots of Palmerston's popularity, a task that Cobden undertook almost in the spirit of a moral crusade late in the 1862 session of Parliament. As one observer said of the climactic confrontation between Palmerston and Cobden at the end of the session, "there they stood, unreconciled and irreconcilable—the representatives of two widely different epochs, and of two widely different types of English life."[21]

That caught it nicely. Cobden attacked the prime minister savagely—among other things, he calculated that Palmerston personally, through his policies and crotchets, had cost the country some £100,000,000—but Cobden denied, rightly, that he was indulging in personal politics in the ordinary sense. He attacked Palmerston because Palmerston "represented himself a policy"[22] and, Cobden might have added, a manner of conducting the affairs of the nation. For it was as much the character of Palmerstonianism as any specific policies that Cobden sought to expose. Parliament itself was being brought into disrepute, he argued. The prime minister professed to lead a Liberal government but ruled illiberally with Tory connivance, and the Tories, by acquiescing in this, had power without responsibility. But it was with the political emasculation of the Liberals that Cobden was especially concerned. "If a party has no principles," he said, "it has been called a faction;—I would call it a nuisance. If a party violates its professed principles, then I think that party should be called an imposture. These are hard words, yet they are precisely the measures which, sooner or later, will be meted out to parties by public opinion; and, late as it now is, it may be well if we . . . should view our position, in order to see how we shall be able to bear the inquest when the day comes, as it will come, for our conduct and our character to be brought into judgement."

Politics on this basis could not last, Cobden warned. It could not last another session, he told the House, and to Bright he suggested that, had

Bright not retreated from Parliament to Scotland before the end of the 1862 session, they might already have placed Palmerston on the defensive. In these predictions, as in the tone of his valedictory address that session, there was a strong resemblance to the later phases of the anti–Corn Law campaign. In 1862, as then, with a curious mixture of passionate commitment and Olympian detachment, Cobden was foretelling the imminent demise of a system that he abhorred. There was this difference: early in the 1840s he had commanded the means of helping to fulfill his prophesy. In 1862 he could speak, with certainty, only for himself. He commanded respect but no significant forces in or out of Parliament. Cobden adjusted to this well and quickly, as his increasing confidence during the 1862 session of Parliament shows, but there is no question that he had expected until well into 1861 to be able to bring greater weight to bear. That this effort, like the peace movement a decade earlier, should have ended in failure, and that the Commercial Treaty, like the repeal of the Corn Laws, should have come to be seen as an end in itself rather than as an opening to other achievements, were among the great disappointments in Cobden's life.

In that sense the politics of the third panic and British rearmament belong less to the life of Cobden than to that of Gladstone, for whom this period was decisive in his movement away from his Conservative past, his Whig colleagues, and even his Peelite friends toward a redefined Liberalism strongly influenced by the radicalism of the Manchester school. As the chief student of Gladstone's rise to power put it, the invasion scare and British rearmament and, above all, the Commercial Treaty and its negotiation, "through bringing him [Gladstone] closer to Cobden, brought him close to Bright."[23] Even that compensation for the frustrations of 1860–61 was not to be realized in full immediately, however, for the process was deflected by a crisis that even Cobden regarded as more pressing than the question of the naval arms race in Europe, the American Civil War.

CHAPTER 23

Britain and the American Civil War

No event during Cobden's thirty-year career more deeply affected him than the American Civil War. That America—to which he had looked ever since he wrote the pamphlets with which he began his public life as the practical corrective to the abuses of old world politics and diplomacy—might actually destroy itself was to Cobden an almost unimaginable disaster, as much for the world at large as for the American people. At first, from the moment the secession of the southern states became likely, and even for a time after hostilities broke out, Cobden believed that the North should let the South go in peace. War, any war, was so abhorrent to him and the costs of war, especially a civil war, appeared so certain to outweigh any benefits, that he would have conceded almost anything to the Confederate states. Cynics might suggest that he was influenced in this by his stake in the future of the Illinois Central Railroad, which depended on peaceful North-South commerce, but that is to apply economic determinism of the crudest kind. Cobden's investments reflected his vision of America, not the other way around. A union preserved by force would be no union; the wounds of a civil war would heal slowly, if at all. Better, in Cobden's view, that the North—his America—should preserve its own strength than weaken itself in the process of subduing a proud and unrepentant South.

Bright disagreed, passionately, and the two friends continued to see the war—the overriding issue of these years for both of them—differently almost until its final stages. This did not strain their friendship, however, as had their differences in the postrepeal years. In the interim they had shared the trials of lonely opposition to the Crimean war, and each had passed through terrible personal trials. They valued their friendship more than ever. Also they now dealt with one another as equals. Indeed, since Cobden was consciously past the summit of his career, he often deferred to Bright tactically. Cobden continued to tender advice to Bright but he did so in the tone of an older to a younger and still rising statesman, not as master to pupil. There was no longer any question of Bright's having to step out from under Cobden's shadow, as had been the case a decade earlier, a process that would have strained their relationship even had there been no disagreements between them.

Certainly their differences over America were no less deep. Bright identified with the North and with its methods during the Civil War in a way that Cobden, for all his love of the United States, never allowed himself to do. This has often been misunderstood, not least by Cobden's official biographer, John Morley, who believed that "Cobden did not at first seize the true significance of the struggle," that "his sympathies wavered," and that he was "slow to take the side of the North," in part because of the free trade tradition of the South, but primarily because he was so anxious to avoid war. Morley also recounted how it was that Cobden "tolerably soon came round to a correct view of the issues at stake, partly under the influence of Mr. Bright," who, in conversations with Cobden during the summer of 1861, purportedly persuaded Cobden to a view of the war similar to his own.[1] The upshot of all this was Cobden's first comments on the war, delivered in a speech to his constituents at Rochdale late in the year.

Virtually all of this is misleading, as Donald Read has shown. In his Rochdale speech, most of which was devoted to Anglo-French relations, Cobden mentioned the Civil War only in passing and then only to suggest a policy of nonintervention by the other powers. This was hardly evidence of a change in Cobden's attitude toward the war; quite the contrary in fact. As to the conversations between Bright and Cobden on the war, Morley gave no source for his account but presumably got the information from Bright, who, not for the first time, recollected his relationship with Cobden in self-serving terms. Read made much of this, comparing the incident with Bright's faulty recollection of his first meeting with Cobden in 1837 and of their Leamington compact in 1841. What Read, unfairly to Bright, did not say was that Bright could quite innocently have misinterpreted the change that did take place in Cobden's thinking during the summer of

1861. Following the battle of Bull Run, Cobden had finally to abandon the hope that the conflict could be settled peacefully and to accept the inevitability of a long and bloody war. To Bright, who certainly wanted unanimity with Cobden, this could easily have been interpreted as evidence that Cobden was moving his way. But it was not: whereas Bright identified with the North in its war effort, Cobden identified with the North in spite of or beyond the war. The difference was fundamental.

That Morley should have misinterpreted Cobden's views on the war is puzzling, since he had access to the full Bright-Cobden correspondence and was writing twenty years after the event. Perhaps, as in part of his account of the early days of the league, Morley was writing too much from hindsight, for in the final stages of the war the prospect of an imminent northern victory produced a practical identity of views between Cobden and Bright that obscured their differences. In any case, by accepting the notion of a radical change in Cobden's thinking in 1861, Morley misrepresented both his earlier and later views on the war. Cobden never wavered in his sympathies, nor did he have to be brought round to siding with the North; but to be pro-North did not necessarily mean being pro-war, at least not at first, nor, uncritically, even much later on. A year and a half after his supposed conversion, Cobden was still urging Bright not to become too closely identified with the Union:

> The Federals . . . have shown frightful incapacity; we cannot shut our eyes to the fact that they are very unsound and ignorant on economical questions . . . and they have launched a weapon of warfare in the abolition proclamation, which, although we approve the object aimed at, may lead to excesses which we may deplore. I am strongly impressed with the conviction that we must avoid being thrust into the attitude of either partisans or champions of the Federal party, if we would hold a position favorable for the advocacy of neutrality.[2]

If Cobden remained so cautious even after the battle of Antietam and the Emancipation Proclamation, it is inconceivable that he would have committed himself to the Union in the early stages of the war. After Bull Run he may have become resigned to the war, but he remained far from certain (as Bright was certain) that the North could win more than a Pyrrhic victory. Nor did he view the war itself with less horror. On the contrary, to his growing certainty that the two sides could never again live in harmony was added a fear that the

North, in the wake of military reverses, would come increasingly under the control of the radical abolitionists, thus opening the way to a bloody slave uprising in the South. That this would end the war, secession, and slavery itself, Cobden of course recognized, and he always maintained that only the abolition of slavery could justify a great civil war; but the likely cost of victory even in such a just cause was more than he could bear to contemplate.

Unable to reconcile his hopes and fears about the war, Cobden retreated to what was in any case his natural position, advocating a policy of nonintervention in America by the other powers. As Cobden frequently pointed out to his friends—and occasionally hinted in public—he did not regard nonintervention in this instance as equivalent to neutrality (any more than he had regarded nonintervention as a policy of inaction a decade earlier). Whatever the military outcome or the success of the South in establishing its independence in the short run, Cobden was certain that the future of America was in the North, with its overwhelming advantages in wealth and economic development and, above all, in its possession of a vast pool of free labor. Slavery was not only evil, Cobden believed, it was doomed economically. Left to itself, America was bound to be dominated by the North, at least in the long run. Nonintervention was also far from being neutrality in that any foreign interference in the American Civil War was bound to favor the Confederacy. As the North tightened its blockade of southern ports and supplies of cotton to Europe dried up, the likelihood increased that one or more European states might intervene, either militarily to break the blockade or diplomatically to recognize the Confederacy. Cobden himself opposed the blockade: on principle—because he believed wartime restrictions on trade should extend only to contraband goods; as an instrument of warfare—because he was certain that it would be circumvented as Napoleon's continental system had been; and on diplomatic grounds—because he feared that it might provoke a wider war.

But much as he might dislike this and other methods of the North in fighting the war, Cobden did not regard it as sufficient reason for military preparations by the European powers, let along for military action, or even for concerted pressure on the American government. Thus, as the war moved rapidly toward total war during 1861, he became increasingly concerned, although he said little and did nothing as long as he judged that the European powers were likely to act with restraint. In November, however, the Confederate commissioners to Britain and France, Mason and Slidell, were seized from the English vessel, *Trent*, by an American warship. Cobden, fearing not only that the incident might lead to conflict but that it would bring all the latent resentment against Union policies, especially the blockade, to the surface, immediately began to do what he could to avert a crisis. For the third time in as many years, he embarked on a campaign of personal diplomacy.

Cobden was in an unusually good position to do something behind the diplomatic scenes during the American Civil War. He had excellent and recent contacts at or near the highest levels in all three of the countries most immediately involved, Britain, France, and the United States itself, and his reputation as an internationalist allowed him a latitude in dealing with the French and the Americans that few other Englishmen could match (although the same reputation probably limited his effectiveness at home). Still, with the British cabinet divided on American policy throughout the war, Cobden was likely to be able to use his access to Milner Gibson, Villiers, Gladstone, and, to a lesser degree, Russell to good effect. He was scarcely less well placed to monitor and influence French policy. Between Chevalier, Persigny, and Rouher, Cobden could be certain of a hearing in government circles.

His American connections were perhaps the most impressive, because the most unexpected. While in the United States in 1859, he had met a number of the men who were soon to serve in Lincoln's cabinet. His most important American friend was Charles Sumner, the chairman of the Senate Foreign Relations Committee and an advisor to Lincoln in matters of foreign policy equal to Secretary of State Seward. Sumner and Cobden had been occasional correspondents for more than a decade before the Civil War, drawn together by their shared interest in the international peace movement. Although they met personally only a couple of times in their lives, by the time the war broke out, each was so confident of the discretion and fundamental sympathy of the other that they felt able to communicate their private sentiments freely and to rely on one another as unofficial conduits of information and ideas to and from their respective governments.

By chance, while in Boston in 1859, Cobden had also met Lincoln's ambassador to London during the war, Charles Francis Adams. They were not overly impressed with one another on first meeting. Adams thought Cobden "a man of capacity and information, but without any of the lighter graces and refinements which are only given by a first class education, a modern Englishman of the reform school."[3] Although Cobden was also ambivalent, he was the only British politician of consequence Adams knew when he arrived in England in 1861, and their regard for each other grew through regular contacts during Adams's four years as ambassador. Cobden had known John Bigelow, the American consul in France during the war, both longer and far better than Adams. They first met on one of Bigelow's earlier trips to Europe and cemented their friendship while Cobden was in Paris negotiating the Commercial Treaty. Like most of Cobden's American contacts, Bigelow did not always take seriously or take kindly to Cobden's criticisms and suggestions. At one point during the war Bigelow noted that Cobden "anticipates a financial crisis in America, which nothing can remedy, of course, but his favoriate panacea, free trade."[4] There was, however, as much affection as irritation in that observation, and they remained close until Cobden's death at the end of the war.

Cobden had been reluctant to use these contacts before the *Trent* affair made it riskier not to do so. His bitter personal experience with the politics of war led him to favor a policy of personal as much as of national nonintervention. As late as the end of November 1861, he refused to "say . . . one word about your troubles" to Sumner. "I made a vow during the Crimean War," he explained, "that if ever another war broke out between England and any other power I should not utter a word with a view of shortening its duration, for reason and argument are lost in the clash of armed men, whose struggle can only be concluded by the exhaustion of one or both parties."[5] In the midst of writing this letter, however, Cobden received news of the *Trent* affair, and although it did not alter his determination never "to utter a word about the merits of a war after it begins," he did "not less feel it my duty to try to prevent hostilities occurring," so suddenly had war become possible between Britain and the United States.

That it was peculiarly his duty to intervene followed, he believed, not only from his nearly unique contacts at home and abroad but also from the fact that he thought the United States to be in the wrong in the *Trent* affair and that he was one of the few Englishmen in a position to say so with some effect to his American friends. For the remainder of the war, he told Sumner, "I write to you what I would not write to any other American—nay, what it would be perhaps improper for any other Englishman than myself to utter to any other American but yourself. But we are," he concluded, "both more of Christians and Cosmopolitans than British or Yankee."[6] Having written nothing to Sumner during the first half year of the war, Cobden sent him seven letters in the two months leading up to the settlement of the *Trent* affair. Bluntly he pointed out that the United States was wrong, probably in law and certainly morally, and that the seizure of Mason and Slidell violated America's best maritime traditions, while vindicating the British practice of narrowly circumscribing the rights of neutrals. For its own sake, he argued, the United States must submit the matter to arbitration.

At the same time he was urging this course on Sumner, Cobden put what pressure he could on the British government to respond with forbearance. On 29 November, the day the cabinet first discussed the *Trent* affair, Cobden called twice at Downing Street to urge avoidance of provocative measures. Furious at what he regarded as the unnecessary bellicosity of some of the longer term measures that were, nonetheless, ordered by Palmerston—such as sending reinforcements to Canada in the dead of winter, months before hostilities were possible—Cobden wrote to Gladstone and Villiers pleading with them not to be drawn into supporting illiberal policies. Cobden played with particular skill on Gladstone's sensibilities, reminding the former Peelite of how bitterly Lord Aberdeen had come to regret his part in the origins of the Crimean war, reminding the coauthor of the French Commercial Treaty of how their joint work had been almost wrecked by Palmerston's anti-French policies, reminding the politician of conscience that "if we force a war on the twenty millions of the free states . . . it will be remembered against us to all future generations," since "for the South and Slavery—if Christianity is to survive—there can be no future."[7] Cobden also spoke out publicly. Although illness prevented him from attending a dinner for Bright in Rochdale in December, he wrote his constituents condemning the government for reacting hastily before it was even certain whether the seizure of the *Trent* was the act of an individual naval captain or sanctioned by the United States.

Cobden and Bright had no direct effect on the outcome of the *Trent* affair, which was resolved not by arbitration (as they suggested) but— largely through Prince Albert's influence—by wording the British ultimatum in such a way as to allow the United States to back down gracefully. Nonetheless, they contributed to the climate in which this solution was hit upon and, beyond that, to a moderating of the public temper, which would have made a resort to war by the British government increasingly unlikely, even had the American response been unfavorable. More specifically, if Horace Rumbold was correct, Cobden's calls at Downing Street on 29 November were "so far successful that he prevailed on Lord P., through Sir G. Cornewall Lewis, not to order out the channel fleet . . . which he had at first intended to do."[8] As for the letter to Gladstone, although it did not alter his thinking, since he was already an advocate of a wait-and-see attitude, it did strengthen his resolve and may have strengthened his hand with his colleagues. He was impressed with Cobden's arguments, and we know that he passed the letter on to at least one other member of the cabinet. Cobden's correspondence also had an influence on the other side of the Atlantic, where, along with Bright's, it was read by Sumner to the critical cabinet meeting at which it was decided to release Mason and Slidell.

The importance to be attached to all this depends, in the end, on an assessment of how likely it was that either the British or the American government was willing to risk war over an individual incident such as the *Trent* affair. For his part Cobden tended to discount the possibility in this case, except as the result of miscalculation by one side or the other. He intervened to prevent such miscalculation, not the war that he thought both sides wished to avoid. More serious, in his view, was what lay behind the *Trent* affair: the growing determination of the Union to cut off the Confederacy from the rest of the world and the inevitable reaction that such action would produce in western Europe. He therefore used the *Trent* affair as an occasion to raise with his American friends and the British public the issues of the blockade and of international maritime law that he hoped could be pushed to the forefront of Anglo-American and Franco-American relations.

For a year after the *Trent* affair, until the battle of Antietam and the Emancipation Proclamation began to tip the military as well as the moral balance of the war against the South, Cobden was haunted with good reason by the possibility of European intervention to circumvent or break the blockade, which he assumed would follow almost inevitably once supplies of cotton dried up and Lancashire and

Picardy were thrown into depression. He did not share the common Confederate assumption that cotton was king, however. Britain's need for northern grain almost balanced off her need for southern cotton, in his view, and the British governing class was ambivalent about the blockade itself, since northern policy provided both an endorsement of past British practice and a precedent for restrictive commercial policies in future wars. If European intervention was to take place, Cobden believed that it was quite likely to be at the instigation of France, which was historically averse to blockades, was more one-sidedly linked to the southern economy than Britain, and saw in American disunity a route to empire in Mexico. At home, however, the danger lay in a temporary and superficial but nonetheless dangerous alignment between cotton-starved industrial interests and that segment of the upper class that disliked the urban and democratic North but felt a kinship with the hierarchical society of the agrarian South.

Broadening the private initiatives that he had begun with the *Trent* affair, Cobden did what he could to prevent a conjunction of these forces, which remained a possibility even after Antietam. He wrote frequently to Chevalier in Paris, although he questioned whether his old friend was close enough to the center of power to be of much use as a source of information or as a transmitter of Cobden's ideas. Thus, when Chevalier too succumbed to the lure of empire in Mexico, Cobden turned to his French counterpart in the Commercial Treaty negotiations, Rouher. Cobden had better sources of information as well as a more receptive audience within the British government; the noninterventionist wing of the cabinet, led by the Duke of Argyll, Milner Gibson, and Villiers, never wavered. Cobden was unable to do as much publicly as he would have liked, however. His health no longer allowed him to stump the country, and even in Parliament a recurrence of his throat condition forced him to cancel important speeches on the blockade and maritime law on at least two occasions in 1862. He compensated for this as best he could by writing for the *Star* and through letters to business leaders and local chambers of commerce.

His message to all his correspondents, English and French, and to his rare public audiences was essentially the same. He emphasized the enormous power of the North and its determination to carry on with the war, almost regardless of cost. This being the case, he argued, whatever anyone might think of that determination, any attempt at foreign interference would have the effect of galvanizing northern opinion, thus prolonging, not shortening, the war and ensuring that supplies of cotton, far from being made available, would become virtually unobtainable. Intervention, Cobden believed, was not only morally wrong but could be economically disastrous.

Not that even Cobden was unaffected by the pressure for some sort of intervention. In the autumn of 1862, at the height of the European clamor against the war, when distress in the cotton districts was worsening every day and there seemed to be no prospect of an end to the conflict, Cobden suggested to Chevalier "an appeal made by all Europe to the North to put an end to the blockade of the South against legitimate commerce on the grounds of humanity—accompanied with the offer of making the abolition of commercial blockades the principle of international law for the future."[9] But that was as far as he would go. Indeed, in the same letter he clearly stated, "I am against violence to put an end to the war. We should not thereby obtain cotton. Nor should we coerce the North. We should only intensify the animosity between the two sections."

Even his suggestion of moral suasion by the powers was an aberration. Both earlier and later in the war, he thought in less formal, more personal terms and specifically of capitalizing on his and Bright's position as foreign friends of the United States. That Cobden, the most principled of noninterventionists, should have considered the use of public and concerted pressure at all is the best evidence of just how intense the feeling was in England that something had to be done.

To his American contacts, therefore, Cobden argued that the blockade could not win the war for the North and might well lose it for them or at least encourage the South to fight on by inviting foreign interference. That this did not happen early in 1862, as Cobden had at first predicted, was not proof that it would not. Action had been delayed, but perhaps only delayed, until the results of the peninsula campaign were known and because there were larger stocks of cotton in Europe than most observers, Cobden included, had at first been aware of. By the summer of 1862, however, all this had changed. McClellan had withdrawn in failure from the outskirts of Richmond, and cotton stocks in Europe had been nearly exhausted. The time of crisis had arrived, and in the absence of a northern victory, it could only be passed through safely, Cobden believed, if the North lifted or drastically modified the blockade.

Cobden was correct in thinking that the autumn of 1862 was the season of greatest danger and equally correct in his assessment that the North could only avert the danger of foreign intervention by adjusting its policies or demonstrating that it could win the war. Yet there was little he could do beyond reiterating these warnings and attempting to educate anyone who would listen on either shore of the Atlantic as to the state of thinking on the other shore. He called a number of times on Adams to state his case but the ambassador, although acknowledging that "much of what he [Cobden] said is wise and practical,"[10] refused to budge on the principle of the blockade and fobbed his insistent caller off with vague assurances that the enforcement of the blockade might be modified once the North had captured more southern ports.

One of Cobden's frustrations during 1862 was that there was no dramatic event comparable to the *Trent* affair that he could use to strengthen his case for restraint. Thus, although he had felt justified in inundating Sumner with letters during the *Trent* crisis, Cobden wrote his chief American contact only once during the remainder of 1862. Sumner had already been made perhaps too well aware of Cobden's views; to have repeated them without the justification of some major new development might have proved counterproductive. Cobden's one letter was written following what was certainly the most important event affecting the blockade, the capture of New Orleans. This allowed the North to develop a more flexible blockade policy, and because it was by now clear that the blockade itself would never be lifted entirely, Cobden took what comfort he could from the thought that his letter (and a similar one from the Duke of Argyll) may have contributed to that flexibility.

At home the most serious threat to peace came and largely went before Cobden was even aware of it. During September the three most powerful men in the British government, Palmerston, Russell, and Gladstone, substantially agreed on a proposal for a joint Anglo-French offer of mediation, followed by some form of recognition of the South, which but for the battle of Antietam they would very likely have pursued even at the risk of conflict with the North. As it was, the news of Lee's retreat south of the Potomac had the effect of strengthening the advocates of a wait-and-see policy within the cabinet, largely because Palmerston temporarily joined them. The moment for European intervention had in fact passed for good, although no one could have been certain of that at the time. The discussion of possible British interference continued for some months not only within the government but, for the first time, by individual members of the government in public.

The first and most dramatic hint of what was afoot came from Gladstone in a speech in Newcastle early in October. Speaking only for himself, although it was widely assumed that he must be speaking for the government, he referred to the South, in a famous phrase he was later to regret, as having "made a nation."[11] Cobden was aghast not only because of what this revealed about the trend of official thinking but because it undermined his confidence in Gladstone's judgment, a confidence built up during the negotiation of the Commercial Treaty but already somewhat eroded by the recent controversy over military spending. The problem was not that Gladstone was wrong in principle but, in Cobden's view, that, as with the issue of military spending, Gladstone came to the wrong practical conclusion, despite his agreement in principle with Cobden.

Gladstone's initial response to the Civil War was similar to Cobden's, closer in many respects than Cobden's was to Bright's. Like both Cobden and Bright, Gladstone favored the preservation of the Union, but unlike Bright and very much like Cobden, he was ambivalent about the use of force to preserve that Union against the desire of the South for self-determination and skeptical of the North's ability to win the war. Also like Cobden, Gladstone was appalled at the length and cost of the conflict and fearful of a slave uprising should it go on. It was therefore understandable that Gladstone should have looked to concerted action by the European powers as a means of bringing an end to the horrors of an apparently interminable war, but this, in Cobden's view, did not make such intervention practicable. As the war dragged on, Cobden became even more firmly convinced that the Americans, North and South, would have to learn the lessons of the war for themselves and that any attempt to dictate a peace from the outside would only add to the legacy of bitterness. Nor was there any guarantee that it would succeed. Indeed, given the power and determination of the North, Cobden was certain that foreign interference, far from shortening or containing the war, would have the opposite effect.

That is a judgment in which most later historians and, in the long run, Gladstone himself concurred. That Gladstone failed to recognize this in 1862 marked, for Cobden, the breaking point in an already strained relationship. "I am sometimes inclined to suspect," he wrote Bright, "that we have had his quota of usefulness as a public man from Gladstone."[12] This was no temporary disillusionment. Cobden's correspondence with Gladstone, a staple of both their political lives since 1859, was broken off for more than a year. In view of how many of his political hopes Cobden had invested in Gladstone, this estrangement left him more cut off from the centers of policy making than he had been since the years of semiretirement following the Crimean war.

Luckily for his peace of mind during the winter of 1862–63, the trend in Anglo-American relations moved steadily away from confrontation. The process had begun even before Gladstone's Newcastle speech and was given further impetus a week later by George Cornewall Lewis, Secretary for War and leader of the cautious middle group in the cabinet, who publicly dismissed the suggestion of recognition of the South as dangerously premature. Since the debate was now at least partly out in the open, Cobden was kept informed of the balance of opinion in the cabinet by Villiers and Gibson, and, although their reports of Gladstone's views continued to disappoint, the general trend was encouraging. As early as February 1863 Cobden felt able to assure Sumner "that any unfriendly act on the part of our Government . . . towards your cause is not to be apprehended."[13]

Cobden attributed this primarily to the effect of the Emancipation Proclamation and the enthusiastic public response to it in England in closing "the mouths of those who have been advocating the side of the South." Although almost no one would now accept that interpretation of events uncritically, Cobden's emphasis on the central importance of the Emancipation Proclamation in transforming public attitudes in England toward the Civil War is understandable, given his view of the war and of the dynamics of English politics. As he had often told his American friends, Europeans saw little to choose in principle early in the war between a protectionist North and a slaveholding South and therefore tended to judge the war entirely in terms of their economic interests. Hence the danger of intervention.

Furthermore, Cobden had always believed that the traditional English governing class—antidemocratic and therefore antinorthern in the Civil War—was able to dominate English politics only so long as the English middle class was not stirred to action. The importance of the Emancipation Proclamation in England was that it provided precisely that distinction in principle between North and South that was most likely to rouse the moral fervor of the English middle class. Thus, as Cobden would have answered the modern revisionists, it mattered little that some in England criticized the proclamation as opportunistic and potentially dangerous or that there remained a large residue of sympathy for the South and antipathy toward the North even among the English middle and working classes. The Emancipation Proclamation had placed the South morally on the defensive, and that would have made it exceedingly difficult for the British government to recognize the Confederacy, even had the South won the battle of Antietam. In combination with Antietam, the Emancipation Proclamation placed the South beyond the pale.

Although the danger of foreign intervention on behalf of the South was over, Cobden had failed to get the benefits he had hoped for from the blockade controversy. Characteristically, almost from the moment the blockade was imposed, he saw it as a potential opening through which to pursue an issue that linked his work as a free trader directly with his later efforts in the peace movement, the reform of maritime law. Specifically he hoped to broaden what had been achieved by the Congress of Paris at the end of the Crimean war in limiting the right of blockade and extending the rights of neutrals in time of war to include the protection of all private property at sea and further restrict the right of blockade. Ironically the United States had made just such a proposal to the Paris Congress, only to have Britain, with its long tradition of waging economic warfare on the high seas, reject it. Had this not happened, Cobden enjoyed pointing out, there would have been no northern blockade and thus no cotton famine.

Now, however, with the United States conducting economic warfare and powerful British interests suffering as a result, Cobden felt that the time might have arrived to establish a consensus in favor of commercial freedom in time of war among the great trading nations. Especially at this moment it was easy to demonstrate that England, as the world's greatest commercial power, had the most to gain from unrestricted commerce at all times and the most to lose if traditional policies were adhered to. Cobden did not expect a revolution in thinking, let alone in policy, to come about quickly and almost certainly not in time to affect the conduct of the American Civil War. Rather he hoped that in the process of dealing with the crisis brought on by the northern blockade, England might be induced to take the lead in—or at least no longer obstruct—enlarging the scope of international law and further limiting the range (and thus the purpose) of warfare. As he said to Henry Ashworth, "If out of this sad civil war we could pluck so great and beneficent a prize as the establishing of the principle of free ports and free seas in future wars, it would be some consolation for the temporary sufferings and disappointments we are obliged to undergo."[14]

To this end he suggested in his letters to Sumner that the Americans lift or modify the blockade as part of a broad initiative to rewrite maritime law, thus forcing the hand of the British government. He also called on Ambassador Adams to suggest the same policy and corresponded with Chevalier in the hope of enlisting French support. At home Cobden wrote articles for the *Star* and prepared the ground for a major debate on maritime law in the House of Commons. (The debate was held in March 1862, but without Cobden as the central figure. Another M.P. had already proposed a similar motion and parliamentary etiquette required Cobden to withdraw his. Then, on the day of the debate he lost his voice.) Cobden also tried to press his friends into taking up the cause. He wrote to Henry Ashworth and Robertson Gladstone, the presidents of the Manchester and Liverpool chambers of commerce, and asked Bright to do the same. The letter to Ashworth was also widely disseminated in the press and published as a pamphlet. And finally, Cobden appeared in person before the Manchester Chamber of Commerce to urge them to take up this issue, as twenty-four years before they had taken up the issue of the Corn Laws: "We had to fight the battle for Free Trade, in time of peace, with our own governing class; and you will have to fight the battle again for Free Trade, in time of war, with the same class, as the only way of obtaining such a change in maritime law as will put it in harmony with the spirit and the exigencies of our age."[15]

Little came of all this effort, which occupied much of Cobden's time throughout 1862. Neither the British nor the United States government wanted to deal with the issues of free seas and free ports, and the economic interests most affected were too preoccupied with the immediate problems raised by the shortage of cotton to be interested in trying to force the hand of the British government on a question of principle. Cobden's researches into the recent history of maritime law were not entirely wasted, however. While studying the Parliamentary papers he came across a note sent to the United States during the Crimean war by England on behalf of the allies, warning the Americans not to violate neutrality by resupplying Russian privateers. When, in 1863, the United States was trying to put a stop to the foreign victualling of Confederate raiders, Cobden informed Bigelow in Paris of the note as a way of helping him put pressure on the French to end the practice and, beyond that, of furthering his own aim of securing legitimate commerce from all forms of attack at sea.

Whatever the frustrations of Cobden's attempts to limit the scope of economic warfare, he proved very effective when it came to helping the innocent victims of that warfare in his political home ground of Lancashire. Indeed, throughout the worst period of distress in the cotton districts, in late 1862 and early 1863, he had considerable and at one point a decisive influence on the conduct of relief policy. Like many others, Cobden at first expected the blockade to produce a sudden crisis affecting the whole of the British economy. He underestimated cotton stocks on hand and overestimated the dependence of the British economy as a whole on the cotton industry. By the end of 1861, however, he had scaled down his predictions to a fairly accurate estimate of the scope and duration of the crisis to come, which he nonetheless continued to see as an extraordinary event in itself and therefore in the means required to deal with it.

Thus, as the situation worsened early in 1862, he joined a number of Lancashire M.P.s in urging the government to act, and when this pressure produced a modest measure, the Union Relief Bill, to spread the financial burden of poor relief more evenly among the areas affected, Cobden took a leading role in seeking to have the bill broadened. In an emergency of this magnitude, he argued, and especially in an emergency that all agreed was temporary, the ordinary regulations governing poor relief should not be applied. To require that the full cost be borne by current poor rates or to spread part of the burden over a wider area would only add to the weight of distress by impoverishing the most vulnerable ratepayers: shopkeepers whose customers were in arrears and frugal factory hands who owned their own homes. Instead, Cobden suggested, the local Poor Law authorities had to be given the power to borrow against future payments, as well as the right to lend money to the honest unemployed. All of the

Lancashire M.P.s supported amendments along these lines, and the relief bill as passed incorporated most of their suggestions. Even then, however, the local Poor Law authorities were not in a position to cope with the full burden of distress during the cotton famine. Nor was it intended that they should be. Private charity was expected to step in to ease the plight of the deserving poor, as virtually all the victims of the cotton famine were acknowledged to be, and in July, just before the relief bill was debated in the Parliament, a relief committee was founded under the chairmanship of Lord Derby. Cobden played no part in forming the committee but he profoundly affected its character as a national institution when nearly four months later he was drawn into its deliberations.

This happened almost by chance. After the end of the 1862 parliamentary session the Cobdens spent a long holiday in Scotland. On his way back south Cobden stopped in Lancashire, briefly so he thought, in part to press the Manchester Chamber of Commerce on the issue of maritime law, in part to report to his Rochdale constituents, and also to see for himself the effects of the cotton famine. Even before visiting Lancashire he had been sufficiently troubled about conditions there to chastise Bright for not taking a prominent role "in some of the more public proceedings respecting the state and prosperity of the districts to which you belong,"[16] and Cobden continued to press the issue indirectly through mutual friends such as Henry Ashworth well into the autumn. (All this was before, and perhaps contributed to, Bright's public relations coup in December of arranging with a number of Yankee merchants to donate and transport food for the unemployed cotton workers of Lancashire.)

For his part, Cobden was so appalled by his firsthand encounter with the effects of the cotton famine that he extended his stay in Lancashire into November—at considerable risk to his health—in the hope of spurring the public and private agencies responsible for relief into adopting more ambitious policies. His opportunity came when, as a courtesy, he was invited to become a member of the largely ceremonial general committee of the relief campaign. Immediately after his name was added to the committee's roll, as he told his fellow members at the end of the meeting, "the first thing I asked my neighbor here was—'What are the functions of the General Committee?' And I have heard that they amount to nothing more than to attend here once a month, and receive the report of the executive committee as to the business done and the distribution of funds."[17] That inspired Cobden to use his chance to speak, ostensibly in support of a vote of thanks to the mayor of Manchester, to make a bold proposal—as unexpected to him as it was to his audience—to recast completely the purpose of the General Committee and the scale of its operations.

In essence he suggested that the committee take on itself the management of an unprecedentedly large and truly national fund-raising campaign. That this was urgently needed he had no doubt. The loss of wages was running at an annual rate of £7,000,000, and there was no way that this could be compensated for out of the poor rates of Lancashire without throwing additional thousands into pauperism. Indeed, he argued, not only the Poor Law in the cotton districts but the entire local economy was in danger of collapsing in upon itself. "It is totally exceptional," he warned the committee. "There has been nothing like it in the history of the world for its suddenness, for the impossibility of dealing with it, or managing it in the way of an effective remedy." The nation had to be made aware of this, he concluded, and sufficient funds raised sufficiently rapidly to prevent what he feared the most: a mass exodus of the unemployed work force from Lancashire.

Cobden had no doubts how this should be done because he had a model in mind (a model he did not name to a nonpartisan committee headed by the Earl of Derby): the Anti–Corn Law League. The General Committee in its capacity as a fund-raising committee should circularize the lord lieutenants of every county and the mayors of every borough, send delegations to the more important local officials, and co-opt them onto the General Committee if that was necessary to ensure the creation of local committees all over the country. Cobden also advocated a fund-raising goal that in itself would galvanize public opinion; it was entirely fitting that he, who in an act of political intuition had set the first fund-raising goal of the league at an unheard-of £50,000, should have closed his speech to the General Relief Committee by suggesting the figure of £1,000,000. The effect was all he could have asked for. Three days later, Derby, Cobden, and a few others met over dinner to work out a specific plan of campaign based on Cobden's suggestions, which was adopted unanimously by a specially convened meeting of the General Committee held the following week. Once the new system was securely under way, Cobden finally felt free to journey south with some sense of satisfaction, to retire to Dunford for the winter.

A few old-line Tories at the time, chronically suspicious of the cotton manufacturers, and a good many historians more recently ascribed much of the crisis in Lancashire to overproduction before the war, but Cobden never accepted this argument. Like most of his contemporaries, he assumed that the cotton famine was entirely genuine and the sole cause of distress, and he therefore rejected the notion that emigration should be looked to as a partial solution. "My experience," he observed acidly, "is that almost everybody wants everybody else to emigrate."[18] Stressing as he had from the beginning the temporary nature of the crisis, he looked to proposals that would keep the Lancashire work force and, so far as was possible, the Lancashire economy intact. He therefore endorsed a public works program in the cotton districts when it was proposed in the spring of 1863, at least as long as the projects involved real not make work, and he actively supported the Public Works Bill introduced by the government in June. Cobden's significant contribution to relieving the crisis had been made with his speech in Manchester seven months before, however, for the worst of the distress was over by the time the Public Works Act was passed. Unemployment reached its highest levels at the end of 1862 and began to decline the following spring, as alternative sources of cotton opened up and the price, driven up by panic, began to drop. Although there were subsequent ups and downs in the cotton industry until the end of the war and the relief committee did not disband until June 1865 (or approach the goal of £1,000,000 until two years after Cobden had set it), the greatest extent of distress had clearly been reached and coped with during the winter of 1862–63.

That, coming on top of the battle of Antietam and the Emancipation Proclamation, should have gradually diminished the importance of the American Civil War as an issue in Anglo-American relations. It did not, owing to a new source of tension that threatened war in 1863 and soured relations for a decade thereafter: the building of Confederate vessels of war in British shipyards. The issue first arose in 1862 when, despite pressure from the United States, the most famous of these ships, the *Alabama*, escaped from British jurisdiction to prey on northern commerce, largely because the British government delayed in deciding whether to take a broad or a narrow view of its own law governing neutrality, the Foreign Enlistment Act. Cobden, of course, had no such hesitation. Since his aim throughout the Civil War was to prevent foreign intervention and, beyond that, to expand the rule of international law as a means of narrowing the field of future wars, he argued that the prohibition against "equipping, furnishing, fitting out or arming" vessels to be used against a nation with which Britain was at peace should clearly extend to vessels built in Britain but armed elsewhere for that purpose.[19]

Thus when the depredations of the *Alabama* and the imminent completion of a number of additional ships—including two specially designed blockade breakers or rams—raised the issue with renewed urgency in 1863, Cobden inevitably took an active part in the controversy. On the diplomatic front he hoped to supplement normal channels of communication, which he distrusted throughout the war in view of the difficult personalities of Russell and Seward, by acting as an unofficial go-between for Russell and Sumner. Immediately after Sumner wrote Cobden in March 1863 concerning the ships then being built, Cobden "communicated privately with Lord Russell, urging him to be more than passive in enforcing the law respecting the building of ships for the Confederate Government."[20] Cobden came away from their meeting impressed with Russell's grasp of the situation and determination not to allow another *Alabama* incident. "He seems to promise fairly," Cobden concluded.

That being the case, Cobden did not confine himself to bringing pressure in favor of the American view on his own government or to giving his American contacts reassurances that they might not have believed coming from official quarters. On the contrary, because Russell appeared to be on the right side on this issue, Cobden placed equal pressure for moderation on Sumner, urging him to overlook the often brusque tone of the foreign secretary's dispatches and, more important, not to mix up the matter of ships with the larger question of munitions (as Ambassador Adams had already done), since that would cloud the issue and allow shipbuilders and Confederate sympathizers in Britain "to divert attention from the real question at issue . . . You must really keep the public mind right in America on this subject. Do not let it be supposed that you have any grievance against us for selling munitions of war . . . which it is not in the power of governments to prevent." If the Americans limited themselves to the issue of ships, Cobden believed, they would succeed, because the

British government was in its own interests moving toward a broad interpretation of the Foreign Enlistment Act. "It is necessary that your Government should know all this," Cobden concluded, "and I hope public opinion in England will be so alive to the necessity of enforcing the law that there will be no more difficulty in the matter."[21]

To help mobilize that public opinion, Cobden raised the issue in Parliament. He had to move with care, because, like Bright, he had earned the reputation of being too pro-Union in the war and even of consulting America's interests before those of his own country. He may have been correct in his assertion that Britain was largely responsible for its sufferings at the hands of the Union blockade, because Britain had long been the major obstacle to limiting the use of blockades, but that was a view that could easily be used against him, especially with his Lancashire constituents (a consideration that may have contributed to his taking, and urging Bright to take, a large role in the cotton famine relief efforts). In any case, Cobden was careful to preface a speech in which he endorsed the American interpretation of British law with assurances that he was looking only to British interests and with criticism of the mistakes of American policy as practiced by Adams and Seward.

Although Cobden did not limit himself to arguing from enlightened self-interest, the essence of his speech was that because of the extent of British overseas commerce "no other country in the world . . . has a quarter . . . of the interest in upholding the system of international law, of which the Foreign Enlistment Act is the basis."[22] In law and in practice, he demonstrated with many examples, America had adhered to a policy of genuine neutrality vis-à-vis Britain during earlier wars, and Britain, in doing less, would invite retribution in the event of future wars. Only in closing did Cobden go beyond this to talk of the body of international law, indeed of the very concept of neutrality, established so recently and with such effort, that was now at stake. "Shall we," he asked the House, "be the first to roll back the tide of civilisation, and thus practically go back to barbarism and the middle ages, by virtually repealing this international code, by which we preserve the rights and interests of neutrality?"

At the time of this speech and of his diplomatic intervention between Sumner and Russell, Cobden was all but certain that Russell and even Palmerston would do the right thing in this instance, at least if their feet could be kept to the fire. However, action was delayed, pending a legal decision in the case of one vessel, and when that went against the government, the whole matter was thrown back into a state of uncertainty and confusion. Inevitably, tempers flared on both sides of the Atlantic. Sumner wrote angrily to Cobden, who "called on Lord Russell and read every word of your last long indictment against him and Lord Palmerston to him. He was a little impatient under the treatment," Cobden noted, "but I got through every word. I did my best to improve on the text in half an hour's conversation."[23] Although Cobden doubted that in the end the British government would let the rams put to sea, the delays and prevarications appalled him nonetheless because they seemed to indicate little concern or understanding for American feelings, a point that Cobden repeatedly tried to get across to Russell. At the end of one of his meetings with the foreign secretary that spring, as Cobden later informed Bright, "I told him on leaving, with all the emphasis I could muster, 'I tell you, as the result of much reflection and of considerable knowledge of the country, that your policy toward the United States will lead either to war or a general humiliation.' "[24]

Here, if understandably, Cobden was being less than fair to Russell, who had always been inclined to stop the traffic in warships and had only been deterred by the ambiguities of the law. In the end, for reasons of state and with the support of Palmerston, he decided to seize the rams and worry about the legalities later. Unfortunately this did not come in time to prevent Adams from making his famous threat of war or Sumner from making a savagely anti-British speech in New York. The latter was too much, even for Cobden. "Was it politic," he asked his friend, "to array us in hostile attitudes just at the moment when the hopes of the South were mainly founded on the prospect of a rupture between yourselves and Europe? . . . Would it not have been better to have shown . . . the strength of the alliance between the masses of England, led by so much of the intellect and the moral and religious worth of the kingdom, and the Federals, and to have demonstrated the impossibility of the aristocracy, with all their hostility, drawing us into a war with each other?"[25]

Such questions were by this time rhetorical. The rams had been seized and that, coming on top of the Union victories at Gettysburg and Vicksburg, meant not only that the South could not win the war but that it could no longer hope to prevent the North from winning. Whatever chance had remained for foreign involvement after Antietam had finally been eliminated. For the first time since late 1861 America's foreign friends could relax their guard. Even the hitherto cautious Cobden, in his year-end address to his constituents, spoke of a northern victory as an all-but-accomplished fact, somewhat misrepresented his earlier views by claiming that he had "never believed that the South should succeed,"[26] and roundly condemned "the upper ten thousand . . . the ruling class," as much for their ignorance of the realities of power in America, as for their sympathy with "an aristocratic rebellion against a democratic Government."

Cobden's newfound confidence at the ultimate outcome of the Civil War did not mean that either he or Bright paid any less attention to the course or conduct of the war. On the contrary, as it dragged on through 1864, Cobden feared that war weariness or political division in the North might lead to a compromise peace, which could threaten the emancipation of the slaves. "Any compromise on that question," he wrote Sumner, "would cover your cause with eternal infamy, and render the sanguinary Civil War with which you have desolated the North and South useless butchery, and the greatest crime against humanity recorded in the world's annals."[27] Even with a northern victory assured, Cobden was hardly more reconciled to the war itself than he had been at its start. "There is," he told Sumner in the summer of 1864, "a constant struggle in my breast against my paramount abhorrence of war as a means of settling disputes . . . If it were not for the interest which I feel in the fate of the slaves . . . I should turn with horror from the details of your battles, and wish only for peace on any terms. As it is, I cannot help asking myself whether it can be within the designs of a merciful God that even a good work should be accomplished at the cost of so much evil to the world."[28]

For assurance that the North would not lose sight of the goals that alone could legitimize the war to Cobden, he looked increasingly to Lincoln. Like many Europeans, Cobden came to this view of the American president late in the war. Early in 1861, as war approached, Cobden dismissed him as a "backwoodsman of good sturdy common sense, but evidently unequal to the occasion."[29] Even late in 1862, after Antietam and the Emancipation Proclamation, Cobden still feared that the South might win, not through its own strength but as a result of poor leadership in the North. "Lincoln has a certain moral dignity," he remarked, "but is intellectually inferior, and as men do not generally measure those correctly who are above their own cali-ber, he has chosen for his instruments mediocre men."[30] Two years later, on the eve of the presidential election, Cobden had changed his view, to the point of deriding those among whom "it is the fashion to underrate Lincoln intellectually,"[31] as Cobden himself had often done. In fact, citing Lincoln's handling of foreign provocations in particu-lar, Cobden concluded that he "seems to have honesty, self control and common sense in an eminent degree." Cobden's growing admi-ration for Lincoln was as much a matter of perspective as of policy. "I always thought his want of enlarged experience was a disadvantage to him," Cobden admitted to Sumner, "but he knows his own coun-trymen, evidently, and that is the main point . . . I hope you will re-elect Mr. Lincoln," Cobden concluded ten months before the elec-tion.[32] In the following months, somewhat to his own surprise, Cobden found himself almost obsessed with American politics. "It is the only public incident," he told a no-less-single-minded Bright, "which for a very long time has so engrossed my thoughts that I have had a difficulty sometimes in attending to other matters."[33] Only after the election was over did Cobden feel able to wait quietly, if impatiently, for the now inevitable outcome of the war.

He did not live to see the end; he died a week to the day before Lee's surrender at Appomattox. But there were clear intimations in the weeks of mentally alert semi-invalidism before Cobden's death that the end of the slaughter was near. Of his own part in containing that slaughter, Cobden spoke modestly. In what proved to be his last letter to Sumner, he wrote: "It is nothing but your great *power* that has kept the hands of Europe off you. When a deputation of free traders applied to Minister Guizot in 1846 for authorisation to hold meetings to agitate for Free Trade, they received permission, with the benediction 'Soyez fort, et nous vous protégerons.' This is about the amount of what your friends in Europe have been able to do for you."[34] That they had in fact done far more than this almost everyone (including Cobden) would have agreed, then and since, and if they have not always received their due, that is perhaps because it is im-possible to demonstrate that, but for the counsels of restraint of cer-tain individuals, events that did not take place would have, let alone what the consequences would have been.

The nature—and limitations—of Cobden's and Bright's special roles are easier to define. So far as their effect on British policy was concerned, one interested observer, Charles Francis Adams, was inclined to diminish its importance. Adams regarded W. E. Forster, the freshman radical M.P. from Bradford, as the Union's "firmest and most judicious friend. We owe to his tact and talent more than we do to the more showy interference of Messrs. Cobden and Bright."[35] Even after allowing for the personal animus evident in this comment (Cobden, for example, did not hestitate to criticize American policy or the ambassador's conduct to his face or in public), Adams had a point. Young Forster brought no extraneous associations with him to the discussion of the Civil War, whereas the views of Cobden and Bright on questions of war and peace and their identification with America were so well known and considered by many so idiosyncratic that their influence at home was bound to be limited. But that in a way misses the real point for both men, each of whom discounted their lack of influence in England, although for different reasons.

Bright sought out the role of isolated supporter of the North because he was certain of a northern victory and therefore that he would be vindicated and strengthened in the end, as indeed he was. Cobden, however, although regretting his limited influence on his own government and people, accepted it as a part of the price he had to pay in order to assume the role that he desired and perhaps alone could perform, that of an Atlantic rather than an English public figure, committed not to any one party in diplomacy or war but to the pursuit of peace within a frame of reference transcending the particular issues of the conflict. That did not endear him to the deeply committed of any persuasion, nor was he able to impress his frame of reference on others, but it did give him access to all parties as a trusted medium of informed communication and as a disinterested offerer of good offices. Thus, more than any other individual acting in an unofficial capacity, Cobden was able to play a part in almost every major international ramification of the American Civil War. As in his negotiation of the Commercial Treaty, this peculiar status and the achievements it made possible were to Cobden the most persuasive evidence of the worth of his concept of internationalism.

CHAPTER 24

The Elder Statesman
of Radicalism

Although preoccupied first with Anglo-French and then with Anglo-American relations in the early 1860s, Cobden never lost sight of a variety of other issues, some of great importance in themselves, others of special interest to him. In addition to old and close friends such as Bright, Ashworth, and Paulton, with whom he shared a wide range of concerns, he kept in touch on particular subjects of mutual interest with a number of acquaintances, many of them made in earlier agitations and maintained since by a fairly constant exchange of letters, in some cases stretching back almost twenty years. Cobden's age and poor health meant that he was no longer on the lookout for new worlds to conquer but, as had been true since the beginning of his public career, he liked to be in a position to recognize new issues as they arose and to take advantage of any opening that presented itself to resuscitate a dormant cause. Thus, as the American crisis finally promised to recede in 1863, there was a noticeable revival of his habit of dusting off old issues, of casting about for targets of opportunity, and above all of playing with and playing off the ceaseless flow of information and commentary that was the substance of his best political friendships.

Colonel Fitzmayer, a professional soldier of unorthodox views, was an unusual member of Cobden's roster of regular correspondents. Cobden first came to know him as a source of information on the fighting in the Crimea, and he continued thereafter to serve as Cobden's chief advisor and friendly critic on imperial and military questions. After Fitzmayer was posted to Ireland, the Irish question became the primary topic of their correspondence, at a time, early in the 1860s, when it was taking on new urgency. Ireland was hardly a new concern for Cobden, who had written about it extensively in his first pamphlet, but he believed that the challenge to British policy that it represented had been revolutionized since then by the influx into the United States of vast numbers of Irish immigrants, ready to support the nationalist movement with money and, in the event of an Irish rebellion, with pressure on the American government to do at least what Britain had done for the Confederacy, grant belligerent rights to the insurgents.

Although the particular circumstances of the Irish problem might have changed, however, its fundamental nature had not. Even more than in England, Cobden had always believed, the enemy was the aristocracy and in particular its ecclesiastical and landed monopolies, "the two great monster evils out of which the disaffection of Ireland springs," as he described them to Fitzmayer.[1] Nothing short of their destruction could reconcile the Irish to British rule, Cobden was certain, yet he saw no signs of progress in that direction. Nonetheless, there seemed to be some reason for hope, if only in the long run and probably at terrible cost, even in Ireland's present difficulties, and not for Ireland alone. For Ireland was the weakest link in the system of aristocratic power, as Cobden noted in sending one of Fitzmayer's letters on to Bright: "As Ireland repealed the Corn Laws for us at the cost of some hundreds of thousands of the people's lives, and the transportation of a million or two more, so I suppose the relation of the soil to the aristocracy, and of the Church to the State will find their first solution in that island."[2]

With John Robertson of Manchester, who had first approached him back in the years of optimism shortly after repeal, Cobden shared an interest in national education and particularly in the Manchester program of the late 1840s, which there was talk of reviving in the early 1860s. As with the Irish question, Cobden's views on education had not changed, and again as with the Irish question, he saw almost no hope for immediate progress. "Now I don't believe," he wrote, "in the possibility of carrying any general measure of education with the present constituencies, and with the present temper of the religious bodies, and with the instinctive indifference if not repugnance of the ruling class to the elevation of the mass of the people."[3]

For a time in 1863 Cobden was more optimistic about the prospects for another of his old objectives, the further reduction of indirect taxes, specifically the malt tax, which was taken up at this time by C. H. Lattimore, a progressive Hertfordshire farmer whom Cobden had met on one of his rural speaking tours for the league. In April 1863 Cobden unearthed his People's Budget of fifteen years before and discovered to his surprise that all the cuts in duties he had proposed had since been carried, except for the repeal of the malt tax. Citing the evil inherent in excise taxes, and the desirability of reducing government profligacy in general and of aiding Gladstone in his battles with Palmerston over spending in particular, Cobden pressed Lattimore to get up an agitation and promised to give whatever support he could. Their little campaign had hardly begun, however, before both of them realized how little parliamentary or public interest there was in it. "You have not a county Member [of Parliament]," Cobden concluded, "who either believes in the possibility of total repeal or who in his heart desires it . . . The farmers as a class have very little power over the county elections."[4] Early in 1864 they let the matter drop.

It was not only with old allies of his own generation that Cobden kept up this kind of dialogue. In 1862 he was invited to visit Oxford and went with some trepidation, only to find that he thoroughly enjoyed himself. In particular he was delighted to meet two liberally minded professors, both nineteen years his juniors, the historian and political essayist, Goldwin Smith, and the political economist, J. E. Thorold Rogers. Smith was often to disagree with Cobden but admired him more than any other political figure he knew; Rogers, like Louis Mallet, another exact contemporary, quickly became a disciple, one of those who attempted to perpetuate Cobdenism into our own century and along with Bright was to edit Cobden's collected speeches. (A brief essay by Smith was also included in that collection, and a longer essay by Mallet prefaced the volume of Cobden's collected writings.) All three of these younger Liberals were, almost from the moment Cobden met them, drawn into that intimate circle of confidants and correspondents who played so central a role in his public life.

Although Cobden had always enjoyed developing ideas and political strategies through correspondence, this became indispensable during the last decade of his life, as family tragedy followed by his own infirmity confined him to Dunford much of the time. His parliamentary career was even more directly affected. Cobden had always looked on Parliament as only one of many means to his ends, which was lucky, for he hardly had a career there after 1855, except during the last three years of his life. The death of his son in 1856, electoral defeat in 1857, and the negotiation of the Commercial Treaty kept him away from Westminster for the better part of six years, and even thereafter his health imposed severe limitations. He hesitated to attend the opening winter months of the session and was sometimes physically unable to speak when he wanted to. Only once in his later years, in 1863, did he participate actively in a full session of Parliament.

Personal reasons aside, there were sound considerations of policy for husbanding his parliamentary resources. On reflection he believed that his efforts in the postrepeal years to control government spending through detailed scrutiny of the estimates had been wasted. The results, if any, were short lived; prosperity and pressure from the service departments had led to a rapid restoration of whatever funds were cut. The only ways, he now believed, were either to eliminate entire categories of spending, so that there was nothing to grow back from, or perhaps still better, "by witholding the means of extravagance."[5] Hence much of his interest in the repeal of the malt tax, although he also supported it as a free trade measure. Hence also his motion in 1863 to eliminate the wooden vessels still in the Royal Navy and thereby the cost of maintaining, berthing, and manning them. In the following session he proposed a similar resolution, calling on the government to replace its armament manufactures with an efficient system of procurement from private industry through competitive bidding.

Cobden was no more hopeful for the passage of these resolutions than he was that any progress could be made on purely domestic questions. More even than in the late phases of the peace campaign, he was speaking for the record and to the future. Only now it appeared that this was no longer a merely noble but futile effort. In 1863, quite suddenly, the future began to take on shape and reality as the Palmerstonian system, which had grown inexorably in power and support ever since 1850, showed signs of serious weakness. And particularly gratifying to Cobden was that this suggestion of decay appeared most dramatically in an area where Palmerston had hitherto been unassailable, the conduct of foreign policy.

The turning point was the Schleswig-Holstein crisis. The Austro-Prussian invasion of Denmark in 1864, following Danish mistreatment of the German population of these provinces in violation of the London protocol of 1852, placed the British government in an awkward position. Although a party to the earlier settlement and favorable to the Danes in the crisis, Britain was diplomatically all but isolated by the caution, ulterior motives, or outright hostility of the two major powers it might have worked with, France and Russia, and militarily it was not in a position unilaterally to affect the outcome, even had it been willing to go to war, which a majority of the cabinet consistently was not. Reduced therefore to bluffing, Russell and Palmerston had their bluff called by Bismarck, with the result that Britain was made to appear even more isolated and ineffectual than it was. Compelled in the end to admit the Britain could do nothing, Palmerston survived a Conservative motion of censure less through his own efforts—he spoke badly—or popularity—much diminished—than, ironically, because of the passage of a substitute motion, drafted by radicals led by Cobden, who were almost as critical of the opposition as of the government and therefore simply expressed their satisfaction that war had been avoided.

That the preservation of peace reflected no credit on the British government was implicit in the neutral wording of the radical motion and explicitly the theme of most speeches in nearly a week of debate on Denmark. Disraeli, echoed a few days later by the future Lord Salisbury, was especially effective in accounting the costs of the government's adopting a policy of nonintervention not out of choice or conviction but by default. As in his attack on Peel's government as an "organised hypocrisy" two decades earlier, Disraeli declared his preference for a Cobdenite policy conducted by those who believed in it, since, "as the consequences would be almost the same, our position would be more consistent; it would certainly be more profitable and in my opinion it would really be more dignified. At least these hon. Gentlemen [Cobden and Bright] would threaten nobody . . . at least they would not lure Denmark by delusive counsels and fallacious hopes."[6]

Inevitably there was a sharp public reaction against the policies of "those two dreadful old men," as the Queen characterized her prime minister and foreign secretary.[7] Seven years after Palmerston had snatched victory from defeat following the *Arrow* incident and twice that time since he had routed his enemies in the Don Pacifico debate, his run of luck appeared to have ended. Observers then sensed what later events confirmed, that the Danish crisis marked a turning point in the history of British policy in Europe. Cobden was delighted, for not only had the crisis illustrated almost perfectly the dangers and follies of interventionism, it also appeared to demonstrate the bankruptcy of traditional diplomacy in the changing conditions of mid-nineteenth-century Europe:

> With this question of Denmark and Germany, two issues are brought clearly before us—I mean, the question as to the dynastic, secret, irresponsible engagements of our Foreign Office, and also the question which is not ancient but new, and which must be taken into consideration in all our foreign policy from this time—the question of nationalities—by which I mean the instinct, now so powerful, leading communities to seek to live together, because they are of the same race, language, and religion.[8]

The protocol of 1852 was irrelevant and unenforceable, he argued, because it had aimed at deciding the fate of the people of Schleswig-Holstein without consulting their wishes. "It will not be repeated again," he concluded. "I mean that there will never again, in all probability, be a conference meeting together to dispose for dynastic purposes of a population whose wishes they do not take into account."

Cobden had sought to enlist English sympathy with nationalism on the side of a noninterventionist foreign policy before, cautiously at the time of his continental journey in 1846–47, more boldly during Kossuth's visit to England in 1851 and against Turkey just before the Crimean war. But never before had he given nationalism the central place in his indictment of traditional foreign policy, which he normally reserved for arguments from economic determinism or from the need to establish a system of international law. The reason for this shift may have been the Russian repression of the Polish revolt of 1863. For reasons of practicality as well as principle, Cobden advocated a policy of nonintervention during that crisis, but the Polish rising awakened a sympathy for the Poles he had never felt before, and he followed the news of their subjugation with sorrow and anger. The Schleswig-Holstein crisis was a different matter. There the principles of national self-determination and nonintervention by England were mutually supportive. The outcome was almost all to the good, he believed, and not only or even primarily for the people of the region: "I am of the opinion that what has happened—I mean the exposure of the utter futility of our foreign policy—the complete breakdown of our diplomacy—will have the effect of extracting these foreign questions from this time henceforth, from the dark recesses of the Foreign Office to the publicity of this House, and will therefore afford, probably, a better guarantee for peace than anything else that could have occurred."

Although the revulsion against the Palmerstonian style in foreign policy was the most hopeful sign of 1864 to Cobden, it was not the only one. For the first time in years there were indications of movement on domestic issues. The succession of antislavery and pro-American meetings early in 1863, culminating in a great meeting in London in March at which Bright shared the platform with leading trade unionists, the formation of the National Reform Union under George Wilson's leadership in Manchester a year later and the support it immediately won in middle-class circles, and Gladstone's announced conversion to political reform in May 1864 all indicated that something of substance was afoot. Cobden took little direct and no public part in these developments. Although invited to join in every major meeting and new association, he declined for reasons of health or because he did not wish to offend any one group of reformers by becoming too closely associated with another or because of his conviction that new movements needed new men. Nonetheless, he followed and encouraged these developments with growing interest and growing hope because he felt that, although nothing could be accomplished as long as Palmerston was around, virtually anything would be possible once he was out of the way—a condition that was bound to be fulfilled soon, since the prime minister was already eighty years old.

Cobden's greatest concern was that his old adversary might abort the birth of a new Liberal party after his death by pursuing Tory policies with tacit Tory support while remaining nominally Liberal, and in the process so compromise other members of his government and its Liberal supporters that they would become dispirited and leaderless. These were far from new concerns for Cobden, who had hardly made his uneasy truce with Palmerston in the summer of 1859 before his old animosity was reawakened by their differences over Anglo-French relations. However, whereas his concern with the completion of the French treaty had compelled Cobden at that time to rein in his feelings, he was under no such constraints in 1864. Ever since his attack on Palmerston in the summer of 1862, Cobden had been officially an independent, and the elimination of any possibility that England might intervene in the American Civil War during 1863 removed the only reason remaining why he should keep on civil terms with the Whig leadership. He felt free to speak out and moreover had the incentive of impending political changes to do so. Thus, in July 1864, he told the House of Commons what he had for some time been saying in private, that Palmerston, "after he has thoroughly demoralized his own party . . . intends when he makes his political will to make over office to . . . [the Tories] as his residuary legatees."[9]

Cobden could hardly have been more blunt, and the same directness characterized his correspondence with Gladstone, which the hopeful political situation as well as the waning of the American problem led Cobden to resume at the end of 1863 after a break of more than a year. This renewed exchange of letters was different in tone and content, however, at least on Cobden's side. At the beginning of the decade he had written to Gladstone on a variety of topics: the budget, the Anglo-French naval race, the future of Liberalism, and so on. In 1864 Cobden was most concerned with putting some distance between Gladstone and Palmerston, as a means of ensuring Gladstone's political future and through him the integrity of Liberalism. When Gladstone raised issues such as the budget or urged Cobden to use his influence to get the French to moderate their naval building program, Cobden wearily or even angrily dismissed Gladstone's suggestions. These were dead topics to him now; he had done what he could with them and failed. If the French were undertaking large-scale rearmament, that was only because Britain had already built on an even larger scale in response to the spurious invasion scare. There was no point in attempting to alter policies on either side of the channel so long as Palmerston was in power; the most that could be done was to hold the old reprobate in check. "And now," Cobden concluded one of his letters, "I really doubt if you will ever induce me to resume my pen on this hopeless theme."[10]

If Cobden in 1864 was less concerned with his own influence than with ensuring that Palmerston's did not extend beyond the grave, that was probably because he sensed his powers were failing badly. Still, he must have hoped that he would outlive his old enemy. He did not. Although twenty years Palmerston's junior, Cobden died seven months earlier, in April 1865, two months short of his sixty-first birthday.

The severity of his last illness came as a shock even to Cobden, and his death, after a partial recovery, stunned his friends and the political world, but neither his illness nor his death could in truth have been called surprising. Cobden's health had been a constant problem for more than five years and a matter of public knowledge for almost that long. Rarely appearing before large audiences, apart from his annual visits to his constituents in Rochdale, unable to rely on his voice even in the House of Commons, and compelled to hibernate at Dunford for four or five months a year, as the circle of his public life narrowed in the years after he returned from Paris, Cobden was increasingly thought of as an elder statesman even by his friends.

He even began to look the part. Until well into middle age, Cobden retained the trim figure and energetic gait of a much younger man. Edward Watkin, a young disciple of Cobden's in league days but well on his way to becoming one of England's great railway magnates by the early 1860s, later recalled how "Cobden at forty-five or fifty, was still to be seen half skipping along a pavement, or a railway platform, with the lightness of a slim and dapper figure, and a mind full bent upon its object."[11] Thereafter, the passage of time, family tragedies, and a succession of illnesses slowed him down with a rapidity that startled his contemporaries. Not that he ever lost his mental agility or powers of concentration. Lady Dorothy Nevill, a near neighbor to Dunford, was astonished at how he "used to work under what to anyone else would have been very disturbing surroundings, writing his letters in the drawing room of his house whilst his children romped about and constantly interrupted his labors by their shouting and laughter, which however never seemed to disturb him at all."[12] If age affected his mental abilities in any way, it was to exaggerate his lifelong tendency toward monomania, which had always been a weakness as well as a strength to Cobden. As the speaker of the House of Commons put it, not unfairly, "it is a fault of Cobden's mind to see one object so strongly that his view cannot embrace another at the same time."[13] Physically, if not mentally, however, the changes during Cobden's last years were marked. Compelled to live a sedentary life for much of the year, he put on weight and by the early 1860s, Disraeli noted, "may be described as decidedly a stout man, with grey hair, full and rather long."[14] The resilience, the bounce, was gone.

Cobden himself necessarily became preoccupied with the state of his health, as the most important factor limiting his public life, and he came to assess the relationship of one to the other much as an accountant might tote up the debit and credit columns of a ledger. So much time accumulated at Dunford during the winter might afford him the chance to spend a normal spring and early summer in London; his long vacation in Scotland in 1862 was in part insurance against having to go abroad again for the winter and might even allow him to skimp on his time at Dunford. Such calculations were rarely absent from his thoughts even in the finest weather, and unfortunately for Cobden the climate did not cooperate. The winter of 1863-64 was harsh, and he found it impossible to balance off the debit side of the ledger. Having come up to London to take at least some part in the proceedings of the House early in 1862 and 1863 and having paid dearly for it on both occasions, Cobden did not speak in Parliament in 1864 until April, at which time he also acknowledged that he could no longer perform all his duties as an M.P., in a letter to Gladstone asking to be relieved of committee work.

In the circumstances he understandably became moody and irritable at times. Cobden had always been somewhat abrupt with those who disagreed with him and persisted in their disagreement even after his best efforts to change their minds, but his later letters to Gladstone betrayed an unwillingness to consider opposing views bordering on rudeness, which was almost unprecedented. The most important instance of his new testiness, because it was played out in public, was his skirmish with John Delane, the editor of *The Times*, at the end of 1863. Cobden dated their mutual hostility back some fifteen years to the period just after he returned from his tour of Europe. "It was at a dinner party in London," he later recalled, "at which I took the chair; and I took the opportunity of launching this question of the press, and saying that the newspaper press of England was not free, and that this was a thing which the Reformers of the country ought to set about—to emancipate it. Well, I got a most vicious article next day from the *Times* newspaper for that, and the *Times* has followed us . . . with a very ample store of venom ever since."[15]

Whether or not this was the reason for the animosity of *The Times*, it did become by far his most important press critic. His increasing identification with the peace movement, culminating in his opposition to the Crimean war, and his leading role in the campaign to repeal the newspaper taxes, a campaign *The Times* bitterly opposed and Cobden supported in part as a way of breaking the power of *The Times*, led to such hostility that the paper sometimes lost its balance, as in its early coverage of the Anglo-French Commercial Treaty. Cobden always denied that his dislike of *The Times* was personally motivated, despite its often vicious attacks on him, especially after the revelations of his financial troubles in 1860, although he would not allow the paper in his home in his last years. He was equally scornful of the suggestion that *The Times* opposed him and supported Palmerston out of conviction. Rather, he believed, its sycophantic owners and staff were motivated by personal social ambition and perhaps by the hope or actuality of government patronage.

In short, Cobden had long desired to bring *The Times* down a peg or two, and in December 1863 he saw his chance. At Cobden's annual meeting with his constituents in late November, he and Bright referred in passing to the desirability of broadening the base of land ownership in England. A few days later *The Times*, also in passing, referred to Bright's "proposition for a division among the poor of the lands of the rich."[16] A visitor to Dunford brought a copy of this issue of the paper with him the following day and Cobden, seizing on the offending phrase, wrote to the editor, accusing *The Times* of grossly misrepresenting Bright's views. In the exchange of letters that followed, Cobden was able easily to demonstrate that *The Times* had maligned not only Bright but himself (in earlier editorials Cobden did not see until after he had written his first letter). Far from even hinting at expropriation or social violence, as *The Times* had suggested, Cobden and Bright had spoken with great care and rejected radical solutions. At each challenge, Delane had to retreat from indefensible positions, although neither he nor *The Times* ever made a public retraction. Even the author of the official history of *The Times* admitted that "the facts were with Cobden."[17]

Whether Cobden was vindicated by the facts was in a sense beside the point. What is interesting about the Cobden-Delane correspondence is not the ostensible issue between them but the relentlessness with which Cobden pursued it. His first letter was insulting: he accused *The Times* of a "groundless and gratuitous falsehood" and a "foul libel," which, he asserted, was all too typical of "a tone of pre-eminent unscrupulousness in the discussion of political questions, a contempt for the rights and feelings of others, and a shameless disregard for the claims of consistency and sincerity on the part of its writers . . . long recognised as the distinguishing characteristics of *The Times*."[18] There was more of the same in the later letters, and not surprisingly Delane and the proprietor of *The Times* decided not to publish any of them. Normally that would have been the end of the matter, but Cobden was not about to let it drop. When Delane replied (almost as testily as Cobden) anonymously in his capacity as editor, Cobden ignored that convention and addressed his second letter to Delane by name, on the grounds that the editor must accept personal responsibility for his words and that it was precisely such lack of accountability that led to the abuse of its power by the press. In addition Cobden set about ensuring that the correspondence was published. This, in itself, was a source of additional trouble. The *Daily Telegraph*, for example, refused to print his opening letter to Delane (yet criticized him for having written it), but Cobden rightly judged that "my letter will be only the more generally read from having been excluded"[19] from any individual paper, and he had no trouble finding London and provincial outlets eager to publish every word. He also published the entire correspondence with both papers as a pamphlet.

Cobden was after bigger game than the anonymous writer of scurrilous editorials, however. Anonymity had become offensive to him because its original purpose of protecting unbridled comment had been perverted not only to shield irresponsible hacks but to hide a too-close relationship of patronage that he was convinced existed between the government and *The Times*. That was the issue he ultimately wished to raise, and he was surprisingly frank in making his intentions known. His first letter to Delane closed with a threat "to lift the veil and dispel the illusion by which *The Times* is enabled to pursue this game of secrecy to the public, and servility to the Government—a game (I purposely use the word) which secures for its connections the corrupt advantages, while denying to the public its own boasted benefits of the anonymous system."[20]

Cobden had every intention of leading this fight and busied himself during his winter confinement at Dunford with plans to raise the issue in Parliament as a means of embarrassing not only *The Times* but the government. The friends to whom he confided his plans were taken aback. Bright waded into the controversy with a speech mocking Delane's pretensions but clearly not intended as the opening shot of a protracted war with *The Times*, an approach that Cobden, very much in earnest, deplored. What Bright and others saw, that Cobden clearly did not, was that Cobden could only hurt himself by pursuing the larger issue of "illicit intercourse"[21] between the government and *The Times.* He had little evidence apart from a few examples of petty patronage and a large amount of gossip concerning social connections between certain *Times* men and government ministers. To have proceeded on such evidence would have appeared either stupid or vindictive. Of all the hobbyhorses Cobden rode during his career, this was the one that, had he not been persuaded to dismount, would most likely have thrown him, much to his embarrassment and perhaps with serious damage to his public reputation.

Of this entire episode Morley wrote, "We need not resort to private grudges to explain what is perfectly intelligible without them."[22] That was an evasion. The flare-up with Delane would not have taken place had Cobden been at the height of his powers. Here and in a few other instances near the end of his life he reverted to some of the less attractive attributes of the young agitator of a quarter century before—intemperance, intolerance, and narrowness of vision—which experience and maturity had all but eliminated in his vigorous middle years. As Joseph Parkes put it in a letter to Delane, Cobden's "temperament was naturally vehement and irascible and he contracted the most vehement and silly personal dislikes."[23] This was not unfair, although it was harsh coming from an old friend and especially so in that it was written the day after Cobden's death.

What was both unfair and untrue was Parkes's further assertion that Cobden's "mind certainly had been off its balance ever since he went to Algiers." The irascibility of his later letters to Gladstone and of his correspondence with Delane was something new, a function perhaps of the unprecedentedly long period of hibernation he spent (and knew he would have to spend) at Dunford during the winter of 1863–64. Before that, although he was often obsessed with certain topics almost to the exclusion of other concerns and relentlessly pressed his battle with Palmerston, Cobden always weighed his moves carefully and was well aware of the likely consequences of his actions. Parkes may not have liked the direction Cobden was moving after the negotiation of the Commercial Treaty, but that was no indication his judgment was impaired. Indeed, his part in the diplomacy, domestic politics, and relief policy of the American Civil War would seem to prove just the opposite.

It is important here to understand the peculiar nature of the stresses that Cobden was under during these years. After he recovered from the unexpected seizure of November 1859, he found that he could live something close to his normal life a great deal of the time. For a couple of years thereafter, even when he lost his voice, there were no other ill effects, and in warm weather he felt almost as energetic as ever. The cold damp and fogs of winter were his great enemies and sources of real dread. Throughout the winter he had trouble breathing and was prone to congestion. Even so, his long withdrawals to Dunford were not so much the effects of illness as precautions against it. If he took care of himself he felt well, even then. The exception was the winter of 1863–64, during which he experienced a measurable decline.

Yet, even after that, in the better weather of spring, the tension dissipated along with the likelihood of further illness, and he went up to London in a mood of optimism, which was perhaps almost as much the cause as the result of his favorable reading of the diplomatic and political portents. His dark and difficult temper the preceding winter was an indicator, in short, but remained anomalous; by and large, Cobden had come to terms with his failing health as well as most men. In early 1860 he deliberately chose to go on with the French treaty negotiations, even at great risk to his health, and a year later, while in Algeria, he wrote reflectively to Henry Ashworth:

> The truth must be told, my dear friend . . . my work is nearly done. I am nearly 57 and not of a long lived family. Since I passed my meridian a few years ago I have found my powers sensibly waning . . . If, however, I could pass the remainder of my days with only the labor of an average person of my years, I could I daresay nurse myself into a good old age. The question is whether I ought rather to content myself with a briefer span and the satisfaction of trying to do something a little beyond my strength. It is a nice question for casuists—for the home duties affecting one's small children intrude.[24]

In spite of these reservations, Cobden did not hesitate long before renewing his campaign against the naval arms race or, six months later, throwing himself into the controversy over the American Civil War. He (and his health) made certain he would not neglect his family, however. There was little he could do to ensure their financial future; that had been taken out of his hands by his friends. But the long periods of enforced rest at Dunford thrust him into the daily round of family life to an extent that he had never lived it before. Both he and his daughters benefited from the experience. For him the constant presence of the children robbed the winters of much of their gloom and foreboding. For the girls the unaccustomed presence of their father could hardly have come at a better time, since all of them were still young. Because he married relatively late and his first two children had died, at the time Cobden went to Paris in 1859, at the age of 55, the eldest of his four daughters was only fifteen, the youngest a mere six. Two years later, following much anxiety for Catherine Cobden's health, yet another child, also a girl, was born.

Perhaps to his own surprise, Cobden thoroughly enjoyed his enhanced responsibility as paterfamilias. It also improved his marriage. The first sixteen years had often been lonely for Catherine Cobden, and although the death of young Richard in 1856 brought the parents closer together, it imposed strains of its own. Catherine never got over her mixed emotions about Dunford with all its associations, and Cobden was often impatient with her morbid preoccupation. In the last years of his life, her unplanned pregnancy and the birth of their last child, together with his growing dependence on his family, established a basis for intimacy that had been all but impossible when young Catherine had had to compete with the Anti–Corn Law League. At no time in his life probably had Cobden achieved a balance more satisfactory to all concerned between his public and his private life. Morley, wishing to suggest something of the flavor of these last years, recounted a little anecdote of how Catherine, journeying up to London with her husband at this time, suggested that they might have done better after all, in spite of his fame and good works, if they had gone off to Canada after their marriage. Cobden did not answer her immediately but stared pensively out the window. After a time he agreed that perhaps she was right and for the moment, at least, he surely meant it.

This little incident took place in the last year of Cobden's life. Although he could not have known that, he certainly knew that his health could only get worse and that it would probably be his bronchial asthma that would kill him. He was not therefore surprised when he took ill following his last public appearance of 1864, his trip north late in the autumn (although no later than the previous year) to speak to his constituents in Rochdale. It was an exhausting visit. His speech was long and ranged widely, as always on such occasions, and the meeting was especially large. Furthermore, he was obliged to attend a reception in his honor the following evening. Worn out, he rushed back to Dunford, not even stopping in London for fear poor health might keep him there. If his exhaustion, although excessive, did not startle him, the near-collapse that followed certainly did. It was far worse then anything he had experienced (and so carefully prepared against) the winter before—worse, for that matter, than anything since the attack that had first signaled a physical decline four years before. For some weeks he could only move about the house with difficulty, and for more than two months he dared not leave it at all.

Another bitter winter further slowed his recovery, but by early March he was able to take short walks on good days and receive visits from close friends. He also corresponded as briskly as ever, not only on familiar topics such as the waning of the American Civil War and, so it appeared, of Palmerstonianism, but on new subjects such as the planned confederation of Canada. This especially interested Cobden because it touched on a variety of issues he had long been concerned with: relations with the post–Civil War United States, the defensibility of Canada, and the implications of colonial self-government on British responsibility for imperial defense. In February he wrote a number of letters on the subject to Gladstone, who was sufficiently impressed that he passed two of them on to Gibson and one to Russell. When the issue arose in the House of Commons, however, letter writing no longer seemed enough, and on 21 March Cobden traveled up to London to take part in a debate on Canadian fortifications.

It was a fatal decision. The day was bitterly cold, and on his arrival in London he suffered a severe attack of asthma. Prostrated for a week, he began to show signs of recovery on 29 March and was able to receive a few friends. But it was a short-lived improvement. Relapse alternated with recovery over the next couple of days, until, on the afternoon of Saturday, 1 April, his asthma complicated by congestion and bronchitis, he began to sink irretrievably. Of Cobden's friends, only Moffat and Bright were there at the end. "I was with him soon after 8 o'clock," on Sunday morning, Bright recorded:

> I found him insensible and dying . . . There was a stertorous breathing which gradually became shorter. There was no apparent pain. Not a

limb stirred. He lay breathing out his precious life, and for 3 1/4 hours I watched my greatest friend of more than 20 years as his life ebbed away. At 1/4 past 11 o'clock the breathing ceased. There was a moment of suspense: a pallor spread over the face, and the manly and gentle spirit of one of the noblest of men passed away to the rewards which surely wait upon a life passed in works of good to mankind . . . It was a scene never to be forgotten. His hands were still warm, and the warmth of life was still on his forehead after life had fled. We stood, and looked, and wept with almost breaking hearts . . . I pressed his hand for the last time, and kissed his forehead, and left him with a sense of the loss I have suffered.[25]

The observances of the days that followed were as appropriate to Cobden as they—like his death—were seemly to the sense of the age of what the death of a great man should entail and signify. There were no state ceremonials and certainly no suggestion that he be buried or memorialized in Westminster Abbey (which was too full of military heroes for his taste). Instead, he was entombed alongside his son Richard in the churchyard at West Lavington, near Midhurst, at a ceremony at which the intimate circle of family and friends who had attended him during his final illness or rushed to London on learning of his death was widened to include representatives of every facet of his career. The twelve pall bearers were themselves a microcosm of that career. There was Bright, of course, and Gladstone. Villiers and Milner Gibson followed. Thomas Bazley, M.P. for Manchester, and A. W. Paulton, free trade lecturer and radical journalist, had both been Cobden's colleagues since the beginning of the anti–Corn Law struggle. Henry Ashworth and George Wilson were friends and coagitators of even longer standing. George Moffat and Thomas Thomasson had been personal even more than political friends and advisors. T. B. Potter, the son of the first mayor of Manchester, represented the rising political generation. Through his work as president of the Union and Emancipation Society in 1863, he had, Cobden believed, "done more than any other man in the North of England to produce that reaction of public opinion in favor of the North" in the American Civil War.[26] Potter was soon to succeed Cobden in the representation of Rochdale and played a leading part in seeking to perpetuate Cobdenism by founding the Cobden Club. The last of the pall bearers was William Evans, chairman of the Emancipation Society.

Among the many mourners there was only one peer, Lord Kinnaird, and only one representative of a foreign government, Charles Francis Adams, facts that Adams thought significant:

> The deceased statesman had fought his way to fame and honor by the single force of his character. He had nothing to give. No wealth, no honors, no preferment. A lifelong contempt of the ruling class of his countrymen had earned for him their secret ill-will, marked on this day by the almost total absence of representatives here. And of all foreign nations, I alone, the type of a great democracy, stood to bear witness to the scene. The real power that was present in the multitude crowding around this lifeless form was not the less gigantic for all this absence. In this country, it may be said to owe its very existence to Mr. Cobden. He first taught them by precept and example that the right of government was not really to the few, but to the many.[27]

Four days earlier, on the day following his death, Cobden was honored in the House of Commons. Only three members spoke. Palmerston frankly (if too frequently) alluded to their differences but predictably stressed Cobden's two greatest achievements, his contributions to the repeal of the Corn Laws and to the French Commercial Treaty. Disraeli rose to the occasion more impressively. Looking to Cobden's historical reputation, Disraeli called him "without doubt the greatest political character that the pure middle class of this country has yet produced," and speaking more directly to the emotions of fellow members, he suggested that "there are Members of Parliament who, though not present in this body, are still members of this House: independent of dissolutions, of the caprice of constituencies, even of the course of time. I think, Sir, Mr. Cobden was one of these men."[28] The leaders of the government and opposition having spoken, all eyes turned to Bright. He rose and, barely able to speak, promised to say more at a later time. "I little knew how much I loved him until I found that I had lost him," Bright concluded.[29]

As might be expected, Cobden's death inspired a surfeit of bathetic commentary in the press; but there were a few essays that still bear reading—notably Walter Bagehot's brief appreciation in the *Economist*—and some balanced, even pointed, articles as well, especially in newspapers that had long been his critics, such as *The Times* and the *Manchester Guardian*. Both papers inevitably emphasized his two greatest achievements, and although the *Guardian* acknowledged his contribution to the "political reputation and power of Manchester,"[30] it was, curiously, *The Times* that placed greater emphasis on repeal, while the *Guardian* made more of the French treaty, especially its importance in redeeming Cobden's political reputation after the failures of the postrepeal years. Neither paper glossed over these public disappointments or, for that matter, his private embarrassments. *The Times* even attempted to explain his inability to sustain the influence he had won through the repeal movement, ascribing it partly to his having achieved so much so early but primarily to a lack of breadth in his view of the role of the state, born of the narrowness of his education and social background. As for his private failings, both papers wrote with superficial charitableness of his too trustful nature but did not neglect to hint at his weakness as a manager or to suggest that Cobden might therefore have been wise (as well as principled) to refuse cabinet office. Under the circumstances, neither paper could end on such a note, and both chose their perorations well. *The Times* singled out his freedom from cant and from slavish adherence to a doctrine or party. "He was in everything independent and original," it said.[31] The *Guardian* emphasized integrity of another sort. Although Cobden had derived enormous power from the people, it noted, he never abused it or descended to the demagoguery that would have tempted lesser men.

One other matter that both papers chose to comment on deserves mention. *The Times* at length and the *Guardian* in passing noted that Cobden's death was premature. No one could call sixty-one young, of course, but this was an age dominated by old politicians. The leaders of both parties had been born in the eighteenth century, and the coming men, Gladstone and Disraeli, neither of whom had yet held the highest office, were Cobden's contemporaries. By the standards of the time Cobden could have expected another decade of active public life, had he lived on in reasonable health. A cynic might suggest that it was perhaps a good thing for his historical reputation that he did not. Certainly the record of other Liberal leaders would support such a view: Palmerston, Russell, Bright and Gladstone did little to enhance their images in their final years.

To suggest that Cobden might have been the exception had he lived may at first seem surprising. Of all nineteenth-century Liberal leaders he was by far the most ideologically inclined, and although a comprehensive political and economic philosophy may have been an asset to a young radical politician in the 1830s, its retention virtually unaltered into old age, during the transition period from mid- to late-

Victorian politics, might have made him an anachronism, had he lived. That was the view of one of his biographers, who, while noting his independence of mind, criticized him as having a "limited and dogmatic originality," which left him at sixty with the same ideas he had held at thirty.[32] To the extent that this was true it is a telling criticism; but in fact it was becoming less not more the case in the final years of his life. Cobden experienced the beginnings of a philosophical revolution during these years, a process that, if carried to its conclusion—and given his cast of mind it would have been—might significantly have altered the content of mid-Victorian radical Liberalism, which he himself had done so much to define.

In domestic affairs Cobden was becoming an ardent democrat, not only theoretically—he had long been that—but as a matter of deep emotional commitment. This was in part a negative process, the result of disillusionment with the middle class, which he had once hoped would be the social vehicle of his ideas. The willingness of the middle class to accommodate itself to the traditional governing class in the decade after repeal, even to the point of abandoning the traditional watchwords of peace, retrenchment, and reform, was the greatest disappointment of Cobden's political career. Inevitably he began to look elsewhere, to the class that, because it lived near the edge of poverty, would never tolerate a profligate government. The working class might be swept up in war hysteria once a war began, he admitted, but it was naturally economy-minded in peacetime.

Cobden did not become enamored of the working class entirely on the rebound, however. Particularly during the American Civil War he developed considerable understanding and regard for distinctly working-class ideas and institutions. This had not always been the case. Early in his career he too readily assumed that the middle and working classes were natural allies against the aristocracy, and when working-class leaders persisted in asserting the distinct interests of their followers, Cobden was either hostile, if his own plans were affected, or simply indifferent. In 1836, for example, when he first thought of running for Parliament, he prepared an address to the electors of Stockport covering a wide range of topics of interest to the middle class but omitted to mention the factory acts, the most important issue to the working class of the North at the time.

Realizing his oversight shortly afterward, he sent a long explanation of his views on the subject to the chairman of his election committee.

As might be expected, they reflected utilitarian thought at its most enlightened. To protect the health and promote the education of the young he favored an absolute ban on child labor in factories, but, as for adults, he was equally firm in opposing interference with the free market in labor. To the charge that this left workers defenseless against their employers, Cobden had a ready response: "I would advise the working classes to make themselves free of the labor market of the world . . . by accumulating twenty pounds each, which will give them the command of the only market in which labor is at a higher rate than in England—I mean that of the United States."[33] It was a curious suggestion in view of Cobden's later denunciation of those who unfeelingly advocated emigration during the cotton famine.

As for the alternative of the workers' protecting themselves through collective action in trade unions, Cobden disliked that as much as he did legislative interference. He frequently denounced unions as effective only at intimidation, since they could not overcome the law of supply and demand by which wages were ultimately determined. Cobden had no more use for the other major working-class movements of the period. He dismissed those who feared and fought the New Poor Law in the North as lunatics and the leaders of Chartism, especially Feargus O'Connor, as demagogues who damaged their own cause. Understandably, virtually all working-class organizations during the 1830s and 1840s looked on Cobden with suspicion not only or perhaps not even primarily because he did not support their programs but because he failed to understand the passion that inspired them.

With the collapse of militant Chartism and the rise in its stead of working-class institutions based largely on principles of self-help— bread and butter trade unions, cooperative societies, friendly societies—Cobden's attitude began to change. Not only did he see these movements as more compatible with his own concerns, but with the middle class deserting the field of reform he began to look to working-class organizations as possible models for future agitations. The movement for the abolition of the taxes on knowledge won his support almost as much because he hoped to shape the nature of such movements as because he shared their goals.

That such tutelage was required Cobden did not doubt. However sympathetic he may have been becoming to working-class radicals, it was for the sake of the unfinished business of radicalism as he defined it, pursued by means he had done much to perfect, that he hoped to enlist their aid. The masses might provide the troops but almost until the end of his life he assumed that the leadership, like the agenda of reform, would come from above. Of the workers he asked, sympathetically but condescendingly, in 1861:

> Have they no Spartacus among them to lead a revolt of the Slave class against their political tormentors? I suppose it is the reaction from the follies of Chartism which keeps the present generation so quiet. However it is certain that so long as five millions of men are silent under their disabilities, it is quite impossible for a few middle class members of Parliament to gain them liberty . . . The middle class have never gained a step in the political scale without long labor and agitation out of doors and the working class may depend on it they can only rise by similar efforts, and the more plainly they are told so the better.[34]

The final stage in the evolution of Cobden's attitude toward working-class politics came during the American Civil War. Like many others, Gladstone most famously, Cobden was deeply impressed by the fortitude and the principled support for the northern cause of the cotton workers of Lancashire. That the extent of that support has been exaggerated is really beside the point. The image of the cotton operatives risking their livelihood by opposing the Confederacy generated a potent myth that Cobden himself did much to propagate. To him, as to most of his contemporaries, the exceptions did not count. What mattered was that those who spoke most eloquently for the working class declared themselves for the North, both more strongly and sooner than most middle-class reformers. Rightly as it turned out, Cobden sensed a possible turning point in the great antislavery meetings held in London early in 1863. "Tell me what you think of those Cockney Trade Unionists whom you met," he asked Bright after one of these meetings. "Their representatives on the platform . . . struck me as being very able logical talkers. It was refreshing to read such straightforward utterances, after the namby-pamby middle class oratory we have been so long used to. Did you have any talk with these men to elicit their political tendencies?"[35]

Over the next two years Cobden's increasing regard for the new generation of working-class leaders developed into something even more significant, an appreciation of working-class institutions for themselves. He no longer complained at the lack of a Spartacus at their head but marveled instead at what was being achieved without such charismatic leadership: "Is not the working class, with that instinct that belongs to multitudes, abandoning the old direct mode of attacking the strong holds of power, and seeking to attain their end by flank movements, such as cooperation, working men's clubs, and industrial exhibitions? There will come a great crisis ... and everything will be conceded by our cowardly ruling class to panic fear, as has always been the case."[36] This was written only three months before his death, and inevitably one wonders what role Cobden would have assumed in the reform movements that were just beginning to emerge in the spring of 1865. George Howell, one of the speakers at the antislavery meeting that had so impressed Cobden two years earlier and secretary of the Reform League founded six weeks before Cobden's death, recalled in his published recollections that "it was thought at one time that Mr. Cobden might be our president."[37] Donald Read understandably made much of this statement, since it was strong evidence for the major contention of his study of Cobden and Bright, that Cobden was the more radical of the two.

So he was, although that did not necessarily mean that he would have taken a prominent part in the agitation leading up to the second reform act. Indeed, Howell's biographer and even Howell himself, in another place, an unpublished memoir, were cautious in their claims. Although Bright was cool toward the radical program of the Reform League, Howell noted, "Mr. Cobden was favorable, and had he lived it is probable that his manly eloquence and his influence would have been used in favor of the Reform League. However his well known sympathy was of service in the earlier stages of the formation of the League and especially in regard to subscriptions, with regard to such men as Professor Cairnes, William Hargreaves, A. W. Paulton, Frederick Pennington, T. B. Potter, Samuel Morley and others."[38] That Cobden would have kept to such a behind-the-scenes role seems likely. It accorded better with his longstanding dictum that the leaders of the Anti–Corn Law League would best serve the future of radicalism by encouraging the spontaneous emergence of other leaders and movements. There is every reason to suppose that he would have continued to act with the Reform League much as he had with the Association for the Repeal of the Taxes on Knowledge.

That said, there is no doubt that Cobden would have enthusiastically endorsed a measure of parliamentary reform more radical than anything Bright, let alone Gladstone, would have been comfortable with. So far as it went, the Reform Act of 1867 would have delighted him. Thereafter he would happily have closed ranks with his more moderate Liberal colleagues, for the agenda of Gladstone's first government was almost entirely concurrent with his own. For that matter, he would surely have joined that government (and probably Russell's government of 1865 as well). Much beyond the achievements of these administrations Cobden could not have gone, however. Suspicious of the power and profligacy of the state, he could not have accommodated himself to the social welfare liberalism of the late nineteenth century. Cobden may have been the most advanced of mid-nineteenth-century radical Liberals, but he remained squarely within that tradition. His original contribution in domestic politics was made to the arts of agitation, where his inventiveness in pursuit of a single goal and his understanding of the potential uses of modern means of communication provided a model for later mass movements that would-be popular leaders could still profitably study. Programmatically, however, he remained a man of his generation.

The same cannot be said of his views on international affairs. He saw both sooner and more clearly than all but a few of his contemporaries the likely shape of things to come. Cobden had never fully shared the easy optimism of many mid-nineteenth-century Liberals. Inherent in the spread of modern industrial civilization, he believed, there were tendencies toward greater internationalism. But these were only tendencies, and in the major crises of the last years of his life he discerned the outline of an alternative future. The Anglo-French naval arms race threatening to spin out of control, the American Civil War, involving the mobilization of resources on a scale that Cobden had previously believed impossible, and the Schleswig-Holstein affair, during which a militaristic Prussian government manipulated the liberal forces of German nationalism for its own purposes, all raised the terrifying prospect that the economic revolutions of the nineteenth century, far from undermining aggressive nationalism, might be enlisted in its service.

Cobden did not live long enough to see his dark vision realized or even to adjust his thinking to accommodate that vision. But nothing that happened in the half century after his death would have surprised him; unlike most Liberals he was intellectually prepared to do battle against the spread of European imperialism throughout Africa and south Asia, the institutionalization of the arms race, and the drift of his own country into a hardening system of European military alliances. Already an advocate of alternatives to traditional foreign policy and one of the few such critics to understand that his criticisms and proposals had to be both hard-headed and specific, Cobden would have responded to the dangerous new world that was only just beginning to take shape at the time of his death not by turning away in horror but by subjecting the conduct of British policy to ceaseless and rigorous scrutiny and by a persistent search for practical alternative courses of action. It is because of this that radical critics of British policy continued to look to Cobden's example for more than two generations after his death. It is because of this also that our own generation might do well to look to that example.

ABBREVIATIONS

SELECTED BIBLIOGRAPHY

NOTES

INDEX

ABBREVIATIONS

BL   British Library
CP   Cobden Papers, West Sussex Record Office
FO   Foreign Office
M   Manchester Central Library
MS   Smith Papers, Manchester Central Library
PP   Palmerston Papers, University of Southampton
PRO   Public Records Office
WSRO   West Sussex Record Office

Selected Bibliography

Manuscript Collections

Adams, Charles Francis, Massachusetts Historical Society.
Bright, John, British Library (Add. MSS 43383-4).
Cobden, Richard, British Library (Add. MSS 43647-78 and 50748-51); Dunford House (CP 1-961), West Sussex Record Office, Chichester; Manchester Central Library (M 87); West Sussex Record Office (WSRO 6009-72 and 2760-7); University of California at Los Angeles (UCLA 1040).
Cowley, Henry R. C. Wellesley, Earl, Public Records Office (FO 519/300).
Gladstone, William Ewart, British Library (Add. MSS 44135-6).
National Public Schools Association—Manchester Central Library (M 136).
Palmerston, Henry John Temple, Viscount, (PP, GC/CO), University of Southampton.
Place, Francis, British Library (Add. MSS 35151 and Place Collection, set 48).
Russell, Lord John, Public Records Office (PRO 30/22).
Smith, John Benjamin, Manchester Central Library (MS 923.2.S330-45).
Sturge, Joseph, British Library (Add. MSS 43722 and 50131).
Wilson, George, Manchester Central Library (M 20).

Primary Sources

Ashworth, Henry. *Recollections of Richard Cobden, M.P., and of the Anti–Corn Law League*. London, 1878.
Beaconsfield, Benjamin Disraeli, First Earl of. *Disraeli's Reminiscences*, Helen M. and Marvin Swartz, eds. New York, 1976.
Bigelow, John. *Retrospections of an Active Life*. New York, 1909.
Bright, John. *The Diaries of John Bright*, ed. R. A. J. Walling. London, 1930.
Cobden, Richard. *The American Diaries of Richard Cobden*, ed. E. H. Crawley. Princeton, 1952.
—— *Mr. Cobden and The Times: Correspondence between Mr. Cobden, M.P., and Mr. Delane, Editor of The Times*. Manchester, 1864.
—— *The Political Writings of Richard Cobden*. London, 1867.

———— *Speeches on Questions of Public Policy by Richard Cobden, M.P.*, ed. John Bright and J. E. Thorold Rogers. London, 1870.

Cole, Henry. *Fifty Years of Public Work of Sir Henry Cole*, ed. A. S. and Henrietta Cole. London, 1884.

Collet, Collet Dobson. *History of the Taxes on Knowledge*. London, 1899.

Derby, Edward Henry Stanley, Fifteenth Earl of. *Disraeli, Derby, and the Conservative Party: Journals and Memoirs of Edward Henry, Lord Stanley, 1849–1869*, ed. John Vincent. New York, 1978.

Gladstone, William Ewart. *The Prime Minister's Papers: W. E. Gladstone I: Autobiographica*, ed. John Brooke and Mary Sorensen. London, 1971.

Greville, Charles. *The Greville Memoirs*, ed. Lytton Strachey and Roger Fulford. London, 1938.

Hill, Sir Rowland, and Hill, George Birkbeck. *The Life of Sir Rowland Hill and the History of Penny Postage*. London, 1880.

Holyoake, George Jacob. *Bygones Worth Remembering*. New York, 1905.

Nevill, Lady Dorothy. *The Reminiscences of Lady Dorothy Nevill*, ed. Ralph Nevill. London, 1906.

Palmerston, Henry John Temple, Third Viscount. *The Palmerston Papers: Gladstone and Palmerston: Being the Correspondence of Lord Palmerston and Mr. Gladstone, 1851–1865*, ed. Philip Guedalla. London, 1928.

Peel, Sir Robert. *Sir Robert Peel from his Private Papers*, ed. Charles Stuart Parker. London, 1891–99.

Prentice, Archibald. *History of the Anti–Corn Law League*. London, 1853.

Russell, Lord John. *The Later Correspondence of Lord John Russell*, ed. George Peabody Gooch. London, 1925.

Salis-Schwabe, Julie. *Reminiscences of Richard Cobden*. London, 1895.

Smiles, Samuel. *The Autobiography of Samuel Smiles*, ed. Thomas Mackay, London, 1905.

Smith, Goldwin. *Reminiscences*. New York, 1910.

Victoria. *The Letters of Queen Victoria: A Selection of Her Majesty's Correspondence between the Years 1837 and 1861*, ed. A. C. Benson and Viscount Esher. London, 1908.

Watkin, Absolom. *Extracts from His Journal*, ed. A. E. Watkin. London, 1920.

Watkin, Edward W. *Alderman Cobden of Manchester: Letters and Reminiscences*. London, 1891.

Watts, John. *The Facts of the Cotton Famine*. London, 1866.

Secondary Sources

Adams, Charles Francis, Jr. *Charles Francis Adams*. Boston, 1900.

Adelman, Paul. *Victorian Radicalism: The Middle Class Experience, 1830–1914*. London, 1984.

Apjohn, Lewis. *Richard Cobden and the Free Traders*. London, 1881.

Ashton, Thomas Southcliffe. *Economic and Social Investigation in Manchester*. London, 1934.

Ausubel, Herman. *John Bright, Victorian Reformer*. New York, 1966.

Axon, William E. A. *Cobden as a Citizen: A Chapter in Manchester History.* Manchester, 1907.

Bowen, Ian. *Cobden.* London, 1935.

Boyson, Rhodes. *The Ashworth Cotton Enterprise: The Rise and Fall of a Family Firm, 1818–1880.* Oxford, 1970.

Briggs, Asa, ed. *Chartist Studies.* London, 1959.

Calkins, W. N. "A Victorian Free Trade Lobby," *Economic History Review,* 2nd ser., 13 (1960–61), 90–104.

Clark, George S. R. Kitson. "Hunger and Politics in 1842," *Journal of Modern History,* 25 (1953), 355–374.

Connell, Brian. *Regina V. Palmerston: The Correspondence between Queen Victoria and Her Foreign and Prime Minister.* London, 1962.

Crook, David Paul. *The North, the South, and the Powers.* New York, 1974.

Dawson, William Harbutt. *Richard Cobden and Foreign Policy.* London, 1926.

Derry, John W. *The Radical Tradition.* London, 1967.

Dunham, Arthur Louis. *The Anglo-French Treaty of Commerce of 1860 and the Progress of the Industrial Revolution in France.* Ann Arbor, 1930.

Edsall, Nicholas C. "A Failed National Movement: The Parliamentary and Financial Reform Association, 1848–54," *Bulletin of the Institute of Historical Research,* 49 (1976), 108–131.

——— "Varieties of Radicalism: Attwood, Cobden and the Local Politics of Municipal Incorporation," *Historical Journal,* 16 (1973), 93–107.

Fraser, Derek. *Urban Politics in Victorian England.* Leicester, 1976.

Frick, Stephen. "Joseph Sturge and the Crimean War. 2. The Founding of *The Morning Star*," *Journal of the Friends Historical Society,* 53 (1975), 335–58.

Gash, Norman. *Reaction and Reconstruction in British Politics, 1832–1852.* Oxford, 1965.

——— *Sir Robert Peel.* London, 1972.

Gates, Paul Wallace. *The Illinois Central Railroad and Its Colonisation Work.* Cambridge, Mass., 1934.

Gibbon, Charles. *Life of George Combe.* London, 1878.

Gillespie, Frances Elma. *Labor and Politics in England, 1850–1867.* Durham, N.C., 1927.

Hamer, David Allan. *The Politics of Electoral Pressure.* London, 1977.

Harrison, Brian. *Drink and the Victorians.* London, 1971.

Henderson, Gavin Burns. *Crimean War Diplomacy and Other Historical Essays.* Glasgow, 1947.

Hirst, Francis W. *Richard Cobden and John Morley.* Swindon, 1941.

Hobson, John Atkinson. *Richard Cobden, the International Man.* London, 1919 (reprinted 1968).

Hollis, Patricia, ed. *Pressure from Without in Early Victorian England.* London, 1974.

Huch, Ronald. *The Radical Lord Radnor.* Minneapolis, 1977.

Huch, Ronald, and Ziegler, Paul. *Joseph Hume: The People's M.P.* Philadelphia, 1985.

Hughes, Edward. "The Development of Cobden's Economic Doctrines and His Methods of Propaganda: Some Unpublished Correspondence," *Bulletin of the John Rylands Library*, 22 (1938), 405–418.

Iliasu, A. A. "The Cobden-Chevalier Commercial Treaty of 1860," *The Historical Journal*, 14 (1971), 67–98.

Jephson, Henry. *The Platform, Its Rise and Progress*. London, 1892.

Jordan, H. Donaldson. "The Political Methods of the Anti–Corn Law League," *Political Science Quarterly*, 42 (1927), 58–76.

———— "Richard Cobden and Penny Postage: A Note on the Processes of Reform," *Victorian Studies*, 8 (1965), 355–360.

Kemp, Betty. "Reflections on the Repeal of the Corn Law," *Victorian Studies*, 5 (1962), 189–204.

La Nauze, J. A. "Some New Letters of Richard Cobden: A Comment," *The Australian Journal of Politics and History*, 3 (1958), 197–203.

Leader, Robert Radon. *Life and Letters of John Arthur Roebuck*. London, 1897.

Maccoby, Simon. *English Radicalism, 1832–1852*. London, 1935.

———— *English Radicalism, 1853–1886*. London, 1938.

Maltby, Samuel Edwin. *Manchester and the Movement for National Elementary Education, 1800–1870*. London, 1918.

McCord, Norman. *The Anti–Corn Law League, 1838–1846*. London, 1958.

———— "Cobden and Bright in Politics," *Ideas and Institutions of Victorian Britain*, ed. Robert Robson. London, 1967.

McGilchrist, John. *Richard Cobden*. New York, 1865.

Miall, Charles. *Henry Richard, M.P.: A Biography*. London, 1889.

Morley, John. *The Life of William Ewart Gladstone*. London, 1903.

———— *The Life of Richard Cobden*. London, 1906.

Morrison, Stanley. *The History of The Times, Vol. II: The Tradition Established, 1841–1884*. London, 1939.

Phelps, Christine. *The Anglo-American Peace Movement in the Mid Nineteenth Century*. New York, 1930.

Prest, John. *Lord John Russell*. London, 1972.

———— *Politics in the Age of Cobden*. London, 1977.

Read, Donald. *Cobden and Bright: A Victorian Political Partnership*. London, 1967.

———— *The English Provinces, c. 1760–1960: A Study in Influence*. London, 1964.

Robbins, Keith. *John Bright*. London, 1979.

Salevouris, Michael. *Riflemen Form: The War Scare of 1859–60 in England*. New York, 1982.

Simon, Shena Dorothy. *A Century of City Government*. London, 1948.

Southgate, Donald. *The Passing of the Whigs, 1832–1886*. London, 1962.

Steer, Francis W., ed. *The Cobden Papers: A Catalogue*. Chichester, 1964.

Taylor, Alan J. P. "John Bright and the Crimean War," *Bulletin of the John Rylands Library*, 36 (1953–54), 501–522.

———— *The Trouble Makers: Dissent Over Foreign Policy, 1792–1939*. London, 1957.

Thompson, Francis M. L. "Whigs and Liberals in the West Riding," *English Historical Review*, 74 (1959), 214–239.

Trautz, Fritz. "Richard Cobden's Associations with Germany," *Bulletin of the John Rylands Library*, 34 (1952), 459–468.

Trevelyan, George M. *The Life of John Bright*. London, 1913.

Vincent, John. *The Formation of the Liberal Party, 1857–1868*. London, 1966.

Wallace, Elisabeth. "The Political Ideas of the Manchester School," *University of Toronto Quarterly*, 29 (1960), 122–138.

Walmsley, Hugh M. *The Life of Sir Joshua Walmsley*. London, 1879.

Walpole, Spencer. *Studies in Biography*. London, 1907.

Williams, William E. *The Rise of Gladstone to the Leadership of the Liberal Party*. Cambridge, 1934.

Newspapers

Leeds
  Leeds Mercury
London
  Herald of Peace
  The League (first published in Manchester as the *Anti–Corn Law Circular*)
  Morning Star
  The Times
Manchester
  Anti–Corn Law Circular (later called the *Anti–Bread Tax Circular*)
  Manchester Guardian
  Manchester Times

Notes

1. Family and Finances

1. Cobden to Lindsay, 24 March 1856 (CP 121).
2. Cobden to F. Cobden, Sept. 1832 (CP 19).
3. Cobden to F. Cobden, 6 Jan. 1832 (WSRO 2762).
4. Asa Briggs, *Victorian Cities* (1963), p. 92.
5. Thomas Carlyle, *Past and Present* (1843), book III, chap. 15.
6. Benjamin Disraeli, *Coningsby* (1844), book IV, chap. 2.
7. Carlyle, *Past and Present*, book III, chap. 15.
8. Alexis de Tocqueville, *Journeys to England and Ireland*, ed. J. P. Mayer (New Haven, 1958), pp. 107–108.
9. Cobden to W. Cobden, 11 Aug. 1831 (WSRO 2760).
10. Cobden to F. Cobden, 30 Jan. 1832 (WSRO 2762).
11. Cobden to F. Cobden, 12 April 1832 (M 87).
12. Cobden to W. Cobden, undated 1822 (WSRO 6019).
13. Cobden to W. Cobden, 6 May 1822 (WSRO 6019).
14. Cobden to F. Cobden, 3 Sept. 1824 (WSRO 6011).
15. *Manchester Courier*, 8 April 1865. This account, published thirty-five years later, blends elements from the founding of the business in 1828 and its expansion in 1831. Thus, it is uncertain when Lewis lent Cobden the money, although the earlier date seems more likely. Whatever the truth, it does not affect the point of the story.
16. Cobden to W. Cobden, 20 May 1829 (M 87).
17. Cobden to F. Cobden, 6 June 1833 (CP 19).
18. John McGilchrist, *Richard Cobden* (New York, 1865), p. 20.
19. Cobden to F. Cobden, 5 Feb. 1826 (M 87).
20. Cobden to F. Cobden, 26 Aug. 1825 (CP 19).
21. Cobden to F. Cobden, 16 Oct. 1838 (CP 25).
22. Cobden to F. Cobden, 26 Oct. 1838 (M 87).
23. Cobden to F. Cobden, 28 Jan. 1837 (CP 24).
24. Cobden to F. Cobden, 26 Oct. 1838 (M 87).

2. Education, Travel, and Authorship

1. Richard Cobden, *The Political Writings of Richard Cobden*, 4th ed. (London, 1903), p. 26.

2. Combe to Andrew Combe, April 1837, in Charles Gibbon, *The Life of George Combe* (London, 1878), II, 11.

3. Donald Read, *Cobden and Bright* (London, 1967), pp. 4–5.

4. John Morley, *The Life of Richard Cobden*, 13th ed. (London, 1906), pp. 93–94.

5. Cobden to F. Cobden, 3 March 1837 (CP 24).

6. Travel diaries of Cobden, Smyrna, 9 Feb. 1837 (BL, Add. MSS 43672).

7. Cobden to F. Cobden, 5 July 1835 (CP 20).

8. Cobden to F. Cobden, 11 Sept. 1838 (CP 24).

9. Cobden, "Russia," *Writings*, p. 203.

10. Cobden, "America," *Writings*, p. 5.

11. Cobden, "Russia," *Writings*, p. 163.

12. Ibid., p. 221.

13. Cobden, "America," *Writings*, p. 21.

14. Cobden, "Russia," *Writings*, p. 256.

3. The Political Setting

1. Cobden, "Russia," *Writings*, pp. 149–150.

2. Ibid., p. 151.

3. Cobden, "America," *Writings*, p. 118.

4. Ibid. p. 34.

5. Cobden to Ashworth, 7 Oct. 1850 (BL, Add. MSS 43653).

6. Cobden, "America," *Writings*, p. 108.

7. Cobden at Aylesbury, 9 Jan. 1853, in Richard Cobden, *Speeches on Questions of Public Policy by Richard Cobden, M.P.*, ed. John Bright and J. E. Thorold Rogers (London, 1870), pp. 225–226.

8. Cobden to Smiles, 21 Oct. 1841, in Samuel Smiles, *The Autobiography of Samuel Smiles* (London, 1905), p. 112.

9. Cobden, "America," *Writings*, p. 102.

10. Cobden, "Russia," *Writings*, p. 250.

4. Political Beginnings

1. McGilchrist, *Cobden*, p. 23. See also the slightly different account in Archibald Prentice, *History of the Anti–Corn Law League* (London, 1853), I, 46–47.

2. Watkin, *Journal*, pp. 191–192 (8 Sept. 1837).

3. Cobden, "America," *Writings*, p. 94.

4. First annual report of the Manchester Statistical Society, as quoted in T. S. Ashton, *Economic and Social Investigation in Manchester* (London, 1934), p. 13.

5. James Heywood in Manchester, 26 May 1837 (*Manchester Guardian*, 27 May 1837). Edward Watkin, *Alderman Cobden of Manchester* (London, 1891), chap. 7, is a valuable record of Cobden's role in the atheneum.

6. Cobden in Manchester, 28 Oct. 1835 (*Manchester Guardian*, 31 Oct. 1835).

7. *Manchester Guardian*, 27 Feb. 1836.

8. *Manchester Guardian*, 30 April 1836. S. E. Maltby, *Manchester and the Movement for National Elementary Education, 1800–1870* (London, 1918), is the best account of the education movement.

9. Cobden to Stowall, 24 Oct. 1837 (*Manchester Guardian*, 25 Oct. 1837).

10. As he recalled fifteen years later in a speech to education reformers in Manchester, 22 Jan. 1851 (Cobden, *Speeches*, p. 592).

11. See above, note 9.

12. Resolution adopted by the Manchester Society for Promoting National Education, 16 Nov. 1837 (*Manchester Guardian*, 18 Nov. 1837).

5. Advances and Setbacks

1. Cobden, "Russia," *Writings*, p. 219.

2. Cobden, "America," *Writings*, p. 116.

3. J. B. Smith papers: Corn Laws, MS 923.2.S333, III, 91. Smith's account rings true in spirit but not in detail. It was written much later, compresses events into too small a span of time, and gives no indication of when this took place. Also Smith may have been self-serving in his account, given that he was so soon to be upstaged by his one-time protégé.

4. Cobden in Manchester, 31 March 1841 (*Manchester Guardian*, 3 April 1841).

5. Henry Ashworth, *Recollections of Richard Cobden, M.P., and of the Anti–Corn Law League* (London, 1878), p. 14.

6. For the text of the petition, see *Manchester Guardian*, 14 Feb. 1838.

7. Parkes to Durham, 13 Sept. 1836, in Stuart Reid, *Life and Letters of the First Earl of Durham* (1906), II, 93.

8. Cobden to the independent electors of Stockport, 10 Oct. 1836 (*Manchester Guardian*, 17 Dec. 1836).

9. Cobden to Charles Cobden, 8 Jan. 1837 (CP 23).

10. Cobden to the Liberal electors of Stockport, 28 July 1837 (*Manchester Guardian*, 5 Aug. 1837).

11. Cobden to F. Cobden, 4 Jan. 1837 (CP 23).

12. Cobden to F. Cobden, 6 June 1837 (CP 24).

13. This and the following references to political leaders are from Cobden to F. Cobden, 12 June 1837 (WSRO 2762).

14. Morley, *Cobden*, p. 117. See also his remarks on the ballot in Bolton, 9 Sept. 1837, and Stockport, 13 Nov. 1837 (*Manchester Guardian*, 13 Sept. and 15 Nov. 1837 respectively).

6. The Incorporation of Manchester

1. Richard Cobden, *Incorporate your Borough* (Manchester, 1837), p. 2. This pamphlet was not included in his collected writings but was reprinted in W. E. A. Axon, *Cobden as a Citizen* (Manchester, 1907), the best account of the incorporation struggle.

2. Cobden, *Incorporate*, p. 12. For the national context of the incorporation movement, see Nicholas C. Edsall, "Varieties of Radicalism: Attwood, Cobden and the Local Politics of Municipal Incorporation," *Historical Journal*, 16 (1973), 93–107.

3. Cobden, *Incorporate*, p. 5.

4. Cobden to Tait, 3 July 1838 (BL, Add. MSS 43665).

5. Cobden to Wilson, 5 May 1838 (M 20).

6. Cobden to Wilson, 11 Jan. 1838 (M 20).

7. Cobden to Tait, 3 July 1838 (BL, Add. MSS 43665).

8. Cobden to Tait, 17 Aug. 1838 (BL, Add. MSS 43665).

7. Founding the Anti–Corn Law League

1. Cobden to Parkes, 11 Nov. 1856 (BL, Add. MSS 43664).

2. Recollections of the league by Sidney Smith, 1880 (MS 923.2.S333, III, 138).

3. In Norman McCord, *The Anti–Corn Law League 1838–1846* (London, 1958), the first systematic account of the inner workings of the league (as opposed to the anecdotal narrative of Prentice's *History of the Anti–Corn Law League*).

4. Cobden to Smith, 1 June 1840 (MS 923.2.S333, IV, 246).

5. By Smith's own account in MS 923.2.S333, II, 47.

6. Resolution adopted by a conference of delegates from anti–Corn Law associations, Manchester, 23 Jan. 1839 (Prentice, *League*, I, 102).

7. Resolutions adopted at a meeting of the Manchester Anti–Corn Law Association, Manchester, 28 Jan. 1839 (Prentice, *League*, I, 104).

8. Cobden to Smith, 3 Feb. 1839 (MS 923.2.S333, IV, 193). For Parkes's views see Parkes to Cobden, 31 Jan. 1839 (M 20).

9. Resolution adopted by a conference of delegates from anti–Corn Law associations, Manchester, 7 March 1839 (Prentice, *League*, I, 122).

10. Cobden to Smith, 3 Feb. 1839 (MS 923.2.S333, IV, 193).

11. Cobden to Smith, 8 Feb. 1839 (MS 923.2.S333, IV, 194).

12. Cobden in London, 20 Feb. 1839, in Harriet Martineau, *Pictorial History of England during the Thirty Years' Peace 1816–1846* (London, 1858), p. 570.

13. Villiers in the House of Commons, 12 Mar. 1839 (Hansard, *Parliamentary Debates*, Third Series, 1839, XLVI, 361).

8. Building an Agitation

1. Cobden in Manchester, 19 Oct. 1843 (Cobden, *Speeches*, p. 49).

2. Morley, *Cobden*, p. 140.

3. Resolution adopted at a conference of delegates from anti–Corn Law associations, London, 20 March 1839 (Prentice, *League*, I, 124).

4. *Anti–Corn Law Circular*, 14 May 1839.

5. *Anti–Corn Law Circular*, 30 April 1839. For the Chartist view, see Donald Read, "Chartism in Manchester," in *Chartist Studies*, ed. Asa Briggs (London, 1959), chap. 2.

6. This and the following quote are from Cobden to Wilson, 14 June 1840 (M 20).

7. Cobden to Wilson, 10 June 1840 (M 20).

8. This and the two following quotes are from Cobden to Smith, 1 June 1840 (MS 923.2.S333, IV, 246).

9. Cobden to Wilson, 14 June 1840 (M 20).

9. The League and Electoral Politics

1. Prentice, *League*, I, 167.

2. This and the following quote are from the *Anti–Corn Law Circular*, 24 Sept. 1840.

3. Cobden to Place, 17 Sept. 1840 (BL, Add. MSS 35151).

4. Resolution adopted at a conference of delegates from anti–Corn Law associations, London, 4 April 1840 (Prentice, *League*, I, 158).

5. J. B. Smith at Bolton, 3 Nov. 1840 (*Anti–Corn Law Circular*, 5 Nov. 1840).

6. *Anti–Corn Law Circular*, 28 Jan. 1841. For the earlier, more conciliatory approach, see *Anti–Corn Law Circular*, 3 Dec. 1840, and Smiles, *Autobiography*, pp. 97–98.

7. This and the following quote are from Sidney Smith's Recollections (MS 923.2.S333, III, 148, 148–149).

8. Cobden to Smith, 12 Jan. 1841 (J. B. Smith papers: Elections, MS 923.2.S336).

9. Cobden to Smith, 29 Jan. 1841 (MS 923.2.S336).

10. MS 923.2.S333, I, 19–20.

11. Cobden in Manchester, 18 Feb. 1841 (Prentice, *League*, I, 187).

12. *Anti–Bread Tax Circular*, 21 April 1841.

13. Cobden to F. Cobden, 5 Oct. 1838 (CP 25).

14. Cobden to Villiers, 6 June 1841 (BL, Add. MSS 43662). On the agreement between the league and the British India Society, see John Ludlow, *The Autobiography of a Christian Socialist*, ed. A. P. Murray, (London, 1981), pp. 65–66 and Prentice, *League*, I, 231.

15. Watkin, *Cobden*, p. 77.

16. *Anti–Corn Law Circular*, 11 Feb. 1841.

17. Cobden to Sturge, 4 Oct. 1841 (*Anti–Bread Tax Circular*, 7 Oct. 1841).

18. Cobden to Smith, 2 May 1841 (MS 923.2.S333, VI, 373).

19. Cobden to Wilson, 14 June 1840 (M 20). On the efforts to get Cobden adopted in Manchester, see Watkin, *Cobden*, chap. 12.

20. Cobden to F. Cobden, 16 June 1841 (BL, Add. MSS 50750). Cobden's letter to the workingmen and nonelectors of Stockport, 1 March 1841, was published in the *Anti–Corn Law Circular*, 11 March 1841.

21. Cobden to F. Cobden, 3 July 1841 (CP 26). The result: H. Marsland 571, Cobden 541, Major T. Marsland 346 (Dod, *Electoral Facts*, p. 296).

22. Cobden to F. Cobden, 26 Sept. 1841 (BL, Add. MSS 50750).

23. Benjamin Disraeli, *Disraeli's Reminiscences*, ed. Helen and Marvin Swartz, (New York, 1976), p. 108.

24. Cobden to F. Cobden, 26 Aug. 1841 (CP 26).

25. Disraeli, *Reminiscences*, p. 108.

26. Cobden in the House of Commons, 24 Sept. 1841 (Hansard, *Parliamentary Debates*, 1841, LIX, 796).

27. This and the following quote are from Cobden to Wilson, undated [Sept. or Oct.] 1841 (M 20).

10. The Crisis of 1842

1. Cobden to Wilson, 9 Oct. 1841 (M 20).

2. This and the following two quotes are from Cobden to Smith, 4 Dec. 1841 (MS 923.2.S333, VII, 424).

3. Cobden to Taylor, 15 Oct. 1841 (CP 70).

4. Cobden to Smith, 4 Dec. 1841 (MS 923.2.S333, VII, 424).

5. Cobden to Wilson, 16 Oct. 1841 (M 20).

6. Cobden to Smith, 4 Dec. 1841 (MS 923.2.S333, VII, 424).

7. Bright at Bradford, 25 July 1877, in G. M. Trevelyan, *The Life of John Bright* (London, 1913), pp. 43–44. See also Read, *Cobden and Bright*, part II, section 2.

8. Cobden to Smith, 4 Dec. 1841 (MS 923.2.S333, VII, 424).

9. Ferrand in the House of Commons, 24 Feb. 1842 (Hansard, *Parliamentary Debates*, 1842, LX, 422–423).

10. Report of the Select Committee on the Payment of Wages (*British Parliamentary Papers*, 1842, IX, 85, question 1776).

11. Cobden to Wilson, 24 Feb. 1842 (M 20).

12. Cobden to Bright, [?] April 1842 (BL, Add. MSS 43649).

13. Cobden to Bright, 21 June 1842 (BL, Add. MSS 43649).

14. Cobden to Ashworth, 7 April 1842 (BL, Add. MSS 43653).

15. Bright to Cobden, 9 March 1842 (BL, Add. MSS 43383).

16. Cobden to Wilson, 27 Feb. 1842 (M 20).

17. Bright to Cobden, 11 Aug. 1842 (BL, Add. MSS 43383).

18. Cobden to F. Cobden, 15 Aug. 1842 (BL, Add. MSS 50750).

19. Bright to Cobden, 16 Aug. 1842 (BL, Add. MSS 43383).

20. Cobden in Manchester, 25 Aug. 1842 (Prentice, *League*, I, 385).

21. Norman Gash, *Sir Robert Peel* (London, 1972), pp. 327–329.

22. Cobden in the House of Commons, 24 Feb. 1842 (Cobden, *Speeches*, p. 9).

23. Roebuck in the House of Commons, 8 July 1842 (Hansard, *Parliamentary Debates*, 1842, LXIV, 1233).

24. This and the following four quotes are from Cobden in the House of Commons, 8 July 1842 (Hansard, *Parliamentary Debates*, 1842, LXIV, 1213, 1217–18, 1217, 1216, 1220).

25. Peel in the House of Commons, 11 July 1842 (Hansard, *Parliamentary Debates*, 1842, LXIV, 1345–46).

26. Cobden to F. Cobden, 11 April 1842 (CP 26).

27. Cobden in the House of Commons, 11 July 1842 (Hansard, *Parliamentary Debates*, 1842, LXIV, 1361).

11. The Long Haul

1. Cobden to Wilson, 27 Feb. 1842 (M 20).
2. Cobden to McLaren, 21 Nov. 1842 (CP 71).
3. Cobden to Villiers, 16 Feb. 1840 (BL, Add. MSS 43662). For Cobden's testimony before the select committee, see Second Report from the Select Committee on Postage, *British Parliamentary Papers*, 1837–38, XX, part 2, pp. 46–63. On his role in the campaign, see H. Donaldson Jordan, "Richard Cobden and Penny Postage: A Note on the Processes of Reform," *Victorian Studies*, 8 (1965), 355–360.
4. Parkes to Cobden, 2 Feb. 1843 (CP 11).
5. Cobden in the House of Commons, 17 Feb. 1843 (Cobden, *Speeches*, pp. 21–22).
6. Cobden to F. Cobden, 23 Feb. 1843 (WSRO 6011).
7. Peel and Cobden in the House of Commons, 17 Feb. 1843 (Hansard, *Parliamentary Debates*, 1843, LXVI, 839).
8. Ibid., p. 880.
9. Cobden in the House of Commons, 17 Feb. 1843 (Cobden, *Speeches*, p. 17).
10. Roebuck in the House of Commons, 17 Feb. 1843 (Hansard, *Parliamentary Debates*, 1843, LXVI, 880).
11. Cobden in the House of Commons, 17 Feb. 1843 (Ibid., pp. 885–886).
12. Brougham to Stansfield, 20 Feb. 1843 (*Anti–Bread Tax Circular*, 28 March 1843).
13. Cobden in the House of Commons, 17 Feb. 1843 (Cobden, *Speeches*, pp. 19–20).
14. Cobden in the House of Commons, 15 May 1843 (Cobden, *Speeches*, pp. 24–26).
15. *Anti–Bread Tax Circular*, 14 March 1843. That this biographical sketch was written by Cobden is clear from a letter to his brother Fred, 11 March 1843 (WSRO 6011).
16. Lady Dorothy Nevill, *The Reminiscences of Lady Dorothy Nevill*, ed. Ralph Nevill (London, 1906), p. 190.
17. *Anti–Bread Tax Circular*, 28 March 1843.
18. Cobden to F. Cobden, 10 April 1843 (WSRO 6011).
19. Radnor to Cobden, 17 Nov. 1842 (BL, Add. MSS 43667). See also Ronald Huch, *The Radical Lord Radnor* (Minneapolis, 1977), chap. 10.
20. Cobden in Manchester, 28 Sept. 1843 (Cobden, *Speeches*, p. 37). The electoral program was outlined in an address from the council of the league to the people of the United Kingdom (*The League*, 30 Sept. 1843).
21. *The Times*, 18 Nov. 1843.
22. Recollections of the league by Sidney Smith, 1880 (MS 923.2.S333, III, 150–151).
23. Cobden in Manchester, 28 Sept. 1843 (Cobden, *Speeches*, p. 37).
24. Bright to Cobden, 13 Feb. 1843 (BL, Add. MSS 43383).
25. Cobden to Wilson, 24 Oct. 1843 (M 20).

26. Cobden to Wilson, 9 April 1844 (M 20).

27. Cobden to Wilson, 9 April 1844 (M 20).

28. Cobden to F. Cobden, 4 June 1844 (BL, Add. MSS 50750).

29. Cobden to Wilson, 23 April 1845 (M 20).

30. Cobden to Wilson, 2 April 1844 (M 20).

31. O'Connor to the working classes (*Northern Star*, 10 Aug. 1844).

32. R. G. Gammage, *History of the Chartist Movement* (London, 1854), p. 255.

33. Lucy Brown, "The Chartists and the Anti–Corn Law League," in *Chartist Studies*, ed. Asa Briggs, pp. 367–368.

34. Cobden to Watkin, 9 Oct. 1841 (Watkin, *Cobden*, p. 81).

35. Cobden in Manchester, 19 Oct. 1843 (Cobden, *Speeches*, p. 55).

12. The Key to Victory?

1. Cobden in London, 26 Nov. 1849 (Cobden, *Speeches*, p. 553). John Prest, *Politics in the Age of Cobden* (London, 1977), chap. 5, gives the freehold campaign the centrality it deserves but perhaps too readily accepts Cobden's assessment of its influence on government tactics.

2. Cobden in London, 11 Dec. 1844 (Cobden, *Speeches*, p. 124). Cobden first announced the new strategy in Manchester, 24 Oct. 1844 (Cobden, *Speeches*, pp. 108–109).

3. This and the two following quotes are from Cobden in London, 15 Jan. 1845 (Cobden, *Speeches*, pp. 128, 132, and 132).

4. Cobden in London, 18 June 1845 (Cobden, *Speeches*, p. 147).

5. Cobden in London, 11 Dec. 1844 (Cobden, *Speeches*, p. 125).

6. Cobden to C. Cobden, 11 March 1845 (BL, Add. MSS 50748).

7. Cobden to Wilson, 28 Feb. 1845 (M 20).

8. This and the following quote are from Cobden to Lattimore, 20 April 1864 (CP 90).

9. Gash, *Peel*, p. 471. W. R. Greg, evaluating Peel's career in the *Westminster Review* (July 1852), gave a slightly different version of this incident.

10. David Cresap Moore, *The Politics of Deference* (London, 1976), p. 328.

11. Cobden in the House of Commons, 13 March 1845 (Cobden, *Speeches*, p. 141).

12. Disraeli in the House of Commons, 17 March 1845 (Hansard, *Parliamentary Debates*, 1845, LXXVIII, 1028).

13. Cobden in the House of Commons, 10 June 1845 (Hansard, *Parliamentary Debates*, 1845, LXXXI, 358).

13. Victory

1. Cobden to Smith, 23 May 1845 (MS 923.2.S333, VIII, 441–442).

2. Cobden to Smith, 27 May 1845 (MS 923.2.S333, VIII, 443).

3. Cobden in Manchester, 28 Oct. 1845 (Cobden, *Speeches*, p. 161).

4. Cobden to C. Cobden, 26 June 1845 (BL, Add. MSS 50748).

5. Cobden to F. Cobden, 7 April 1845 (Morley, *Cobden*, pp. 330–331).
6. Cobden to F. Cobden, 18 April 1845 (CP 27).
7. Cobden to F. Cobden, 28 June 1845 (Morley, *Cobden*, p. 332).
8. Bright to Cobden, 20 Sept. 1845 (BL, Add. MSS 43383).
9. Cobden to Smith, 18 March 1846 (MS 923.2.S333, VIII, 448).
10. Cobden in the House of Commons, 27 Feb. 1846 (Cobden, *Speeches*, p. 190).
11. Ibid., p. 191.
12. Cobden to C. Cobden, 28 Jan. 1846 (BL, Add. MSS 50748). For the decisive influence of public opinion on Cobden, see Cobden to Russell, 6 Feb. 1846, in *The Later Correspondence of Lord John Russell*, ed. G. P. Gooch (London, 1925), I, 107–108; Charles Greville, *The Greville Memoirs*, ed. Lytton Strachey and Roger Fulford (London, 1938), V, 291; and J. B. Smith to Cobden, 29 Jan. 1846 (CP 1).
13. Cobden in the House of Commons, 25 June 1846 (Hansard, *Parliamentary Debates*, 1846, LXXXVII, 1026–1027).
14. Peel in the House of Commons, 29 June 1846 (Hansard, *Parliamentary Debates*, 1846, LXXXVII, 1054).
15. Cobden in Manchester, 28 Oct. 1845 (Cobden, *Speeches*, p. 159).
16. Cobden in Birmingham, 13 Nov. 1845 (Cobden, *Speeches*, p. 166).
17. Cobden in London, 17 Dec. 1845 (Cobden, *Speeches*, p. 176).
18. Cobden in Stockport, 11 Dec. 1845 (*Manchester Guardian*, 13 Dec. 1845).
19. Cobden to Combe, 2 Feb. 1846 (BL, Add. MSS 43660).
20. Peel and Cobden in the House of Commons, 27 Feb. 1846 (Hansard, *Parliamentary Debates*, 1846, LXXXIV, 248–249). See also *Harriet Martineau's Autobiography*, ed. Maria Weston Chapman (Boston, 1877), I, 523–527.
21. Cobden to Combe, 7 March 1846 (BL, Add. MSS 43660).
22. Cobden to Peel, 23 June 1846 (BL, Add. MSS 43667).
23. Peel to Cobden, 24 June 1846 (BL, Add. MSS 43667).
24. Cobden to Sturge, 10 June 1846 (BL, Add. MSS 50131).
25. Cobden in London, 18 June 1845 (Cobden, *Speeches*, p. 157).

14. Transitions

1. Cobden to Hunter, 12 March 1846 (CP 55).
2. Cobden to Combe, 7 March 1846 (BL, Add. MSS 43660).
3. Cobden to Crawford, 30 April 1846 (CP 77).
4. Parkes to Cobden, 26 July 1846 (CP 11). On the testimonial fund see Ashworth, *Cobden*, pp. 221–224, and Cobden to Combe, 14 July 1846 (BL, Add. MSS 43660). On his closely related decision to remain in Parliament, see Cobden to Coppock, 9 July 1846 (CP 41).
5. Cobden to Ashworth, 4 July 1846 (Morley, *Cobden*, pp. 408–409).
6. Cobden to Simpson, 4 July 1846 (CP 83).
7. Cobden to Paulton, 4 July 1846 (BL, Add. MSS 43662).
8. Cobden in Manchester, 15 Jan. 1846 (Cobden, *Speeches*, p. 187).
9. Cobden to Ashworth, 4 July 1846 (Morley, *Cobden*, p. 409).

10. Cobden to Parkes, 6 July 1846 (BL, Add. MSS 43664).

11. Cobden to Coppock, 17 July 1846 (CP 41). See also Bright to Cobden, 29 July 1846 (BL, Add. MSS 43383), and Cobden's reply, 30 July 1846 (BL, Add. MSS 43649). For the machinations of the Manchester Reform Association, see *Manchester Guardian*, 15 Aug. and 26 Sept. 1846.

12. Bright to Cobden, 29 Nov. 1846 (BL, Add. MSS 43383). That Bright felt badly used is clear from his letters to Villiers, for which see Keith Robbins, *John Bright* (London, 1979), pp. 71–73.

13. Read, *Cobden and Bright*, chap. 3, part 1.

14. Travel diaries of Cobden, Rome, 11 Feb. 1847 (BL, Add. MSS 43674).

15. Venice, 21 June 1847 (BL, Add. MSS 43674).

16. Naples, 27 Feb. 1847 (BL, Add. MSS 43674).

17. Berlin, 29 July 1847 (BL, Add. MSS 43674).

18. Luz, 20 Sept. 1846 (BL, Add. MSS 43674).

19. Berlin, 28 July 1847 (BL, Add. MSS 43674).

20. Dieppe, 6 Aug. 1846 (BL, Add. MSS 43674).

21. St. Petersburgh, 20 Aug. 1847 (BL, Add. MSS 43674).

22. Vienna, 10 July 1847 (BL, Add. MSS 43674).

23. St. Petersburgh, 15 Sept. 1847 (BL, Add. MSS 43674).

24. This and the following quote are from Cobden to Ashworth, 4 July 1846 (Morley, *Cobden*, p. 409).

25. Cobden to Combe, 26 June 1847 (BL, Add. MSS 43660).

26. Leipzig, 24 July 1847 (BL, Add. MSS 43674).

27. Memorandum by Prince Albert, 30 June 1846, in *The Letters of Queen Victoria: A Selection of Her Majesty's Correspondence between the Years 1837 and 1861*, ed. A. C. Benson and Viscount Esher (London, 1908) II, 84.

28. Diary of Lord Morpeth, London, 2 July 1846, as quoted in John Prest, *Lord John Russell* (London, 1972), p. 223. See also Clarendon's memorandum to his Whig colleagues, as quoted in Herbert Maxwell, *The Life and Letters of George William Frederick, fourth Earl of Clarendon* (London, 1913), I, 265–267.

29. Russell to Cobden, 2 July 1846 (Morley, *Cobden*, pp. 403–404).

30. Russell to Victoria, 14 Oct. 1847 (Victoria, *Letters*, II, 130).

31. Victoria to Russell, 14 Oct. 1847 (Victoria, *Letters*, II, 131).

32. F. M. L. Thompson, "Whigs and Liberals in the West Riding 1830–1860," *English Historical Review*, 74 (1959), 231.

15. The Manchester School and Post-Repeal Politics

1. Cobden to Wilson, 8 May 1848 (M20).

2. Cobden in the House of Commons, 6 July 1848 (Cobden, *Speeches*, p. 547).

3. Ibid., p. 541.

4. Cobden to Sturge, 16 July 1846 (BL, Add. MSS 50131).

5. Cobden to C. Cobden, 11 March 1848 (BL, Add. MSS 50749).

6. Cobden to Wilson, 17 Jan. 1848 (M20). See also Cobden's letters to Sturge, Dec. 1847–Feb. 1848 (BL, Add. MSS 43656).

7. Cobden in Manchester, 27 Jan. 1848 (Cobden, *Speeches*, pp. 240–241).

8. Cobden to Greg, 15 May 1848 (Morley, *Cobden*, p. 487–488).

9. Resolution passed at a meeting of radical members of Parliament, 13 April 1848 (*The Times*, 15 April 1848).

10. Cobden to Sturge, 21 Sept. 1848 (BL, Add. MSS 43656). For a contemporary account of the freehold movement, see J. E. Ritchie, *Freehold Land Societies: Their History, Present Position and Claims* (London, 1853). Prest, *Politics in the Age of Cobden*, chap. 6, provides a modern account. The Liverpool Financial Reform Association has also been well served by modern scholarship: W. N. Calkins, "A Victorian Free Trade Lobby," *Economic History Review*, 2nd ser., 13 (1960–61), 90–104.

11. Cobden to Bright, 16 Nov. 1848 (BL, Add. MSS 43649).

12. Cobden to Robertson Gladstone, 18 Dec. 1848 (*The Times*, 22 Dec. 1848). The budget was published as one of the *Tracts of the Liverpool Financial Reform Association* (Liverpool, 1853).

13. Cobden to Bright, 16 Nov. 1848 (BL, Add. MSS 43649).

14. Bright to Wilson, 24 Dec. 1848 (M20).

15. Cobden to Bright, 23 Dec. 1848 (BL, Add. MSS 43649).

16. Trevelyan, *Bright*, p. 176.

17. Papers Headed Financial and Parliamentary Reform (Place Collection, set 48, p. 13). This collection is the major source of original material on the Parliamentary and Financial Reform Association. H. M. Walmsley, *The Life of Sir Joshua Walmsley* (London, 1875), chaps. 18–23, which contains a number of letters from Cobden, is also valuable. For a modern study, see N. C. Edsall, "A Failed National Movement: The Parliamentary and Financial Reform Association," *Bulletin of the Institute of Historical Research*, 49 (1976), 108–131.

18. Cobden to Combe, 8 Feb. 1849 (BL, Add. MSS 43660).

19. Cobden in the House of Commons, 12 July 1849 (Hansard, *Parliamentary Debates*, 1849, CVII, 277–278). For Cobden's service on select committees, see "A Return of the Number of Public Committees Appointed in the Session of 1847/8" and similar returns for subsequent years in the *British Parliamentary Papers*. See also reports from the Select Committees on Navy, Army, and Ordnance Estimates, 1847–48, XXI; Army and Ordnance Expenditures, 1849, IX, 1; 1850, X, 1; 1851, VII, 735; Steam Navy, 1849, XVII, 453; Official Salaries, 1850, XV, 179.

20. Cobden to Combe, 8 Feb. 1849 (BL, Add. MSS 43660). On Cobden's role in the freehold movement, see Cobden to Lattimore, 15 Oct. 1849 (CP 87).

21. Roebuck to his wife, 12 July 1849, in Robert Radon Leader, *Life and Letters of John Arthur Roebuck* (London, 1897), p. 230.

22. This and the two following quotes are from Bright to Cobden, 7 Dec. 1849 (BL, Add. MSS 43383).

23. This and the following quote are from Cobden to Bright, 8 Dec. 1849 (BL, Add. MSS 43649).

24. Bright to Cobden, 12 Oct. 1850 (BL, Add. MSS 43383).

25. Cobden to Bright, 1 Oct. 1849 (BL, Add. MSS 43649).

26. Cobden in London, 26 May 1851 (NPFRA, *National Reform Tracts* (London, 1851), Proceedings of the Fourth Monthly Soiree).

27. Cobden to Bright, 23 Sept. 1851 (BL, Add. MSS 43649).

28. Cobden to Bright, 7 Nov. 1851 (BL, Add. MSS 43649).

29. Cobden to Smith, 4 March 1852 (MS 923.2.S345).

30. Cobden to Sturge, 11 March 1852 (BL, Add. MSS 43656).

31. Villiers in the House of Commons, 23 Nov. 1852 (Hansard, *Parliamentary Debates*, 1852, CXXIII, 351). On Cobden's insistence on this wording, see Arthur Hamilton Gordon, Baron Stanmore, *Sidney Herbert, Lord Herbert of Lea; A memoir* (London, 1906), I, 165, and Greville, *Memoirs*, VI, 370–371.

32. Cobden to Bright, 13 Jan. 1853 (BL, Add. MSS 43660). That Bright was "annoyed" (and worse) with Cobden is clear from the Jan. 1853 entries in *The Diaries of John Bright*, ed. R. A. J. Walling (London, 1930), pp. 132–133.

33. Cobden to Walmsley, 16 Oct. 1853 (Walmsley, *Walmsley*, p. 279).

34. Cobden in Manchester, 23 Jan. 1851 (Cobden, *Speeches*, p. 538).

16. The Manchester School and Educational Reform

1. Cobden to Bright, 10 Oct. 1851 (BL, Add. MSS 43649).

2. Cobden to Bright, 29 Dec. 1853 (BL, Add. MSS 43650).

3. Cobden in London, 26 Nov. 1849 (Cobden, *Speeches*, pp. 555–556).

4. Cobden to Combe, 5 Jan. 1849 (BL, Add. MSS 43660). See also his letters to Combe of 24 April and 17 July 1848.

5. Cobden to Robertson, 25 March 1854 (BL, Add. MSS 43665).

6. Cobden to Combe, 9 Nov. 1850 (BL, Add. MSS 43660). For a report of the conference, see *Manchester Guardian*, 2 Nov. 1850.

7. Cobden to Gibson, 15 Nov. 1850 (CP 77).

8. Cobden in Manchester, 22 Jan. 1851 (Cobden, *Speeches*, pp. 589–590).

9. Ibid., pp. 595–596.

10. Cobden to R. W. Smiles, 5 Sept. 1851 (M 136/2/3).

11. Address of the People's Charter Union to Richard Cobden, 19 Jan. 1849, as quoted in C. D. Collet, *History of the Taxes on Knowledge* (London, 1899), I, 83.

12. Collet, *Taxes*, p. 85.

13. George Jacob Holyoake, *Bygones Worth Remembering* (New York, 1905), II, 268.

14. Cobden to Collet, 5 Dec. 1853 (BL, Add. MSS 43677). Cobden's letters to Collet were published in Watkin, *Cobden*, chap. 8.

15. Cobden to Collet, 2 April 1853 (BL, Add. MSS 43677).

16. Cobden to Collet, 5 Dec. 1853 (BL, Add. MSS 43677).

17. Cobden to Collet, 5 June 1854 (BL, Add. MSS 43677).

18. Cobden to Collet, 6 Feb. 1854 (BL, Add. MSS 43677).

19. Cobden to Collet, 22 Nov. 1853 (BL, Add. MSS 43677).

20. Cobden to Collet, 5 Dec. 1853 (BL, Add. MSS 43677).

21. G. J. Holyoake in the introduction to Collet, *Taxes*, I, vii.

17. The Pursuit of Peace

1. Cobden to Sturge, 16 Sept. 1848 (BL, Add. MSS 43656). Intended by Cobden to be read to the Brussels Peace Congress, this letter was included in an account of the congress in the Oct. 1848 edition of the *Herald of Peace*, the most important source on the history of the movement. The only full-length study, Christine Phelps, *The Anglo-American Peace Movement in the Mid-Nineteenth Century* (New York, 1930), is poorly organized and poorly written. Briefer but better is Gavin Burns Henderson, *Crimean War Diplomacy and Other Historical Essays* (Glasgow, 1947), essay 6, "The Pacifists of the Fifties." For Cobden's part in the movement, see especially his letters to Joseph Sturge and Henry Richard. Many of the latter were published in J. A. Hobson, *Richard Cobden: The International Man* (1968 reprint of 1919 edition), but although Hobson transcribed the text of the letters accurately, he often misread the dates, and many of the letters are out of sequence.

2. Cobden to Sturge, Sept. 1848 (BL, Add. MSS 43656).

3. Cobden to Combe, 19 June 1849 (BL, Add. MSS 43660).

4. Cobden in the House of Commons, 12 June 1849 (Cobden, *Speeches*, p. 398).

5. Cobden to Combe, 19 June 1849 (BL, Add. MSS 43660).

6. Cobden in Paris, 24 Aug. 1849 (*Herald of Peace*, Sept. 1849).

7. Diary of Cobden at the Paris Peace Congress, Paris, 22 Aug. 1849 (BL, Add. MSS 43674).

8. This and the following quote are from Cobden in London, 18 Jan. 1850 (Cobden *Speeches*, pp. 407, 414). His speech on the Austrian loan, delivered in London, 8 Oct. 1849, is also in his collected speeches.

9. Kingsley to Ludlow, Dec. 1849, in Frances Eliza Kingsley, *Charles Kingsley: His Letters and Memories of His Life* (London, 1877), I, 222–223.

10. Cobden to Richard, 28 Nov. 1849 (BL, Add. MSS 43657).

11. Cobden in the House of Commons, 19 July 1850 (Hansard, *Parliamentary Debates*, 1850, CXII, 42).

12. Palmerston in the House of Commons, 25 June 1850 (Hansard, *Parliamentary Debates*, 1850, CXII, 444).

13. This and the following quote are from Cobden in the House of Commons, 28 June 1850 (Cobden, *Speeches*, pp. 420, 422–423).

18. Protecting the Peace

1. Cobden to Hadfield, 5 July 1850 (BL, Add. MSS 43668).

2. C. Cobden to Julie Schwabe, 27 Dec. 1849, in Julie Salis-Schwabe, *Reminiscences of Richard Cobden* (London, 1895), p. 150.

3. Diary of Lord Hatherton, 28 March 1850, Russell Papers (PRO 30/22/8D).

4. Cobden in London, 2 May 1850 (*The Times*, 3 May 1850).

5. Henry Cole, *Fifty Years of Public Work of Sir Henry Cole*, ed. A. S. and H. Cole (London, 1884), II, 146.

6. Cobden to Sturge, [?] June 1850 (BL, Add. MSS 50131).

7. Cobden to Richard, 14 May 1850 (BL, Add. MSS 43657). See also Bright, *Diaries*, p. 123.

8. Cobden to Sturge, 8 July 1850 (BL, Add. MSS 50131).

9. Cobden to Sturge, [?] July 1850 (BL, Add. MSS 50131). For the Frankfurt and London Peace Congresses see the *Herald of Peace* for Sept. 1850 and Aug. 1851 respectively.

10. Cobden to Richard, 13 March 1851 (BL, Add. MSS 43657). For Cobden's speech on the reduction of armaments, delivered 17 June 1851, see Cobden, *Speeches*, pp. 263–269.

11. Cobden in Winchester, 27 Oct. 1851 (*The Times*, 28 Oct. 1851).

12. Cobden to Richard, 10 Oct. 1850 (BL, Add. MSS 43657); for his efforts in support of the mission, see Cobden to Chevalier Bunsen, 3 Oct. 1850 (Salis-Schwabe, *Reminiscences*, pp. 120–121).

13. Cobden to Bright, 6 Nov. 1851 (BL, Add. MSS 43649).

14. Cobden to Richard, 9 Nov. 1851 (BL, Add. MSS 43657). The article to which Cobden objected was in the Oct. 1851 *Herald of Peace*.

15. Cobden to Richard, 18 Nov. 1851 (BL, Add. MSS 43657).

16. Cobden to Richard, 9 Nov. 1851 (BL, Add. MSS 43657).

17. *Herald of Peace*, Feb. 1852.

18. Osborne in the House of Commons, 16 Feb. 1852 (Hansard, *Parliamentary Debates*, 1852, CXIX, 591).

19. Cobden to Sturge, 14 Sept. 1852 (BL, Add. MSS 43656).

20. Cobden to Thomasson, 27 Sept. 1852 (CP 29).

21. This and the three following quotes are from Cobden, "1793 and 1853, in Three Letters," *Writings*, pp. 281, 323–324, 347, 370.

22. Cobden to Richard, 25 Jan. 1853 (BL, Add. MSS 43657).

23. This and the two following quotes are from Cobden, "1793 and 1853," *Writings*, pp. 349, 355, 363.

24. Cobden to C. Cobden, 31 Jan. 1853 (BL, Add. MSS 50749).

25. Cobden to Wilson, 4 Dec. 1852 (M20). For the Manchester Conference, see the Feb. 1853 *Herald of Peace*.

26. This and the four following quotes are from Cobden to Richard, undated, but internal evidence indicates 1 June 1853 (BL, Add. MSS 43657).

27. Cobden, "How Wars are got up in India," *Writings*, pp. 457–458.

28. Diary of Henry Richard, London, 27 June 1853, as quoted in Charles Miall, *Henry Richard, M.P.: A Biography* (London, 1889), p. 95.

29. Cobden to McLaren, 19 Sept. 1853 (CP 29).

30. Cobden to Richard, 17 Oct. 1853 (BL, Add. MSS 43657).

19. War

1. Palmerston in the House of Commons, 16 Aug. 1853 (Hansard, *Parliamentary Debates*, 1853, CXXIX, 1809).

2. Cobden in Edinburgh, 12 Oct. 1853 (*The Times*, 14 Oct. 1853).

3. Ibid. Cobden was so pleased with this passage that he used it in a later pamphlet (Cobden, "The Three Panics," *Writings*, pp. 580–581).

4. Cobden in Edinburgh, 12 Oct. 1853 (*The Times*, 14 Oct. 1853).

5. Cobden in Edinburgh, 13 Oct. 1853 (*The Times*, 15 Oct. 1853).

6. Diary of Lord Stanley, London, 20 Feb. 1854, *Disraeli, Derby and the Conservative Party: Journals and Memoirs of Edward Henry, Lord Stanley 1849–1869*, ed. John Vincent (New York, 1978), p. 120.

7. Cobden to Richard, 9 March 1854 (BL, Add. MSS 43657).

8. Cobden to Richard, 9 Dec. 1854 (BL, Add. MSS 43657).

9. This and the following quote are from Cobden to Richard, 21 Oct. 1854 (BL, Add. MSS 43657).

10. Cobden to Richard, 3 Dec. 1854 (BL, Add. MSS 43657).

11. Cobden in the House of Commons, 22 Dec. 1854 (Cobden, *Speeches*, pp. 310–320).

12. Cobden in Manchester, 17 Jan. 1855 (*Manchester Guardian*, 20 Jan. 1855).

13. Cobden in Leeds, 15 Jan. 1855 (*Manchester Guardian*, 20 Jan. 1855).

14. Cobden to Richard, 6 Jan. 1855 (BL, Add. MSS 43657).

15. Cobden in the House of Commons, 6 July 1855 (Hansard, *Parliamentary Debates*, 1855, CXXXIX, 581–582).

16. Cobden to the editor of *The Times*, 7 Aug. 1855 (*The Times*, 9 Aug. 1855). The offending editorial was in *The Times* of 6 Aug.

17. Cobden to Baines, 31 Oct. 1855 (*The Times*, 5 Nov. 1855); Cobden, "What Next—and Next," *Writings*, pp. 459–536.

18. Cobden to Bright, 1 Oct. 1854 (BL, Add. MSS 43650).

19. Graham to Clarendon, 16 Aug. 1853 (Maxwell, *Clarendon*, II, 16).

20. Palmerston to Seymour, 24 Jan. 1856, in Evelyn Ashley, *Life and Correspondence of Henry John Temple, Viscount Palmerston* (London, 1879), II, 325.

21. Diary of Charles Greville, 4 April 1857, *The Greville Memoirs*, VII, 284.

22. Cobden to Wilson, 23 Dec. 1856 (M20).

23. Morley, *Cobden*, p. 626.

20. Postwar Casualties

1. Cobden to Bright, 28 March 1856 (BL, Add. MSS 43650).

2. Cobden to Bright, 8 March 1856 (BL, Add. MSS 43650).

3. Cobden to Bright, 7 May 1856 (WSRO 2767).

4. Cobden to Robertson, 26 July 1856 (WSRO 2767).

5. Cobden to Bright, April 1856 (WSRO 2767).

6. Cobden to Moffat, 26 May 1856 (CP 119).

7. Cobden to F. Cobden, 10 June 1856 (BL, Add. MSS 50751).

8. Cobden to Sale, 22 May 1856 (WSRO 6014).

9. Cobden to his sister, Priscilla Sale, 5 May 1856 (WSRO 6012).

10. Cobden to Bright, 7 May 1856 (WSRO 2767).

11. Cobden to Sturge, 7 May 1856 (BL, Add. MSS 43722).

12. This and the following quote are from Cobden to Moffat, 17 Nov. 1856 (CP 119).

13. Cobden to F. Cobden, 8 Dec. 1856 (BL, Add. MSS 50751).

14. Cobden to Parkes, 11 Nov. 1856 (BL, Add. MSS 43664).

15. Cobden to Moffat, 22 Dec. 1856 (CP 119).

16. Cobden to Bright, 17 Sept. 1855 (BL, Add. MSS 43650). This account of the early history of the *Star* owes much to the work of Randall Cash, a graduate student at the University of Virginia.

17. Cobden to Bright, 28 Dec. 1855 (BL, Add. MSS 43650).

18. Diary of Chicester Fortescue, later Lord Carlingford, London, 28 Feb. 1857, "*. . . and Mr. Fortescue*", *a Selection from the Diaries from 1851 to 1862 of Chichester Fortescue*, ed. Osbert Wyndham Hewett (London, 1958), p. 104. Fortescue, a moderate Whig and sometime junior minister under Palmerston, had intended to support Cobden but so disliked the tone of the attack on the government that he voted for the prime minister.

19. This and the two following quotes are from Cobden in the House of Commons, 26 Feb. 1857 (Cobden, *Speeches*, pp. 386, 381, 388).

20. Palmerston in the House of Commons, 3 March 1857 (Hansard, *Parliamentary Debates*, 1857, CXLIV, 1812).

21. Cobden to Chevalier, 5 Oct. 1855 (BL, Add. MSS 43674).

22. Cobden to Richard, 18 June 1856 (BL, Add. MSS 43658).

23. Cobden to Bright, 6 March 1857 (BL, Add. MSS 43650).

24. Cobden in Manchester, 18 March 1857 (Cobden, *Speeches*, pp. 345–346).

25. Cobden to Fitzmayer, 14 Nov. 1856 (BL, Add. MSS 43665).

26. Bright to Cobden, 16 April 1857 (BL, Add. MSS 43384).

27. Cobden to Moffat, 7 April 1857 (CP 119).

28. Cobden to Vaughan, 20 May 1857 (BL, Add. MSS 43669).

29. Cobden to Parkes, 9 Aug. 1857 (BL, Add. MSS 43664).

30. Cobden to Sturge, 4 June 1857 (BL, Add. MSS 43722).

31. Cobden to Sturge, 31 Aug. 1857 (BL, Add. MSS 43722).

32. Cobden to Ashworth, 16 Oct. 1857 (BL, Add. MSS 43657).

33. Cobden to Sturge, 15 Oct. 1857 (BL, Add. MSS 43722).

34. Cobden to Paulton, 8 Jan. 1858 (WSRO 6014).

35. Cobden to Bright, 22 Sept. 1857 (BL, Add. MSS 43650).

36. Cobden to Bright, 10 April 1858 (BL, Add. MSS 43650).

37. Cobden to Sale, April 1858 (WSRO 6014).

38. Cobden to F. Cobden, 30 Jan. 1830 (WSRO 6011).

39. Cobden to Sturge, 22 May 1856 (BL, Add. MSS 43722).

40. Cobden to Sturge, 22 April 1858 (BL, Add. MSS 43722).

41. Cobden to Sturge, 31 Aug. 1857 (BL, Add. MSS 43722).

42. Cobden to Bright, 31 March 1858 (BL, Add. MSS 43650).

43. Cobden to Moffat, 20 May 1857 (CP 119).

44. Cobden to Moffat, 16 Sept. 1857 (CP 119). On the Illinois Central and Cobden, see Paul Wallace Gates, *The Illinois Central Railroad and Its Colonisation Work* (Cambridge, Mass., 1934), chap. 4.

45. Cobden to Moffat, 20 May 1857 (CP 119).

46. Cobden to Moffat, early 1858 (Morley, *Cobden*, pp. 686–687).

47. Cobden to Moffat, 16 Sept. 1857 (CP 119).

48. Cobden to Moffat, 31 March 1858 (CP 119).

49. Cobden to Moffat, 10 June 1858 (CP 119).

50. Cobden to Ashworth, 3 Feb. 1859 (BL, Add. MSS 43653).

51. Cobden to Parkes, 5 Feb. 1859 (BL, Add. MSS 43664).

52. Cobden to Bright, 5 Feb. 1859 (BL, Add. MSS 43651).

53. Cobden to Parkes, 5 Feb. 1859 (BL, Add. MSS 43664).

54. Chicago, 14 May 1859, in *The American Diaries of Richard Cobden*, ed. E. H. Crawley (Princeton, 1952), p. 190.

55. On the Mississippi, 26 and 27 March, 1859 (Ibid., p. 158).

56. En route from Boston to Montreal, 10 or 11 June 1859 (Ibid., p. 208).

57. Boston, 8 June 1859 (Ibid., p. 205).

58. Cobden to Gilpin, 22 Aug. 1859 (WSRO 6014).

59. Ashworth, *Cobden*, p. 243. See also Bright, *Diaries*, p. 433.

60. Palmerston to Russell, 4 Dec. 1863, in Philip Guedalla, *The Palmerston Papers* (London, 1928), p. 276.

61. *The Times*, 1 Feb. 1861.

21. Negotiating a Treaty

1. Cobden to C. Cobden, 30 June 1859 (Morley, *Cobden*, p. 692).

2. Russell to Cobden, 25 June 1859 (BL, Add. MSS 43669).

3. Cobden to C. Cobden, 30 June 1859 (Morley, *Cobden*, p. 693).

4. This and the three following quotes are from Cobden to Sale, 4 July 1859 (BL, Add. MSS 43669). See also Palmerston to Victoria, 1 July 1859 (Victoria, *Letters*, III, 348).

5. Cobden to Bright, 16 Dec. 1859 (BL, Add. MSS 43651).

6. Cobden to Sale, 4 July 1859 (BL, Add. MSS 43669).

7. Goldwin Smith, *Reminiscences* (New York, 1910), p. 247.

8. Cobden to Gladstone, 5 Sept. 1859 (BL, Add. MSS 44135).

9. Hawarden, 12 Sept. 1859, in *The Gladstone Diaries*, Vol. V, ed. H. C. G. Matthew (Oxford, 1978), p. 424.

10. Penmaenmawr, 13 Sept. 1859 (Ibid.).

11. Cobden to Gladstone, 11 Nov. 1859 (BL, Add. MSS 44135).

12. For this and the following quote, see the diary of Cobden during the French treaty negotiations, Paris, 2 Nov. 1859 (BL Add. MSS 43675). The diary, supplemented by his correspondence with Gladstone, is the most important source on the negotiations, an excellent study of which was written by Arthur Louis Dunham, *The Anglo-French Treaty of Commerce of 1860* (Ann Arbor, 1930).

13. Paris, 27 Oct. 1859 (BL, Add. MSS 43675).

14. Cobden to Palmerston, 29 Oct. 1859 (PP).

15. Cobden to Gladstone, 29 Oct. 1859 (BL, Add. MSS 44135).

16. Paris, 8 Nov. 1859 (BL, Add. MSS 43675).

17. A. A. Iliasu, "The Cobden-Chevalier Commercial Treaty of 1860," in *The Historical Journal*, 14 (1971), 67–98.

18. Paris, 23 Jan. 1860 (BL, Add. MSS 43675).

19. Cobden to Palmerston, 22 Dec. 1859 (PP).

20. Cobden to Palmerston, 29 Oct. 1859 (PP).

21. Paris, 25 Nov. 1859 (BL, Add. MSS 43675).

22. Paris, 26 Dec. 1859 (BL, Add. MSS 43675).
23. Cobden to Gladstone, 23 Nov. 1859 (BL, Add. MSS 44135).
24. Cobden to Parkes 11 Feb. 1860 (BL, Add. MSS 43664).
25. Cobden to Lord Cowley, 9 April 1860 (FO 519/300).
26. *The Times*, 23 Jan. 1860.
27. Paris, 11 Aug. 1860 (BL, Add. MSS 43675).
28. Paris, 10 Sept. 1860 (BL, Add. MSS 43675).
29. Paris, 26 Sept. 1860 (BL, Add. MSS 43675).
30. Paris, 5 Oct. 1860 (BL, Add. MSS 43675).
31. Paris, 12 Oct. 1860 (BL, Add. MSS 43675).
32. Paris, 22 Oct. 1860 (BL, Add. MSS 43675).
33. Cobden to Gladstone, 12 Nov. 1860 (BL, Add. MSS 44136).
34. Cobden to Gladstone, 5 Dec. 1859 (BL, Add. MSS 44135).
35. Cobden to Bright, 31 Dec. 1860 (BL, Add. MSS 43651).
36. Cobden to Bright, 4 Feb. 1861 (BL, Add. MSS 43651).
37. Cobden to Palmerston, 13 April 1861 (PP).
38. This and the two following quotes are from Cobden to Bright, 4 Feb. 1861 (BL, Add. MSS 43651).

22. The Third French Invasion Panic

1. Cobden to Chevalier, 1 Sept. 1860 (CP 46). The third panic has recently been given its due in Michael Salevouris, *Riflemen Form: The War Scare of 1859–60 in England* (New York, 1982).
2. These recollections were written in 1897. *The Prime Minister's Papers: W. E. Gladstone I; Autobiographica*, ed. John Brooke and Mary Sorensen, (London, 1971), p. 85.
3. Cobden to Bright, 29 Dec. 1859 (BL, Add. MSS 43651).
4. Cobden to Gladstone, 29 Jan. 1860 (BL, Add. MSS 44135).
5. Cobden to Palmerston, 12 July 1860 (PP).
6. Cobden to Bright, 22 June 1860 (BL, Add. MSS 43651).
7. Cobden to Bright, 30 June 1860 (BL, Add. MSS 43651).
8. Cobden to Bright, 29 Dec. 1859 (BL, Add. MSS 43651).
9. Cobden to Bright, 23 Jan. 1860 (BL, Add. MSS 43651).
10. Cobden to Richard, 27 Jan. 1857 (BL, Add. MSS 43658).
11. Gladstone to Cobden, 14 Jan. 1860 (BL, Add. MSS 44135).
12. Cobden to Bright, 30 Jan. 1860 (BL, Add. MSS 43651).
13. Cobden to Gladstone, 15 Jan. 1862 (BL, Add. MSS 44136).
14. Cobden to Gladstone, 22 Dec. 1863 (BL, Add. MSS 44136).
15. Prince Albert to Palmerston, 24 Jan. 1861, in Brian Connell, *Regina v. Palmerston* (London, 1962), p. 298.
16. Diary of Cobden, Paris, 11 Sept. 1860 (BL, Add. MSS 43675).
17. Cobden to Chevalier, 12 June 1861 (CP 46).
18. This and the following quote are from the memorandum of Cobden to Lord Palmerston and Emperor Napoleon III, Oct. 1861 (Cobden, *Writings*, p. 703).

19. Richard Cobden, "The Three Panics: An Historical Episode," *Writings*, p. 608.

20. Palmerston in the House of Commons, 23 July 1860 (Hansard, *Parliamentary Debates*, 1860, CLX, 18).

21. Mountstuart Elphinstone Grant Duff, *Elgin Speeches* (Edinburgh, 1871), p. 25.

22. This and the following quote are from Cobden in the House of Commons, 1 Aug. 1862 (Cobden, *Speeches*, pp. 440, 438).

23. W. E. Williams, *The Rise of Gladstone to the Leadership of the Liberal Party* (Cambridge, 1934), p. 20. However, the most important study of the Liberal party during this period argues that Cobden's "teaching . . . meant nothing to Gladstone": see John Vincent, *The Formation of the Liberal Party, 1857–1868* (London, 1966), pp. 34–35.

23. Britain and the American Civil War

1. Morley, *Cobden*, pp. 836–837. See also Read, *Cobden and Bright*, pp. 219–221.

2. Cobden to Bright, 29 Dec. 1862 (BL, Add. MSS 43652).

3. Charles Francis Adams, Jr., *Charles Francis Adams* (Boston, 1900), p. 264.

4. Bigelow to Seward, 29 May 1862, in John Bigelow, *Retrospections of an Active Life* (New York, 1909), I, 494.

5. This and the following quote are from Cobden to Sumner, 27 Nov. 1861 (BL, Add. MSS 43676). Cobden's letters to Sumner were published in Hobson, *Cobden*, chap. 12. For the context in which Cobden operated, see D. P. Crook, *The North, the South, and the Powers, 1861–1865* (New York, 1974).

6. Cobden to Sumner, 5 Dec. 1861 (BL, Add. MSS 43676).

7. Cobden to Gladstone, 11 Dec. 1861 (BL, Add. MSS 44136).

8. Sir Horace Rumbold, *Recollections of a Diplomatist* (London, 1902), II, pp. 84. See also Gladstone to Cobden, 13 Dec. 1861 (BL, Add. MSS 43136) and Sumner to Cobden, 31 Dec. 1861 (CP 13).

9. Cobden to Chevalier, 25 Oct. 1862 (CP 47). Cobden wrote or spoke in similar terms to others; see, for example, Stanley, *Journals*, p. 191.

10. Diary of C. F. Adams, London, 24 Feb. 1862 (Massachusetts Historical Society).

11. Gladstone in Newcastle, 7 Oct. 1862, in John Morley, *The Life of William Ewart Gladstone* (London, 1903), II, 79.

12. Cobden to Bright, 9 Oct. 1862 (BL, Add. MSS 43652).

13. This and the following quote are from Cobden to Sumner, 13 Feb. 1853 (BL, Add. MSS 43676).

14. Cobden to Ashworth, 17 Oct. 1861 (BL, Add. MSS 43654).

15. Cobden in Manchester, 25 Oct. 1862 (Cobden, *Speeches*, p. 458). His letter to Ashworth, 10 April 1862, was printed as a pamphlet: Cobden, *Writings*, pp. 380–393.

16. Cobden to Bright, 28 Aug. 1862 (BL, Add. MSS 43652).

17. This and the following quote are from Cobden in Manchester, 3 Nov.

1862, in John Watts, *The Facts of the Cotton Famine* (London, 1866), pp. 173, 176. On his role in Parliament, see Stanley, *Journals*, pp. 185, 196.

18. Cobden in the House of Commons, 18 June 1863 (Hansard, *Parliamentary Debates*, 1863, CLXXI, 1080).

19. Crook, *The North, the South, and the Powers*, p. 259.

20. This and the following quote are from Cobden to Sumner, 2 April 1863 (BL, Add. MSS 43676).

21. Cobden to Sumner, 2 May 1863 (BL, Add. MSS 43676).

22. This and the following quote from Cobden in the House of Commons, 24 April 1863 (Cobden, *Speeches*, p. 350).

23. Cobden to Sumner, 22 May 1863 (BL, Add. MSS 43676).

24. Cobden to Bright, 26 Oct. 1863 (BL, Add. MSS 43652).

25. Cobden to Sumner, 8 Oct. 1863 (BL, Add. MSS 43676).

26. This and the two following quotes are from Cobden in Rochdale, 24 Nov. 1863 (Cobden, *Speeches*, pp. 362, 361, 363).

27. Cobden to Sumner, 7 Jan. 1864 (BL, Add. MSS 43676).

28. Cobden to Sumner, 18 Aug. 1864 (BL, Add. MSS 43676).

29. Cobden to Bright, 25 March 1861 (BL, Add. MSS 43651).

30. Cobden to Bright, 7 Oct. 1862 (BL, Add. MSS 43651).

31. Cobden to Bright, 4 Oct. 1864 (BL, Add. MSS 43652).

32. Cobden to Sumner, 7 Jan. 1864 (BL, Add. MSS 43676).

33. Cobden to Bright, 19 Nov. 1864 (BL, Add. MSS 43652).

34. Cobden to Sumner, 2 March 1865 (BL, Add. MSS 43676).

35. Diary of C. F. Adams, London, 25 Jan. 1865 (Massachusetts Historical Society).

24. The Elder Statesman of Radicalism

1. Cobden to Fitzmayer, 30 March 1864 (BL, Add. MSS 43665).

2. Cobden to Bright, 30 March 1864 (BL, Add. MSS 43652).

3. Cobden to Robertson, 22 Jan. 1864 (BL, Add. MSS 43665).

4. Cobden to Lattimore, 20 Feb. 1864 (CP 90).

5. Cobden to MacQueen, 13 May 1863 (University of London Library, autograph letters 351).

6. Disraeli in the House of Commons, 4 Feb. 1864 (Hansard, *Parliamentary Debates*, 1864, CLXXVI, 354).

7. Victoria to the king of the Belgians, 25 Feb. 1864, in *Letters of Queen Victoria: Second Series*, ed. George Earl Buckle (London, 1926), I, 168.

8. This and the two following quotes are from Cobden in the House of Commons, 5 July 1864 (Hansard, *Parliamentary Debates*, 1864, CLXXVI, 828–829).

9. Cobden in the House of Commons, 5 July 1864 (Hansard, *Parliamentary Debates*, 1864, CLXXVI, 837).

10. Cobden to Gladstone, 9 Jan. 1864 (BL, Add. MSS 44136).

11. Watkin, *Cobden*, p. 8.

12. Nevill, *Reminiscences*, p. 185.

13. This comment was made in a letter to Charles Greville in Aug. 1860 (Greville, *Memoirs*, VII, 482).

14. Disraeli, *Reminiscences*, p. 108.

15. Cobden in Manchester, 18 March 1857 (Cobden, *Speeches*, p. 347).

16. *The Times*, 3 Dec. 1863.

17. [Stanley Morrison], *The History of The Times, Vol. II: The Tradition Established, 1841–1884* (London, 1939), p. 335.

18. Cobden to the editor of *The Times*, 4 Dec. 1863, in Richard Cobden, *Mr. Cobden and The Times: Correspondence between Mr. Cobden, M. P., and Mr. Delane, Editor of The Times* (Manchester, 1864), pp. 1–2.

19. Cobden to Delane, 9 Dec. 1863 (Ibid., p. 7).

20. Cobden to the editor of *The Times*, 4 Dec. 1863 (Ibid., p. 2).

21. Cobden to the editor of the *Daily Telegraph*, 12 Dec. 1863 (Ibid., p. 29).

22. Morley, *Cobden*, p. 884.

23. Parkes to Delane, 3 April 1865 (Morrison, *Times*, p. 336).

24. Cobden to Ashworth, 26 April 1861 (BL, Add. MSS 43654).

25. London, 2 April 1865 (*The Diaries of John Bright*, p. 286).

26. Cobden to Potter, 28 March 1863 (Bigelow, *Retrospections*, I, 616).

27. Diary of C. F. Adams, London, 7 April 1965 (Massachusetts Historical Society).

28. Disraeli in the House of Commons, 3 April 1865 (Hansard, *Parliamentary Debates*, 1865, CLXXVIII, 677). This regard for Cobden as a representative of his class was hardly a new theme for Disraeli, whose fictional manufacturer, Millbank, in *Coningsby* may have been based on Cobden. Cobden certainly thought so and thanked Disraeli for the compliment when the novelist-politician visited the Manchester Atheneum in 1844 (Watkin, *Cobden*, p. 135).

29. Bright in the House of Commons, 3 April 1865 (Hansard, *Parliamentary Debates*, 1865, CLXXVIII, 677).

30. *Manchester Guardian*, 4 April 1865.

31. *The Times*, 3 April 1865.

32. Ian Bowen, *Cobden* (London, 1935), p. 15.

33. Cobden to Hunt, 21 Oct. 1836 (BL, Add. MSS 43667).

34. Cobden to Hargreaves, 1 March 1861 (BL, Add. MSS 43655).

35. Cobden to Bright, 30 March 1863 (BL, Add. MSS 43652).

36. Cobden to Hargreaves, 5 Jan. 1865 (BL, Add. MSS 43655).

37. George Howell, *Labor Legislation, Labor Movements and Labor Leaders* (London, 1902), p. 144. See also Read, *Cobden and Bright*, pp. 160–161.

38. "Autobiography of George Howell," vol. C/C, "The Reform League" (Bishopsgate Institute, London: Howell Papers), p. 2. See also F. M. Levanthal, *Respectable Radical: George Howell and Victorian Working Class Politics* (Cambridge, Mass., 1971), p. 63.

Index